CW00648091

To my children, grandchildren, and those still to come—
may you follow Jesus all the days of your life.
—C. B.

To the Belsky family—may you grow in the grace and
knowledge of our Lord Jesus Christ.
—T. M.

To my grandma. Without your faith I would never have
found mine.
—A. S.

Our Daily Bread for Kids: 365 Devotions from Genesis to Revelation
©2023 by Crystal Bowman and Teri McKinley
Illustrations by Anita Schmidt. © 2023 by Our Daily Bread Publishing

Requests for permission to quote from this book should be directed to:
Permissions Department, Our Daily Bread Publishing, PO Box 3566, Grand
Rapids, MI 49501, or contact us by email at permissionsdept@odb.org.

Design by Jody Langley

Library of Congress Cataloging-in-Publication Data Available

Printed in Europe
23 24 25 26 27 28 29 30 / 8 7 6 5 4 3 2 1

Introduction

Did you know that the Bible is the best-selling book of all time? More than six billion copies have been sold since the printing press was invented by Johannes Gutenberg in 1440. But the Bible is really a collection of sixty-six smaller books that have been divided into two groups called the Old Testament and the New Testament. It's more than just a collection of exciting stories though. Together, those sixty-six books tell *one* big true story.

Our Daily Bread for Kids is not the Bible, but it has 365 devotions to help you learn more about the Bible. As we look at some of the stories and verses from Genesis to Revelation, you will learn how they fit together to tell the story of God's amazing love for you. With one reading for each day of the year, you can have a special time with God every day and grow closer to Him as you learn more about who Jesus is and all He did.

The words *Our Daily Bread* come from the prayer Jesus said when He was teaching His disciples how to pray. In Matthew 6:11, Jesus prayed, "Give us today our daily bread" (NIV). Just as we need to eat food every day for our bodies to be strong, we need "spiritual food" to have strong belief and trust in God. As you read the devotions and open your Bible, ask God to help you understand what He wants you to know so you can be spiritually strong.

You can read the devotions on the following pages by yourself or have a grown-up read them with you. You might want to read this book with your family at mealtime or bedtime. You can start on today's date or at the very beginning of this book on January 1. If you read it in order, you may understand the stories better. We take you from the beginning of the Bible in a book called Genesis and end with the last book of the Bible, which is Revelation. However you use it, our prayer is that you will learn how much God loves you and how Jesus makes a way for you to be a part of God's family.

Are you ready to go on an unforgettable journey through the Bible? Let's get started!

Crystal and Teri

If you come across words you don't understand, look them up in the glossary at the back of the book.

The Beginning

In the beginning, God created the heavens and the earth. The earth didn't have any shape. And it was empty. There was darkness over the surface of the waves. At that time, the Spirit of God was hovering over the waters. —Genesis 1:1–2 NIrV

The book of Genesis is the first book of the Bible, and this is where everything begins. We don't know what the earth looked like, but we know it was dark and empty and didn't have any shape. Maybe it looked like a giant blob! No matter what it looked like, God was there, and He did something only He can do. God said, "Let there be light," and just like that, light appeared. Then He separated the light from the darkness. He called the light *day*, and He called the dark *night*.

The next day God divided the water into two places and put a huge space between them. He named the space *sky*. Then God gathered the water together so dry land would appear. He named the dry land *earth* and the water *seas*. Then God created plants and trees on the land that would grow delicious food.

When God looked at His creation, He said, "It is good." But He wasn't finished. He placed two great lights in the sky. The larger light (the sun) ruled the day, and the smaller light (the moon) ruled the night. He also put billions of stars in the sky.

Then God filled the waters with sea animals and created birds to fly in the air. On the last day of creation, God made every kind of animal on the land. But God saved the best for last! He made humans to take care of creation and enjoy everything He had made. God created the world in six days, and on the seventh day He rested.

TALK TO GOD
Tell God what you like best about His creation.

EXPLORE MORE: What did God tell the birds to do in Genesis 1:22?

Everything God made was good.

DID YOU KNOW?
Our galaxy, the Milky Way, has around 100 to 400 billion stars.

Jesus Was There

Then God said, "Let us make human beings in our image and likeness. And let them rule over the fish in the sea and the birds in the sky. Let them rule over the tame animals, over all the earth and over all the small crawling animals on the earth. —Genesis 1:26 ICB

The story of creation tells us how our world began. On the sixth day God said, "Let us make human beings in our image and in our likeness." Did you notice the word *us*? Who was God talking to since there were no people?

There is only one God, but He exists in three persons—Father, Son, and Holy Spirit. Genesis 1:2 says that God's Spirit was hovering over the waters. A verse from the New Testament says that Jesus is exactly like God. Jesus is higher than all things. God created everything through His Son (see Colossians 1:15–16).

The Son is Jesus, who is also God. He made the sun, moon, and stars appear in the sky. He made the plants and trees on the land. He created whales to splash their tails and eagles to soar through the sky. He watched tigers race across the land and koala bears climb gum trees. So when God said, "Let us make human beings in our image," the word *us* refers to the Father, Son, and Holy Spirit. This is called the *Trinity*, which means "three in one."

TALK TO GOD
Thank God for making you in His image.

Because God made people in His "image," we can know God in a way that's different from the rest of creation. He created us with a spirit so we can talk to Him and learn about Him from the Bible and from His creation. God created the world by speaking words, but He created a human being by breathing life into him. The first person was made in God's image, and so are you.

EXPLORE MORE: Read Genesis 2:7 to find out how God created the first person.

DID YOU KNOW?
The cheetah is the fastest animal on land and can run up to 70 miles (113 kilometers) per hour.

Jesus is my creator.

As Seasons Change

He made the moon to mark the seasons, and the sun knows when to go down. —Psalm 104:19 NIV

When God put the sun, moon, and stars in the sky and made the planets start turning, that was the beginning of days, months, and seasons. As the whole solar system revolves and rotates, temperatures change, and our days get longer or shorter.

In places like Japan and Canada, the four seasons bring a wide variety of weather. Summer months can be warm and sunny when kids go for hikes and splash in the water. After summer comes autumn, when trees are full of colorful leaves that eventually fall to the ground. Winter can be cold and snowy with icicles and blizzards. And when spring follows winter, the rainy days make flowers pop out of the ground.

TALK TO GOD
Tell God which season you like best.

In some parts of the world, it's cold most of the year, and in other areas it's always hot. In places like Argentina and Australia, winter begins in June, and summer begins on the first day of December. But no matter where you live or what your seasons are like, summer, autumn, winter, and spring always follow the same order and each season follows God's plan.

Psalm 102:27 says that God will never change. As we go from one season to the next, remember that even though seasons change, God's love for you never changes. He loves you every hour and every day of the year. What God wants us to do never changes either. God wants us to love Him with all our hearts, and to show His love to others every day.

EXPLORE MORE: What does Genesis 8:22 tell us about seasons?

God loves me all year long.

DID YOU KNOW?
Snowflakes can fall at about 9 miles (14.5 kilometers) per hour.

Adam and Eve in the Garden

The Lord God gave the man a command. He said, "You may eat fruit from any tree in the garden. But you must not eat the fruit from the tree of the knowledge of good and evil. If you do, you will certainly die." —Genesis 2:16–17 NIrV

God named the first man Adam, and he was different from the rest of God's creation. Unlike the animals, Adam could talk to God, and God talked to Adam. God made Adam perfect in every way. But it wasn't good for him to be alone, so God created the first woman, Eve. God placed them in a beautiful garden called Eden. The garden had rivers, trees, and animals. God wanted Adam and Eve to take care of the garden and enjoy it. He told them to eat the delicious fruit from all the trees—except for one. But one day, Adam and Eve ate fruit from that tree. For the first time, they disobeyed God—the Bible calls that sin—and that changed everything. Now they had to work hard for their food, and they would experience sickness, pain, and death.

Adam and Eve were sorry they didn't listen to God. But God still loved them even though He had to discipline them. God knew that all people would sin, so He made a way for their sins to be forgiven. As time went on, God asked people to bring their best lamb or goat as an offering, or sacrifice, to Him. This would make things right between them and God for a while. But it was something they needed to do over and over again, because they kept on sinning. They would need a lot of lambs or goats!

Today we still disobey God, but we don't have to bring God sacrifices anymore. God loves us so much that He gave His son for our sin instead of lambs and goats. When Jesus died on the cross, He gave His life for us and paid for all our sins. His sacrifice was enough to last forever! Jesus's sacrifice is all we need to be right with God, and believing in Him as our Savior gives us eternal life.

TALK TO GOD
Ask God to help you do what is right, and thank Him for making things right through Jesus.

EXPLORE MORE: Read Genesis 3:21 to find out what God made for Adam and Eve after they sinned.

DID YOU KNOW?
In the English language, the name Adam means "man." It comes from the Hebrew name Adamah which means "land" or "red earth."

Jesus makes things right.

Noah Builds an Ark

Noah had faith. So he built an ark to save his family. He built it because of his great respect for God. God had warned him about things that could not yet be seen. . . . Because of his faith he was considered right with God. —Hebrews 11:7 NIrV

The story of Noah's ark is a well-known story from the book of Genesis. You may have heard it at church or read it in one of your Bible storybooks. Perhaps you drew a picture of the ark with giraffe heads peeking out of the windows. God told a man named Noah to build a huge ark for him and his family. God also told Noah to take two of every animal and bring them into the ark. That's why the ark had to be big!

This story takes place many years after God created the world. The people had turned away from God and didn't listen to Him anymore. Genesis 6:6 says that God was sorry He put people on the earth. He decided to wash everything away in a flood except for Noah and his family, because Noah loved and obeyed God.

Noah believed what God said even though he didn't understand everything. Noah built the ark just like God told him to. When Noah finished the ark, he and his family went inside. The pairs of animals went into the ark too. Then God closed the door. The rain poured down and flooded the earth. The ark kept Noah and his family and the animals safe because Noah had faith in God.

TALK TO GOD
Ask God to give you faith to believe in Him.

Do you know how Jesus is like the ark? Jesus can keep us safe too. When bad things happen in the world, we can trust in Jesus to help us. Jesus protects us from danger just like God protected Noah from the flood. It takes faith to believe because, like Noah, we don't always understand everything in our world. The next time you hear the story of Noah and the ark, remember that God keeps us safe. We can be like Noah and trust and obey God.

EXPLORE MORE: Can you guess how old Noah was when the flood was over? Read Genesis 8:13 for the answer.

God keeps me safe.

DID YOU KNOW?
Some people think there were as many as 30,000 animals on the ark.

God's Colorful Promise

"This is my promise to you: All life on the earth was destroyed by the flood. But that will never happen again. A flood will never again destroy all life on the earth." —Genesis 9:11 ERV

It must have been exciting for Noah and his family to finally come out of the ark after being inside for more than a year with all those animals. The animals were probably happy too! The lions and zebras could run across the dry land. Donkeys had room to kick their legs. Birds could fly from one tree to another, and giraffes could find fresh leaves to nibble on.

Noah was thankful that God kept his family safe during the flood. To thank God and to honor Him, Noah gave an offering. When the offering was burned, it smelled good. God was pleased with the sweet smell of the sacrifice. Then God made a promise to Noah, to all the animals, and to every living thing on earth. God promised that He would never send a great flood to destroy the earth again.

TALK TO GOD
Thank God for rainbows.

Then God did something awesome!

God wanted to give Noah a sign that would be a reminder of His promise. So God stretched a beautiful rainbow of colors across the sky—red, orange, yellow, green, blue, indigo, and violet. Can you imagine how amazing it was for Noah and his family to see the very first rainbow? From then on, whenever they saw a rainbow, they could remember God's wonderful promise. They didn't have to worry about a flood destroying the earth again.

The promise God made to Noah and his family is also for us. Every time you see a rainbow in the sky, you can remember how God kept Noah safe in the ark. The rainbow is a reminder to us that God will never send another flood to destroy the whole earth. And God always keeps His promises.

EXPLORE MORE: What does Genesis 9:18–19 tell us about Noah's three sons?

DID YOU KNOW?
In a double rainbow, the second one is less bright, and the colors are reversed.

The rainbow is a sign of God's promise.

Many More Promises

We can trust God to do what he promised. —Hebrews 10:23 ERV

God's promise to Noah is great. There are even more promises in the Bible that help us understand how much God loves us and cares about us. No one knows exactly how many promises there are, but some people have counted more than three thousand!

In Isaiah 41:10 God says, "Don't worry. I am with you. Don't be afraid or scared because I am your God. I will help you. I will make you strong. I will hold you with my steady hand." There's more than one promise packed into that verse, but knowing God's always with us means we are never alone.

Did you know God promises to be your counselor? In Psalm 32:8 He says, "I will teach you and guide you. I will show you how to live." When you talk to God and read His Word, you can ask God to help you make good decisions. God promises to help you.

TALK TO GOD
Thank God for one of His special promises to you.

In 1 Peter 5:7 it says: "Give all your worries to God. He cares about you." Everyone faces problems now and then—at home, at school, and even when you're playing sports. You may feel like there's no one who cares or is willing to listen. Well, guess what? God cares and He promises to listen!

Another great promise is God's promise to forgive our sins. In 1 John 1:9 it says, "If we confess our sins, God will forgive us. We can trust God to forgive us. He always does what is right. He will make us clean from all the wrong things we have done."

Those are only a few of God's promises, but you can read more in the Bible—about 3,000 more!

EXPLORE MORE: What does God promise in John 3:16?

God gives me thousands of promises.

The Tower That Didn't Get Finished

"Come on! Let's build a city for ourselves. Let's build a tower that reaches to the sky." —Genesis 11:4 NIrV

After the flood, Noah's sons had more children, grandchildren, and great-grandchildren. Many people lived on the earth, and they all settled in a land called Babylon. One day someone said, "Let's build a city and a tower to reach into the sky. Then we can all live in one place and be famous!" Everyone thought that was a good idea.

At this time, the people all spoke the same language, so they worked together to build their big city and mighty tower. But that is not what God wanted them to do. When Noah's family came out of the ark, God told them to fill the earth. By building the city and tower, they were not listening to God. They were trying to stay in one place and be famous.

TALK TO GOD
Ask God to help you understand His ways.

When God saw what they were doing, He did not like it. They were not obeying God. So God mixed up their language, which made them very confused. "What did you say? I don't understand you," one of the workers said. With different languages it was hard for them to work together, so they stopped building the city and the tower. The land was now called Babel and the people were confused. They ended up spreading out all over the world instead of staying in one place.

God always knows what's best, and the best thing we can do is obey Him. If you don't know what God wants you to do, ask Him to show you. You can also talk to your parents or another trustworthy adult. Before you make your plans, read the Bible and pray. That's called "seeking God's will." Once you are sure you understand what God wants you to do, then do it! And when you do things God's way, you can avoid a lot of confusion!

EXPLORE MORE: What does Isaiah 55:8–9 tell us about God's ways?

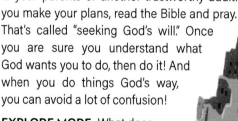

DID YOU KNOW?
The word *babel* means "a confused noise made by a number of voices."

God's ways are best.

A Big Surprise

"Is anything too hard for the Lord? I will return to you at the appointed time next year, and Sarah will have a son." —Genesis 18:14 NIV

Abraham was one of Noah's distant relatives who loved God very much. One day he was sitting under a tree when he saw three visitors walking toward him. He bowed to greet them and offered to get water to wash their feet. In those days people wore sandals and walked along dusty roads so their feet were often dirty. Abraham told his wife, Sarah, to bake some bread, and he told his servant to prepare some meat for the visitors to eat.

As Abraham talked with the men, they had some surprising news! They told Abraham that Sarah was going to have a baby the following year. Sarah was listening, and when she heard the news, she laughed because she was way too old to have a baby.

Many years before, God had promised Abraham that his family would become a great nation. Abraham didn't see how that could happen since he and Sarah didn't have any children and he and Sarah were old. But God kept His promise, and Sarah had a baby boy one year later. Abraham named him Isaac, which means laughter. The huge family God promised to give Abraham would come through Isaac.

TALK TO GOD
Thank God that He can do impossible things.

When things seem impossible to us, we need to remember that God can do anything. He is not limited like we are. When He says something is going to happen, it will. The Bible is filled with God's words and promises, and we can believe they are true.

Almost two thousand years after Isaac was born, another baby boy was born who was also promised by God. He is one of Abraham's distant relatives, a descendant, and His name is Jesus.

EXPLORE MORE: What does Psalm 127:3–4 say about children?

God can do things that are impossible for us.

DID YOU KNOW?
In Abraham's day, sandals were made from leather or wood. People used leather straps to tie them to their feet.

More Than We Can Imagine

God is able to do far more than we could ever ask for or imagine. He does everything by his power that is working in us. —Ephesians 3:20 NIrV

We know that God can do amazing things because He created the world and everything in it. He put the sun, moon, and stars in the sky. He keeps the planets in space as they revolve around the sun, creating seasons and years. He keeps the earth spinning, so we have both day and night. God puts glowing rainbows in the sky and paints orange and pink sunsets. He puts on a nighttime show with the Northern Lights when swirls of blue and green light dance across the sky. He makes rain fall from the clouds and tells the wind which way to blow. There is no way we can count all the things that God can do.

TALK TO GOD
Ask God to help you with a problem you have.

We can read in the Bible about what God has done in the past, and God is still doing amazing things today. Every snowflake that falls has its own design. The animals find food and water that God provides for them. And every newborn baby is a gift from God.

God does amazing things for you too. He wants to help you with whatever you need. If you are struggling with a math problem, you can ask God to help you figure it out. God may send just the right person to show you how to work out that problem. If a friend gets upset with you, ask God to show you ways that you can get along better. If a loved one is sick, you can ask God to make that person well.

God always listens when you talk to Him, but sometimes we have to wait to see how God will answer our prayers. Just remember that God can do anything, and sometimes He does more than we can imagine or even think about!

EXPLORE MORE: What does Psalm 147:4–5 tell us about God?

DID YOU KNOW?
The Northern Lights are also known as Aurora Borealis. The giant swirls of green, red, purple, or blue are most visible to people living in the far north.

God can do more than I can imagine.

A Long Hike

Abraham answered, "God himself will provide the lamb for the burnt offering, my son." And the two of them went on together.
—Genesis 22:8 NIV

Abraham was filled with joy when his son, Isaac, was born. Years later, God told Abraham to go to the region of Moriah and take Isaac with him. Abraham must have been sad and confused when God said the purpose of the trip was to offer Isaac as a sacrifice, just as people offered animals to God. How could God ask Abraham to give up the son He had promised?

Abraham trusted God and did what God asked even though he didn't understand. After walking for three long days, Abraham saw the place where God wanted him to build an altar. When Abraham placed the wood on the altar, Isaac asked, "Where is the lamb for the offering?" Abraham told Isaac, "God will provide the offering."

Abraham tied Isaac to the altar. But as he raised his knife, an angel of the Lord called out, "Abraham! Do not harm your son! Now I know you love God more than anything else."

Abraham looked up and saw a ram caught in the bushes. Instead of his son, Abraham sacrificed the ram. Abraham named that place The Lord Will Provide. The angel told Abraham that because he obeyed God, he would have many descendants. And people throughout the world would be "blessed," or cared for and happy, because Abraham obeyed God.

TALK TO GOD
Tell God how much you love Him.

This story of Abraham and Isaac is a symbol, like a picture that shows us what our salvation is like. The Lamb that God provides for our sacrifice is Jesus, His one and only Son. In the New Testament, John the Baptist said that Jesus is "the Lamb of God, who takes away the sin of the world" (John 1:29). Through Jesus, every person can have salvation.

EXPLORE MORE: Read Genesis 22:16–18. How did God describe the number of Abraham's descendants?

DID YOU KNOW?
In the days of Abraham, altars were made of dirt or stones found in a field, and no tool could be used to make them.

God will provide.

Happy Days and Hard Days

The Lord is close to all who call on him, yes, to all who call on him in truth. —Psalm 145:18 NLT

If you could describe a happy day, what would that look like? A day at the zoo? A day at the beach? Going camping with your family? Maybe you like playing in your neighborhood or going to a park. Almost everyone has something they enjoy doing. But the truth is that some days are not as much fun as other days, and some days can be really hard.

TALK TO GOD
Tell God about your day, and what makes it a happy or hard day for you.

The day that Abraham walked up the mountain to sacrifice his son Isaac must have been the hardest day of Abraham's life. Grown-ups have hard days sometimes—and so do kids. You may have to leave your home and neighborhood if your family needs to move someplace else. You may miss a friend's birthday party if you're sick. You might have to give your pet away if you find out you're allergic to it. Whether you are enjoying your favorite day, or experiencing a hard day, God is with you, and He cares about you.

When you are having a hard day, it helps to talk to someone like a parent or a friend. And you can also talk to God because He is close to you. He loves to hear your praises on happy days, and He also wants you to talk to Him on days that are hard. You can always tell God how you feel because He already knows. Is today a happy day, a hard day, or an in-between kind of day? You can be honest and truthful with God. He is waiting to hear from you.

EXPLORE MORE: Read James 5:13. When should we pray? When should we praise God?

DID YOU KNOW?
Some of the most popular outdoor activities kids enjoy are biking, hiking, camping, and fishing.

God knows what kind of day I am having.

A Wife for Isaac

Then he prayed, "Lord, you are the God of my master Abraham.
Make me successful today. Be kind to my master Abraham."
—Genesis 24:12 NIrV

Abraham was getting very old. His wife, Sarah, had passed away, and he wanted to find a wife for Isaac, his son. They were living in the land of Canaan, but Abraham wanted Isaac to marry someone from Harran, where his relatives lived. He wanted Isaac to have a wife who obeyed God.

Abraham asked his servant to travel to Harran to find a wife for Isaac. The servant loaded up ten camels with expensive gifts for the family of Isaac's soon-to-be bride. The servant traveled for weeks until he arrived at a well just outside of town.

Can you imagine how hard it might have been for Abraham's servant to find the right wife for Isaac? How would he know who she was, and what if she didn't want to go with him?

TALK TO GOD
Ask God to help you with something you need to do.

The servant prayed, "Oh Lord, please show kindness to my master Abraham. As I watch young women come to get water, I will say, 'May I have a drink from your jug?' If she says, 'Yes, and I will give water to your camels too,' let this be the one you have chosen for Isaac's wife."

Before the servant finished praying, a young woman named Rebekah came to the well. When the servant asked for a drink, she said, "Yes, have a drink, and I will also give water to your camels." The servant told Rebekah and her family about his prayer. They believed God had sent him and agreed to let Rebekah marry Isaac.

The servant depended on God to help him with this important assignment. Sometimes kids have important assignments or projects too. Just like the servant, we can ask God to help us complete what we need to do.

EXPLORE MORE: What does Genesis 24:67 say about Isaac's feelings for Rebekah?

God will help me complete my assignments.

DID YOU KNOW?
In countries such as India, Korea, and Bangladesh, some families still arrange marriages for their children.

Just Keep Praying

Do not worry about anything. But pray and ask God for everything you need. And when you pray, always give thanks. —Philippians 4:6 ICB

Grown-ups have many decisions to make, and so do kids. Some decisions, like what kind of cereal to eat or which pajamas to wear, are usually not a big deal. But as people get older and need to decide where to live, what school to attend, or what career to choose, that's a bigger deal.

When you have a big decision to make and don't know what to do, you might feel worried. But God tells us we can pray instead of worrying. God knows what you are thinking, so you can talk to Him about anything. Tell Him exactly what's on your mind. Ask Him to help you make the best decision, and then say thank you. You can say something like this: "Thank you, God, because I know you care about me. Thank you for helping me make good decisions. Thank you that you always listen to me and answer my prayers."

TALK TO GOD
Ask God to help you with a decision you need to make.

Sometimes God answers our prayers right away, and it's exciting to see how He helps us make good decisions. But sometimes we have to wait. Do you know what you can do while you wait for God to answer your prayer? Just keep praying. God never gets tired of hearing your prayers, even if you say the same prayer over and over.

It's true that God is our almighty creator. It's true that He is a holy God. But it's also true that He is your Father and friend. So talk to Him like you talk to a parent, or talk to Him like you talk to a friend. He loves to listen when you talk to Him.

EXPLORE MORE: Read 1 Thessalonians 5:16–18 to find out what God wants us to do in every situation.

DID YOU KNOW?

Playing board games helps you learn how to think and make decisions while having fun.

I can pray about my decisions.

It's Twins!

"May he give you and your children after you the blessing he gave to Abraham." —Genesis 28:4 NIrV

Abraham's son, Isaac, married Rebekah. When Rebekah was unable to have a baby, Isaac prayed and asked God to give them children. God answered Isaac's prayer and gave them twin sons named Esau and Jacob. Even though they were twins, they were very different. Esau was rugged and hairy. He loved the outdoors and became a skillful hunter. Jacob was quiet and liked to stay home cooking stew with his mother.

Just like many siblings, the brothers didn't always get along. Jacob was the younger twin, but he wanted the birthrights that belonged to Esau, who was the oldest. One day while Esau was out hunting, Jacob cooked a pot of lentil stew. When Esau came home, he was very hungry. Esau smelled the delicious stew and wanted some at once. If Jacob had been a good brother, he would have given Esau a bowl of stew right away. But instead, Jacob made Esau promise to give Jacob his birthright before he would give Esau a bowl of the stew.

Esau was so hungry he agreed to give Jacob his birthright. This meant that Jacob would be the head of the family and own the family's property instead of Esau. Then years later, Jacob took the blessing, which is a special prayer about the future, that was supposed to be for Esau. Isaac was about to die so Jacob tricked his father into believing he was Esau. This is how Isaac ended up blessing Jacob instead of Esau. It's no surprise that Esau was angry with his brother!

TALK TO GOD
Ask God to help you be kind to the people in your family.

Rebekah knew that Esau was furious, so she told Jacob to flee to Harran and live with her brother, Laban. Before Jacob left home, Isaac prayed over him. The blessings God had promised to Abraham would now be passed down from Isaac to Jacob and his descendants. And one of his descendants would be Jesus, the Messiah.

EXPLORE MORE: Read Genesis 27:15–16 to find out how Rebekah helped Jacob pretend to be Esau.

God's promises continue through many generations.

DID YOU KNOW?
Lentils are beans that are high in protein, rich in minerals, and a good source of fiber.

Love in the Family

Dear friends, let us love one another, because
love comes from God. Everyone who loves has
become a child of God and knows God.
—1 John 4:7 NIrV

It's pretty common for brothers and sisters to bother each other. Sometimes they fight over the last cookie or who has to feed the dog. But God's plan for the family is to love and support one another.

God puts families together in different ways. Some children are born into a family with a mom and dad. Some children become part of a family through adoption or foster care. When two families come together, it's called a blended family. Some kids might have one parent, and some kids live with their grandparents or other relatives. Families can be big, small, or in-between.

No matter what your family is like, God wants you to show love and kindness toward them, and there are many ways to do that! You can help your brother find his shoes or help your sister pick up her toys. You can read books or play games with your siblings while your parents have work to do. If you don't have a brother or sister, you can help by cleaning your room or putting your clothes away.

TALK TO GOD
Thank God for
your family.

We can show love to others with our words. Saying "please" and "thank you" are ways to respect each other. Saying "I love you" lets others know how you feel. We can also stay calm and use kind words when people do things that frustrate us. And if you're ever upset about something, it's okay to talk about it to help you feel better.

The Bible says that love comes from God. When we have God's love within us, we can ask Him to help us show love to our family—even if it's sharing the last cookie!

EXPLORE MORE: Why should we love others? See 1 John 4:19 to find the answer.

DID YOU KNOW?
Philadelphia is a city in Pennsylvania. The name Philadelphia means "city of brotherly love."

God wants me to love my family.

Jacob's Dream

"What an awesome place this is! It is none other than the house of God, the very gateway to heaven!" —Genesis 28:17 NLT

After he stole Esau's birthright and blessing, Jacob left home and traveled to Harran. As the sun was going down, he found a good place to camp for the night. After he fell asleep, Jacob had a dream. In his dream he saw stairs that reached down from heaven to earth. He saw angels going up and down the stairs, and he saw the Lord standing at the top.

Jacob heard the Lord speak to him. "I am the Lord," He said. "I am the God of your grandfather Abraham and the God of Isaac. I will give you and your children after you the land you are lying on. They will be like the dust of the earth that can't be counted. They will spread out to the west and to the east. They will spread out to the north and to the south. All nations on earth will be blessed because of you and your children after you. I am with you. I will watch over you everywhere you go. And I will bring you back to this land. I will not leave you until I have done what I promised."

TALK TO GOD
Say thank you to Jesus for being the stairway to heaven.

Doesn't this sound a lot like the promise God gave to Abraham? That's because it's the same promise! Jacob is Abraham's grandson, and God's promise would continue through Jacob's children, grandchildren, and great-grandchildren.

The stairway in Jacob's dream is a symbol of Jesus. Jesus can connect us to God like the stairs connected earth to heaven. When we believe in Jesus, He connects us to God.

When Jacob woke up, he was sure that God would always be with him. He was connected to God.

EXPLORE MORE: Read Genesis 28:11 to find out what Jacob used for a pillow.

Jesus is the stairway to heaven.

DID YOU KNOW?
The average person has about four dreams a night. Many people don't remember their dreams after they wake up.

Jacob Meets Rachel

He was still talking with [the shepherds] when Rachel came with her father's sheep. It was her job to take care of the flock.
—Genesis 29:9 NIrV

As Jacob traveled toward Harran, he stopped at a well where shepherds were waiting to water their sheep and goats. A heavy stone covered the mouth of the well, so they waited for more shepherds to come before they moved the stone. As Jacob waited with the shepherds, he asked some questions. "Where are you from?"

"We are from Harran," they answered.

"Do you know a man named Laban?" asked Jacob.

"Yes, we do," they answered. "And here comes his daughter Rachel with his flocks."

Jacob thought Rachel was beautiful. He told her that he was the son of Rebekah. Rachel quickly ran home to tell her father, Laban, about Jacob.

TALK TO GOD
Ask God to help you be patient as you wait for things you want or need.

Jacob lived with his uncle Laban and began working for him. When Laban wanted to pay him, Jacob said, "I will work for seven years if you give Rachel to me as my wife." Laban agreed. But at the end of seven years, Laban tricked Jacob and gave him Rachel's sister, Leah, to marry instead.

Jacob was angry Laban had tricked him. Do you think he remembered how he had tricked his brother Esau and his father Isaac? Laban said Jacob could marry Rachel after one week, but he would have to work for Laban another seven years. Jacob loved Rachel very much, so he agreed.

As Jacob worked for Laban, God helped him to be successful. Jacob began having children, and his family started to grow. God's promise to make his family into a great nation was beginning to unfold, but it would be many years before his descendants would be like the stars in the sky or sand on the seashore.

EXPLORE MORE: Read Genesis 29:26 to find out why Laban wanted Jacob to marry Leah.

DID YOU KNOW?
The land around Harran was dry, so heavy stones were placed over wells to prevent them from being filled with sand.

Sometimes God's promises take time.

What Will You Be?

The Lord says, "I will make you wise. I will show you where to go. I will guide you and watch over you." —Psalm 32:8 ICB

Jacob worked hard as a shepherd for his uncle Laban for many years. Being a shepherd was common in Bible times, but it is less common today. Do you know what you want to be when you grow up? Some kids might want to be a teacher, doctor, soccer player, scientist, artist, or an engineer—there are so many possibilities! If you don't know what you want to be yet, it's okay. You don't need to decide now, and you may change your mind many times. The important thing to remember is that God will grow you into the person He has created you to be.

TALK TO GOD
Ask God to help you discover your special talents.

Some people go to school for many years to earn degrees. Some work as assistants or aides before they reach the positions they hope to have. Others find work they enjoy without spending years in college.

While you are growing and learning, you will discover the special talents God has given you. Maybe you are a strong athlete, or maybe you enjoy music and art. God might have created you with a mind for learning about scientific things, or maybe you have a desire to care for children or animals.

God created you for a reason, and it will be exciting to find out who He wants you to be. As you grow into an adult, you can also grow in your love for God. Read the Bible and talk to Him often. Ask Him to show you the best path for your life. It can be a fun surprise to see where He leads you.

EXPLORE MORE: What good advice can you learn from Proverbs 3:5–6?

God will help me become who He wants me to be.

DID YOU KNOW?
One of the most common jobs in South Africa is a plumber.

Jacob Leaves Harran

Then the Lord said to Jacob, "Go back to the land of your fathers and to your relatives, and I will be with you." —Genesis 31:3 NIV

Jacob's family was growing. He wanted to bring his wives and children to his own country, but his uncle Laban didn't want him to leave. One day God spoke to Jacob and told him to return to the land of his father, grandfather, and relatives. God promised to be with him.

Jacob packed up his belongings and put his flocks of animals ahead of him. He put his wives and children on camels and set out for the land of Canaan. Three days after Jacob left, Laban realized he was gone. So, Laban chased after Jacob. Laban finally caught up with Jacob seven days later. Laban was angry that Jacob left without saying goodbye, but God warned him in a dream to leave Jacob alone. When they talked to each other, Jacob reminded Laban that he worked hard for him for twenty years, taking good care of his sheep and goats.

"Let's make an agreement," said Laban. Jacob set up a stone monument and told his family to gather stones and pile them in a heap. They ate a meal beside the pile of stones to celebrate the agreement. The pile of stones would be a reminder that Jacob and Laban agreed to live in peace and would not bring harm to each other.

The next morning, Laban kissed his daughters and grandchildren and blessed them. Then he returned home. As Jacob went on his way, angels came to meet him. "This is God's camp," he said. Jacob named the place *Mahanaim*, which means "two camps."

TALK TO GOD
Thank God that He goes with you wherever you go.

EXPLORE MORE: What did Jacob and Laban name the place where they built the pile of stones? See Genesis 31:45–47 for the answer.

DID YOU KNOW?

The Gateway Arch in St. Louis, Missouri, is the world's tallest monument at 630 feet (192 meters) high.

The God of Abraham, Isaac, and Jacob goes with me.

Jacob and Esau Meet Again

Jacob thought, "If I send this gift ahead of me, maybe Esau will forgive me. Then when I see him, perhaps he will accept me."
—Genesis 32:20 ICB

As Jacob traveled back toward Canaan, he came to the land of Edom. Do you know who lived in Edom? His brother Esau whom Jacob had not seen since he ran away. The last time they saw each other, Esau was angry because Jacob had tricked their father, Isaac, into giving him the birthright that belonged to Esau. It's no surprise that Jacob was afraid to see his brother again!

Jacob had an idea. He thought if he sent goats, rams, camels, and donkeys to Esau as a gift, maybe Esau would forgive him. Jacob sent his servants to tell Esau he wanted to see him. The servants returned and said that Esau was coming with an army of four hundred men. Now Jacob was more afraid than ever! He stayed where he was for the night and told his servants to bring the animals to Esau.

TALK TO GOD
Ask God to help you show love to the people in your family.

During the night, a man came and wrestled with Jacob. The man changed Jacob's name to Israel and blessed him. In the morning, Jacob realized that man was God. He named the place *Peniel*, which means "face of God."

Jacob saw Esau coming with his army. He divided his family into groups and went ahead of them. Esau ran to meet Jacob. He threw his arms around him and kissed him. Esau was not angry with Jacob anymore because God had changed his heart. He didn't even want the animals Jacob had offered as a gift. "I have enough," he told Jacob. But he accepted the gifts because Jacob insisted.

Jacob finally reached the land of Canaan and settled in a town where he built an altar to God.

EXPLORE MORE: In Genesis 33:15, what did Esau offer to do for Jacob?

God can change the hearts of people.

DID YOU KNOW?
The ancient land of Edom is now southwestern Jordan and lies between the Dead Sea and the Gulf of Aqaba.

What's Your Name?

God said to him, "Your name is Jacob. But you will not be called Jacob any longer. Your new name will be Israel." So he called him Israel. —Genesis 35:10 ICB

When we meet someone new, the first thing we ask is their name. Names are important because they tell others who we are. Some people are named after relatives or famous people. Some parents give their kids a name just because they like it. Names have meanings, too, and many people like to find out what their name means.

In the Bible most people only had first names. A person would be called, "Isaac, son of Abraham," or "Jacob, son of Isaac." We also read in the Bible that God sometimes changed a person's name. God changed Abram's name to Abraham, and Sarai's name to Sarah. In the New Testament, Jesus changed Simon's name to Peter. In the story of Jacob, we learn that God changed his name to Israel.

God promised Jacob that his descendants would become a great nation. Since his name was changed to Israel, his sons were known as the sons of Israel. His descendants were known as Israelites.

Today people have a first and last name, and most people have a middle name. Our last name tells what family we are from. Different cultures have different ways of naming their children, but every culture believes names are important.

TALK TO GOD
Thank God for being your Father.

Another name we can have is the name Christian. People who are Christians are followers of Christ. Any person can be called a Christian if they believe that Jesus is the Son of God who died to forgive our sins. If you are a Christian, it means that God is your Father, and you are part of His family. It's the most important name of all!

EXPLORE MORE: Read Genesis 17:3–6 to find out why God changed Abram's name to Abraham.

DID YOU KNOW?
The name Jesus means "God saves us."

My name is important.

Joseph and His Brothers

"You planned to harm me. But God planned it for good. He planned to do what is now being done. He wanted to save many lives."
—Genesis 50:20 NIrV

Jacob had twelve sons and one daughter. One of his sons was named Joseph. Joseph's brothers were jealous when their father gave Joseph a colorful robe. One day the brothers threw Joseph into a pit. When a group of traders came by, the brothers pulled Joseph out of the pit and sold him to the traders for twenty pieces of silver. The traders traveled to Egypt and sold Joseph to a man named Potiphar. The man let Joseph live in the palace and put Joseph in charge of his other servants.

Joseph worked in the palace and was successful until a woman lied about him. He was sent to prison, but God was with him and helped him. When God helped Joseph explain the meaning of the king's strange dreams, the king let Joseph out of prison. The king put Joseph in charge and trusted Joseph to get the people and the land ready for a big famine.

TALK TO GOD
Ask God to help you forgive people who are unkind.

When the famine came there was not enough food for everyone to eat. But Joseph had told the people in Egypt to save some food, so people from other lands came to Egypt to buy food. The famine brought Joseph's brothers to Egypt too. They did not recognize him, but Joseph knew who they were. The brothers bowed down to Joseph because he was a great leader. After several visits, Joseph finally told his brothers who he was. They were afraid he would be angry that they had treated him so badly. But Joseph showed love to his brothers. He said it was all part of God's big plan to save many people's lives.

Like Joseph, Jesus was treated badly. Jesus suffered and died so that people could live. It was all part of God's big plan to save us.

EXPLORE MORE: Joseph had some dreams about his brothers. Read Genesis 37:5–11 to find out what they were.

We can trust God's plans.

DID YOU KNOW?
The most common cloth in biblical times was wool. It was easy to dye, which made it possible to make a coat of many colors.

Forgive Others

Be kind and tender to one another. Forgive one another, just as God forgave you because of what Christ has done. —Ephesians 4:32 NIrV

No one wants to be friends with someone who is mean. Sometimes when a person is mean to us, we feel like being mean back. If someone is mean to you, tell your parents or another grown-up so they can help you. Talking about the problem can help a lot, but sometimes it doesn't make it go away.

Many times when kids are mean, it's because they are not happy. Maybe they feel like no one likes them. Maybe they have a problem at school or at home. You can try being kind to a mean person. But sometimes it takes more than just being kind.

TALK TO GOD
Ask God to help you show kindness and forgiveness to others.

What can you do if someone is being mean to you? You can pray for them and ask God to change their heart. You can forgive them for being mean. And you can find other kids to play with who are nice.

No one is perfect, and we all do things that are wrong. But God loves us so much that He forgives us when we sin. Jesus died on the cross to take away all the wrong things we do. Because God forgives us, He wants us to forgive others. When you forgive someone for being mean, you're not saying the way they treated you is okay. Rather, you are deciding not to be mean back to them or carry anger toward them in your heart.

Joseph could have treated his brothers badly when they came to Egypt to buy grain. But instead, he forgave them and was kind to them. You can be like Joseph and forgive those who are mean to you.

EXPLORE MORE: Read Genesis 47:5–6 to find out how Pharaoh treated Joseph's father and brothers.

DID YOU KNOW?
Forgiveness is good for your health. It helps you sleep better.

God wants me to forgive others.

Moses and the Burning Bush

"I am sending you to Pharaoh. I want you to bring the Israelites out of Egypt. They are my people." —Exodus 3:10 NIrV

Jacob's family lived in Egypt for more than four hundred years and became a big nation called Israel. Many years passed after Joseph died, and a new king called Pharaoh, didn't know that Joseph had helped the Egyptians. All he knew was that too many Israelites lived in his land, and he was afraid they would take over his kingdom. He treated the Israelites like slaves and didn't want them to have more children.

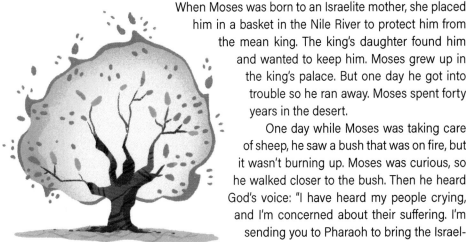

When Moses was born to an Israelite mother, she placed him in a basket in the Nile River to protect him from the mean king. The king's daughter found him and wanted to keep him. Moses grew up in the king's palace. But one day he got into trouble so he ran away. Moses spent forty years in the desert.

One day while Moses was taking care of sheep, he saw a bush that was on fire, but it wasn't burning up. Moses was curious, so he walked closer to the bush. Then he heard God's voice: "I have heard my people crying, and I'm concerned about their suffering. I'm sending you to Pharaoh to bring the Israelites out of Egypt."

Moses was not happy about this assignment! He was afraid to talk to Pharaoh and the Israelites. God told Moses that He would be with him. But Moses said, "What should I say when they ask who sent me?" God told him, "Say this to the Israelites: 'I Am has sent me to you'" (Exodus 3:14). I Am is a name for God, and many centuries later, Jesus said, "Before Abraham was born, I Am!" He said this to show that He was God.

God promised to help Moses, and God will help you serve Him, too, even if it's a big assignment.

EXPLORE MORE: God told Moses to do something at the burning bush. Read Exodus 3:4–5 to find out what it was.

TALK TO GOD
Thank God that He will help you with your big assignments.

When God asks me to do something, He will help me.

DID YOU KNOW?
Moses's baby basket was made from a plant called papyrus. It was covered with sticky tar to make it float.

Go with God

"Now go! I will help you speak. I will tell you what to say."
—Exodus 4:12 ICB

God has created each of us with special talents that we can use to help and serve others. People who are good singers are often asked to sing in church or school. If a coach wants a good baseball team, he tries to find the best players. Artists are often asked to paint pictures for hospitals or community centers. People who understand how computers work can create fun and helpful apps.

But do you know what? God doesn't always look for the smartest or most talented people to do His work.

Moses didn't want to go to Egypt. When he talked to God at the burning bush, he said, "I am not very good at speaking and my words get all tangled." God told Moses that He would be with him and help him know what to say. Moses kept making excuses and finally said to God, "Please send someone else!"

TALK TO GOD
Thank God for doing great things through His people.

When Moses kept making excuses, God said He would send Moses's brother, Aaron, with him. God also gave them special signs to perform that would show they had God's power. Once again God said, "Go! And I will be with you." So, Moses finally agreed.

Someday God might ask you to do something you don't feel like you can do. Maybe you think that you are too young or not talented enough. But just as God promised to be with Moses, God will also be with you. God can do great things in our lives, but it's not because we are great. It's because God is great!

EXPLORE MORE: Read Exodus 4:1–5 to learn about one of the signs God gave to Moses.

DID YOU KNOW?
In 1508, Pope Julius II asked Michelangelo to paint the Sistine Chapel's ceiling. It took four years for him to paint scenes from the Old Testament, including the creation story and Noah's ark.

God can use me to do great things.

Pharaoh's Stubborn Heart

"The blood on your houses will be a sign for you. When I see the blood, I will pass over you. No deadly plague will touch you when I strike Egypt." —Exodus 12:13 NIrV

Moses and his brother, Aaron, went to Egypt to talk to Pharaoh. They asked him to let the Israelites leave Egypt. Pharaoh said no! That's when God sent lots of trouble—known as plagues. First, the rivers turned to blood. Then frogs, gnats, and flies took over the land. Every time God sent a plague, Pharaoh said he would let the people leave. But each time God stopped a plague, Pharaoh changed his mind.

TALK TO GOD
Thank God that we can celebrate His goodness every day.

God sent more plagues. The animals got sick and died, people got sores on their skin, and a fierce storm pounded Egypt. Then God sent a plague of locusts. Grasshoppers covered the land and ate all of the plants in Egypt. In the next plague, God made Egypt very dark. The Egyptians could not see anything for three days. But even with all these troubles, Pharaoh didn't let the Israelites leave.

God gave Moses some special instructions. He said that each family had to choose a lamb without flaws. At sundown, they were told to paint the sides and top of the doorways with blood from the lamb. They needed to cook the lamb over a fire and eat it while they were dressed and ready to leave.

The Israelites did what God said. That night, the angel of the Lord passed through Egypt, killing the firstborn male in every Egyptian family. But the Israelites, who had the blood on their doorframes, were saved. Their sons did not die. This was the tenth plague that God sent to Egypt. Pharaoh knew he was no match for God and begged the people to leave.

This event is known as the Passover, and the lamb is called the Passover lamb. In the New Testament, the apostle Paul calls Jesus "our Passover Lamb" (1 Corinthians 5:7). Jesus is the Lamb whose blood was shed on the cross for our sins.

EXPLORE MORE: What instructions did God give to the Israelites on celebrating the Passover? Read Exodus 12:14–16 to find out.

Jesus is the Lamb of God.

DID YOU KNOW?
The Egyptians were so eager for the Israelites to leave that they gave them clothing, gold, and silver.

Follow the Pillar

The pillar of cloud was always with them during the day. And the pillar of fire was always with them at night. —Exodus 13:22 ICB

God brought the children of Israel out of Egypt just as He had promised Moses at the burning bush. God had seen how the people were mistreated and wanted to lead them to the land of Canaan. This land was known as the promised land. It had lots of good stuff like milk and honey, and fresh fruits and vegetables. To get to the promised land, the people had to travel through the wilderness.

God did not lead the Israelites on the shortest route. He wanted to protect them from the Philistines who might want to fight with them. God led them through the wilderness toward the Red Sea.

TALK TO GOD
Ask God to lead you on the right path.

Back then, people didn't have GPS or maps on their phones to help them know where to go. There were no road signs in the wilderness telling them how far it was to the Red Sea. But God didn't leave them on their own. He was with them. During the day, He moved with the people in a long, tall cloud, called a pillar of cloud. At night, He moved with them in a long, tall pillar of fire. The pillars reminded the people that God was always with them.

Did you know that the Holy Spirit is like the pillars of cloud and fire? The Holy Spirit is always with us and leads the way. Sometimes our lives can change. Maybe your family needs to move to another home away from friends and relatives. Or maybe you need to go to a new school where you don't know anyone. If your life changes, don't worry. Just trust and follow God. He will lead you on the right path.

DID YOU KNOW?
The big, white puffy clouds we see floating in the sky are called cumulus clouds. They look like giant balls of cotton.

EXPLORE MORE: Read Exodus 14:19–20 to find out how the pillar of cloud protected the Israelites.

God leads me.

A Walk through the Sea

And when the Israelites saw the mighty hand of the Lord displayed against the Egyptians, the people feared the Lord and put their trust in him and in Moses his servant. —Exodus 14:31 NIV

Soon after the Israelites left Egypt, Pharaoh changed his mind and went after them. He got his chariots, rounded up his troops, and began the chase. Pharaoh and his army caught up to the Israelites as they camped for the night near the Red Sea. The people were afraid. They didn't see any way to escape. They cried out to Moses, "Why did you bring us out here to die? It's better to be a slave in Egypt than to die in the wilderness!" But Moses told them to stay calm and watch what God would do.

TALK TO GOD
Tell God what He does that amazes you.

God told Moses to pick up his staff and raise his hand over the sea. Moses did what God told him to do. As he raised his staff, God sent a strong east wind to split the sea in half. Now the people had a path in the sea to walk on. The wind blew all night long, holding back the water so the Israelites could walk through the sea on dry land.

When the last person reached the other side, God told Moses to raise his staff over the sea again. This time the water fell back into the sea. The path was gone, and the water swallowed the Egyptian army. The Israelites were finally free from the Egyptians.

When the people saw how God had parted the water to make a path for them, they were amazed. They put their trust in God and in Moses as their leader. The Israelites sang a song of praise to the God who had saved them from their enemies.

EXPLORE MORE: What did the people say about God in Exodus 15:2–3?

God delivers His people.

DID YOU KNOW?
The Red Sea is a popular spot for divers and snorkelers from all over the world. It has old shipwrecks, coral reefs, and hundreds of underwater species.

The God of Miracles

He alone is your God, the only one who is worthy of your praise, the one who has done these mighty miracles that you have seen with your own eyes. —Deuteronomy 10:21 NLT

Can you imagine what it was like for the Israelites to see the waters of the Red Sea split into two sides leaving a dry path for them to walk across? The Israelites were amazed at God's power as they watched this awesome miracle happen right before their eyes. Do you think there were any fish flopping on the path or sea turtles wondering what happened? What an exciting night that was for the Israelites!

The Bible is filled with miracles that show us how awesome and powerful God is. He used His powers to create the entire world and continues to show His power today. God is the one who makes rain and snow fall from the clouds. He flashes lightning across the heavens and makes the thunder roar. He tells the ocean waves where to stop and tells the sun when to rise. He guides a flock of noisy geese through the air and sends a gust of wind so eagles can soar. God provides food and water for the animals and cares for every living creature. And God cares about people too!

TALK TO GOD
Thank God for miracles.

In today's verse from Deuteronomy, Moses reminded the people how God performed amazing miracles for them. Moses told the people that God is worthy of our praise. Moses said, "He alone is the God of gods, and the Lord of lords. He is a great and mighty and awesome God who owns everything in heaven and on earth."

The next time you go for a walk and see the miracles of His creation, remember that God is great and worthy of your praise.

EXPLORE MORE: Who should praise God? See Psalm 145:21 to find the answer.

DID YOU KNOW?
There are more than 120 miracles recorded in the Bible.

God alone is worthy of praise.

Waiting for God's Promises

Wait for the Lord. Be strong and don't lose hope. Wait for the Lord.
—Psalm 27:14 NIrV

When God promised Abraham his descendants would be as many as the stars in the sky and the grains of sand on the shore, Abraham didn't even have a child. But the promise God made to Abraham continued through his son Isaac, his grandson Jacob, and the Israelites. Hundreds of years later, God's promise came true. Jacob's family arrived in Egypt with around 70 people. By the time the Israelites left, there were more than 3 million people, and the numbers kept growing.

TALK TO GOD
Thank God for keeping His promises.

When Jacob and his family moved from Canaan to Egypt during the famine, God told Jacob that he would die there, but God would bring his descendants back to Canaan. Four hundred years later, God chose Moses to lead the children of Israel out of Egypt. That was the beginning of their return to Canaan and the fulfilling of God's promise.

In the Old Testament, God also made many promises of a Messiah, and those promises came true when Jesus was born two thousand years later. It's exciting to read the Bible and see how many of God's promises came true, even if it took hundreds or thousands of years.

The Bible is more than stories about people who lived a long time ago. The Bible is God's Word to us, and many of His promises are for us today. God promises to listen when we talk to Him, and He promises to answer our prayers. But sometimes we need to wait for His answers. As we read the stories in the Bible, and see how God's promises always come true, we can trust God to keep His promises.

EXPLORE MORE: What did Moses bring with him out of Egypt? Read Exodus 13:19 to find out.

God keeps His promises.

DID YOU KNOW?
Joseph was seventeen when he went to Egypt.

Thirsty People

"I am the Lord, who heals you." —Exodus 15:26 NIV

Have you ever gone a long time without drinking water? If you have, were you thirsty? Our bodies need water every day in order for them to work well. When we don't get enough water, we can feel tired and dizzy or have a bad headache.

After Moses led the Israelites across the Red Sea, they went into the Desert of Shur. They traveled for three days without finding water, and they became thirsty. They probably didn't feel very well either.

They finally came to a place called Marah where there was water, but the people couldn't drink it because the water was bitter. They grumbled and asked Moses, "What are we supposed to drink?"

TALK TO GOD
Thank God for water to drink when you are thirsty.

Moses cried out to God, and God showed Moses a piece of wood. He told Moses to throw the wood into the water. Moses did what God told him to do, and the bitter water became sweet so the people could drink it. Then God said to Moses, "If you listen carefully to the Lord your God and do what is right in his eyes, if you pay attention to his commands and keep all his laws, I will not bring on you any of the diseases I brought on the Egyptians. I am the LORD, who heals you" (Exodus 15:26).

When the people left Marah, they came to a place called Elim. And guess what? There were twelve springs of water and seventy palm trees in Elim! Can you imagine how excited the people of Israel were? That night, the people camped near the water and were no longer thirsty.

EXPLORE MORE: What else can we thirst for besides water? Read Psalm 42:2 to find out.

DID YOU KNOW?
A person can live without water for about three days, but some people have lived a few days longer without water.

God takes care of His people.

Bread from Heaven

"I am the living bread that came down from heaven. Everyone who eats some of this bread will live forever. This bread is my body. I will give it for the life of the world."
—John 6:51 NIrV

At first, the Israelites were happy to be free from their lives of slavery in Egypt. They no longer had to work hard for the Egyptian king, who was called Pharaoh. But after a while their empty stomachs rumbled, and they became tired of living in the desert.

On the fifteenth day of the second month after coming out of Egypt, they grumbled against Moses and Aaron. "We were better off in Egypt because we had food to eat!" they said.

God heard their complaining and told Moses He would send food for the people. So, at night, God sent a kind of bird called quail for the people to eat. In the morning dew covered the ground. When the dew was gone, thin flakes of bread appeared. The people looked at it and said, "What is it?" That's how this food got the name *manna*, which means "what is it?" The manna tasted like wafers made with honey. God told them to pick up the manna every morning for six days. On the sixth day they needed to pick up enough for two days so they could rest on the seventh day, called the Sabbath.

TALK TO GOD
Tell Jesus thank you for being our Living Bread.

Did you know that manna is also a symbol for Jesus? When Jesus lived on earth, He said He was the Living Bread that came down from heaven. Just like manna fed the people to keep them alive, Jesus gives us what we need to live with God forever and ever. The Israelites had to collect manna six days a week, but we only need to accept Jesus one time. Once we believe in Him, the life He gives us lasts forever.

EXPLORE MORE: What did God tell Moses to do with some of the manna? You can find the answer in Exodus 16:32–33.

Jesus is the Living Bread.

DID YOU KNOW?
Before erasers were invented, people used a moist, rolled-up piece of bread as an eraser.

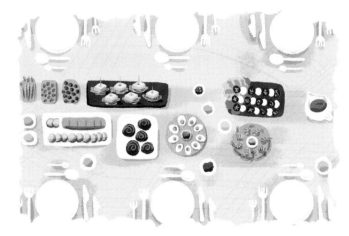

God Provides

You take care of the land and water it. You make it very fertile. The rivers of God are full of water. Grain grows because you make it grow. —Psalm 65:9 ICB

Moses prayed to God to provide food and water for the Israelites, and God answered his prayer. Even in the middle of a dry desert, God led them to water and sent bread from heaven. God is all-powerful, and He can do anything, anywhere.

Just as God provided for the Israelites, He also provides for us today. Some people buy their food from a grocery store or farmers market, while others walk into fields or gardens to pick fresh grain, fruits, and vegetables from the ground. Some people turn on a faucet to get a drink, while others pump the handle of a well until fresh water comes spilling out. No matter how or where we get our food and water, it all comes from God.

TALK TO GOD
Thank God for the food He provides.

God controls the weather, sending rays of sunshine and drops of rain to make the crops grow. He controls the seasons that allow farmers to plant seeds at the right time and gather crops at harvest time. And He provides a way for all that food to get on our dinner tables. God takes care of us through every detail!

As Moses led the people of Israel through the wilderness, they were fully dependent on God. They lived one day at a time, not knowing what the next day would bring. They knew that everything they had came from God. Sometimes it's hard for us to remember that everything we have comes from God too. The next time you sit at the table to eat a meal, or unwrap a tasty snack, you can thank God for all He provides.

DID YOU KNOW?
Some of the most important crops in the world are potatoes, rice, wheat, and corn.

EXPLORE MORE: Besides people, who does God provide food for? Look up Psalm 147:9 for the answer.

Our food and water come from God.

Water from a Rock

They all drank the same spiritual drink. They drank from that spiritual rock that was with them. That rock was Christ. —1 Corinthians 10:4 ICB

For many years, God continued to lead Moses and the Israelites through the wilderness. When they camped at a place called Rephidim, they once again found themselves without water to drink. This time they not only complained, but they were angry at Moses and demanded that he give them water. So once again, Moses cried out to God for help.

God gave Moses some special instructions. He said, "Walk ahead of the people and take some elders with you. Take the walking stick in your hand that you used to strike the Nile River. I will stand before you at the rock of Horeb. When you strike the rock, water will come out for the people" (Exodus 17:5–6). Moses did exactly what God told him to do. Enough water poured out of the rock for thousands of people and cattle.

TALK TO GOD
Ask God to give you both spiritual food and physical food.

In the New Testament, the apostle Paul writes about this miracle in 1 Corinthians 10:1–4. He reminds his readers of the time when God led the people of Israel through the sea as they followed the cloud before them. They ate and drank in the wilderness as God provided for their physical needs. But God provided even more. The way He provided for them through miracles taught the people that He was their God, and they were His people. They could depend on Him and trust Him for everything. God fed them physical food for their bodies as well as spiritual food for their souls.

The rock in this story was more than a giant mass of stone and minerals. It represented Jesus, who offers living water to all who believe in Him.

EXPLORE MORE: Read Exodus 17:7 to discover the two names Moses gave the place at Mount Horeb.

Jesus is my rock.

DID YOU KNOW?
The three main rock groups are igneous rock, sedimentary rock, and metamorphic rock.

Smoke on the Mountain

The Lord spoke to Moses. He said, "I am going to come to you in a thick cloud. The people will hear me speaking with you. They will always put their trust in you." —Exodus 19:9 NIrV

Three months after the Israelites left Egypt, they came to the Desert of Sinai and camped in front of a mountain. Moses climbed the mountain, then God called out to him. God said to Moses, "Tell the people of Israel that they have seen what I did to Egypt and how I carried you out like an eagle carries its young. If they obey me and keep my covenant, they will be my treasured possession." Moses delivered God's message to the people who said, "We will do everything the Lord says."

God told Moses He would come to him in a thick cloud and the people would be able to hear His voice. God wanted the people to trust Moses as His chosen leader. But before God appeared to them, He told Moses the people needed to get ready for two days by washing their clothes. Moses gave the people God's message, so that's what they did.

TALK TO GOD
Ask God to help you be more aware of His presence.

On the morning of the third day, lightning flashed and thunder boomed. A thick cloud hung above the mountain, and a loud trumpet blast was heard throughout the land. Mount Sinai trembled as the Lord came down to the mountain. God told Moses to warn the people not to come close to the mountain.

The mountain was set apart as holy because God was on it. Only Aaron was allowed to go up the mountain with Moses.

Moses and Aaron went up the mountain to meet with God, while the people stayed below. And just like the mountain trembled, the people trembled in God's presence.

DID YOU KNOW?
The most popular time to climb Mount Sinai is during the night, so that climbers can reach the top in time to see a beautiful sunrise.

EXPLORE MORE: What does Hebrews 10:22 tell us about coming near to God?

God's presence is powerful.

Our Holy God

"Holy, holy, holy is the Lord Almighty; the whole earth
is full of his glory." —Isaiah 6:3 NIV

We can learn a lot about God by reading the Bible. The words in the Bible are one way God speaks to us. As we read different books in the Bible, we learn that God is our creator, Father, shepherd, healer, Savior, and friend. God is someone we can talk to anytime or anywhere because He loves us, and He is always with us. The Bible also teaches us that God is a holy God.

The word *holy* comes from the Hebrew word *kedush*, which means "separate." God is holy because He is separated from evil or anything that is unclean. To be holy means to be pure and perfect. When we say God is holy, it refers to His power, perfection, and majesty.

TALK TO GOD
Praise God that He
is a holy God.

There are many verses in the Bible that we can read to learn about God's holiness. But we can also see evidence of His holiness in the world He created. We call this God's *glory*. Colorful sunsets, glowing rainbows, bright flowers, tiny white snowflakes, and millions of stars show us God's glory. Only a holy God could create such magnificent things.

God's glory is all around us and we can see it everywhere. We see it in blue skies, wispy clouds, and golden sunbeams. Some people find God's glory in beautiful oceans and sandy beaches, while others may see His glory in tall oak trees, large mountains, or colorful birds. No matter where we see God's glory, it reminds us that we worship a holy God. How will you see God's glory today?

EXPLORE MORE: What does Psalm 97:12 tell us to do?

God is holy.

DID YOU KNOW?
The hymn "Holy, Holy, Holy" was written in the 1800s by Reginald Heber. The word *holy* is used in the song more than fifteen times.

The Ten Commandments

God spoke all these words: "I am the Lord your God, who brought you out of Egypt, out of the land of slavery." —Exodus 20:1–2 NIV

God spoke to Moses while he was on Mount Sinai. God gave Moses special rules for the people. These rules are called the Ten Commandments. God gave His people these rules to live by so they would understand how to love God and each other. The first four commandments are about loving God: "You shall have no other gods before me. You shall not make idols or bow down to them. You shall not use my name in a way that disrespects me. Keep the Sabbath day holy for this day belongs to me."

The next six rules are about loving others: "Honor your father and your mother so you will live long in the land I am giving you. Do not kill anyone. Do not take another person's husband or wife for yourself. Do not steal. Do not lie. Do not want the things your neighbors own."

After God gave these rules to Moses, thunder rumbled, lightning flashed, trumpets blared, and smoke was all around the mountain. The Israelites did not go near the mountain. They knew God was on it and they respected God's presence.

God wrote the Ten Commandments on two stone tablets and gave them to Moses so the people would remember how He wanted them to live. We can read the commandments in the Old Testament books of Exodus and Deuteronomy. They can also be found hanging on walls in churches and other buildings.

God didn't give the Ten Commandments as a list of rules to keep us from doing things we want to do. Following God's rules helps us to make good choices so we can have safe and happy lives.

EXPLORE MORE: What did God tell Moses after He gave him the Ten Commandments? Read Exodus 20:22–24 to find out.

TALK TO GOD
Thank God for the Bible and for commandments that help you make good choices.

DID YOU KNOW?
The largest display of the Ten Commandments is in Murphy, North Carolina, in the Fields of the Wood. The letters are 5 feet tall and 4 feet wide (about 1.2 by 1.5 meters).

God gives me commandments to help me make good choices.

It's the Right Thing to Do

Children, obey your parents the way the Lord wants, because this is the right thing to do. —Ephesians 6:1 ERV

The fifth commandment that God gave to Moses is this: "You must honor and respect your father and your mother. Do this so that you will have a full life in the land that the Lord your God gives you" (Exodus 20:12).

The way to honor and respect your parents is to obey them. Your parents love you and care about you. They want to protect you and keep you safe. This commandment comes with a promise that children who obey their parents will live a long and happy life. When kids disobey and get into trouble, it can cause problems. But when kids obey their parents, it's a better way to live.

TALK TO GOD
Thank God for the grown-ups who are raising you.

Not all kids have parents who raise them. Some children live with grandparents, other relatives, or grown-ups who have chosen to love and care for them. Whoever it is that's caring for you, God wants you to listen to them and obey them.

Many grown-ups who raise children also teach them things that will help them as they get older. They teach their children how to be polite and helpful. They remind their kids to do their homework, practice the piano, clean their room, or feed the dog. These may seem like more rules to follow, but these rules help kids to grow into responsible adults.

When you remember that your parents' rules come from a place of love, it makes them easier to obey. The same is true for God. He loves you and wants to protect you. When you obey, it shows Him that you love Him too.

EXPLORE MORE: What does Psalm 103:17–18 tell us about God?

I show my love for God when I obey my parents.

DID YOU KNOW?
In the United States, more than 13 million children live with their grandparents. In many Asian cultures grandparents live in the same house with their children and grandchildren.

The Israelites Build a Tent

"The people must build a holy place for me. Then I can live among them. Build this Holy Tent and everything in it by the plan I will show you." —Exodus 25:8–9 ICB

In the book of Genesis, we learn how God gave Noah special instructions for building an ark. God told Moses to build something, too, but it wasn't a giant boat. God told Moses He wanted the Israelites to build a tent where they could meet with Him. This tent was not the kind people use when they go camping. It was known as the Holy Tent or tabernacle, and it would be God's dwelling place.

God gave instructions on how to build the tent and what needed to go inside. He asked people to bring offerings of gold, silver, bronze, fine linen, and purple and red thread. They also needed to bring cloth made from goat's hair, olive oil for lamps, sheepskins, and acacia wood. The people could give as much or as little as they wanted. They were so excited to give that they brought more than enough.

TALK TO GOD
Thank God that you can meet with Him anywhere.

The yard around the tent was where the people offered sacrifices to God. The tent had two rooms: the Holy Place and the Most Holy Place. A thick curtain separated the two rooms. Only the priests were allowed in the Holy Place. Only the leader of the priests, called the *high priest*, was allowed to enter the Most Holy Place.

Did you know that the tabernacle was a symbol for Jesus? When Jesus was born, God came to earth in human form. Jesus's body was like a tabernacle where God lived. When people met with Jesus, they were also meeting with God. If you believe in Jesus as your Savior, then God also lives in you.

EXPLORE MORE: What colors of yarn were used to make the curtain for the entrance to the courtyard? Read Exodus 27:16 to find out.

DID YOU KNOW?
The people were able to move the tabernacle because it was "portable." Whenever the people moved to another place, they would take the tabernacle down and set it up again.

God lives in His people.

Cheerful Givers

Each one of you should give what you have decided in your heart to give. You should not give if it makes you unhappy or if you feel forced to give. God loves those who are happy to give. —2 Corinthians 9:7 ERV

When God asked the Israelites to give items to help build the tabernacle, they were happy and excited to give. Even though the Israelites often grumbled and complained in the wilderness, this time their hearts were filled with joy. They gladly brought their gifts and worked to construct the Holy Tent.

The men and women used their skills to build the tabernacle. Those who were skilled at crafts carved artistic designs in gold and wood. Their work was an offering, which means it was a gift to God. Many years later, in the New Testament, the apostle Paul writes to the church to remind them to be cheerful givers too.

When we think about giving an offering to God, we often think it means money. But there are other ways you can give offerings to God. Like the Israelites, you can use your talents and abilities to help others. If you are a good reader, you can listen to a friend or sibling as they learn to read. If you are good at sports, you may be able to help someone learn how to play soccer or basketball.

TALK TO GOD
Ask God to help you use your skills for Him.

Do you play the piano or another musical instrument? If so, you can play a song for your family or youth group. Are you an artist? Giving someone a picture you created will make them smile. When you share your gifts and talents with others, you are not only giving good things to them, but you are also giving to God.

Whether you give money, a song, or a colorful picture, giving with a cheerful heart is the best way to give. It will put a smile on your face too.

EXPLORE MORE: Read Exodus 36:1 to learn the names of two skilled workers who helped build the tabernacle.

I will give with a happy heart.

DID YOU KNOW?
Studies have shown that giving to others can make us happier and healthier.

A Calf Made from Gold

So the people collected all their gold earrings and brought them to Aaron. He took the gold from the people and used it to make an idol. Using a special tool, he shaped the gold into a statue of a calf. —Exodus 32:3–4 ERV

When Moses was on Mount Sinai meeting with God, the people of Israel began to think he was not coming back. They asked Aaron to make a god for them that they could see. Aaron could have reminded them that God was the one true God, and the *only* God they worshiped, but he didn't. He agreed to make a god for the people.

The people brought their gold jewelry to Aaron. He melted the gold and shaped it to look like a small cow. The next day the Israelites brought offerings to the gold calf and had a grand celebration with food and drink. They worshiped the gold calf like they should have worshiped God. God saw what they were doing, and He told Moses to go down the mountain right away.

TALK TO GOD
Thank God that He is the one true God.

When Moses saw the people dancing and having a wild party in front of the calf, he became angry. He had the Ten Commandments written on stone tablets in his hands. He threw the tablets to the ground, and they broke into pieces. He melted the golden calf and turned it into dust. Then he mixed the dust into their drinking water and made the people drink it.

It must have broken God's heart to see His people worshiping a fake god. Moses pleaded with God to forgive the people. Moses stood at the front of the camp and asked everyone who wanted to follow God to come to him. The people from the tribe of Levi came to Moses, and from that day on the Levites were chosen to serve God.

DID YOU KNOW?
Gold begins to melt when the temperature is about 1,943° Fahrenheit (1,064° Celsius). That's a lot of heat!

EXPLORE MORE: How did Aaron explain the golden calf to Moses? Read what he said in Exodus 32:24.

God is the only true God.

No Other Gods

"Do not put any other gods in place of me. Do not make for yourself statues of gods that look like anything in the sky. They may not look like anything on the earth or in the water either."
—Exodus 20:3–4 NIrV

When God gave Moses the Ten Commandments, the first commandment was "You shall have no other gods before me." That commandment was not just for the Israelites. It's for everyone. God is the only true God, and we should not worship any other gods. We shouldn't make anything or anyone more important than God.

The Israelites made other gods because they wanted a god they could see. Even though they could not actually see the one true God, they had seen what God had done for them. He parted the Red Sea and brought them out of Egypt. He led them with a cloud by day and a pillar of fire by night. He gave them food and water in the wilderness, and they saw His holiness in the thunder clouds on Mount Sinai.

We can't see God either, but we can enjoy the food and water He provides. We can see His beauty in rainbows and sunrises. We see His power in waterfalls and ocean waves. And we see His greatness in high and mighty mountains. Even though we might not make a statue of gold or worship another god, anything that's more important to us than God is like an idol. It's okay to enjoy video games, soccer, or a new bike. But loving God means we desire Him more than anything else. Matthew 6:33 says, "What you should want most is God's kingdom and doing what God wants you to do. Then he will give you all the other things you need." When you put God first, it doesn't mean you will get everything you want. It means that you believe God will take care of you and give you everything you need.

TALK TO GOD
Tell God He's first in your life.

EXPLORE MORE: What did Jesus say in Luke 4:8?

I will put God first in my life.

A Shining Face

Aaron and all the people of Israel saw that Moses' face was shining.
So they were afraid to go near him. —Exodus 34:30 ICB

God told Moses to climb Mount Sinai early in the morning. God told Moses to bring two new stone tablets to replace the ones that had broken. Moses did what God told him to do. He listened as God gave instructions for the Israelites. God told Moses what feasts they should celebrate and how they should bring offerings to Him. God gave Moses the Ten Commandments again too. Moses wrote them on the new tablets of stone.

Moses was on Mount Sinai meeting with God for forty days and nights. When Moses came down from the mountain, he didn't know that his face was bright from being with God. Moses's face was so bright that the people were afraid to come near him.

TALK TO GOD
Ask God to let His love shine through you.

Moses covered his face so the people would not be afraid to look at him. But, whenever he talked with God, he would uncover his face. Then he would cover it again when he was with the people. The people knew when Moses met with God because Moses's face would always be bright.

You don't need to climb a mountain to spend time with God. You can talk to Him wherever you are. You can also read the Bible or listen to worship music. Sometimes going to a quiet place and being still helps us feel closer to God. When you talk to God and spend time with Him, He fills you up with His love. When you are filled with His love, it shows on your face. Maybe your face won't shine like Moses's did, but your smile will be bright enough for people to see.

EXPLORE MORE: What does 1 John 1:5 tell us about God?

DID YOU KNOW?
Drinking water can make your face glow and look brighter.

I want to shine for God.

Let's Celebrate!

The Lord said to Moses, "Speak to the Israelites. Tell them, 'Here are my appointed feast days. They are the appointed feast days of the Lord. Tell the people that they must come together for these sacred assemblies.'" —Leviticus 23:1–2 NIrV

While the children of Israel lived in the wilderness, God wanted them to celebrate special days that He chose for them. Some of these celebrations were to remind the people how God had delivered them from slavery in Egypt. Other celebrations pointed to Jesus who would deliver the world from sin. These celebrations were called feasts or festivals and many of them required special offerings to God.

The first day that God set apart as holy was the Sabbath day. God created the world in six days, then rested on the seventh day. God wanted His people to do the same. They could work six days a week, but the Sabbath was a celebration day of rest and worship.

The Lord's Passover and the Feast of Unleavened Bread were celebrated each year to remind the Israelites how God brought them from Egypt. The celebration reminded the people how they ate lamb and put blood on their doors on their last night in Egypt. To remember what God did for them, the people would eat bread made without yeast and they would not do any work. The feast lasted for seven days.

TALK TO GOD
Thank God for special days to celebrate His love for us.

There were many other feasts and festivals that God made for the Israelites. He was their God who provided for them, and they were His people. Today we have holidays to celebrate too. We celebrate Christmas to remember the day Jesus came to earth. We celebrate Good Friday when Jesus died on the cross for the sins of the world. And we celebrate Easter when Jesus came back to life. These celebrations help us remember what God has done for us and they remind us of His great love.

EXPLORE MORE: What does Genesis 2:3 say about the seventh day?

Celebrate God's love.

DID YOU KNOW?
Christmas, Hanukkah, and New Years are the top three celebrated holidays in the world.

God's List of Blessings

These are the laws, rules and teachings the Lord gave the people of Israel. He gave these laws to the Israelites through Moses. This was at Mount Sinai. —Leviticus 26:46 ICB

God gave Moses many instructions for the Israelites because He loved them and wanted to protect them. God promised that if they followed His ways, He would bless them. Here are some of the blessings they would receive if they listened to Him:

God said, "I will send rain in the right season. The land will produce many crops. The trees in the field will grow much fruit. Your threshing will continue until it's time to harvest grapes, and your grape harvest will continue until it's time to plant. You will have plenty of food to eat, and you will be safe in your land. You will live in peace, and no one will make you afraid. I will keep wild animals from your land and no armies will pass through your country" (Leviticus 26:3-6).

God continued with more blessings, "I will show kindness to you and give you many children. I will keep my agreement with you. Your crops will last for more than a year. I will walk with you, and you will be my people. I am the Lord your God who brought you out of Egypt" (Leviticus 26:9-13).

TALK TO GOD
Ask God to help you love and follow Him.

God gave commandments to the Israelites because He loved them. He wanted the people to understand that they could live happy and good lives. They could live well knowing God cared for them and was always with them—just like He promised.

Today we can read God's instructions in the Bible. If we follow His commands, we will also live good lives. God loves us just like He loved the Israelites, and He wants to give us His blessings. He will keep His promises to us too.

EXPLORE MORE: Read Deuteronomy 7:9. How long will God keep His promise to bless those who love and obey Him?

DID YOU KNOW?
According to dictionary.com, a blessing is a favor or gift given by God that brings happiness.

I can receive the blessings of God's promises.

The Priestly Blessing

The Lord said to Moses, "Tell Aaron and his sons, 'This is how you are to bless the Israelites.'" —Numbers 6:22–23 NIV

Moses's brother, Aaron, was a high priest. As the high priest, he was the head of the other priests. The priests would offer special sacrifices in the outer courts of the tabernacle and ask God to forgive their sins and the sins of the people. Then they would enter the Holy Place to meet with God.

The priests wore special clothes. The priests would speak to God for the people. Then the priest would give God's words to the people.

One day God spoke to Moses and gave him words for the priests to say to the people. These words are called "the priestly blessing," and many church leaders still say these words today. The blessing is found in Numbers 6:24–27:

> The Lord bless you
> and keep you;
> the Lord make his face shine on you
> and be gracious to you;
> the Lord turn his face toward you
> and give you peace.

TALK TO GOD
Thank God that because of Jesus you can talk to Him and enter His Holy Place.

God told the priests to say these words to the people so His name would be on them. This meant that God would bless them because they had His name with them.

Did you know that Jesus is our High Priest? Jesus made an offering to God for the sins of all people by sacrificing His body on the cross. Because of Jesus, we don't have to make a sacrifice before speaking to God, and we don't need a priest to speak to God for us. Because of Jesus, we can talk to our holy God ourselves. His name is with us, and He blesses us.

EXPLORE MORE: What does Hebrews 4:16 tell us about approaching God?

Jesus is my High Priest.

DID YOU KNOW?
The priestly blessing is also known as the "raising of the hands." When a priest or pastor gives the blessing, they usually raise their hands.

Carry God's Name

"I am the Lord. That is my name! I will not let any other god share my glory. I will not let statues of gods share my praise." —Isaiah 42:8 NIrV

God wanted the Israelites to carry His name. He wanted all nations to know that they belonged to Him. If we belong to God, then we also carry His name. In the Ten Commandments, the third commandment says to respect God's name and not to misuse it. Do you ever hear people misusing God's name? It happens a lot. People use God's name when they are upset or angry. Sometimes they use it when they are super excited or surprised. When people misuse God's name, it does not honor God the way He deserves.

God is a holy and perfect God, and His name is holy. We can honor God by using His name when we pray. We can honor Him when we talk about how wonderful He is. And we honor God's name when we praise Him for His creation, His goodness, and His love.

TALK TO GOD
Ask God to help you honor His name.

Carrying God's name is more than honoring Him with our words. We can also honor Him with our actions. When we respect and honor our parents, grandparents, and teachers, we are also honoring God. Being kind and showing love to others are ways we can carry God's name well. If you go to school, you can be a friend to someone who plays alone. You can stick up for someone who is being bullied, or you can help someone who is struggling with a math problem.

Giving money, food, or clothes to people who need them are other things we can do to carry God's name. There are so many ways we can carry God's name; the list is endless. God's name is the greatest name of all. Carry it well!

EXPLORE MORE: What does Proverbs 18:10 say about God's name?

DID YOU KNOW?
Jehovah is the Hebrew name for God. It means "I am the One who is."

I will carry God's name well.

The Cloud and the Trumpets

The holy tent was set up. It was the tent where the tablets of the covenant law were kept. On the day it was set up, the cloud covered it. From evening until morning the cloud above the tent looked like fire. —Numbers 9:15 NIrV

On the day the tabernacle was set up, God covered it with a cloud. At night, the cloud looked like fire. This was God's way of letting the people know He was with them. Do you remember when the Israelites left Egypt? They followed a cloud by day and a pillar of fire by night. That's how God showed them where to go.

Now that they were living in the wilderness, they didn't need to travel every day. God used the cloud to let them know when it was time to move and when it was time to stay. Whenever the cloud lifted above the tabernacle, the Israelites had to pack up and move. As long as the cloud stayed over the tabernacle, the people stayed where they were. Sometimes the cloud was over the tabernacle for a few days. Sometimes the cloud stayed for weeks, months, or even a year.

God told Moses to make two silver trumpets and use them for calling the people together to let them know how to travel when the cloud lifted. When both trumpets sounded, all the people were to meet at the entrance of the Holy Tent. If one trumpet sounded, only the leaders had to meet. When a trumpet blast sounded again, the tribes camping on the east side were to set out. At the sound of the second blast, the camps on the south side set out.

God guided the Israelites in the wilderness and watched over them. He made His presence known so they would trust Him. God's presence is always with us too. We can trust Him to guide us day and night.

EXPLORE MORE: Read Numbers 10:10 to find out other times the trumpets sounded.

TALK TO GOD
Thank God for always being with you.

God leads me where I need to go.

DID YOU KNOW?
A flammagenitus cloud is also known as a fire cloud and is caused by volcanic eruptions.

The Best Guide

The Lord says, "I will teach you and guide you in the way you should live. I will watch over you and be your guide. —Psalm 32:8 ERV

As we learn more about the Israelites' journey through the wilderness, we can see how God guided them day and night. He led them through the Red Sea as they followed the cloud. Once they were in the wilderness, God told Moses where to lead the people. As they moved from place to place, they knew where to go and what to do.

Today God doesn't use a cloud to tell us where to go. We don't have one leader like Moses who speaks to God for us. But that doesn't mean God won't help us know what He wants us to do. Today we have the Bible, which is God's Word. Psalm 119:105 says that God's Word is a lamp for our feet and a light on our path. When we read and study the Bible, God speaks to us and guides us through His Holy Spirit.

TALK TO GOD
Ask God to guide you today and show you what He wants you to do.

God cares about every detail of your life. He will help your family make decisions like where to live, what school to go to, and what church to attend. You can ask God to help you make the right kind of friends. As you get older, you can ask God to show you what kind of career He wants you to have.

God may also use grown-ups to help you make good decisions. If they love God and you trust them, then listen to their advice and wisdom.

Sometimes the Israelites had to wait for God to lead them, and sometimes we need to wait too. God is never in a hurry, and we can trust that He will guide us to the right place at the right time.

EXPLORE MORE: Read Psalm 25:4–5. How can these verses be used as a prayer?

DID YOU KNOW?
Guide dogs are trained to help guide people with special needs. The most common breeds are golden retrievers, Labradors, and German shepherds.

God is my guide.

Exploring the Promised Land

The Lord said to Moses, "Send men to explore the land of Canaan. I will give that land to the Israelites. Send one leader from each tribe." —Numbers 13:1–2 ICB

After years of wandering, the Israelites were getting close to the land of Canaan. This was called the promised land because it was the land God promised to give Abraham and his descendants. God told Moses to send twelve men, one from each tribe, to explore the land.

Moses sent them into Canaan and told them to bring back a report. "See if the people are strong or weak. See if their cities have walls. Find out if the soil is good and what kind of trees they have. Bring back some fruit if you can."

The men entered the land and began to explore. They were amazed at how big the cities were. The people were big too. They made the Israelite men seem really small— like grasshoppers. But the land was rich with figs, pomegranates, and grapes. The Israelite men cut off a branch of grapes, and it was so large it took two men to carry it!

After forty days of exploring, the men returned. Ten of the men were terrified. "The people are strong. They are so big and tall that they make us look like grasshoppers," they said. The people of Israel wept when they heard this news. They complained to Moses and said they wanted to go back to Egypt.

Two of the spies, Joshua and Caleb, had a different report. They said, "The land is good! It's flowing with milk and honey. Do not be afraid of the people. The Lord will be with us. He will lead us into the land and give it to us."

TALK TO GOD
Ask God to help you trust Him when you face big challenges.

Joshua and Caleb knew that God was stronger and more powerful than the people living in Canaan. They were ready to follow Him and live in the promised land.

EXPLORE MORE: Read Numbers 13:30 to find out what Caleb said when the Israelites were afraid to enter Canaan.

God is stronger than people.

DID YOU KNOW?
The people of Canaan were descendants of Noah's son Ham.

God Is More Powerful

Dear children, you belong to God. You have not accepted the teachings of the false prophets. That's because the one who is in you is powerful. He is more powerful than the one who is in the world. —1 John 4:4 NIrV

Today we get information from many different places—television, internet, books, and social media. We can google to find information on any topic instantly. But how do we know if what we hear or read is true? Some information we get can make us afraid, and it's hard to know what to believe. But whether the reports are true or false, we don't need to be afraid.

Twelve spies went into the land of Canaan. They all saw the same things. They all heard the same things. Ten men were afraid, but two had courage and faith to believe that God would be with them. They knew that no matter how powerful the people were, God was more powerful.

TALK TO GOD
Ask God to help you trust Him when you are afraid.

We may never have to move a whole nation into a new land like Joshua and Caleb did, but we might face other things that make us afraid. It can be hard moving to a new town and going to a new school where you don't know anyone. Have you ever tried out for a play or sports team? That can make you super nervous! It's also scary to stand up for what you believe when others make fun of your faith. But when you are afraid, you can have courage because God is on your side. God's power is greater than your fears, and He will help you to be strong. And if things don't turn out the way you want them to, God will be with you no matter what happens. God wants you to trust Him, just like Joshua and Caleb trusted Him to give them the land He promised.

EXPLORE MORE: What does Psalm 46:1 tell us about God?

DID YOU KNOW?
Google was officially launched in 1998. It is a search engine that helps people find materials or information on the internet.

I can trust in God's power.

Blossoms on a Stick

"I will choose one man. His stick will begin to grow leaves. And I will stop the Israelites from always complaining against you." —Numbers 17:5 ICB

Moses and Aaron were the men God chose to lead the Israelites from Egypt to the promised land. The Israelites had other leaders, too, but Moses and Aaron were the ones who spoke to God for the people. Some of the leaders got angry with Moses and Aaron. They said, "You are making yourselves more important than the rest of the Lord's people."

God was not pleased with the attitude of the other leaders. He told Moses to get twelve sticks—one for each tribe. God said, "Write the name of each man on his stick. On the stick of Levi, write Aaron's name. Place them in the Holy Tent. The stick belonging to the man I choose will sprout."

TALK TO GOD
Ask God to help you respect the leaders He chooses.

Moses did what God told him to do. He placed the sticks in the Holy Tent and left them overnight. The next morning, Aaron's stick, which represented the tribe of Levi, had sprouted buds, blossoms, and almonds. The Lord made it clear to everyone that He chose Aaron to be the leader of Israel along with Moses.

The Lord told Aaron that He had chosen the Levites to serve as priests to care for the Holy Tent and perform all the priestly duties. They would be in charge of the offerings, and God would give them some of every offering that was brought to the temple.

God chooses some people to be leaders and others to be helpers. Everything we do for God matters, and in God's eyes, everyone is important.

EXPLORE MORE: Read Numbers 18:21. What did God promise to give the Levites?

God chooses the people He wants to be leaders.

DID YOU KNOW?
Some doctors say eating almonds can help your heart stay healthy.

Moses Strikes a Rock

"You and your brother Aaron should gather the people. Also take your walking stick. Speak to that rock in front of them. Then water will flow from it. Give that water to the people and their animals." —Numbers 20:8 ICB

When the Israelites traveled through the Desert of Zin, they camped at a place called Kadesh. They couldn't find water to drink, so once again they complained to Moses. "Why did you bring us into this terrible place? It has no fruit or grain, and there is no water!"

Moses and Aaron went to the Holy Tent and fell down before God. God told Moses to take his walking stick and gather the people in front of a rock. God told Moses to speak to the rock and enough water would pour out for everyone.

Moses and Aaron gathered the people together in front of the rock. The people were still complaining—and that made Moses angry. Instead of speaking to the rock, like God had told him to do, Moses hit the rock with his stick. Water gushed out and the people and their livestock had enough to drink.

TALK TO GOD
Thank God that He loves us even when we mess up.

God chose Moses to lead the Israelites though the wilderness. Moses always turned to God when the people complained, and he did what God told him to do. But this time he didn't. He did not honor God as holy in front of the Israelites. Moses did things his own way. Because of this, God told Moses he would not be able to go into the promised land with the Israelites.

It's hard for us to understand that God gave Moses this punishment because of his actions. But as God's chosen leader, he needed to do everything God told him to do. God continued to be with Moses and the Israelites and did not leave them on their own. God continued to love Moses and His people because God's love never ends.

DID YOU KNOW?
Water from wells and natural springs is rich in potassium, sodium, and magnesium but should be filtered before drinking.

EXPLORE MORE: Read Numbers 20:13 to find out the name that was given to this place.

We must respect our holy God.

Nobody's Perfect

Surely there is not a good man on earth who always does good and never sins. —Ecclesiastes 7:20 ICB

Ever since sin entered the world through Adam and Eve, no one can live a perfect life. Even a great leader like Moses did what he wanted to do instead of what God told him to do. We often hear the phrase "nobody's perfect," and it's true.

God gave the Israelites the Ten Commandments to protect them and keep them safe. He wanted them to know how to love God and other people. If they followed God's commandments, things would go well with them. If they didn't, they had to face consequences for their actions.

TALK TO GOD
Ask God to help you do the right things.

It's impossible for us to live a perfect life. That's why God sent Jesus. Jesus was human, but He is also God's Son, so He never sinned. When He died on the cross, He took the punishment for all the sins of the world. When we believe in Him, the wrong things we do are forgiven. We will never be perfect on earth, but that's how God sees us when we become part of His family.

Even though God forgives our sins, we need to ask Him to help us live in a way that shows our love for Him. When we choose to do what we know is wrong, we may face consequences. Cheating on a test will get you in trouble at school. Being mean to other kids will keep you from having friends, and lying to your parents will make it hard for them to trust you.

The Bible teaches us how to love God and love others. We may not be able to do it perfectly, but God will help us when we depend on Him.

EXPLORE MORE: What does 1 John 1:8–9 tell us about sin?

God loves me even though I am not perfect.

DID YOU KNOW?
The Bible and scientists agree that telling the truth is good for your health.

A Snake on a Pole

The Lord said to Moses, "Make a snake. Put it up on a pole. Then anyone who is bitten can look at it and remain alive." —Numbers 21:8 NIrV

When it was time for the Israelites to leave Kadesh, Moses sent a message to the king of Edom. Moses asked the king if the Israelites could pass through his land. Moses said, "If you allow us to pass through your land, we will not walk through your fields or drink from your wells." But the king of Edom said no.

Moses had to lead the Israelites around Edom, and the people grew impatient. They complained against God and Moses and said they hated their food. God heard their grumbling and sent snakes that bit some of the people and made them sick. They soon realized they had sinned against God with their complaining. The people begged Moses to ask God to take the snakes away.

TALK TO GOD
Thank God for sending Jesus to take away our sins.

Moses prayed to God for the people. God told Moses to make a bronze snake and put it on a pole. If anyone was bitten, they could look up at the bronze snake and He would heal them.

The bronze snake was a picture of sin and evil. By putting the snake on a pole, God was offering to deliver them from the consequences of their sin and to heal them. Moses did what God told him to do. When the people who had been bitten chose to look at the pole where the snake was lifted up, God healed them.

Many years later, Jesus was "lifted up" and nailed to a cross. He took sin and evil upon himself to save us from the power of Satan. Anyone who believes in Jesus as their Savior will be healed from sin and will live forever with Him in heaven.

EXPLORE MORE: What did Jesus tell a Jewish leader in John 3:14–15?

DID YOU KNOW?

There are 3,500 different species of snakes in the world. About 600 of them are poisonous.

I will look up to Jesus and be saved.

No More Whining!

Do everything without complaining and arguing. —Philippians 2:14 NLT

As we read stories about the Israelites in the Old Testament, we see that they complained a lot. Sometimes they were hungry. Sometimes they were thirsty. And sometimes they were tired. Wandering in the wilderness for years and years would be hard, so it makes sense that they would grumble and complain. But God wanted them to keep trusting Him to take care of them and give them what they needed.

TALK TO GOD
Ask God to help you be grateful when you feel like complaining.

God provided for the Israelites. He gave them manna from heaven in the morning, quail for dinner in the evening, and water from rocks when they were thirsty. Today we get our food from grocery stores, markets, or gardens. And even though we can pick out the food ourselves, God is the one who provides it.

Do you ever complain about having to eat the vegetables your parents cooked for dinner? Eating ice cream instead of green beans might make you smile, but it won't help you to get the vitamins and minerals you need to grow. Do you grumble when a grown-up makes you spaghetti, but you'd rather have pizza? It's easy to complain when you don't get what you want, but complaining can put you in a bad mood, and no one likes that!

Sometimes kids grumble about other things, too, like having to clean their room or help with dishes. Whether it's eating food you don't like, or doing chores, you can ask God to help you be thankful rather than complain. Being thankful will help you to have a cheerful attitude and will put you in a good mood. It might even help you eat your beans!

EXPLORE MORE: Who were the Israelites complaining against? Read Exodus 16:8 to find out.

It's better to be thankful than to complain.

DID YOU KNOW?
The countries that produce the most food are Brazil, India, China, and the United States.

A Donkey and an Angel

The angel of the Lord said to Balaam, "Go with the men, but speak only what I tell you." —Numbers 22:35 NIV

Balak, the king of Moab, was worried because the Israelites had arrived near his land. He knew they were powerful and could take over his kingdom. Balak sent messengers to a man named Balaam and offered him money to say bad things to the Israelites. At first God told Balaam not to go. Then God told Balaam to go, but he could only speak the words God would tell him to say.

As Balaam traveled, his donkey saw an angel holding a sword. The donkey darted into a field. Balaam hit his donkey and led him back to the road.

As they traveled, the donkey saw the angel again. The donkey squeezed through a narrow pathway near a wall. He didn't want to go near the angel. But the donkey crushed Balaam's foot against the wall. Balaam hit the donkey again. Farther down the road, the donkey saw the angel and lay down in front of him. Balaam was angry and hit the donkey again.

TALK TO GOD
Ask God to help you speak kind words to others.

Then God made the donkey speak. "Why did you hit me three times? I've always been your donkey and have never done this before."

God opened Balaam's eyes to see the angel standing before him. Balaam bowed to the ground. Then the angel said, "Go with the men but speak only what I tell you." So instead of saying bad things to the Israelites, Balaam said the words God told him to say.

It's never okay to speak bad words to others. We need to speak words that are kind and helpful to our friends and family. You can't always do it on your own, but God can help you choose the best words to say.

EXPLORE MORE: Read Numbers 22:38 to find out what Balaam said to King Balak.

DID YOU KNOW?
Donkeys don't like to be alone. They are smart and friendly and like being around people and other donkeys.

God will help me speak the right words.

A New Leader for Israel

The Lord said to Moses, "Take Joshua son of Nun. My Spirit is in him. Put your hand on him." —Numbers 27:18 ICB

Moses was getting very old, and the Israelites would soon need a new leader. Moses asked God to choose someone who would be a good leader. God told Moses that He chose Joshua, the son of Nun, to be the next leader of Israel.

TALK TO GOD
Pray that your leaders would trust in God.

Joshua loved and trusted God. He was one of the twelve spies who went into Jericho and brought back a good report. He believed that God would give the Israelites the land He promised. God told Moses to have Joshua stand before Eleazar the priest and all the people so they could watch Moses lay his hands on him. Then the people would know that Joshua was chosen by God. They would accept Joshua as their new leader.

In Numbers 27:22 it says, "Moses did what the Lord told him to do." This is something we read over and over again about Moses. He was not perfect, but Moses loved and trusted God. Moses brought Joshua before Eleazar and the people. He laid his hands on Joshua to show that he would be the new leader.

For the rest of Moses's life, he continued to remind the people that God was the only God they should worship. He reminded them that God would provide for them, protect them, and fight for them. He told them to follow God's commands so that things would go well for them.

It's important to have good leaders who love God and trust Him. And the best leaders will help you follow God.

EXPLORE MORE: Read Exodus 24:12–13 to find out something important that Joshua did with Moses.

God chooses leaders who trust and follow Him.

DID YOU KNOW?
Leaders of countries have different titles. Some nations have presidents, while others have prime ministers or chancellors. Some countries today still have kings and queens.

Hear, O Israel

"Hear, O Israel: The Lord our God, the Lord is one. Love the Lord your God with all your heart and with all your soul and with all your strength." —Deuteronomy 6:4–5 NIV

Joshua would soon lead the Israelites into the land of Canaan that God had promised to Abraham's descendants. The people who would enter the land were the grown children and grandchildren of the families who left Egypt. The Israelites had been living in the wilderness for forty years. Moses wanted all of the people—young and old—to understand how important it was to love God.

Today's Bible verses from Deuteronomy are known as the *Shema*. The Israelites recited these words as a prayer every morning and evening. Moses told them to remember these commandments and teach them to their children. He said, "Talk about this when you sit in your home and when you walk along the road. Talk about God when you get up in the morning and when you go to bed at night. Tie these words to your hands and wear them on your foreheads. Write them on the doorposts and gates of your homes."

TALK TO GOD
Tell God how much you love Him.

The words of the Shema are still true for us today. Saying a prayer every morning and night is a way to stay close to God and remember that He is always with you. Saying Bible verses or singing songs to God are other ways you can think about God throughout the day. Reading Bible storybooks or devotions will help you to grow and learn more about God too.

God's love is the greatest love in the world. We can enjoy His love the most when we love Him back.

EXPLORE MORE: Who recited the Shema in Mark 12:29–30?

DID YOU KNOW?
It is a custom for Jewish people to cover their eyes with their right hand while saying the first words of the Shema. This allows them to think about the words without being distracted.

I will love the Lord with all my heart.

Moses Sees the Promised Land

"This is the land I promised to Abraham, Isaac and Jacob. I told them, 'I will give this land to your children and their children.' Moses, I have let you see it with your own eyes. But you will not go across the Jordan River to enter it." —Deuteronomy 34:4 NIrV

Have you ever climbed a big hill or a mountain? It takes a lot of energy! When Moses was 120 years old, he was strong enough to climb a mountain. He could see very well. God told Moses to climb Mount Nebo, but first Moses gathered the Israelites together to say a blessing for them. Moses knew he would die soon. This would be the last time he could speak a blessing from God over the people.

After Moses blessed the Israelites, he climbed to the top of Mount Nebo. God told Moses to look out over the land. God showed him the entire land He had promised to give Abraham's descendants. God told Moses that He would keep His promise to the Israelites, even though Moses would not enter the land.

TALK TO GOD
Do you know of a good Christian leader? Thank God for that person.

The Bible tells us that Moses died and God buried him. The people cried because they were sad. In Deuteronomy 34:10–12 it says, "Since then, Israel has never had a prophet like Moses. The Lord knew him face to face. Moses did many amazing things. . . . No one has ever had the mighty power like Moses had. No one has ever done the wonderful acts Moses did in the sight of all the Israelites."

Moses wrote the first five books of the Bible. They tell about the events from the beginning of the world until Moses died. They teach us about God's power, the miracles He performed, and how much He loves His people. And they show how God used a great leader like Moses to help His people follow Him.

EXPLORE MORE: What blessing did Moses give the Israelites in Deuteronomy 33:28–29?

God uses leaders who love Him.

DID YOU KNOW?
The first five books of the Old Testament are also called the Pentateuch or the Torah.

God's Message to Joshua

> "Remember that I commanded you to be strong and brave. So don't be afraid. The Lord your God will be with you everywhere you go." —Joshua 1:9 ICB

Joshua became the new leader after Moses died. God chose him to lead the Israelites into the promised land. But this was not an easy march to the land. This was going to be very hard! It would take three days to prepare. And more than a million people with all their stuff would have to cross the Jordan River on foot.

In the first chapter of the book of Joshua, God speaks to Joshua to remind him of His promise to give the Israelites the land. God told Joshua, "I will give you every place where you set your foot, as I promised Moses. . . . No one will be able to stand against you. . . . I was with Moses and I will be with you too" (Joshua 1:3, 5).

TALK TO GOD
Thank God that He is always with you.

Joshua told the leaders to have the people get their stuff ready to cross the Jordan River. The leaders told Joshua, "We will do whatever you tell us to do, and we will go where you send us. May God be with you as He was with Moses."

God knew that Joshua had a big job ahead of him. Three times God told Joshua, "Be strong and brave." Some Bibles say, "Be strong and courageous." The third time God spoke these words, He added, "Do not be afraid and do not be discouraged, for the Lord your God is with you wherever you go." God wanted Joshua to understand that He would be with him, and he had nothing to fear.

EXPLORE MORE: What does God tell Joshua in Joshua 1:7–8?

DID YOU KNOW?

The Jordan River is 156 miles (251 kilometers) long and flows north to south from the Sea of Galilee to the Dead Sea. It is mentioned in the Bible more than 185 times.

God goes with me everywhere I go.

Be Strong and Brave

All you who put your hope in the Lord be strong and brave.
—Psalm 31:24 ICB

The Israelites lived in the wilderness for forty years. They were finally ready to move into the promised land. It would be hard, but God had promised to be with them. Today we can do hard things too because God promises to be with us.

Most of us will never live in the wilderness. We may never have to cross a river or sea to get to where we need to go. But that doesn't mean our lives are always easy. Maybe you have a problem getting along with some kids at school. Maybe someone in your family is sick. If you are chosen to be a leader or special helper at school, you could be afraid. Trying out for a play or sports team can be scary too. Or maybe you want to work harder in school.

TALK TO GOD
Tell God about a problem you're having. Ask Him to help you be strong and brave to face it.

Sometimes our hard things and the challenges we face can't be seen by others. Maybe you feel like you are not good enough or smart enough. You might be sad or angry because of changes in your home or family. Maybe being around others makes you feel nervous or afraid. These things can be challenging, and they can also be scary. But no matter how hard or scary things may seem, you have a God who loves you and cares about you very much. He is always by your side and will never leave you. God's message to you is the same message He gave to Joshua, "Be strong and brave, because I am always with you!"

EXPLORE MORE: What does God give us through the Holy Spirit? Read 2 Timothy 1:7 to find the answer.

God will help me to be strong and brave.

DID YOU KNOW?
Speaking in front of an audience is one of the most common fears that people have.

Rahab Helps the Spies

"Promise me in the name of the Lord that you will be kind to my family. I've been kind to you." —Joshua 2:12 NIrV

Before the Israelites began their march into the city of Jericho, Joshua sent two spies to check out the land. They stayed at the house of a Canaanite woman whose name was Rahab. She hid the spies on her roof to protect them from the king's messengers who wanted to capture them. Rahab knew the Israelites worshiped a powerful God and she wanted to be on their side.

Rahab told the spies, "I know God has given you this land. Everyone is living in fear because of you. We've heard how the Lord dried up the Red Sea when you came out of Egypt. We know you are more powerful than your enemies."

TALK TO GOD
Ask God to help you trust Him, even when people around you don't.

Even though Rahab was living in a land where the people did not honor God, she knew that the God of Israel was the one true God. She told the spies, "The Lord your God is the God who rules in heaven above and on the earth below."

Rahab asked the spies to make a promise to save her and her family when the Israelites came to take the land. The spies gave Rahab a scarlet rope and told her to hang it from her window. Now the Israelites would know which house to protect. The spies said Rahab's entire family would be saved if they stayed in her house.

When the spies returned, they told Joshua, "Surely the Lord has given us this land. The people are terrified because of us!"

The Canaanites who lived in the promised land did not love or worship God. Like many people today, they did whatever they pleased. But even people like Rahab are able to see how strong and powerful God is. He rules in heaven above and on the earth below!

DID YOU KNOW?
The color "scarlet" is bright red mixed with a bit of orange. On a color wheel it is one quarter of the way between red and orange.

EXPLORE MORE: Read Joshua 2:15–16 to find out how Rahab helped the spies escape.

Everyone can see that God is powerful.

Rahab and Jesus

Salmon was the father of Boaz. Rahab was Boaz's mother. Boaz was the father of Obed. Ruth was Obed's mother. Obed was the father of Jesse. And Jesse was the father of King David. —Matthew 1:5–6 NIrV

The story of Rahab shows that you don't have to be born into a certain family or live in a certain country to be in God's family. No matter where you live or what kind of family you are from, you can love and worship the one true God.

Rahab knew in her heart that the God of the Israelites was the God who rules over heaven and earth. Because of her faith, Rahab's life and the lives of her family were saved. Rahab eventually married an Israelite man named Salmon, who was from the tribe of Judah. Later, Rahab became the great-great-grandmother of King David. And many years later after King David, Jesus was born into the same family.

God doesn't stop anyone from becoming part of His family when they believe in Him. Rahab was not an Israelite, but she believed in God. The scarlet rope that the spies gave Rahab to hang from her window, saved her and her family. This red rope would also represent the blood of Jesus. Someday God would send His Son into the world to make a way for all people to be saved.

TALK TO GOD
Pray for others to know and believe in God.

The Bible doesn't tell us much about Rahab's family, but we know that they chose to stay in her house. Rahab must have loved her family and wanted them to be saved too. If you believe in God like Rahab did, don't keep it to yourself! Tell your friends and family that they can know and worship the one true God like you do. If they choose to believe in Jesus, then they will be saved too.

EXPLORE MORE: What does God want? Read 1 Timothy 2:4 to find out.

I will tell others about God.

DID YOU KNOW?
The countries with the most Christians are the United States, Brazil, and Mexico.

Crossing the Jordan River

The ground there became dry. The priests carried the Ark of the Covenant with the Lord to the middle of the river and stopped. They waited there while all the people of Israel walked across. They crossed the Jordan River on dry land. —Joshua 3:17 ICB

The time had come for the Israelites to cross the Jordan River and enter the city of Jericho. If you were there, would you be excited or a little scared? Remember how God told Joshua to be strong and brave? Now it was time for *all* the Israelites to be strong and brave!

Joshua told the leaders to give orders to the people so they would know what to do. He told the Levites, who were priests, to carry the ark of the covenant. The ark of the covenant was the holy place God told the Israelites to make. It was a reminder that God was with the people. When the Levites reached the edge of the river, they walked into the water and stood still. They held the ark of the covenant because God was with them.

Then something amazing happened! God caused the water from one side to stop flowing. The Levites who carried the ark of the covenant stood on dry ground while the Israelites safely crossed the river.

The Bible says that the Jordan River was at flood stage, which would make it much more dangerous and difficult for the people to cross. But nothing is impossible with God. The Israelites had heard the stories from their parents and grandparents of how God parted the Red Sea so they could escape from Egypt. Now they were walking on dry land, just like their ancestors had done.

TALK TO GOD
Thank God for all of the big and small things He has done.

Can you image how exciting this must have been? Once again, they could see that God was on their side. He was the God who loved them, and He was powerful enough to make a way for them to reach the promised land.

EXPLORE MORE: What instructions did the leaders give the people in Joshua 3:2–4?

DID YOU KNOW?
The ark of the covenant was a holy box from the tabernacle. It was covered with gold and contained the Ten Commandments, a jar of manna, and Aaron's staff.

God will make a way for His people.

Stones from the River

"In the future, when your children ask you, 'What do these stones mean?' tell them that the flow of the Jordan was cut off before the ark of the covenant of the Lord." —Joshua 4:6–7 NIV

After the Israelites had safely crossed the Jordan River on dry land, God told Joshua to have one man from each of the twelve tribes go back to where the priests were standing and pick up a large stone. The men did what Joshua told them to do. They picked up stones from the river and carried them to their camp.

Joshua put the twelve stones in a pile. Do you know why God told Joshua to do this? It was to help the people remember what God had done for them. In the future, when their children and grand-children asked, "What do these stones mean?" the older people could tell them how God stopped the water of the Jordan River so they could walk across. When they remembered what God had done in the past, it would help them to keep trusting Him.

TALK TO GOD
Think of something God has done for you and thank Him for that.

The people watched as the Levite priests finished crossing with the ark of the covenant. As soon as they stepped on the land, the waters of the Jordan began to flow—just like before.

God performed a great miracle that day, and He wanted the people to remember. When God does great things for us, too, it's good to find a way to remember. One way to do that is to keep a "God is great" journal. When God answers your prayers or helps you with a problem, write it down so you can look back and see the ways God has helped you. Remembering what God has done for you helps you to keep trusting Him!

EXPLORE MORE: Look up Psalm 77:13–15 to read a song about remembering God's great works.

I will remember the great things God does for me.

DID YOU KNOW?
A man-made pile of stones built as a memorial or landmark is called a cairn (pronounced *kern*).

The Commander of the Lord's Army

"I am not on either side," he replied. "I have come as the commander of the Lord's army." —Joshua 5:14 NIrV

The Israelites camped near Jericho in a place called Gilgal where they celebrated the Passover. They were no longer slaves in Egypt, and they were no longer in the wilderness where they ate manna every day. They were now in the promised land of Canaan where they could eat fresh fruit and grain. What do you think it was like for the kids to eat a handful of juicy grapes or spread honey on their bread for the first time?

Joshua knew they would face a battle in Jericho soon. He looked up and saw a man standing in front of him with a sword. Joshua asked, "Are you for us or for our enemies?" The man replied, "Neither. I am the commander of the Lord's army."

Joshua realized this man was a heavenly being—maybe an angel or even God himself. He bowed to the ground and asked the man if he had a message for him. The man replied, "Take off your sandals because you are standing on holy ground." So Joshua took off his shoes.

TALK TO GOD
Ask God to help you follow Him.

God sent the commander to remind Joshua that the battle at Jericho was the Lord's battle, and the Israelite army would need to follow His command. God led them to the promised land, but they would face many battles in order to live in the land. Just as they had followed God out of Egypt and through the wilderness, they would now need to follow God in this new land. And just like the Israelites needed to trust and follow God every day, we can trust and follow God as He leads the way for us.

DID YOU KNOW?
The name Gilgal, which is where the Israelites camped, means "rolled away." God had rolled away the Israelites' shame of living as slaves in Egypt.

EXPLORE MORE: Do you remember who else was told to take off his sandals? Read Exodus 3:4–5 to see if you got it right.

I will trust and follow where God leads.

The Best Leader

When people choose to follow the Lord, he shows them the best way to live. —Psalm 25:12 ERV

As we look at the story of the Israelites, we see how they had to follow God and trust Him as their leader, and sometimes it was hard! They had to depend on God to help them cross the Red Sea while the Egyptians were chasing them. They followed the pillars of cloud and fire as God led them into the wilderness. They moved when God told them to move, and they stayed when God told them to stay.

TALK TO GOD
Thank God that you can trust Him to lead you.

The Israelites had to follow God's instructions for forty years to reach the promised land. God told them what to do as He led the way. He never forgot about them. He never left them on their own to figure things out for themselves. He was their leader, and He sent the commander of the Lord's army to remind Joshua who was in charge.

God is your creator, and He loves you. God is also your leader. The Bible gives us many instructions on how to follow God. The more we read and study the Bible, the more we will learn how to follow Him. The most important part of following God is loving Him and showing kindness to others.

Following God doesn't mean your life will always be easy, but God will never leave you on your own to figure things out by yourself. If you are struggling with something you don't understand, talk to a grown-up who loves God. Together you can pray and ask God to show you what He wants you to do. Ask God to lead you because He is the best leader you can follow.

EXPLORE MORE: Read Psalm 143:8 out loud and say it as a prayer.

God is my leader.

DID YOU KNOW?
Follow-the-leader is a popular game for kids. It takes thinking and concentration, and some teachers use it to help students focus.

Seven Days of Marching

The priests blew the trumpets. As soon as the army heard the sound, they gave a loud shout. Then the wall fell down. —Joshua 6:20 NIrV

Have you ever gone to a parade? It's fun to listen to the band playing their instruments while they march in straight rows. God told the Israelites to march in a line, but it was different from the parades we see today.

It was time for the Israelites to take over the land of Jericho. God told Joshua exactly what to do. They probably wondered why God was giving them such strange orders, but the Israelites followed God's instructions.

Seven priests blew trumpets made from rams' horns and marched in front of the ark of the covenant while the people marched behind. Joshua told the people to be quiet and not say a word. For six days they marched around the city of Jericho one time each day.

TALK TO GOD
Thank God that He is more powerful than walls and buildings.

On the seventh day, the people marched around Jericho seven times. After the seventh march, the priests blew a long blast on the trumpets, and all the people gave a mighty shout. Suddenly, rocks began to tumble, and the wall around the city of Jericho came crashing down with a loud boom.

When God wants something to happen, it will happen. Nothing could keep God from giving the city of Jericho to the Israelites—not the strongest city wall or the tightest lock on the gates. But in order for the Israelites to win this battle, they needed to trust and follow God's orders.

We don't always understand God's ways. Sometimes we might think they don't make sense. But just like the Israelites, we need to trust God, believe that His plans are best, and do things His way.

EXPLORE MORE: Read Joshua 6:1 to find out how the people of Jericho responded when they knew the Israelites were nearby.

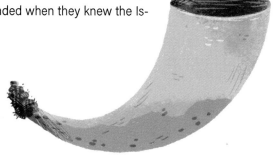

DID YOU KNOW?
In a marching band, the drum major is a leader who tells the band members what to play and when to march.

I will trust God's ways because they are best.

It's Your Choice

"Then choose for yourselves right now whom you will serve. . . . But as for me and my family, we will serve the Lord." —Joshua 24:15 NIrV

Joshua loved and followed God throughout his life. God helped Joshua win many victories for the Israelites in the land of Canaan. The promised land was divided among the tribes, and they were all given their pieces of land.

Before Joshua died, he reminded the people to keep following God so things would go well with them. Joshua said, "Be very strong and be careful to obey all that is written in the law of Moses. Do not worship the gods that other nations worship. Love the Lord your God, because He is the one who fights for you."

TALK TO GOD
Ask God to help you love and serve Him every day.

Joshua knew the people would be tempted to worship other gods and follow the ways of other nations when they moved into new lands. He told the Israelites to make a choice. They could worship and serve other gods, or they could worship the one true God. Joshua said, "As for me and my family, we will serve the Lord."

The Israelites listened to Joshua's speech. They said to him, "We will serve the Lord and obey Him because He is our God." They were at a place called Shechem and Joshua put a stone there. The stone was a reminder to the people that they had chosen to follow God.

God created all the people in the world, and He is the one true God of heaven and earth. God loves us, and He wants us to love Him back. But God doesn't force people to follow Him even though He could. God gives everyone a choice, including you. You can choose to love and serve God, or you can choose to love and serve other things. What do you think is the best choice?

EXPLORE MORE: Read Joshua 24:32 to find out something else that happened at Shechem.

I will choose to serve God.

DID YOU KNOW?
Studies have shown that it's best to make important decisions in the morning after a good night's sleep.

Judges for the People

Then the Lord chose leaders called judges. These leaders saved the Israelites from the enemies who took their possessions. —Judges 2:16 ERV

When people don't have a good leader, things can go wrong. What if schools didn't have any teachers? What if kids lived in a house by themselves without grown-ups? And if a team didn't have a coach, they probably wouldn't win many games.

Moses and Joshua were great leaders that God chose for the Israelites. But after Joshua died, the next generation of Israelites did not follow God because they didn't have a leader. They followed and worshiped the gods of other nations. When they turned away from God, they did not win their battles, and that's what Joshua said would happen.

The Israelites cried out to God to rescue them. God heard their cries and sent a man named Othniel to lead them. He was Caleb's nephew. Do you remember Caleb? He was one of the twelve spies who went into Canaan and came back with a good report like Joshua did. Othniel was the first judge of Israel. The Bible says that Othniel was filled with God's Spirit. His job as judge was to help the Israelites turn back to God, which they did.

TALK TO GOD
Think of some good leaders in your life and thank God for them.

After Othniel died, the Israelites turned away from God again. When things did not go well, they cried out to God, who sent them another judge named Ehud. After Ehud came Shamgar. After Shamgar, a woman named Deborah became the next judge of Israel. While Deborah was leading the Israelites, God was with them in their battles. The judges helped the Israelites turn away from other gods and serve the one true God. When they followed Him, He was with them and helped them face their enemies.

EXPLORE MORE: Whom did Deborah praise in Judges 5:1–3?

DID YOU KNOW?
Deborah is the only female judge mentioned in the Bible, and she was also a prophetess.

Good leaders help people follow God.

An Angel Visits Gideon

The angel of the Lord appeared to Gideon and said, "The Lord is with you, mighty warrior!" —Judges 6:12 ICB

Judge Deborah ruled over the Israelites for about forty years, and during that time the people lived in peace. After Deborah died, the Israelites turned away from God again. For seven years, the people from the land of Midian were mean to the Israelites. They camped on their land and ruined all their crops. They took the Israelites' sheep, donkeys, and cattle. The Israelites were so afraid of the Midianites that they built shelters in the mountains and hid in caves.

A man named Gideon was working in a winepress, which is where grapes are made into wine. He hoped the Midianites wouldn't see him there. God sent an angel to visit Gideon while he was working. The angel said, "The Lord is with you, mighty warrior!" Gideon was surprised and confused. "If God is with us, then why are all these bad things happening?" he asked. The Lord answered, "I am sending you to save your people from the hand of Midian."

TALK TO GOD
Thank God you can be a mighty warrior too.

Now Gideon was even more confused. "How can I save my people?" he asked. "My family is the weakest family in my tribe, and I am the least important person in my family."

"I will be with you," said the Lord.

Have you ever been asked to do something that you felt was too hard for you? That's how Gideon felt! He didn't think of himself as an important leader, and he didn't know why God would choose him for such a big assignment. But Gideon would soon find out that it didn't matter who he was, because God would use him to be a mighty warrior.

EXPLORE MORE: Read Judges 6:5–6 to find out how big and powerful the Midianites were.

God can choose anyone to do His work.

DID YOU KNOW?
Gideon was from the tribe of Manasseh. Manasseh was one of Joseph's sons.

Gideon Asks God for a Sign

Then Gideon said to him, "If you would, please give me some proof that you really are the Lord. Please wait here. Don't go away until I come back to you. Let me bring my offering and set it down in front of you." —Judges 6:17–18 ERV

Gideon wanted to be sure his visitor was from God. Maybe Gideon thought he was having a dream or that the Midianites were trying to trick him. Gideon asked the angel for a sign. He told the angel to wait while he prepared an offering.

After a while, Gideon returned with some cooked goat's meat, a pot of broth, and a loaf of bread. The angel told Gideon, "Place the meat and bread on this rock and pour out the broth." So that's what Gideon did. Then the angel touched the food with the tip of his staff. Suddenly, fire jumped out of the rock and burned up the meat and bread. When the angel disappeared, Gideon said, "I've seen the angel of the Lord face to face!"

TALK TO GOD
Ask God to help you trust Him as you learn more about Him.

Gideon wanted another sign, so he said to God, "I'll put a piece of wool on the ground tonight. If the wool is wet with dew and the ground is dry, I'll know that you will use me to save Israel."

The next morning, the piece of wool was so wet that Gideon squeezed out a bowlful of water, but the ground was dry. Then Gideon said, "Please let me ask one more thing. When I wake up tomorrow, let the wool be dry, while the ground around it is wet." And that's exactly what happened.

God was patient with Gideon and gave him signs so he would trust God. Sometimes it's hard to know exactly what God wants you to do, but you can pray and ask God to help you know His will, or what He wants. God is patient and wants you to trust Him.

EXPLORE MORE: Read Judges 6:25–27 to find out what God asked Gideon to do.

DID YOU KNOW?
It is possible to use rocks to cook food. Many campers know how to do it.

I will seek God's will and trust Him.

For the Lord and Gideon

"I and everyone with me will blow our trumpets. Then blow your trumpets from your positions all around the camp. And shout the battle cry, 'For the Lord and for Gideon!' " —Judges 7:18 NIrV

Gideon was ready to do what God said. Gideon was ready to lead the Israelite army against the people in Midian. When Gideon was ready to go, God said, "You have too many men. I want the Israelites to know that I am the one who will win the battle against Midian and not them."

So Gideon said to the men, "If you're afraid, you may go back home." Thousands of men went back home, but ten thousand stayed.

Then God said, "You still have too many men. Bring them to the water and watch how they drink. Some men will drink the way dogs do, lapping the water with their tongues. Separate them from the men who get down on their knees to drink."

Gideon led the men to the water. Only three hundred men lapped up the water like dogs, so Gideon sent the rest of the men home. Gideon divided the three hundred men into three groups. He gave each man a trumpet and a jar with a burning torch inside. Then they surrounded the Midianites' camp. "Watch me and do what I do," Gideon said. "When my men and I blow our trumpets, you must do the same."

Gideon and his men blew their trumpets, smashed their jars, and held up their torches. They shouted, "For the Lord and for Gideon." The Midianites were confused and afraid when they heard the noise, so they ran away.

TALK TO GOD
Ask God to help you trust Him more than anything else.

The Israelites didn't need a big, powerful army to protect them from the Midianites. They didn't even need to fight! They just needed to trust God because He is stronger and more powerful than thousands of soldiers.

EXPLORE MORE: Read Judges 7:13–14 to find out about a dream a man had that showed God was with Gideon.

God is more powerful than an army.

DID YOU KNOW?
The earliest trumpets were made out of wood, bamboo, bark, clay, bone, or metal.

God Chooses the Weak

Each time he said, "My grace is all you need. My power works best in weakness." —2 Corinthians 12:9 NLT

Gideon didn't think he was an important guy. His family was the weakest in the tribe of Manasseh, and he was the smallest and least important in his family. He wasn't especially strong, rich, or well-known. In fact, when the angel of the Lord came to tell him to save Israel from Midian, Gideon was hiding from the Midianites! Even though Gideon was weak, he was exactly who God wanted to use.

When God called Moses to lead His people many years earlier, Moses was also hiding from people he feared. Like Gideon, Moses saw himself as a weak man. He even asked God to choose someone else when he heard the important job God wanted him to do. Neither Moses nor Gideon thought they were good enough to do the big things God had planned for them. But they soon found out that God uses the weak to do mighty things.

God doesn't always do things the way that people do. The Bible says people look at things on the outside, but God looks at a person's heart. God knows what we are thinking and feeling on the inside. God doesn't choose people who are the biggest and strongest, but He chooses the people who trust and love Him.

TALK TO GOD
Ask God to give you courage to do the big things He wants you to do.

Maybe there are times you feel like Gideon and Moses. Maybe you feel small and unimportant and think you're not good enough to do big things for God. If you ever feel that way, you can remember how strong God is when you feel weak. Just like He helped Moses and Gideon, He will help you do whatever He asks you to do, no matter how big it seems.

DID YOU KNOW?
The dung beetle is considered the strongest animal in the world. It can pull more than one thousand times its body weight.

EXPLORE MORE: What does Isaiah 40:29–31 say about God giving us strength?

God is strong when I feel weak.

Samson's Strength and Weakness

"You will become pregnant. You will have a son. The hair on his head must never be cut. That is because the boy will be a Nazirite. He will be set apart to God from the day he is born. He will take the lead in saving Israel from the power of the Philistines." —Judges 13:5 NIrV

During the time of the judges, the Israelites faced another enemy called the Philistines. After forty years, God raised up a leader to defeat the Philistines. His name was Samson.

When Samson was born, he was set apart to be a Nazirite. This meant he had to follow special rules like not eating certain foods and never cutting his hair. Samson was the strongest man the Israelites had ever seen. He tore apart a lion with his hands and carried a heavy gate up a hill. The secret to his strength was his long hair, and it was important that no one found out.

God had given Samson great strength, but Samson didn't always make wise choices. He fell in love with a Philistine woman named Delilah. The Philistines offered Delilah lots of money to find out what made Samson so strong. Delilah asked Samson about his strength. At first, he did not tell her his secret. But finally, he told her the truth. Delilah told the Philistines, and she had Samson's hair cut while he was sleeping. When Samson woke up, his strength was gone, and the Philistines captured him. Before the end of his life, God gave Samson strength one last time to defeat the Philistines, but Samson died with them.

TALK TO GOD
Ask God to show you the special talents He's given you. Ask for His help in using those talents for His glory.

Samson's strength was a gift from God, but sometimes his heart was full of pride. Samson also made the wrong kind of friends. We can learn from Samson by using our talents wisely and remembering the things that make us special come from God. When we honor God with our abilities, we will use them in the best way.

EXPLORE MORE: How does God want us to use the gifts He's given us? Read 1 Peter 4:10–11 to find out.

I can use my talents for God.

DID YOU KNOW?
Some Bible scholars believe the gates of Gaza that Samson tore down weighed around four tons (8,000 pounds or 3,600 kilograms).

Make Good Friends

Whoever spends time with wise people will become wise. But whoever makes friends with fools will suffer. —Proverbs 13:20 ICB

Most people like having friends. Some people have one or two friends, while others may have lots of friends. It doesn't matter if you have one friend or a bunch of friends. What matters is that you have the right kind of friends.

Samson helped save the Israelites from the Philistines, but he didn't make good choices when it came to having friends. He went against God's rules by marrying a Philistine woman. The Philistines worshiped idols, and God didn't want His people mixing with idol worshipers. Samson made bad choices by spending too much time with the Philistines, and this led to his capture.

The people we choose as our friends are those whom we often spend time with. Proverbs tells us, "Those who spend time with wise people will become wise. But those who make friends with fools will suffer." What kinds of friends are you spending time with? Are they friends who encourage you to do the right thing? Those are the kind of friends you want to be around. Do you ever spend time with someone who tries to make you do things that you know are wrong? Kids who try to make you do bad things are not good friends. Instead, choose friends who treat you like a true friend and help you make good choices.

TALK TO GOD
Ask God to bring good friends into your life and thank Him for the friends He's already given you.

True friends will accept and support you for who you are. They are honest and kind and will work things out if you disagree. The best kinds of friends will point you to Jesus and encourage you to be more like Him. And the best part is, you can be that kind of friend to other kids too.

EXPLORE MORE: Read Ecclesiastes 4:9–12 to find out why good friends are important.

Good friends are good to have.

Ruth Does the Right Thing

Ruth replied, "Don't try to make me leave you and go back. Where you go I'll go. Where you stay I'll stay. Your people will be my people. Your God will be my God." —Ruth 1:16 NIrV

During the time of the judges, the crops stopped growing and there wasn't enough food. A man from Bethlehem named Elimelek moved to Moab with his wife and two sons. Sadly, Elimelek died. Both of Naomi's sons married women from Moab. Their names were Orpah and Ruth. After a while, Naomi's sons died, and she was left with no men in her family, which was hard for a woman during Bible times.

TALK TO GOD
Ask God to help you do the right thing even when it's hard.

Naomi decided to move back to Bethlehem because she heard that God had given food to His people again. She started traveling with Orpah and Ruth but told them, "Both of you go back. May the Lord be kind to you and help you find another husband." At first Orpah and Ruth disagreed. They said, "We will go with you." But Naomi told them to go home. So Orpah said goodbye and stayed in Moab, but Ruth would not agree. She said, "Don't try to make me leave you. Where you go, I'll go. Where you stay, I'll stay. Your people will be my people. Your God will be my God."

It would have been easier for Ruth to stay in Moab. But she chose to go with Naomi because she knew it was right to help her. Ruth didn't know it at the time, but God had good plans for her and used her decision in a powerful way.

Sometimes the right thing is the hardest thing to do. It might take a lot of hard work or make us uncomfortable, but it's always worth it. We might not always see the good results of doing the right thing, but God sees, and it makes Him happy.

EXPLORE MORE: Read Ruth 1:22 to find out what the people were doing in Bethlehem when Naomi and Ruth arrived.

I can do the right thing even when it's hard.

DID YOU KNOW?
The Moabites were descendants of Lot, Abraham's nephew.

Ruth's Blessings

"May the Lord reward you for what you have done. May the Lord, the God of Israel, bless you richly. You have come to him to find safety under his care." —Ruth 2:12 NIrV

When Naomi and Ruth returned to Bethlehem, Ruth walked behind workers who were cutting and gathering grain in a field, and she picked up what was left behind. She was following a special rule God had given the Israelites to help take care of the widows and people who didn't have enough to eat. Ruth didn't know it at first, but the field she worked in belonged to one of Naomi's relatives.

The owner of the field was named Boaz. He noticed Ruth, and one of his workers told him Ruth's story. Boaz told Ruth to keep gathering grain in his field. He promised to take care of her and keep her safe. He gave her food to eat and water to drink and extra grain to take home. When Ruth told Naomi she met Boaz, Naomi was so happy! She explained that he was a close relative who would take care of them. Boaz was a man who loved and followed God. He married Ruth and took care of her. Ruth and Boaz had a son, and they named him Obed. Many years later Obed became the grandfather of King David.

Boaz showed us what Jesus would be like hundreds of years before Jesus was born. He was kind toward the widows and those who didn't have a lot of money. He was fair and good to his workers. He protected the weak and offered them safety. He provided for Ruth and gave her a beautiful life. That is exactly what Jesus does for anyone who comes to Him— He changes their story and gives them a better life.

TALK TO GOD
Thank God for protecting, providing, and taking care of you. Tell Him how happy you are that Jesus can give you a better life!

DID YOU KNOW?
Boaz's mother was Rahab, who the Israelites rescued from Jericho because she helped the spies.

EXPLORE MORE: Read Matthew 1:1-5. Who is listed as a part of Jesus's family in Matthew's gospel?

Jesus gives us a better life.

Wear Compassion and Kindness

Therefore, as God's chosen people, holy and dearly loved, clothe yourselves with compassion, kindness, humility, gentleness and patience. —Colossians 3:12 NIV

Boaz showed kindness and compassion to Ruth, and it changed her life. The love Boaz had in his heart for God was shown by the way he talked to people and helped them. Did you know that God wants us to show kindness and compassion to others too? He wants our love for Him to flow from our hearts and show up in the way we love others.

Showing compassion means you notice when someone is having a hard time and you help them. When your little brother falls and scrapes his knee, you can show compassion by helping him up and hugging him. You can show compassion by making a card for someone who is sad, or by helping your elderly neighbor do yard work when it's too hard for her.

Showing kindness means saying nice things and being a good friend. You can show kindness by sharing your toys with your friends. You can say, "Good job!" when someone shows you something they made. You can show kindness by making a gift for someone just because. You can even show kindness by praying for someone.

TALK TO GOD
Ask God to help you show kindness and compassion to the people in your life.

In the New Testament, the apostle Paul tells us to wear compassion and kindness like clothes. Just like when other people can tell what team you are on by your sports jersey, people will be able to see that you love Jesus by the way you treat others. When we clothe ourselves with the good things of God like compassion, kindness, humility, gentleness, and patience, we will look good from the inside out.

EXPLORE MORE: Jesus told a parable about a man who showed kindness and compassion to someone in need. Turn to Luke 10:30–34 to read the story.

I can show kindness and compassion to others.

DID YOU KNOW?
Compassion International is an organization that helps kids in need. People can send money each month to help kids go to school and learn about Jesus.

God Answers Hannah's Prayer

In due time she gave birth to a son. She named him Samuel, for she said, "I asked the Lord for him." —1 Samuel 1:20 NLT

Hannah was a woman who was sad because she didn't have any children. Every year she would go with her husband to a place called Shiloh to worship God. Another woman would make fun of Hannah because she couldn't have a baby, and that made Hannah upset.

One year Hannah went to the house of the Lord to pray. She cried out to God, "If you will answer my prayer and give me a son, then I will give him back to you. He will be yours for his entire lifetime."

Eli, the priest, saw Hannah praying. He could see Hannah's lips moving but he didn't hear her talking. He thought that was strange, so he went to talk to her.

Hannah told Eli, "I have been praying with great sorrow." When Eli heard Hannah's story, he told her, "Go in peace! May the God of Israel give you what you have asked of Him."

Not long after that, God answered Hannah's prayers and she had a baby boy. She named him Samuel. When Samuel was three years old, Hannah brought him to the temple to live with Eli the priest. She kept her promise to give her son back to God to serve Him.

God answered Hannah's prayers for a son because that was His plan. God always hears us when we pray. He wants us to tell Him everything we're feeling like Hannah did. No matter what you are going through today, you can tell God about it. He loves you and wants what's best for you.

> **TALK TO GOD**
> Talk to God about how you're feeling today. If you're sad or upset, tell God what is bothering you.

EXPLORE MORE: What kind of prayers does God listen to? Read 1 John 5:14 to find out.

DID YOU KNOW?
The name Samuel means "God has heard."

God hears us when we pray.

Tell God How You Feel

I call to you, God, and you answer me. Listen to me now.
Hear what I say. —Psalm 17:6 ICB

Do you ever feel like you have to pray a certain way for God to hear you? Maybe you feel like you have to say certain words or that you can't tell God how you really feel and what you really want. Most people have felt that way at some point. But the truth is, God loves to hear you talk to Him. There are no special words you have to say to get His attention. And He wants you to tell Him everything you think about and everything that's going on in your life.

TALK TO GOD
Tell God about something you desire.

Like Hannah in the Old Testament, you can pray for the things you want and tell God how you feel. You can ask God for anything, and He will listen. He already knows what's in your heart. Sometimes when we pray for things, God doesn't answer the way we want Him to. But He is still listening, and He still cares. God loves us so much that He is always working out His plan for our lives, even if it doesn't make sense right away or match up with what we want. What God wants most is for us to know Him and love Him more and more each day. He can work through anything in our lives to help us do that—whether they are good things, bad things, and even ordinary things. So, keep praying for the things you want, and tell God how you feel. God knows what is best for you, so ask Him to do what is best. God is always happy to listen!

EXPLORE MORE: Read Psalm 139:1–2 to find out what God knows about you. Does knowing this help you feel like you can tell Him anything?

I can tell God how I feel.

Samuel Hears God's Voice

The Lord came and stood there. He called out, just as he had done the other times. He said, "Samuel! Samuel!" Then Samuel replied, "Speak. I'm listening." —1 Samuel 3:10 NIrV

Hannah's son, Samuel, grew up in the temple where he served the Lord with Eli the priest. One night while Samuel was in bed, he heard someone call his name. He ran to Eli and said, "I'm here! You called me." But Eli didn't call for Samuel. Eli told him to go back to bed.

When Samuel got back in bed, he heard his name again. Samuel went to Eli and said, "I'm here. You called me." Eli said, "I didn't call you. Go back to bed." Samuel got in bed and heard his name again. He went back to Eli, but this time Eli realized God was calling Samuel. Eli told Samuel, "Go to bed. If you hear your name again, say, 'Speak, Lord. I am your servant, and I am listening.'"

When Samuel went back to bed, he heard God call his name, "Samuel, Samuel!" Samuel said, "Speak, Lord. I am your servant, and I am listening." God told Samuel that Eli's family would be punished because his sons did not follow Him.

It was hard for Samuel to share this message with Eli, but he told Eli what God had said to him. Samuel became the first prophet of Israel, which meant that God would give him more messages to tell the people. God was with Samuel from that day forward. Every message He gave Samuel came true.

Today God speaks to us through the Bible and the Holy Spirit. You can listen to God like Samuel did. When you feel God's words telling you to do something, you can say, "Speak, Lord, I am listening."

TALK TO GOD
Ask God to speak to you and to help you listen to His words.

EXPLORE MORE: Read 1 Samuel 3:18 to find out how Eli reacted when he heard the message God gave Samuel.

DID YOU KNOW?
Studies have shown that most babies can recognize the sound of their name when they are around six months old.

I can listen to God.

God Still Speaks

Whether you turn to the right or to the left, your ears will hear a voice behind you, saying, "This is the way; walk in it." —Isaiah 30:21 NIV

Have you ever heard someone say God told them to do something? Have you wondered what that means? We don't usually hear God's voice out loud like people did in the Old Testament. But did you know God still speaks to people today? How does He do that?

The way God spoke to people in Bible stories is different from how God speaks to us now. Before the Bible was written, God gave special messages to prophets to share with other people. He also visited people in dreams and sent angels to talk to people, like He did with Abraham, Jacob, and Gideon.

As time went on, God gave us the Bible. He told writers a long time ago what He wanted to say so they could write it down and we could read it. Today many people have Bibles in their homes, and they can read God's Word anytime.

God also gave us a special gift by sending the Holy Spirit after Jesus went back to heaven. The Bible tells us the Holy Spirit helps us talk with God and helps us understand what He wants us to know.

TALK TO GOD
Thank God for giving us the Bible and the Holy Spirit to speak to us.

Even though you might not hear a voice talk to you like Samuel did, or see an angel like Gideon did, God is still speaking today. And He wants to talk to you! When you want to hear from God, you can read the Bible and pray. Ask the Holy Spirit to quiet your heart so you can understand what God wants you to know. God loves to speak to those who are listening!

EXPLORE MORE: What is the biggest way God has spoken to us? Read Hebrews 1:1–2 to find out.

God speaks to me.

DID YOU KNOW?
Currently there are over seven thousand known languages spoken in the world.

Israel Asks for a King

The elders asked for a king to lead them. Samuel thought this was a bad idea, so he prayed to the Lord. The Lord told Samuel, "Do what the people tell you. They have not rejected you. They have rejected me. They don't want me to be their king."
—1 Samuel 8:6–7 ERV

As the nation of Israel grew, they noticed the other countries around them had kings. They wanted a king too. Some of the leaders asked Samuel to choose a king for them. Samuel thought this was a bad idea, but God told him to listen to the people. God wanted the people to see what it was like to follow a human king instead of following Him.

God told Samuel that a man named Saul would rule the Israelites. Samuel anointed Saul by pouring oil on his head. It was a special way of showing that Saul would be the king.

Saul became the first king of Israel. At the start of his reign as king, he followed God, but after a while he became stubborn and wanted to do things his own way. He became jealous and angry and didn't do what God told him to do. Eventually, Saul died and was no longer king. A new king took Saul's place.

The Israelites wanted to be like the people around them, and they forgot that God is the one true King. The earthly leaders they followed were temporary—each one eventually died and someone else had to lead them. Their kings were also imperfect and made mistakes. Some of Israel's kings ended up being evil and leading the people in the wrong direction.

God is the King who will rule forever. No one will ever take His place, and He will never make mistakes. No matter where we live or who our leader is, we can follow God and be a part of His kingdom. God's kingdom will never end.

EXPLORE MORE: Read Luke 1:32–33. What did the angel Gabriel tell Mary about Jesus's kingdom?

TALK TO GOD
Ask God to help you follow Him as your King.

DID YOU KNOW?
There are more than forty countries in the world today that have kings or queens.

God is King forever.

Look on the Inside

"The Lord does not look at the things people look at. People look at the outside of a person. But the Lord looks at what is in the heart." —1 Samuel 16:7 NIrV

God told Samuel there was another king He had chosen to take Saul's place. He sent Samuel to the small town of Bethlehem to visit a man named Jesse. One of Jesse's sons was the next king God had chosen.

Samuel invited Jesse and his sons to offer a sacrifice to God. As he saw Jesse's oldest son, he thought, "This has to be the one the Lord wants." But God told Samuel, "Do not look at how handsome or tall he is. I have not chosen him." Then God told Samuel, "People look at the outside of a person, but the Lord looks at what is in the heart."

One by one each of Jesse's sons walked by Samuel, but God hadn't chosen any of them. Samuel asked Jesse if he had another son. Jesse answered, "My youngest son is taking care of the sheep." Jesse sent for his youngest son, and he stood before Samuel. His name was David. God said, "This is the one." Samuel poured oil on David's head in front of his older brothers. This showed that David would become the next king. From that day on, God's Spirit was with David.

TALK TO GOD
Thank God for making you in His likeness, inside and out. Ask God to help you see people the way He sees them.

Like Samuel, sometimes we judge people by how they look on the outside, but God cares about a person's heart. When someone gives you a present, the wrapping paper doesn't matter as much as the gift inside. When we look at others, we can get to know them on the inside to find a beautiful gift too.

EXPLORE MORE: Read Isaiah 53:2 to find out how Jesus looked on the outside.

God looks at our hearts.

DID YOU KNOW?
Bethlehem is also called the City of David in the Bible and is the place where Jesus was born.

David Serves the King

When David came to Saul, he began to serve him. Saul loved David very much. And David became the officer who carried Saul's armor.
—1 Samuel 16:21 ICB

As Saul's heart grew hard toward God, he became very troubled. His servants said, "We should find someone to play the harp for you. It will help you feel better." King Saul agreed and told his servants to bring a harp player to him. One of his servants said, "Jesse of Bethlehem has a son who plays the harp. He is a brave man and fights well. The Lord's Spirit is with him."

Saul sent messengers to Jesse, and they asked for David to come to the palace. Jesse agreed and sent David on his way. When David began serving King Saul, the king liked David and wanted him to stay. Whenever Saul felt troubled, David played the harp and Saul felt better.

TALK TO GOD
Ask God to help you serve Him no matter what He wants you to do.

David's work for God started small, but one day he became a great king in Israel. No one would have expected a shepherd boy and harp player from a small town to become a king. And even though David knew what God's plans were for him, he stayed humble. He depended on God and was patient. David served God with the small jobs God gave him as he waited patiently for the big job God had planned.

Maybe like David you have big plans and dreams for your life. Sometimes it can feel like those things are so far away they may never happen. But while you wait, you can serve God faithfully like David did. It's not about the size of your job, but the size of your love for God. When you serve Him with all your heart in the small things, He knows you can serve Him with all your heart in the big things too.

DID YOU KNOW?
The instrument David played is often called a lyre in the Bible. A lyre is a U-shaped stringed instrument similar to a harp.

EXPLORE MORE: Read Luke 16:10 to find out what Jesus said about people who are trustworthy with small things.

I can serve God in small and big ways.

God Is Bigger than a Giant

What shall we say about such wonderful things as these? If God is for us, who can ever be against us? —Romans 8:31 NLT

The Philistine army came to fight the Israelites. The Philistines camped on one hill, while the Israelites camped on another hill. In between them was the valley of Elah, which was in the land of Judah near Bethlehem. A Philistine warrior named Goliath was more than 9 feet (2.7 meters) tall! For forty days he shouted to the Israelites and dared them to send someone to fight him.

Every time Israel's army saw Goliath, they ran away. But one day David heard Goliath's challenge as he brought some food to his brothers. David was angry that Goliath teased God's people. David said, "He dares the armies of the living God to fight him. Who does he think he is?"

TALK TO GOD
Thank God that He is on your side and that He helps you.

David decided to fight Goliath, but King Saul tried to stop him. David said, "I fought a lion and a bear while taking care of my father's sheep. The Lord will save me from this Philistine too."

Saul put his armor on David, but it was too heavy, so he took it off. David picked up five stones and grabbed his sling.

Goliath laughed when he saw David standing before him. David said, "You come to fight against me with a sword, a spear, and a javelin. But I come against you in the name of the Lord." David ran toward Goliath, put a stone in his sling and slung it. The stone hit Goliath on the forehead, and the giant fell to the ground—*bam*!

God can help His people do amazing things. When we love and follow God we don't have to be afraid. When we face scary things, God will help us—even when our problems seem gigantic!

EXPLORE MORE: Read 1 Samuel 17:34–35 to learn how David protected his father's sheep.

God helps us.

DID YOU KNOW?
Today the nation of Israel has a missile defense system named David's Sling.

David's Loyal Friend

Jonathan made an agreement with David. He did this because he loved David as much as himself. —1 Samuel 18:3 ICB

David became more and more famous as he continued to do great things. Saul became jealous and was afraid that David would take over as king. Eventually, Saul wanted to get rid of him.

Saul had a son named Jonathan who was David's best friend. The Bible says that Jonathan loved David as much as he loved himself. Jonathan didn't only think of David as one of his father's soldiers, he also thought of him as a close friend. Jonathan gave David his robe, sword, and belt. And whenever Saul had plans to hurt David, Jonathan would keep David safe.

One time Jonathan even helped David hide when he was in danger. They came up with a plan so David would know if it was safe to come back or if he needed to leave for a while. Jonathan found out that Saul wanted to hurt David, so he let David know he had to go away. The two friends cried as they said goodbye to each other.

TALK TO GOD
Ask God to help you be a good friend to others.

Since Jonathan was Saul's son, he was in line to be the next king. But he never let that get in the way of his friendship with David. He knew that God had chosen David to be the next king of Israel. Jonathan loved David and trusted God's plan for both of them.

Because Jonathan was such a good friend, he always protected David when Saul wanted to hurt him. Jonathan cared about David and supported him in the good times and the bad times because that's what good friends do.

DID YOU KNOW?
Animals like baboons, elephants, dolphins, horses, and chimpanzees make friends with the other animals they grow up with.

EXPLORE MORE: Read 1 Samuel 20:18–23 to find out Jonathan's plan to protect David.

God can use friends to help each other.

Loyal Friends

A friend loves you all the time. A brother is always there to help you. —Proverbs 17:17 ICB

Has a friend ever been kind to you when you had a hard day? Maybe you fell down at the park and your friend helped you up. Maybe someone said mean words to you and your friend stood up for you. Or maybe something sad happened and your friend just sat with you so you didn't have to be alone. How did that make you feel?

The Bible tells us that true friends love us all the time. That means they love us when things are good and when they're bad. They stick with us through happy days and sad days, and they forgive us when we mess up.

Just like it feels good to have loyal friends, you can make others feel good by being a loyal friend too. You can love your friends all the time—when they do well on a school project, when they score a goal, when they are sick, when they make a mistake, or when they're going through a hard time. Being a loyal friend means your love for someone doesn't change, no matter what's going on. You treat your friends the same on good days and bad days. It's the kind of friend Jonathan was to David, and one of the best ways we can show God's love to others.

> **TALK TO GOD**
> Think of a friend who has been kind to you and thank God for that person.

And what's even better is that Jesus is always a loyal friend to us. He will never leave us, no matter how hard things get. Even if we feel alone at times, He will always be our friend and stick with us. Jesus is the best friend we can ever have.

EXPLORE MORE: Read John 15:14 to find out how you can be a friend of Jesus.

It's good to be a loyal friend.

DID YOU KNOW?
The Spanish word for friend is *amigo*. In French it is *ami*, and in Italian it's *amico*.

A Corner of the King's Robe

"I know for sure that you will be king. I know that the kingdom of Israel will be made secure under your control." —1 Samuel 24:20 NIrV

King Saul was jealous of David. Saul knew David would be the next king. Saul also knew that God was with David.

Sometimes David had to hide because Saul wanted to hurt him. One day Saul went into a cave where David and his men were hiding. Saul did not see David and his men, but David's men saw Saul. "God has given you a chance to capture your enemy," the men told David. But David didn't want to attack Saul. Instead, he cut off a corner of Saul's robe and snuck away.

David was sorry for cutting Saul's robe. David told his men that Saul was king and deserved to be respected. David called out, "King Saul, my master!" Then he bowed before Saul and said, "Look at this piece of your robe in my hand. I could have hurt you, but I didn't."

TALK TO GOD
Ask God to help you respect all people.

When Saul thought about how kind David was, he wept out loud. "You are a better person than I am, David! You have treated me well and I have treated you badly. I know you will become the great king of Israel. Promise that you will not hurt me or my family." So David made that promise to Saul, and they both went their separate ways.

Just like David respected King Saul, we need to respect others. If someone doesn't like you or if you don't like them, you can be nice and respectful anyway. As you show kindness to people who are hard to get along with, you might even become friends.

DID YOU KNOW?
It is not proper for anyone outside of the royal family to touch a king or queen without permission.

EXPLORE MORE: What did King Saul say to David when he found out that David refused to harm him a second time? Read 1 Samuel 26:21–25.

I will respect everyone.

David Becomes King

"Please, bless my family. Let it continue before you forever. Lord God, you have said these wonderful things. With your blessing let my family be blessed forever." —2 Samuel 7:29 ICB

The Israelites were at a place called Hebron when the time came for David to become their king. The people told David, "We are your family. Even when Saul was the king, you were the one who led us." Then they made David king of Israel.

David was thirty years old when he became king. In 2 Samuel 7 we read how God spoke to David through the prophet Nathan. He said, "I have taken you from tending sheep in the pasture to being the leader of my people. I am with you everywhere you go, and I have helped you win your battles. Now I will make your name famous and will provide a homeland for my people. Your son will build a temple for me, and his kingdom will be strong. Your family and kingdom will continue forever."

TALK TO GOD
Ask God to bless your family.

King David responded by praying to the Lord, "God, you are great! There is no one like you! You have made Israel your very own people, and you are our God. I am your servant. Bless my family with your promise, so it will continue forever."

More than a thousand years later, Jesus was born into the family line of David. When God made this promise to David, He was talking about the kingdom of God that would last forever through Jesus. When we believe that Jesus is the Son of God who died on the cross for our sins, we become part of God's forever kingdom. Jesus is the King who rules over the entire world. No king will ever be greater than He is!

EXPLORE MORE: Who else said, "I am the Lord's servant"? Read Luke 1:38 to find out.

Jesus's kingdom lasts forever.

DID YOU KNOW?
About six hundred years before David was in Hebron, Abraham bought land in Hebron for four hundred pieces of silver.

Kindness from the King

The king asked, "Isn't there anyone still alive from the royal house of Saul? God has been very kind to me. I would like to be kind to that person in the same way."
—2 Samuel 9:3 NIrV

After David became king, he asked, "Is anyone from Saul's family still alive?"

"Yes," said one of the men who had been Saul's servant. "Jonathan's son Mephibosheth is alive. He was hurt when he was a young boy and cannot walk."

In Bible times, people who couldn't walk sat on the ground and begged for food as others walked by. They could not own land or take care of themselves. They were often treated badly. "Bring Mephibosheth to me," said David.

Can you imagine how surprised Mephibosheth must have been when he heard the king wanted to see him? Not only was he surprised, but he was also scared!

When Mephibosheth saw King David, he bowed to the ground. "Don't be afraid!" said David. "I want to be kind to you because of my promise to your father, Jonathan. I'll give you the land that belonged to your grandfather Saul, and you may live with me at the palace."

TALK TO GOD
Say thank you to Jesus for inviting you to be part of His family.

David was the highest ruler in the land, and Mephibosheth was seen by others as the lowest. He even said to David, "Who am I that you would show kindness to a dead dog like me?" But David didn't see him that way. From that day on, Mephibosheth ate at the king's table and David treated him like a son.

David showed love and kindness to Mephibosheth the way Jesus shows love and kindness to us. Jesus is the greatest ruler, yet He invites us to be part of His family and treats us as His children. When we belong to Jesus, He gives us everything we need.

EXPLORE MORE: Read Luke 18:35–43 to find out how Jesus showed kindness to another man who sat and begged for food.

DID YOU KNOW?
King Athelstan was the first king of England from 927–939. He was a Christian man who was known for being kind and compassionate to everyone.

Jesus shows love and kindness to me.

Doing Good

And don't forget to do good and to share what you have with others, because sacrifices like these are very pleasing to God.
—Hebrews 13:16 ERV

The Bible says that David was a man who loved God and wanted the things that would please Him. David was an important king, but he showed that he was kind and caring by inviting Mephibosheth to live with him at the palace.

TALK TO GOD
Ask God to help you find ways to show kindness to others.

God created everyone, and it makes Him happy when we show kindness to others. There are many ways you can do that, and you can start with the people in your family. You can help by doing chores like setting the table or bringing dishes to the sink. If you have a younger brother or sister, you can help them find their shoes or make their bed. You can also show kindness with your words by saying please and thank you and telling others the good things you see in them.

When it comes to caring about people in your community, you can ask your parents to help you bring food or clothes to a shelter for people in need. Do you like to be outside? Then put on a pair of work gloves and pick up trash at a playground. Do you see books lying around when you're at the library? You can collect them and bring them to the librarian's desk. Are you an artist? Create some cards or pictures and give them to your grandparents or someone in your neighborhood. Do you like to bake? Then whip up a batch of cookies and share them with your friends or neighbors.

You don't have to be a king or even a grown-up to find ways to care about others. Like David, you can share God's love by treating others with kindness.

EXPLORE MORE: Read Galatians 5:22–23 to find out where kindness comes from.

I will care about others.

DID YOU KNOW?
Canned meat, canned vegetables, peanut butter, pasta, and baby food are some of the top items needed in many food pantries.

David's Song of Praise

The Lord is my Rock, my fortress, my place of safety. He is my God, the Rock I run to for protection. He is my shield; by his power I am saved. He is my hiding place high in the hills. —Psalm 18:2 ERV

God made David the greatest king of Israel. Toward the end of David's life, he sang a song of praise to God. He sang these words, "The Lord is my rock, my fortress, and my savior; my God is my rock, in whom I find protection" (2 Samuel 22:2–3).

David knew that without God he would not have been a great king. God was his *rock*. A rock is solid, hard, and strong and is not easily moved. God was his *fortress*. That's another word for a strong fort or hiding place. God was David's *Savior*. He saved David from his enemies, and He saved him by forgiving his sins.

David also called God his shield, his strength, and high tower. A *shield* gives protection when someone tries to harm you. God was David's *strength*. David knew he was not strong enough to win his battles on his own, but God would help him when he depended on Him. God was David's *high tower*. In Bible times a high tower was a safe place. When you got to the top, you could see everything. A high tower was also a safe place because others could not enter the tower when it was locked.

> **TALK TO GOD**
> Thank God for being your rock, your strength, and your place of safety.

The God who protected David is the same God who protects us. As you learn more about God, you can know that He is your rock, your strong fort, and your Savior. You can depend on God to be your shield, your strength, and your high tower. And like David, you can sing a song of praise to God for everything He is to you.

EXPLORE MORE: Read Psalm 59:16–17 to find out when David enjoyed singing his praises to God.

DID YOU KNOW?
The tallest building in the world today is the Burj Khalifa in Dubai. It stands at over 2,700 feet (823 meters) tall.

God is my place of safety.

Solomon Becomes the New King

"Then come back up to the city with [Solomon]. Have him sit on my throne. He will rule in my place. I've appointed him ruler over Israel and Judah." —1 Kings 1:35 NIrV

The time had come for a new king to rule over Israel. David was old and could no longer do the things a king needed to do. Adonijah was one of David's sons. Adonijah decided to make himself the king without telling his father. When King David found out, he said that his son Solomon would be the next king of Israel.

David told the priest and Nathan, the prophet, to make Solomon king. David gave them instructions on where to go. He told them to go to Gihon Spring to make Solomon king. When they got to Gihon Spring, Zadok the priest poured oil over Solomon's head. The trumpets sounded and everyone shouted, "Long live King Solomon!"

When Solomon returned to Jerusalem, David gave him some words of advice. He said, "Do everything the Lord requires of you. Follow His laws and commands. Obey the law of Moses, then you will be successful in everything you do. Your sons must be careful how they live. If they are faithful to Him, the Lord will keep His promise. Your family will always sit on the throne of Israel."

TALK TO GOD
Thank God that He gives us instructions to help us love and follow Him.

David's words to Solomon are wise words for all of us. Because God loves us so much, He wants us to follow His rules and commands in the Bible. Loving God, honoring our parents, and being kind to others also helps us to have happier and more peaceful lives. God's ways are always right, and following them is the best thing we can do!

EXPLORE MORE: Read 1 Kings 1:40 to find out how the people celebrated when Solomon became the king.

I will follow God's ways.

DID YOU KNOW?
The Gihon Spring is Jerusalem's major natural source of fresh water. At certain times it flows stronger and faster, which is why it's named Gihon, meaning "gushing."

The King Asks for Wisdom

The Lord appeared to Solomon at Gibeon. He spoke to him in a dream during the night. God said, "Ask for anything you want me to give you." —1 Kings 3:5 NIrV

King Solomon loved God and followed the instructions that David had given him. One of the first things he did as king was offer a sacrifice to God. Solomon went to the most important altar at a place called Gibeon. Solomon didn't offer one or two sacrifices—he offered one thousand sacrifices! How long do you think it took to make that many sacrifices—a few days or maybe even weeks? Solomon did this to show that he wanted to serve God with all his heart.

In 1 Kings 3 it says that God spoke to Solomon in a dream. God said, "You can ask for anything, and I will give it to you." Solomon replied, "You were kind to my father, David, because he was faithful to you. You are kind to me by making me king. But I don't know how to rule over this many people—there are too many to count! Give me wisdom to rule and to know right from wrong. Without you, no one can rule over this great nation."

God was pleased with Solomon's answer. He said, "I will give you wisdom to rule over Israel, but I will also give you riches and honor that you did not ask for. If you follow me as your father, David, did, I will also give you a long life."

TALK TO GOD
Ask God to give you wisdom.

What would you say if God told you to ask for anything you wanted? Would you need to think about it for a while? Solomon knew right away that having wisdom would help him be a better king. And just like Solomon, you can ask God for wisdom too.

EXPLORE MORE: What does James 1:5–6 tell us about asking for wisdom?

DID YOU KNOW?
Wisdom is the ability to make godly choices.

Wisdom comes from God.

Solomon Builds the Temple

"Obey all my laws and commands. If you do, I will do for you what I promised your father David. And I will live among the children of Israel in this Temple you are building. I will never leave the people of Israel." —1 Kings 6:12–13 ICB

In his fourth year as king of Israel, Solomon knew it was time to build a temple to honor God. Like the tabernacle in the wilderness, it would be the place where people would go to meet with God. The temple would also be a sign of God's presence.

The construction of the temple began 480 years after the Israelites left Egypt. It was built in Jerusalem, which is the capital city of Israel. It took thousands of workers seven years to complete the temple. In 1 Kings 6, you can read about the size of the temple and the materials that were used. From cedarwood and olive wood to pure gold on the walls and ceilings, only the finest materials were used to build the temple.

TALK TO GOD
Thank God for churches and places to worship with other believers.

Solomon had so much respect for the holiness of God that he made a special request. Instead of having the stones for the building cut and polished at the site of the temple, Solomon asked for them to be cut and polished away from the temple. This way the sound of hammers, axes, and other iron tools couldn't be heard at the temple site.

Just like the tabernacle, the temple had a Most Holy Place where the ark of the covenant rested. Solomon had gold cherubim figures made which looked like heavenly angels. Their long wings were a sign of God's protection over His people. When the priests brought the ark of the covenant into the temple, it was placed under the wings of the cherubim.

God kept His promise to live among the people in the temple. Today, God's Holy Spirit lives in the hearts of all who believe in Jesus.

EXPLORE MORE: Read 1 Kings 8:5–6 to find out what the people did before the priests brought the ark of the covenant into the temple.

We are God's temple.

DID YOU KNOW?
A large, deep open stone pit is called a quarry. It's where stonecutters go to get pieces of stone to use as building materials.

Solomon Dedicates the Temple

Then Solomon stood in front of the Lord's altar. He stood in front of the whole community of Israel. He spread out his hands toward heaven. —1 Kings 8:22 NIrV

When Solomon finished building the temple, he wanted to honor God for keeping His promise to live among the Israelites. The first thing Solomon did was dedicate the temple to God. With his hands reaching toward heaven, Solomon prayed, "Lord, you are the God of Israel. There is no God like you in heaven above or on earth below."

Solomon knew that God had chosen him to build the temple. He was honored that God allowed him this special blessing. By dedicating the temple to God, Solomon was honoring God.

When we dedicate something to God, it's like giving something back to Him that He has given us. Parents dedicate their children to God by promising to raise them in a Christian home and teach them about God. Some people dedicate their homes to God. They may find ways to invite others into their homes and offer them food or a place to stay. When people build a new church, they might dedicate the church building to God by having a special ceremony like Solomon did.

TALK TO GOD
Ask God to help you dedicate your life to Him.

We can also dedicate our talents and abilities to God by using them in a way that honors Him. Sometimes famous athletes thank God for their victories, and musicians may dedicate their music to God.

DID YOU KNOW?
Sydney McLaughlin won the 2020 Olympic gold medal for Team USA in the 400-meter hurdles. She set a world record. After the race, she said, "I use the gifts God has given me to point all the attention back to Him."

God is pleased when we use what we have to honor Him. But of all the things we can dedicate to God, the most important thing we can dedicate is ourselves. When you love God with all your heart and share His love with others, you will live a life that is dedicated to loving and serving God.

EXPLORE MORE: Read 1 Kings 9:25 to find out what Solomon did at the temple three times a year.

I will dedicate myself to God.

God Is Everywhere

"But, God, will you really live here with us on the earth? The whole sky and the highest heaven cannot contain you. Certainly this Temple that I built cannot contain you either." —1 Kings 8:27 ERV

Solomon prayed a prayer of dedication to God after he had finished building the temple. As he was praying, he realized that although he had built the temple as a place for God to dwell, God's presence is greater than a building.

God created the heavens and the earth, and He rules over them. God is everywhere. King David, Solomon's father, wrote, "Where can I go to get away from your Spirit? Where can I run from you? If I go up to the skies, you are there. . . . If I rise with the sun in the east, and settle in the west beyond the sea, even there you would guide me. With your right hand you would hold me" (Psalm 130:7–10).

TALK TO GOD
Tell God, "Thank you for being everywhere."

Sometimes we feel close to God at church or Sunday school. Some people feel close to God when they go for a walk in the woods or along the ocean. And some people feel close to God when they find a quiet place at home. It's good to go to places where we feel close to God. But no matter where we are, God is always with us.

Whether you're at home painting a picture, at school reading a book, or outdoors kicking a soccer ball across the field with your teammates, you can feel close to God by thinking about Him. You can say, "God, I know you are right beside me. Please help me today in everything I do." God loves it when you think about Him and talk to Him. You never have to look for Him because He is everywhere.

EXPLORE MORE: What does Psalm 145:18 tell us to do to feel close to God?

DID YOU KNOW?
When the Israelites were in the wilderness, Moses would climb up Mount Sinai to be close to God and talk with Him.

No matter where I am, God is there.

One Nation Becomes Two

"Your father put a heavy load on our shoulders. But now make our hard work easier. Make the heavy load on us lighter. Then we'll serve you." —1 Kings 12:4 NIrV

King Rehoboam became the ruler of Israel after his father, Solomon, died. The Israelites promised to be loyal to Rehoboam if he would not make them work so hard. They also wanted him to lower the amount of taxes that King Solomon placed on them. Rehoboam was foolish and listened to bad advice from some of his friends. He told the people he would be a harsh ruler—even harsher than King Solomon.

Ten of the tribes refused to honor Rehoboam as king. They chose another man to be their king. They were called the Northern Kingdom or "Israel." The other two tribes agreed to have Rehoboam as their king. They were called the Southern Kingdom or "Judah."

Rehoboam was angry and ordered his men to fight the tribes who rejected him as king. But God sent a man to tell Rehoboam not to fight Israel because they were his relatives. This time, Rehoboam listened to good advice and sent the fighting men home.

TALK TO GOD
Ask God to help you follow Him all the time.

It had been more than five hundred years since the Israelites left Egypt as one nation, and now they were split in two. The people no longer lived the way God wanted them to. They followed bad leaders and lived in ways that must have broken God's heart. But even though they turned their backs on God, He never stopped loving them. He continued to send people to bring the Israelites back to Him. And one day, God would send His Son, Jesus, to pay for the sins of the world. Jesus would bring people back to God. God's love and forgiveness never end.

EXPLORE MORE: What does Psalm 103:8–10 tell us about God?

DID YOU KNOW?

The name Judah is close to the Hebrew word for "praise," which is *yadah*. When you offer *yadah*, you praise God with lifted hands.

God's love for His people lasts forever.

Good King Asa

Asa commanded the people of Judah to obey the Lord, the God their ancestors followed. Asa commanded them to obey the Lord's teachings and commandments. —2 Chronicles 14:4 ICB

Rehoboam's son Abijam became the king after Rehoboam died. Like his father, Abijam was not faithful to the Lord. He only ruled for three years. Then his son Asa became the king of Judah.

King Asa followed the Lord and commanded the people to follow Him. In every town of Judah, he tore down the idols and altars that were used to worship false gods. He smashed the stone pillars that honored false gods. He also removed his grandmother from her position as queen mother. She had made a pole that was used to worship a false goddess, and Asa knew that was wrong.

King Asa built strong-walled cities with towers and gates. He repaired the altar of the Lord which stood in front of the entrance to the temple. God blessed the land of Judah with peace while Asa was king because he remained faithful to God. Some people from the Northern Kingdom of Israel moved to Judah during Asa's reign because they saw that God was with him.

TALK TO GOD
Ask God to help you find friends who follow Him.

It's good to be with people who love God and follow Him. Being with others who believe the things we believe helps us stay strong in our faith. But sometimes we may find ourselves with people who do not follow God. You may have friends at school or in your neighborhood who do not believe in Jesus. Like King Asa, you can use your words and actions to show that you honor and respect the Lord. When you follow God with all your heart, others will see it. Then you can tell them how they can follow God too.

EXPLORE MORE: Read 2 Chronicles 17:1–5 to find out about the next king of Judah.

I want others to see that I follow God.

DID YOU KNOW?
The Temple Institute is an organization in Israel. Its goal is to build the third Jewish temple in Jerusalem.

Food for Elijah

"Leave this place. Go east and hide in the Kerith Valley. It is east of the Jordan River. You will drink water from the brook. I have directed some ravens to supply you with food there." —1 Kings 17:3–4 NIrV

Elijah was a man who loved and followed God. He was a prophet, which meant that he was one of God's messengers. King Ahab was an evil king who ruled over Israel. Elijah told King Ahab, "I serve the Lord, the God of Israel. There will be no dew or rain for the next few years, until I say so."

God told Elijah to camp by a brook called Kerith. The brook flowed into the Jordan River. God said to Elijah, "Drink from the brook and eat what the ravens bring you." Every morning and evening, ravens came and brought meat and bread for Elijah, and every day he drank fresh water from the brook.

Eventually the brook dried up because there was no rain. God told Elijah to go to the village of Zarephath where a woman would feed him. The woman was called a widow because her husband had died. When Elijah met the widow and asked for food, she said, "I only have a handful of flour and a little oil in my jug." Elijah told her to make some bread anyway. God had told Elijah that the woman would always have enough flour and oil to make more bread. The widow listened to Elijah, and sure enough, her containers of flour and oil were never empty.

Isn't it amazing to see how God provides for His people? He sent bread from heaven when the Israelites lived in the wilderness, He used birds to deliver food to Elijah, and He gave a never-ending supply of flour and oil to a poor widow. What seems impossible to us is never impossible with God. He can do anything.

EXPLORE MORE: Read 1 Kings 17:8–12 to find out what the widow was doing when Elijah met her.

TALK TO GOD
Thank God for the food you have today.

DID YOU KNOW?
Ravens are smart birds. They can copy the sounds of human words as well as other animal sounds. They also like to play and slide down snowy roofs.

God provides in unexpected ways.

The Widow's Son

"Give me your son," Elijah replied. He took him from her arms. He carried him to the upstairs room where he was staying. He put him down on his bed. —1 Kings 17:19 NIrV

The widow in Zarephath who had made bread for Elijah invited him to stay in an upstairs room in her house. After a while, her son became very sick and died. The woman was upset and said, "What have you done to me? Did you come here to point out my sins?" Maybe she wondered if God was punishing her for something she had done. But that's not why her son died.

Elijah took the boy upstairs and laid the boy on his bed. Elijah lay down on top of the boy and cried out to God three times. He prayed, "Lord, please let the child's life return to him!"

God heard Elijah's prayer, and the boy began to breathe. Elijah brought him to his mother and said, "Look! Your son is alive!" The woman was amazed and said, "Now I know that you are a man of God and that He speaks through you."

This is the first time we read of someone coming back to life in the Bible. Elijah had never seen anyone come back to life, yet he believed in the power of God and asked Him for this miracle. And many years later, God would show His power by bringing His own Son back to life.

TALK TO GOD
Thank God that He is able to do more than we can.

The Bible doesn't tell us what happened to the widow and her son. Do you think she told her friends how her son died and became alive again? Maybe she baked bread for her neighbors because she always had enough flour and oil. What we do know is that she believed in God. The words she spoke to Elijah tell us this. She knew that only a man of God could do such amazing miracles.

EXPLORE MORE: Read John 3:1–2. How did Nicodemus know that Jesus was a man of God?

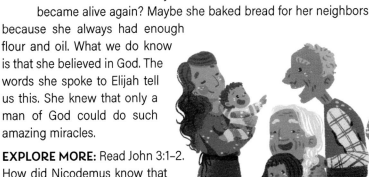

God can make miracles happen.

Fire from Heaven

"Then you pray to your god. And I'll pray to the Lord. The god who answers by sending fire down is the one and only God." —1 Kings 18:24 NIrV

King Ahab, who ruled over Israel, worshiped a fake god named Baal. About 450 prophets followed Baal too. Elijah was a prophet, a messenger of God. Elijah challenged King Ahab to a contest on Mount Carmel. When the people gathered around the mountain, Elijah said, "How long will you serve both Baal and God? If the Lord is the true God, follow Him. But if Baal is the true God, follow him!"

Elijah asked for two bulls. He told Ahab's prophets to place their bull on the altar and pray for Baal to send fire. They prayed from morning until noon. "Answer us!" they shouted, as they danced around the altar. But nothing happened.

"Pray louder," said Elijah. "Maybe your god is sleeping or on vacation." They prayed until evening, but Baal did not send fire.

Then it was Elijah's turn. He used twelve stones to build an altar and dug a ditch around it. He prepared the wood and said, "Pour four jugs of water on the altar." So they did. "Do it again," said Elijah. So they did. "Pour the water again," said Elijah. They poured water a third time.

TALK TO GOD
Tell God that you know He is the only true living God.

When the altar was soaked with water, Elijah asked God to show the people that He alone is God. As Elijah prayed, blazing fire roared from heaven and burned the altar and everything on it. The fire burned the ground around the altar and dried up all the water! The people fell down and cried, "The Lord is God!"

Elijah trusted God. He knew God would hear His prayer and show the people that He is the living God. If He is your God, then you can trust Him too!

EXPLORE MORE: Read Elijah's prayer in 1 Kings 18:36–37.

DID YOU KNOW?
Mount Carmel is a high, wooded mountain range along the Mediterranean coast and is seen as a symbol of beauty.

God shows us that He is the one and only God.

God Is Alive

Before the mountains were born, and before you created
the earth and the world, you are God. You have always
been, and you will always be. —Psalm 90:2 ICB

What do you think it was like to be on Mount Carmel when God sent a fiery blaze from heaven to burn up Elijah's altar? The Israelites must have been amazed as God proved to them once again that He is the only true and living God. As they fell to the ground, they may have felt foolish that they had been worshiping a false god. They had believed Baal could send rain and bless the earth, but only God can do that. After three years of no rain, they should have known that Baal had no power over the earth. Baal was just a statue and not a living being.

TALK TO GOD
Thank God that He has always been alive and will live forever.

The Israelites worshiped the gods of other nations when they lived among the people of those nations. Instead of being strong in their faith, many of them were weak and forgot about God's commandment to worship only Him. Elijah told the Israelites they could not serve both God and Baal. It seems that some of the people thought they could do both.

God is the only true God. He is the God of heaven and earth, and He has been alive forever. It's hard for us to understand that God has always been alive, but we know it's true because the Bible tells us. Kings and presidents and rulers do not live forever, and they cannot do the things that God can do. And a fake god made from wood or stone has never been alive and cannot do anything at all! Our great God in heaven is alive and that will never change—you can count on that!

EXPLORE MORE: What does Psalm 86:8–10 tell us about God?

God has always been alive.

DID YOU KNOW?
After the contest on Mount Carmel, Elijah prayed for God to send rain. God answered his prayer.

A Good Example

Jehoshaphat followed all the ways of his father Asa. He didn't wander away from them. He did what was right in the sight of the Lord. —1 Kings 22:43 NIrV

Jehoshaphat was King Asa's son, and he became the king of Judah after his father died. Jehoshaphat was thirty-five years old when he became king. He ruled in Jerusalem for twenty-five years. The Bible says that Jehoshaphat followed the ways of his father. He did what God wanted him to do. He was a good military leader and built a strong army and sturdy forts.

King Jehoshaphat stayed faithful to God. He kept the commands that God had given Moses. He also sent people away who didn't honor God or His temple. He did many good things for the kingdom of Judah, and he even made peace with Ahab, the king of Israel. The king brought glory to God by doing what was right. Jehoshaphat was a good example to the people of Judah.

TALK TO GOD
Ask God to help you follow the good examples of people who love Him.

All of us have good leaders we can look up to, even if they aren't people we know personally. There are many pastors and teachers and athletes who love God and set a good example for us to follow. Even though no one is perfect, we can learn from the things they do that honor God. We can use those examples to help us honor God too.

Following the examples of good leaders is one way to help us grow as a Christian. The Bible has many stories of good leaders. But the best leader we can follow is Jesus. He lived a perfect life and honored God in everything He did. When you follow Jesus and ask Him to help you honor God, you can be a good example for others.

EXPLORE MORE: Read 1 Timothy 4:12 to find out how kids can set a good example.

DID YOU KNOW?
The name Jehoshaphat means "Jehovah has judged."

I can learn from people who set a good example.

Elijah and the Windstorm

Elijah and Elisha were still walking and talking. Then a chariot and horses of fire appeared. The chariot and horses of fire separated Elijah from Elisha. Then Elijah went up to heaven in a whirlwind.
—2 Kings 2:11 ICB

The time came for Elijah to go to heaven. His student, Elisha, would take over as the prophet of Israel. As they walked together, they came to the Jordan River. Elijah rolled up his coat and hit the water with it. The water split to the right and left, and they crossed the river on dry ground.

"What can I do before I leave you?" asked Elijah.

"Let me be blessed with a double portion of your spirit. I want to be like you," said Elisha.

"You have asked for something hard," said Elijah. "But if you see me when I am taken from you, it will be yours."

TALK TO GOD
Ask God to be with you in the changes you face and thank Him for doing amazing things.

Suddenly, a fiery chariot with fiery horses separated them and a windstorm carried Elijah to heaven. Elisha saw everything and cried, "Master! Master! Israel's chariot and horses!" When Elijah disappeared, Elisha tore his coat. Elijah's coat had fallen off, so he picked it up and went back to the Jordan River. He hit the water with Elijah's coat and said, "Where is the power of the God of Elijah?" Just like that, the water parted to the right and left. This miracle showed that God's Spirit was with Elisha, just like it had been with Elijah.

God can bring people to heaven in a chariot of fire. He can split rivers so people can walk across them. And He can strengthen us when we go through big changes, like Elisha did.

You may be facing a big change, and you may not know how it's going to turn out. When things seem too big, remember that God is bigger. He can do amazing things, and His Spirit is with you.

EXPLORE MORE: Look up Hebrews 13:8. No matter what big changes we face, who will always stay the same?

God is bigger than the changes I face.

DID YOU KNOW?

Chariots of Fire is a 1981 film based on the true story of two British athletes in the 1924 Olympics: Eric Liddell who ran for the glory of God, and Harold Abrahams who ran to overcome prejudice.

Free Refills

Elisha replied to her, "How can I help you? Tell me. What do you have in your house?" "I don't have anything there at all," she said. "All I have is a small jar of olive oil." —2 Kings 4:2 NIrV

Have you ever been to a restaurant with free refills? When you finish your drink, you can get another full cup, and you can get your cup filled as many times as you want without having to pay extra. The Bible tells the story of a woman who received free refills in an unexpected way. The woman was going through a hard time because her husband had died. Before he had died, he owed a man some money. Now the woman had to pay the man, but she didn't have enough money. The man was going to take her sons away and make them work to pay off the money. The woman went to Elisha for help.

TALK TO GOD
Think of two things God has provided for you and tell Him thank you.

"What do you have in your house?" asked Elisha.

The woman replied, "I don't have anything except a small jar of olive oil." The woman knew the olive oil was not worth much, so what Elisha said next must have sounded strange.

He said, "Go to all your neighbors. Ask them for empty jars. Get as many as you can. Then go inside your house and shut the door. Pour oil into all the jars. As each jar is filled, put it to one side."

The woman did what Elisha told her. She kept pouring and pouring until all the jars were full. Somehow that one small jar of oil filled lots of other jars. Elisha said, "Go and sell the oil. Pay what you owe. You and your sons can live on what is left."

God took care of the woman when she needed help. And He will always take care of us.

EXPLORE MORE: Read Psalm 147:9. What creatures does God provide for besides people?

DID YOU KNOW?
Taco Bell was the first restaurant to offer free refills starting in the 1980s.

God provides for us.

Faith to Obey

But Jesus said, "Those who hear the teaching of God and obey it—they are the ones who are truly blessed." —Luke 11:28 ICB

Like the widow who listened to Elisha, there are many stories of people in the Bible who had faith to obey God. They did what God told them to do even though they didn't understand why. Noah had faith when he obeyed God and built the ark. Abraham had faith when he obeyed God by leaving his homeland. Moses had faith when he obeyed God by leading the Israelites out of Egypt.

Sometimes obeying can be hard! We don't always understand why we have to do certain things. We don't always see how listening to God's instructions or our parents' rules will help us. Sometimes we think if we do things our own way, it will be better or easier. But even when we don't understand, we can still obey. We can trust that God is good, and His commands are best for us. We can remember our parents love us, and we can listen to them, even if we don't always agree with their rules.

TALK TO GOD
Ask God to give you faith to obey.

It takes faith for us to obey, just like the people we read about in the Bible. Having faith to obey means we trust God's way even when we don't understand it or it seems impossible—like filling up a bunch of jars with one small jar of oil.

Faith takes time to grow. We grow our faith by asking God to help us love and trust Him more, and by asking the Holy Spirit to fill our hearts with faith. So even when obeying isn't easy, our faith can help us to do what we need to do, and then we will be blessed.

EXPLORE MORE: What story from the Bible shows how the Israelites needed faith to obey God? Read Hebrews 11:30 to find out.

I can obey in faith.

DID YOU KNOW?
Faith is a popular girl's name that goes back to the 1600s. It means "to trust, to believe."

Naaman Needs a Bath

Elisha sent a messenger out to him. The messenger said, "Go! Wash yourself in the Jordan River seven times. Then your skin will be healed. You will be pure and 'clean' again." —2 Kings 5:10 NIrV

Naaman was an important army commander for the king of Aram, but he had a skin disease called leprosy. He wanted to be healed. Naaman's wife had a servant girl who was an Israelite. She knew about Elisha. She told Naaman's wife that a prophet in Samaria could heal Naaman. When Naaman shared this news with the king of Aram, the king said, "You should go!"

Naaman went to Israel and showed the king a letter from the king of Aram. In the letter, the king of Aram asked for Naaman to be healed. The king of Israel was scared. He thought the letter was a trick. The king of Israel said, "Am I God? I cannot heal this man of his skin disease!" When Elisha heard about this, he told the king to send Naaman to him.

Naaman arrived at Elisha's house hoping Elisha would wave his hand over him and call on God to heal him. But that's not what Elisha did. Instead, he told Naaman to wash in the Jordan River seven times. Naaman was mad. "Our rivers are better than the rivers in Israel!" he said as he walked away.

TALK TO GOD
Thank God that He can heal people in many different ways.

Naaman's servants said, "If Elisha had told you to do something hard, wouldn't you have done that? Just listen. Wash in the river seven times and you will be healed."

Naaman listened to his servants and went to the Jordan River. He dipped in the river one time, and nothing happened. He dipped in again and again, but he still had his skin disease. He finally dipped in the river for the seventh time, and when he came up, his leprosy was gone! Once again God showed that He has power over everything, and He can work in ways that amaze us.

EXPLORE MORE: Read 2 Kings 5:5 to find out what Naaman brought with him when he went to see the king of Israel.

DID YOU KNOW?
The Jordan River is the longest and most famous river in Israel.

God has the power to heal.

A Woman Shares Her Home

Share with the Lord's people who are in need. Welcome others into your homes. —Romans 12:13 NIrV

A rich woman who lived in the town of Shunem made meals for Elisha when he traveled through town. The woman told her husband, "I'm sure Elisha is a man of God. Let's make a room for him so he can rest when he comes here."

Elisha was thankful for her kindness. His servant asked the woman if Elisha could do something for her. The woman said, "No. My family takes good care of me."

The woman didn't have a son and her husband was old. Elisha told her, "Next year, you'll be holding a baby boy."

The woman was surprised. "That can't be true," she said. "Please don't lie to me." But the following year, she had a son, just like Elisha had promised.

When the boy was older, he went to look for his father who was working in a field. Suddenly he became sick and cried, "My head hurts!" A servant brought the boy home and he died.

TALK TO GOD
Think of someone you know who shares what they have with others. Thank God for that person.

The woman hurried to find Elisha and begged him to come with her. When they reached home, Elisha went into the boy's room. He lay on top of the boy and placed his face and hands on him. The boy began to get warm. Then he sneezed and opened his eyes. The boy's mother fell to her knees and thanked Elisha for bringing her son back to life.

The woman believed that Elisha was a prophet of God. She shared her home and food with him, and God blessed her for her kindness. God's blessings come in different ways. When we share with others, just knowing it makes them happy is one of those blessings.

EXPLORE MORE: Read another story about the woman from Shunem in 2 Kings 8:1–6.

God blesses people who share.

DID YOU KNOW?
The Bible doesn't tell us the name of the woman in today's story, so she is often referred to as the Shunammite woman.

Practice Hospitality

When we can do good to everyone, let us do it. Let's try even harder to do good to the family of believers. —Galatians 6:10 NIrV

Have you ever heard someone say that it's good to practice hospitality? Practicing hospitality means being friendly or helpful to guests, visitors, or strangers. There are many stories of hospitality in the Bible. People often invited others into their homes and gave them a meal or a place to stay. In the New Testament, Jesus also encourages us to show hospitality, especially to those who are in need.

We can show hospitality to others by inviting them over for dinner, giving them a thoughtful gift, or sharing what we have. Hospitality can be big or small. You can give the clothes you've outgrown to a younger friend who could use them. You could hold the door for a stranger when you walk into a store. You can ask someone how their day is and listen when they answer you. You could invite a friend or relative to stay at your house if they need a place to stay.

TALK TO GOD
Ask God to show you someone you can show hospitality to this week.

When we practice hospitality, we show our love for others and our love for God. People feel loved when we take time to show them that they're important. When we think about their needs, we follow Jesus's command to love others as we love ourselves.

We show our love for God by sharing the things He's given us. We follow Jesus's example by serving others and making them feel important and cared for. When we take the time to get to know people better, they will know they are not alone. God uses us to bless others when we practice hospitality because it shows we love them the way He does.

EXPLORE MORE: Turn to John 13:4-5 to read about a time that Jesus showed hospitality to His disciples.

DID YOU KNOW?
The purpose of a hotel is to offer hospitality to people who are traveling. One of the first modern hotels was the Royal Clarence Hotel, which opened in 1769 in Exeter, Devon, in England.

It's good to practice hospitality.

Soup and Bread

Then Elisha's servant put the food in front of the group of prophets. The group of prophets had enough to eat, and they even had food left over. This happened just as the Lord had said.
—2 Kings 4:44 ERV

Elisha went to small city called Gilgal. He met with a group of prophets there. They were very hungry because there was a famine in the land. Elisha told his servant, "Put the large pot on the fire, and make some soup." One of the men went into a field and collected herbs and wild fruit to put in the pot. The prophets didn't recognize the fruit he found. When they ate the soup, it tasted like poison. "This will kill us!" they cried. But Elisha said, "Bring some flour." He threw the flour into the pot, and it became safe to eat.

TALK TO GOD
Pray for God to provide food for people who are hungry.

After this, a man from another town brought twenty loaves of bread to Elisha. "Give this food to the people so they can eat," Elisha told his servant.

The servant replied, "There are one hundred men here. How can I feed all of them?"

Elisha answered, "The Lord says, 'They will eat and there will still be food left over.'" So Elisha's servant gave the food to the prophets. They had enough to eat and there was bread left over, just as God had said.

God is the one who provides food for all of us. When you're hungry, maybe you go to the pantry to find a snack or look for something delicious in the refrigerator. Maybe your parents go to the grocery store when you start running out of food. Some families have more than enough food, but others don't always have enough to eat. Before you eat your food, thank God for the food you have, and pray for the people who are hungry. Ask God to provide for them in amazing ways.

EXPLORE MORE: Look up Matthew 14:13–21 in your Bible. How did Jesus feed some hungry people?

DID YOU KNOW?
Sinigang has been rated as one of the best vegetable soups in the world. Sinigang is a soup made in the Philippines and flavored with fruit.

I will thank God for my food.

God Provides

And my God will meet all your needs according to the riches of his glory in Christ Jesus. —Philippians 4:19 NIV

The Bible has many stories about God providing for His people in surprising and incredible ways. He sent manna from heaven to the Israelites after they left Egypt. He gave Ruth and Naomi a family when they lost their husbands. He gave poor widows exactly what they needed in hard times, and He gave food to His people during famines. There are almost too many stories to count!

The God who loved and provided for His people is the same God who loves and provides for us today. Sometimes God provides so much for us that we forget He is the one who gives us everything. When we go to the grocery store to buy food—God is the one who provides it for us. When we get dressed to go to school—God is the one who gives us clothes to wear. When we laugh with our family and enjoy special times together—God is the one who gives us those moments.

TALK TO GOD
Do you know someone who has a need? Ask God what you can do to help that person.

Sometimes we need things that are so big, it seems like no one could ever help us. When that happens and we're not sure what to do, we can pray and ask God to provide for us. Sometimes God gives us what we need at just the right time. Sometimes He provides for us by giving us strength and patience to get through our struggle. No matter how He answers our prayers, we can trust that He loves us and promises to take care of us.

Whether we have a lot or a little, we can always find something good that God has given us. And sometimes God will use us to help meet someone else's needs. What is something good God has given you today?

DID YOU KNOW?
Nicholas Lowinger started Gotta Have Sole when he was 12 years old. His organization gives shoes to homeless children so they can go to school.

EXPLORE MORE: Read Matthew 6:25–26 to find out what Jesus said about how God takes care of the birds.

God gives me what I need.

The Invisible Army

Elisha prayed, "Lord, open my servant's eyes so that he can see." Then the Lord opened his eyes. Elisha's servant looked up and saw the hills. He saw that Elisha was surrounded by horses and chariots made of fire. —2 Kings 6:17 NIrV

The Israelites' enemies, the Arameans, kept trying to attack them. Every time they planned to sneak up on the Israelites' camp, God would tell Elisha. Then Elisha would warn the king, and the Israelites would escape.

The king of Aram asked his soldiers, "Which one of you is telling Israel's king my plans?"

An officer said, "Elisha tells the king everything you say." So the king of Aram sent horses, chariots, and soldiers to Dothan to capture Elisha. They surrounded the city at night.

In the morning, Elisha's servant saw the army and said, "Master, what should we do?"

TALK TO GOD
Thank God for helping you and protecting you.

Elisha answered, "Don't be afraid. We have more forces on our side than they have on theirs." Elisha prayed for his servant's eyes to be opened. When his servant looked up, he saw the mountain filled with God's fiery horses and chariots.

As the Arameans came to capture Elisha, he prayed, "Lord, please make them blind." God did what Elisha asked. Then Elisha tricked the soldiers and said they were in the wrong place. He led them to Israel's king in Samaria. Elisha prayed again, "Lord, please let them see." The Lord opened their eyes, and they realized they were in Samaria!

"What should I do with these soldiers?" asked the king.

"Give them food and water, then send them home," said Elisha. After the army had a great feast, they went home and didn't attack the Israelites again.

Elisha prayed and listened to God. His obedience kept the people safe. God was on Elisha's side and used His power to help Elisha. When we belong to God's family, He is on our side too. When we obey God, He will use His invisible power to help us and protect us.

EXPLORE MORE: Turn to Romans 8:31. What does this verse say about God helping us?

God protects His people.

DID YOU KNOW?
Dothan is a city in central Israel and means "two wells." Both wells are still there today.

Joash Repairs the Temple

"Each priest must take the money from the people he serves.
Then the priests must repair any damage they find in the Temple."
—2 Kings 12:5 ICB

Before becoming king of Judah, Joash was hidden as a baby and raised by the priest Jehoiada. An evil queen had tried to take over as ruler, and she damaged the temple and treated it disrespectfully. She used the holy things from the temple to worship a false god.

When Joash became king, he did what was right and listened to the things Jehoiada taught him. One of the most important things he did was repair the temple. Joash told the priests, "Take all the money brought to the temple as offerings. Then use this money to repair any damage you find in the temple." But as time went on, the priests still hadn't repaired the temple.

Joash called the priests together and asked, "Why are you not repairing the damage to the temple? Hand over the money for the repairs." So, the priests agreed not to do the repairs themselves but to hire workers. Then Jehoiada made a box with a hole in the top and put it by the altar for offerings. The priests put all the money given into the box, and when it was full, they gave it to the men in charge of the work on the temple. They paid the carpenters, builders, stoneworkers, and stonecutters. The money paid for everything needed to repair the temple.

Joash knew the temple should be respected and treated with care because it was God's house. He honored God by taking care of the place where people worshiped Him. The churches where we worship God today are sometimes called God's house. We can honor God by treating our churches as special places that bring God glory.

TALK TO GOD
Thank God for the places you can go to worship Him.

EXPLORE MORE: Read Mark 11:15–17. What did Jesus do to keep God's house holy?

DID YOU KNOW?

The temple Joash repaired was built by Solomon. It had been built more than one hundred years before Joash repaired it.

God's house is a special place where we can go to worship God with others.

Israel Rejects God

So the Lord was very angry with Israel. He removed them from his
land. Only the tribe of Judah was left. —2 Kings 17:18 NIrV

After King Hoshea ruled in Israel for nine years, the king of Assyria defeated the Israelites and took them away to Assyria. This was a very sad time for the Israelites, and it happened because they turned away from God's commands.

God had done so many things for Israel. He took them out of Egypt and freed them from Pharaoh's power. He pushed out other countries so there was room for Israel to live in the promised land. But the Israelites chose to be like the evil countries God had removed from their land. They worshiped other gods and followed kings who didn't love and obey Him.

> **TALK TO GOD**
> Ask God to help you love Him and follow Him.

Because God is kind and patient, He gave the Israelites many chances to come back to Him. He sent prophets to tell them to stop doing what was wrong and to follow God. God told them, "Turn from your evil ways and keep my commands and rules. Obey every part of my law." But the people would not listen. They had stubborn hearts and didn't trust God. They broke the promise He made with them. They did not do what God told them to do. Since the people refused to obey, God removed them from His land and handed them over to their enemies.

When people reject God, it costs them a lot. People who don't love God don't receive all the blessings He gives to people who love Him. And worst of all, when people reject God, they're separated from Him. But God is patient and forgiving. He will accept anyone who comes back to Him and let them be a part of His family.

EXPLORE MORE: How long does God show love to those who love and obey Him? Turn to Exodus 20:6 to find out.

God wants us to follow Him.

> **DID YOU KNOW?**
> Hoshea was the last king of Israel. The people were captured and forced to live in other lands after his rule.

King Hezekiah Trusts in God

"Now, Lord our God, save us from the king's power. Then all the kingdoms of the earth will know that you, Lord, are the only God."
—2 Kings 19:19 ICB

Unlike the kings of Israel, Hezekiah, the king of Judah, followed God and obeyed Him. He took down all the altars where the people worshiped false gods, and he broke down their idols. Hezekiah trusted God and was loyal to Him. The Bible says that there were no kings like him in Judah who did what was right the way he did.

Several years after the Assyrians captured the kingdom of Israel, they attacked Judah and broke down the city walls. The king of Assyria sent out his top commanders to scare King Hezekiah and the people of Judah. They tried to trick the people and said that God had told them to capture Judah. The commanders told the people, "Don't listen to Hezekiah. He is fooling you when he says, 'The Lord will save us.' No other god has saved his people from the power of the king of Assyria." The people didn't say a word because Hezekiah had commanded them not to answer the Assyrians.

TALK TO GOD
Ask God to help you trust Him, even when you feel afraid.

When Hezekiah heard the Assyrians' message, he went to the temple and prayed. He asked God to listen to the unkind things the king of Assyria had spoken against Him. Hezekiah asked God to save Judah from the Assyrians' power and show that He was the only true God. The Lord answered Hezekiah's prayer and defeated the Assyrians for Judah.

God was with Hezekiah because Hezekiah loved and served Him. Hezekiah trusted in God's power and knew God could do what no one else could. When we love God the way Hezekiah did, we will see God's power in our lives too.

EXPLORE MORE: Turn to 2 Kings 19:15–19 to read Hezekiah's prayer to God.

DID YOU KNOW?
While Hezekiah was the king of Judah, he built tunnels to bring fresh water into Jerusalem. The people had better lives and better education during his reign.

I can put my trust in God.

Come Back to God

Come back to the Lord your God. He is kind and shows mercy.
He doesn't become angry quickly. He has great love. He
would rather forgive than punish. —Joel 2:13 ICB

King Hezekiah chose to follow God and serve Him when many of the kings before him didn't love God. Hezekiah helped the people of Judah return to God. The king and the whole nation received the blessings of loving and obeying God. Just like there is a cost to rejecting God, there is blessing in returning to God.

> **TALK TO GOD**
> Thank God for being so loving and forgiving.

The Bible tells us that God wants us to come back to Him if we have wandered away. There will be times when we struggle to obey God. There may be times when we don't put Him first in our lives. There may be times when we love the things in the world more than God.

When people have a hard time following God, He is patient. He is kind and wants us to tell Him we're sorry so we can be close to Him again. When we do, He makes everything right. He wipes away all our mistakes and makes us new in Him.

When we return to God, we experience the blessing of having a close relationship with Him. For Hezekiah, that meant he was protected from the Assyrians, and the people of Judah were saved. For us, a close relationship with God may give us peace in our hearts. A close relationship with God can also help us live God's best plans for our lives.

No matter what we have done, God will always let us come back to Him. He has great love for all people and cares about us more than we can understand. He is a good God, and He wants to bless us.

EXPLORE MORE: What message does God give in 2 Chronicles 7:14?

God forgives people when they come back to Him.

DID YOU KNOW?
People who receive forgiveness are happier and healthier. They feel closer to their friends, family, and God.

God Answers Hezekiah's Prayer

"Go back and speak to Hezekiah. . . . Tell him, 'The Lord, the God of King David, says, "I have heard your prayer. I have seen your tears. And I will heal you."'" —2 Kings 20:5 NIrV

King Hezekiah had a bad sore that made him very sick. The prophet Isaiah came to him with a message. Isaiah told Hezekiah, "The Lord says, 'Put everything in order. You are not going to get better.'" When Hezekiah heard Isaiah's words, he turned toward the wall and prayed. "Lord, please remember how faithful I've been to you. I've lived the way you wanted me to and served you with all my heart. I've done what is good in your sight." After Hezekiah said these words, he cried.

Isaiah was leaving the king's courtyard when God gave him another message: "Go back to Hezekiah. Tell him, 'I have heard your prayer. I have seen your tears, and I will heal you.'" Then Isaiah told the king's helpers to make an ointment from figs and spread it on Hezekiah's sore.

Hezekiah asked Isaiah for a sign to prove that God would answer his prayer. Isaiah told Hezekiah, "The Lord will do what He has promised. Here is a sign for you. Do you want the shadow on the sundial to go forward ten steps or back ten steps?"

Hezekiah said, "It's easy for the shadow to go forward ten steps, so have it go back ten steps." Isaiah prayed to God, and God made the shadow go back ten steps. Hezekiah got better and lived fifteen more years. God saved him and his city from Assyria to keep His promise to David.

TALK TO GOD
Tell God how wonderful it is that He answers your prayers.

God heard Hezekiah when he prayed and answered his prayers. We can be sure that God hears us too. He always listens to those who come to Him, and He can answer our prayers in amazing ways.

EXPLORE MORE: Read James 5:17–18 to learn about a time when God answered Elijah's prayers.

DID YOU KNOW?
Sundials measure time by the position of the sun and the shadow the sun creates. In Bible times, people used sundials to mark the passage of hours and minutes.

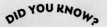

God answers prayer.

A Boy Becomes a King

Josiah did what the Lord said was right. He did good things as his ancestor David had done. Josiah did not stop doing what was right.
—2 Kings 22:2 ICB

Do you like being a leader? Sometimes it's fun to be in charge and tell others what to do. You might have the chance to be a leader in your classroom for a day or be a leader on a team. But you've probably never been the leader of a country since you haven't grown up yet.

TALK TO GOD
Pray that the leaders of your country would follow God.

Did you know that Josiah was only eight years old when he became the king of Judah? He probably had some helpers, but Josiah was the king over the land. Even though Josiah was young, he trusted and followed God and did what was right.

When Josiah was twenty-six years old, he raised money to pay workers to repair the temple. While the people were working in the temple, the high priest, Hilkiah, found the book of the law that Moses had written. Hilkiah gave it to a man named Shaphan who read it to King Josiah. As the king listened, he tore his clothes because he was very upset. He realized that the people had turned away from God and were not following Him.

King Josiah called the people of Judah together and read the book of the law out loud. He made an agreement to follow the Lord, and all the people promised to do the same. Josiah got rid of anything in the temple that did not honor God. He also went through the towns, tearing down altars to other gods and smashing them to pieces. Josiah wanted the people of Judah to be faithful to God. For the rest of his life, Josiah followed God and did what was right.

EXPLORE MORE: Read 2 Kings 23:12 to find out what Josiah did with the smashed altars.

Good leaders help people follow God.

DID YOU KNOW?
Jetsun Pema became queen at age twenty-one in 2011 when she married King Jigme Khesar Namgyel Wangchuck of Bhutan, a small country between India and Tibet. She is the youngest living queen.

Kid Power

Yes, God is working in you to help you want to do what pleases him. Then he gives you the power to do it. —Philippians 2:13 ICB

You probably won't become a kid king like Josiah, but even while you're young, you can make a difference by the things you do and the words you say. That may sound like a hard thing to do, but the good news is you can ask God to help you do what pleases Him. The Bible says God will give us His power, and God has a lot of that!

Have you ever tried racing a remote-control car with dead batteries? It doesn't go anywhere, does it? Have you ever tried to turn on a lamp that wasn't plugged into an outlet? The lamp can't give light if it isn't plugged in. And if you try to mix cupcake batter with an electric mixer, the mixer won't work if you don't turn it on.

TALK TO GOD
Ask God to fill you with the Holy Spirit so you will have His power.

Just like many of the things we use need to be plugged into a power source to work, we need to be plugged into our power source—the Holy Spirit. God gives us His Holy Spirit when we believe in Jesus as our Savior. The Holy Spirit lives in our hearts to guide us and help us live in a way that honors God.

With the power of the Holy Spirit, you can help someone who is being teased on the playground. You can pray with a friend who's having a hard day. And if your parents ask you to feed the dog or take out the trash, you can do it with a smile on your face. When you have the Holy Spirit, you will always have plenty of power!

EXPLORE MORE: Read Acts 1:8 to find out what Jesus told His disciples before He went back to heaven.

DID YOU KNOW?
An Italian physicist named Alessandro Volta invented the first true battery in 1800.

The Holy Spirit gives me power.

The People of Judah Go to Babylon

At that time the officers of Nebuchadnezzar king of Babylon came
up to Jerusalem. They surrounded the city and attacked it.
—2 Kings 24:10 ICB

The kings who ruled after Josiah did not follow God. They were bad leaders who did not encourage the Israelites to love and serve God. When King Jehoiakim was ruling over Judah, the army from Babylon came and surrounded the land. They captured many of the people and brought them to live in Babylon. The Babylonian army destroyed the city walls and the temple of God in Jerusalem. They took some of the treasures from the temple and brought them to Babylon. It was a very sad day for the Israelites who lived in Judah.

TALK TO GOD
Thank God that when we follow Him, we receive His blessings.

When Joshua led the Israelites into the promised land, he warned them to keep following God or He would no longer protect them from other nations. Many of God's prophets had also warned them, but they did not listen. God loved His people and was always willing to forgive them. But they did not come back to Him and continued to worship other gods, so God gave them over to their enemies.

While the people of Judah lived as prisoners in Babylon, God did not forget about them. Some of the Israelites stayed faithful to God and worshiped Him instead of the false gods of Babylon. God blessed them and protected them.

When we don't follow God, it can lead to a life of pain and sadness. When we love and obey God, we stay close to Him and receive His best for us. That doesn't mean we won't have any problems, but God's love and protection are bigger than our problems. God will always help us when we keep following Him.

EXPLORE MORE: What does Jesus tell us in Luke 11:28?

I can follow and obey God.

DID YOU KNOW?
The Babylonians were smart mathematicians. They are credited with creating the system of using sixty seconds for a minute and sixty minutes for an hour.

All Those Names!

"Your name will be Abraham, because I have made you a father of many nations. I will greatly increase the number of your children after you. Nations and kings will come from you." —Genesis 17:5–6 NIrV

It's exciting to read Bible stories about God's amazing miracles—like when He parted the Red Sea or broke down the walls of Jericho with the shouts of His people. It's also fun to read stories of how God provides for His people in unusual ways—like sending manna from heaven or having birds bring food to Elijah. But when we get to chapters 1–9 of 1 Chronicles, many readers could be tempted to skip those chapters. Who wants to read pages and pages of names that are hard to pronounce?

You might wonder why all these names are in the Bible, but there is a reason they are included. Way back in the book of Genesis, God promised Abraham that he would be the father of many nations, and kings would be among his descendants. This long list of names shows that God kept His promise to Abraham. It also shows that Abraham's descendants came from other nations, and not just the nation of Israel. This list of names ties the Old and New Testaments together, and when we read other lists of names in the Bible, they show us how Jesus came through Abraham's family line.

TALK TO GOD
Pray that people all over the world will come to know Jesus as their Savior.

The lists of names that lead to Jesus include people from different countries and nations. God's plan of salvation is for everyone who believes in Jesus as their Savior. It doesn't matter what country your great-great-great grandparents came from. What matters is that you love God with all your heart and believe that Jesus came to forgive your sins.

It's hard to count how many kings descended from Abraham, but the greatest King is Jesus!

EXPLORE MORE: According to Psalm 67:1–3, who should praise God for His power to save us?

DID YOU KNOW?
The list of names found in 1 Chronicles 1–9 includes 130 names that begin with the letter A, 110 names that begin with the letter J, and 105 names that begin with the letter S.

There are many nations in God's family.

Going Back Home

"If any of God's people are living among you, I pray God will bless them. You must let them go to Jerusalem in the country of Judah. You must let them go build the Temple of the Lord, the God of Israel, the God who is in Jerusalem." —Ezra 1:3 ERV

The people of Judah lived in Babylon as prisoners for seventy years. As you keep reading through more passages of the Bible, you will learn about some of the things that happened while they were living there. After Nebuchadnezzar died, a few more kings ruled over Babylon until it was captured by the Medes and the Persians. King Cyrus of Persia became the new ruler and made an important announcement. He said that God had given him all the kingdoms of the earth and had chosen him to rebuild the temple at Jerusalem in the land of Judah.

TALK TO GOD
Pray for Christians who may be in danger because of their faith, and thank God if you can worship Him freely.

The people must have been overjoyed to hear this announcement! The leaders of the tribes of Judah and Benjamin got ready to go to Jerusalem with their families right away. Many of their neighbors gave them gifts of gold, silver, and animals. King Cyrus also gave them the treasures that King Nebuchadnezzar had taken from the temple.

It took almost seven months for the people to get settled in their hometowns. Then everyone met in Jerusalem to rebuild the altar of God in the place where it had been before it was destroyed. The people were so happy to be back home! After not being able to worship God the way they were supposed to, they were eager to offer sacrifices and celebrate their festivals again.

Sometimes people don't appreciate the freedom they have to worship God until it's taken away. If you can go to church and pray whenever you want to, be thankful for that freedom. Sing and pray out loud, and let others know who you worship!

EXPLORE MORE: Read Ezra 1:9–11 to see the list of items that King Cyrus gave to the people returning to Judah.

I will be thankful for my freedom to worship.

DID YOU KNOW?
When the people of Judah returned home, they celebrated the Festival of Shelters, also known as the Festival of Tabernacles. For seven days, they lived in tents to remind them how their ancestors lived in the wilderness after leaving Egypt.

Where Is Your Home?

But our homeland is in heaven, and we are waiting for our Savior, the Lord Jesus Christ, to come from heaven. —Philippians 3:20 ICB

The world is a very big place where billions of people live. With seven continents and 195 different countries, there are many places people call home. Some families spend most of their lives living in one area of the world. They may grow up with sisters and brothers, grandpas and grandmas, and dozens of cousins who live close by. Other families move around because of jobs or because they want to live in warmer or cooler areas.

Families who serve in the military move to different places where their service is needed. Missionaries move to other countries to tell people about Jesus. Some families like to live in the mountains, and others want to live near an ocean. But no matter where families live, they all want to have a place they call home.

TALK TO GOD
Thank God that someday we can live in heaven with Him.

The Bible tells us that our homes on earth will not last forever. If we believe in Jesus, then we have a forever home in heaven where we'll live someday. We don't know everything there is to know about heaven, but we do know it's more wonderful and beautiful than we can imagine. Not only that, it's always light in heaven because God is there. In heaven, no one gets sick or hurt. No one is sad or afraid. Heaven is only filled with good things.

The Bible tells us about some amazing people like Abraham, Moses, and King David who lived long ago. Someday, when we get to heaven, we will meet them and many other great people! We will dance on streets of gold and sing songs of praise with the angels. Heaven is the best home in the universe!

EXPLORE MORE: What did Jesus say about heaven in John 14:2–4?

DID YOU KNOW?

Antarctica is the coldest continent in the world. Scientists work at research stations in Antarctica for short periods of time, but no one else lives there because it's covered with ice.

Heaven is my forever home.

Working with Joy

With praise and thanksgiving, they sang to the Lord: "He is good; his love for Israel continues forever." And then all the people shouted loudly, "Praise the Lord! The foundation of his Temple has been laid." —Ezra 3:11 ICB

When the people returned to Judah from Babylon, they were excited to rebuild the temple that had been destroyed. They hired stonecutters and carpenters to begin working on the foundation. King Cyrus gave them permission to ask for help from the cities of Tyre and Sidon. These cities were on the Mediterranean Sea, and the people could float cedar logs to the town of Joppa, which was near Jerusalem. The people from Judah gave food, wine, and oil to the people in Tyre and Sidon to pay for the logs.

Everyone who had returned from Babylon began to help. The Levites who were twenty years old or older were put in charge of rebuilding the temple. When the foundation of the temple was finished, the people had a huge celebration. The priests put on special robes and got their trumpets ready to play. The Levites had their cymbals. Then all the people came together and praised the Lord like King David had done when the first temple was built. They praised God, shouting, "Praise the Lord! The foundation of the Lord's Temple has been laid. He is good and His love for Israel continues forever."

The younger people shouted with joy, but some of the older priests and family leaders cried. They had seen the first temple and were sad that it had been destroyed. The singing and cheering and crying were so loud that it could be heard far away.

The temple reminded the people that God had not forgotten about them. They had turned away from Him many times, but He never turned away from them. He delivered them from the Babylonians and gave them another chance to follow Him.

EXPLORE MORE: Read part of King David's prayer when the people gave their resources to build the first temple in 1 Chronicles 29:10–13.

TALK TO GOD
Praise God for His greatness, power, glory, and victory.

DID YOU KNOW?
Today, Tyre and Sidon are both located in Lebanon. They are 20 miles (32 kilometers) apart, and the cities are smaller than they were in Bible times.

God lets His people come back to Him.

God's Faithful Love

Lord, who is a God like you? You forgive sin. You forgive your people when they do what is wrong. You don't stay angry forever. Instead, you take delight in showing your faithful love to them. —Micah 7:18 NIrV

The more we read about how the Israelites turned away from God, the more we can see that God is full of love and forgiveness. When God's people turned away from Him, they had to experience some sadness and hardships because of their bad choices. But God was always waiting to forgive them when they came back to Him. God is a God of mercy, which means He not only forgives our sins, but He also forgets about them.

When people do not follow God's ways, their lives can become a big mess. But when people turn to God and choose to love and follow Him, He can clean up their big messes and bless them with a better life.

Like the Israelites, some people turn away from God more than once. It must break God's heart when people who love Him stop following Him. But God is patient and waits for His people to come back to Him. When they do, He forgives them because His love continues forever.

Just like God is always faithful to us, we can be faithful to Him. Our love is not perfect like God's love is, but we can show our love for God by praising Him and thanking Him for His many blessings. We can show our love for God by being kind to people in our family, school, and neighborhood. We can also show kindness to people we don't even know. We can ask God to help us keep following Him and doing the things that bring Him joy. Aren't you glad God's love lasts forever? How can you show your love for Him today?

TALK TO GOD
Say thank you to God for His faithful love, and then tell Him why you love Him.

EXPLORE MORE: What does God do with our sins? Read Micah 7:19 to find out.

DID YOU KNOW?
World Kindness Day was started in 1998 to encourage people to be kind to each other. In countries like Australia, Canada, Japan, and the United States, it is celebrated on November 13.

God's love and forgiveness never end.

Dedication and Celebration

Then the people of Israel celebrated. They gave the Temple to God to honor him. Everybody was happy: the priests, the Levites and the rest of the Jews who had returned from captivity. —Ezra 6:16 ICB

Have you ever worked on a puzzle for a really long time and then finally finished it? It's a great feeling of accomplishment, and it makes you feel like celebrating!

The people of Judah continued to build the temple of God, and they worked hard until it was completed. The kings from Persia helped them by supplying many of the materials. When the temple was finally finished, they were ready for a grand celebration!

TALK TO GOD
Thank God for something He has done for you.

The people had a dedication ceremony for the temple of God. They sacrificed rams, lambs, and goats. Following the dedication, the people celebrated the Passover and the Feast of Unleavened Bread to remind them how God had brought their ancestors out of Egypt.

The Israelites were filled with great joy because God had softened the hearts of foreign kings who allowed them to return to their homeland. They were filled with great joy because God had forgiven them for turning away from Him. They were happy to worship the one and only true God who loved and cared about them.

We don't need to experience bad things in our lives like the Israelites did in order to realize the great things God can do. We can be filled with joy every day because God cares about every detail of our lives. He cares when you celebrate your birthday. He cares when you get a good grade on a spelling test. And He even cares when you complete a big project that you've been working on for a long time. When you have something to celebrate, remember to praise God and thank Him for caring so much about you.

EXPLORE MORE: Read Psalm 126:3. Why should we be filled with joy?

I will celebrate God's love and care.

DID YOU KNOW?
During the Feast of Unleavened Bread, the Israelites ate bread without leaven, which is an ingredient that makes bread rise. They made this bread when they left Egypt because they didn't have time to wait for the bread to rise.

Nehemiah Prayed

"Send me to the city in Judah where my ancestors are buried. I will rebuild it. Do this if you are willing and if I have pleased you."
—Nehemiah 2:5 ICB

Nehemiah was an Israelite who was a servant to King Artaxerxes of Babylon. He continued to live in Babylon even though many Israelites had returned to Judah. Nehemiah's brother came to see him and gave him some sad news. "Things are not going well for the people. The wall of Jerusalem has been torn down and the gates have been burned."

Even though the temple had been rebuilt, without walls and gates around the city, the people could not protect the temple from their enemies. Nehemiah cried when he heard the news. He prayed for four days and didn't eat anything. In Nehemiah 1:9, Nehemiah prayed to God and asked Him to remember the promise He had made to Moses. "If you return to me and obey my commands, I will gather your people from the far ends of the earth. I will bring them back to the place I have chosen for my name to be honored." Before Nehemiah finished his prayer, he asked God to give him success in asking the king for a big favor.

TALK TO GOD
Think of something that's hard for you and ask God to help you.

King Artaxerxes noticed that Nehemiah was sad and asked him what was wrong. Nehemiah explained that the wall in Jerusalem needed to be rebuilt. He asked the king to let him go and help the people. The king agreed.

It was a scary thing for Nehemiah to ask the king for this big favor, but he prayed for God to help him, and God answered his prayer. Whenever you face something hard, it's important to ask God to show you what to do and what to say. When something seems hard for you, remember that nothing is too hard for God.

EXPLORE MORE: Read Nehemiah 6:15–16 to find out how long it took to build the wall and how the other nations responded.

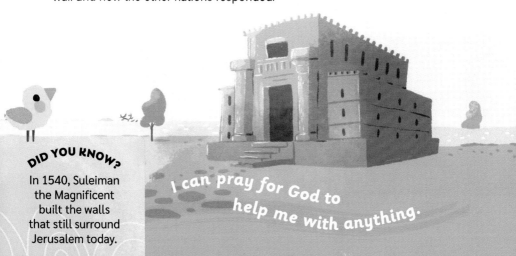

DID YOU KNOW?
In 1540, Suleiman the Magnificent built the walls that still surround Jerusalem today.

I can pray for God to help me with anything.

Pray First

**My God, I call out to you because you will answer me.
Listen to me. Hear my prayer. —Psalm 17:6 NIrV**

Nehemiah was a faithful servant of God. He loved God, and he loved God's people. Like David's words in today's Bible verse, Nehemiah also prayed for help, wisdom, and guidance. God answered Nehemiah's prayers.

TALK TO GOD
Thank God that He loves to hear your prayers.

Nehemiah's story reminds us that we can talk to God about anything. God loves it when we pray and talk to Him, and He will always listen to us. Whenever you need to make a decision, or whenever you need courage to tackle something hard, do what Nehemiah did and pray first.

There are many things you can pray about, and you can pray anytime of the day or night. Do you get nervous before taking a test? Pray first and ask God to help you remember the things you studied and learned. Do you have to play in a piano recital? Pray first and ask God to help you play your song. Are you going to be in a program at church or school? Pray first and ask God to help you speak clearly so everyone can hear you.

You don't have to wait until you are nervous or scared to pray. You can thank God for your breakfast and ask Him to help you have a good day. You can pray for God to help your parents with the work they need to do. You can pray for God to keep you safe on the playground. And you can ask God to help you be kind to your brother or sister. No matter what you need to do, whether it's something fun or a little scary, be like Nehemiah and pray first!

EXPLORE MORE: Read Romans 8:26–27. Who is praying for us as we pray?

DID YOU KNOW?

Praying out loud when you are alone will make it easier for you to pray out loud in front of other people.

I will pray first.

Joyful People

Ezra the priest brought the Law out to the whole community. It was the first day of the seventh month. The group was made up of men, women, and children old enough to understand what Ezra was going to read. —Nehemiah 8:2 NIrV

When the people who had returned from Babylon finally settled in their towns, they all met together at a place called the Water Gate. This was a place where fresh water flowed into the city, providing clean water for the people to drink and use to take baths.

A priest named Ezra stood on a wooden platform and opened a scroll which had the words to the book of the law. When the people saw Ezra open the scroll, they stood up to show honor to God's Word. Ezra praised the Lord, saying, "He is the great God!" and all the people said, "Amen!" They lifted their hands toward heaven, then bowed down to worship the Lord.

TALK TO GOD
Ask God to make you clean on the inside and thank Him for the joy He gives.

The people listened and cried as Ezra read from the book of the law. The Levites also took turns reading the Law and explaining it to the people. Ezra and Nehemiah said, "Don't be sad because this is a special day to celebrate. Have a feast and share your food. The joy of the Lord is our strength!"

A few weeks later, the people gathered as Ezra read the Law again. They listened for many hours and confessed their sins to God. Then they were filled with great joy and praised the name of the Lord.

The people were happy because confessing their sins was like washing their hearts and making them clean. Just like they needed the fresh water at the Water Gate to be washed clean on the outside, they needed God's Word and His forgiveness to be washed clean on the inside. Being clean inside and out makes us joyful.

EXPLORE MORE: Read some of the praises that the people said to God in Nehemiah 9:5–6.

DID YOU KNOW?
Today, the old city walls in Jerusalem that were built in the 1500s have eight different gates. Seven of the gates still allow people to enter the city and visit the markets and historical sites.

God's forgiveness gives me joy.

A Queen Saves Her People

"Who knows? It's possible that you became queen for
a time just like this." —Esther 4:14 NIrV

Xerxes was the king of Persia, and he needed a new queen. The king's helpers searched for beautiful young women and sent them to the palace. Of all the young women, Esther was the one King Xerxes chose to be his queen.

Esther was an orphan who was raised by her cousin Mordecai. He was one of the Israelites who was taken to Babylon when King Nebuchadnezzar captured the people from Judah. They were also called Jews. A man named Haman didn't like the Jews and made an evil plan to get rid of them. That was a big mistake! Queen Esther was a Jew, but neither Haman nor the king knew this.

Mordecai learned about Haman's plan and told Esther to tell the king. During those days, people could only visit the king if he invited them, even the queen. Esther was afraid because if the king didn't want to see her, she could be killed. Mordecai believed that God had put Esther in this position so she could save His people. He told Esther, "Who knows? Maybe you were chosen to be queen for such a time as this!"

TALK TO GOD
Thank God that His plans are always bigger and better than plans for evil.

Esther went to see the king, and he allowed her to speak with him. She invited the king and Haman to a party. During dinner, Esther told the king about Haman's plan to destroy the Jewish people. Then she told the king that she was a Jew. The king was angry with Haman and made a new law to protect the Jewish people. Then he chose Mordecai to be an important leader.

God's plans are always greater than anyone's plans for evil. He loves and protects His people.

EXPLORE MORE: What does Esther 10:3 tell us about Mordecai?

God uses His people for good.

DID YOU KNOW?
Esther was the queen's Persian name. Her Hebrew name was Hadassah.

Here for a Reason

All the days planned for me were written in your book before I was one day old. —Psalm 139:16 ICB

As we read stories in the Bible, we can see how God uses people for special assignments. He used Joseph to help Pharaoh prepare for a seven-year famine. He used Moses to rescue the Israelites from slavery in Egypt. He used Joshua to lead the Israelites into the promised land. And He used Esther to save the Jewish people from an evil plan.

These stories show how God uses ordinary people to do big things for Him. God doesn't use whoever happens to be there. God plans the events of our lives even before we are born. And just like God had plans for people in the Bible, He has plans for you.

Did you know that God knew exactly when you would be born? He planned the day, the hour, the minute, and the second! You are here now because God created you for a reason. You might not become a king or queen, and you might not lead a nation across a river or sea, but God created you for today—right now! If you keep loving and following God, you will discover how God can use you in your family, church, school, or community.

TALK TO GOD
Thank God for creating you and ask Him to help you know His plans for you.

Maybe someday God will lead you to go somewhere to serve Him in a special way. Maybe the job you have will give you opportunities to do something only you can do. Whether these opportunities seem big or small, they are important because God chose you to do them. The next time you celebrate your birthday, remember that the day you were born was chosen by God and you are here for a reason.

EXPLORE MORE: What do you learn from reading Ephesians 2:10?

DID YOU KNOW?
More people are born in August and September than in the other months of the year.

God planned the days of my life.

Job Trusts God

In all this Job did not sin. He did not blame God. —Job 1:22 ICB

A man named Job loved God with all his heart. He lived in the land of Uz and was very rich. He owned thousands of sheep, camels, oxen, and donkeys. He and his wife had ten children who enjoyed having fancy celebrations. We can read his story in the book of Job in the Old Testament.

Job enjoyed a good life, but he eventually lost everything except his wife and three friends. He even had sores all over his body. In his pain and sadness, he tore his clothes and shaved his head to show how sad he was. Then he bowed down to worship God, saying, "The Lord has given, and the Lord has taken away. Praise the name of the Lord."

Job's friends came to see him. They cried with him and stayed with him in order to comfort him. Those are good things for friends to do. But when they tried to give him advice, their words were not helpful because they were not true. Job's friends said that God was punishing him for something he did wrong. They said, "Tell God your sin and ask God to forgive you." But Job knew better. Even though he didn't understand why these bad things were happening, he never turned away from God or blamed Him for his problems. Through all his pain and misery, Job still loved and trusted God.

TALK TO GOD
Ask God to help you keep trusting Him even when life is hard.

Job's story has a happy ending. God blessed Job by giving him twice as much as he had before. Job's story shows us that even in bad times, we can trust God and believe that He loves us.

EXPLORE MORE: Why is James 1:12 a good verse for people who are going through hard things?

I will trust God no matter what happens.

DID YOU KNOW?
"The patience of Job" is a common phrase that is still said today. It comes from today's story and means that someone is being patient even though they are having problems.

True Words

All your words are true. All your laws are right. They last forever.
—Psalm 119:160 NIrV

Many people believe in God, but not everything they say about God is true. Job's friends said that God was punishing him for doing something wrong, but that was not why Job was having problems. We need to be sure the things people say about God are true.

If someone tells you that God doesn't love you, that is not true! When people say that the Bible is full of stories that people made up, that's not true either. We know everything written in the Bible is true, so we can believe what we read. The prophets, kings, and disciples of Jesus who wrote the Bible were guided by the Holy Spirit. They wrote down the words that God told them to write.

When Jesus came into the world, many Old Testament prophesies were fulfilled by Him. Details of His birth, His teaching, and His death were predicted in the Old Testament. When they came true, it showed we can trust what the Bible says. We can also believe every word that Jesus said because He is God. Jesus not only spoke what is true, He is the truth. In John 14:6 Jesus says, "I am the way and the truth and the life. No one comes to the Father except through me."

TALK TO GOD
Ask God to help you learn what is true.

The way to know if something is true or false is to study the Bible and search for the answers to your questions. If you don't understand something, ask God to show you. You can also talk to a parent, pastor, or teacher who understands the Bible. It's impossible for God to lie, so we know every word He says is true!

EXPLORE MORE: What did Jesus tell His followers in John 8:31–32?

DID YOU KNOW?
In some courts of law, witnesses place their hands on the Bible and promise to tell the truth.

God's Word is true.

God Speaks to Job

"I know that you can do anything. No one can keep you from doing what you plan to do." —Job 42:2 NIrV

God created us to do many amazing things. But nothing we do can compare to what God can do. When Job was going through the hardest time of his life, God asked him some questions to remind him of God's power over creation. In Job 38 God asked Job, "Where were you when I laid the earth's foundations? Who stretched a measuring line across it? Who created the ocean? I said, 'You can come this far. But you can't come any farther. Here is where your proud waves have to stop.' Have you ever commanded the morning to come? Have you ever shown the sun where to rise?"

Job listened as God asked him more questions. "Have you traveled to the springs at the bottom of the ocean? Have you walked in its deepest parts? Do you understand how big the earth is? Can you bring out all the stars in their seasons? Can you lead out the Big Dipper and the Little Dipper? Who provides food for ravens when their babies cry out to me? Tell me if you know."

TALK TO GOD
Thank God that He is in control of everything.

What would you say if God asked you those questions? Would it make you realize how God's power is so much greater than we can understand? God created the universe and rules over all His creation. He controls the rain, hail, and snow. He makes the lightning and thunder, and gives orders to the clouds. He tells the sun when to rise and the stars when to shine. If God can do all that and more, then we can trust Him to be in control of our lives.

EXPLORE MORE: What questions did God ask Job in Job 38:33–37?

DID YOU KNOW?
The two constellations Ursa Major and Ursa Minor are also known as the Great Bear and Little Bear. The Big Dipper and Little Dipper make up part of these constellations, or group of stars, and can only be seen in the northern skies.

God is in control.

A Strong Tree

That kind of person is like a tree that is planted near a stream of water. It always bears its fruit at the right time. Its leaves don't dry up. Everything godly people do turns out well. —Psalm 1:3 NIrV

Have you ever seen a tree so big and strong, you can't even wrap your arms around the trunk? Trees like that need important ingredients to grow—like sunlight and water. When a tree has the right nutrients, it's a healthy tree. Its leaves stay green, and it doesn't fall over when the wind blows hard.

The Bible says that people who obey the law of the Lord are like a healthy tree planted by a stream of water. A tree growing near a stream will have an endless supply of water for its roots. For people who love God, the Bible is like that. It gives them what they need to be spiritually strong over and over and never stops. When we stay close to God through reading the Bible, praying to Him, and doing things His way, it helps us grow strong in our spirits. We have hope when hard things happen. We remember God is with us when we feel tempted to do the wrong thing. And people can see our love for God flowing out of our hearts, just like a tall green tree grabs our attention with its size.

TALK TO GOD
Ask God to help you grow into a strong person of faith.

Psalm 1 tells us more ways we can be a fruitful person—a person who grows in the things of God. We don't follow the advice of people who don't love God or do things that go against God's direction for our lives. We don't join with others who make fun of God and His law. Instead, we find joy in God's Word and think about it day and night. When we live our lives that way, there's no limit to how strong we can grow.

EXPLORE MORE: Read John 15:5. What does Jesus say He is in this verse? What does He say we are?

DID YOU KNOW?
Not all trees grow well near water, but some species handle wet soil very well. Pine, oak, dogwood, and sycamore trees grow well near water.

I can stand strong in my faith.

Wake Up with God

Lord, every morning you hear my voice. Every morning, I tell you what I need. And I wait for your answer. —Psalm 5:3 ICB

What do you do when you wake up in the morning? Do you stretch your arms and legs before you get out of bed? Do you peek out the window to see what the weather is like? Do you say good morning to your family or your pets?

There are many things we can do when we first wake up in the morning. And the very best thing we can do is wake up with God. In Psalm 5, King David talked about starting his day by praying to God. He said, "Every morning I tell you what I need. And I wait for your answer."

TALK TO GOD
Tell God how wonderful it is to start your day with Him each morning.

Waking up with God means we start our day by thinking about Him and talking to Him. We can even say, "Good morning, God!" when we first open our eyes. We can say, "Thank you for giving us another day." We can ask God to help us be close to Him as we go through our day. And like King David, we can tell God what we need in the morning and then look for His answer.

When we wake up with God, it's a way we can show God how important He is. We can read a Bible story and pray with our families at breakfast. We can choose a Bible verse to think about during the day, and we can sing a song to God on our way to school.

Even though God is the ruler over the universe, He always wants to talk to us and listen to us. Tomorrow when you wake up, see how wonderful it is to start your day with God!

EXPLORE MORE: Read Psalm 90:14. What did Moses ask God to do every morning?

I will wake up with God.

DID YOU KNOW?
Kids ages six to thirteen should get about nine to eleven hours of sleep each night to be well rested in the morning.

How Majestic Is God's Name

O Lord, our Lord, your majestic name fills the earth! Your glory is higher than the heavens. —Psalm 8:1 NLT

Have you ever heard the word *majestic*? It comes from the word *majesty* and is used to describe something that is very beautiful, grand in size, and worthy of respect. In Psalm 8:1, King David called God's name *majestic*. As David thought about God's greatness, he listed some of the ways God is majestic.

David noticed how young children and babies sing praises to God. And when young people speak truth about God and praise Him, David said they silence God's enemies. That means they make them be quiet.

David also realized how great God is when he looked into the night sky. When David saw the moon and stars, it made him feel so small. He was amazed that God would even care about people because we are so tiny compared with the huge universe He created. But even though people are so small, David knew that God crowned them with glory and honor. God put people in charge of His creation, including the animals that swim in the sea and roam the earth.

TALK TO GOD
Praise God for being so majestic. If you know a song about His majesty, sing it to Him.

God showed His full majesty when He sent His Son, Jesus, to earth. Jesus was full of God's glory and filled with love for all people. He lived a sinless life and took the punishment for our sins upon himself. God's majestic name was on Jesus as He made a way for people to be saved through His death on the cross.

David ends this psalm with the words, "O Lord, our Lord, your majestic name fills the earth!" When we read this psalm, we can stop and think about all the ways we see God's majesty. We serve a majestic God!

EXPLORE MORE: Psalm 93:1 says God is robed in something. What is it?

DID YOU KNOW?
The RMS *Majestic* was an ocean liner launched in 1914 for a British shipping company. At that time, it was the largest ship in the world.

God is majestic.

The Path of Life

You will teach me the right way to live. Just being with you will bring complete happiness. Being at your right side will make me happy forever. —Psalm 16:11 ERV

If you have ever been hiking, you know there are different paths you can take. Some trails are easier and shorter. And some are longer and more difficult. The path you take changes the type of hike you have.

The Bible tells us that the decisions we make and the way we live our lives is like choosing a path to walk down. Some decisions and ways of living will lead us down a good path, while other decisions and ways of living can lead us down a bad path. In the Psalms, David wrote about the idea of these paths and the different ways our lives might go as we make choices.

TALK TO GOD
Ask God to show you the right way to live and to help you follow the path of life.

In Psalm 16:11, David wrote, "You make known to me the path of life." Some other versions of the Bible say, "You will teach me the right way to live." God will help us know the right things to do and the things that are best for us. He doesn't want us to be confused and end up on the wrong path by mistake. Through reading God's Word, prayer, and listening to adults who love you, you will know the right way to live.

In Psalm 16 David also talks about what happens to people who do not choose the right way to live. King David said people who worship other gods will have many troubles and be very sad. That's because they will not be close to God. But David tells us when we follow God's right way of living, we will be close to Him—and that means we will be happy with God forever.

EXPLORE MORE: What does God tell us in Psalm 32:8?

DID YOU KNOW?

Sweden's longest and most famous hiking trail is called the King's Trail (also known as Kungsleden). It is about 65 miles (105 kilometers) long, and sometimes reindeer can be seen along the way.

God shows me the right way to live.

The Apple of God's Eye

Keep me as the apple of your eye; hide me in the
shadow of your wings. —Psalm 17:8 NIV

The book of Psalms is filled with prayers and songs, and King David wrote many of them. Even though these psalms were written thousands of years ago, they sound like they could have been written today. The thoughts and feelings King David had are thoughts and feelings many of us have too.

But in Psalm 17, David says something that sounds kind of funny today. As he calls out to God, David says, "Keep me as the apple of your eye." We don't usually see people walking around with an apple in their eye. What was King David talking about?

The meaning of "the apple of the eye" has to do with the part of our eyes called the pupil. The pupil is the black circle in the middle of your eye. When you stand very close in front of someone, you can actually see your own reflection in the pupil of their eye. That reflection was known as "the little man of the eye" in the Hebrew language. That phrase has been translated to "the apple of the eye" in English.

Being the apple of someone's eye means more than seeing your reflection. It means that person *cherishes* you or loves you very much. David wanted God to watch over him and to protect him. He wanted to be precious to God.

> **TALK TO GOD**
> Think of a special way to ask God to care for you (keep me close like a mother bird protects her babies; show me your love is bigger than the mountains), and pray it to Him today.

Like David, we can pray to God using words that are important to us. We can ask God to watch over us and protect us too. And we can remember that God always has His eyes on us.

DID YOU KNOW?
Shakespeare wrote the phrase "apple of his eye" in *A Midsummer Night's Dream* in the 1600s.

EXPLORE MORE: Read Deuteronomy 32:10. What is the nation of Israel called in the song of Moses?

I am precious to God.

Creation Speaks

The heavens tell about the glory of God. The skies show that his hands created them. —Psalm 19:1 NIrV

Did you know that nature can talk? We don't hear the trees saying hello in the morning, or the sky say, "It's good to see you!" But the Bible tells us that God's creation speaks. Psalm 19 tells us that day after day creation is pouring out speech and giving us knowledge without words. What is creation saying so loudly without words? Creation is shouting about the glory of God!

TALK TO GOD
Go outside today or look out your window. What do you see that God made? Thank Him for being a wonderful creator.

When David, the writer of Psalm 19, looked into the heavens, he could see God's work. He could see the beauty of God's creation in the daytime sky with wispy clouds floating by. He could see God's greatness in the glowing sun that rises and sets each day. He could see it in the night sky with the thousands of stars twinkling above him and the moon shining in the quiet dark. David could see how big God is in making our giant world and the objects in space. He could see how powerful God is to make something so grand. And He could see how creative God is to make something so awesome.

Today we still see God in creation. When we stop and look around, it's almost like we can hear the trees and the sunset and the ocean and the mountains telling us God exists. Have you ever felt small when you saw something amazing in creation? That feeling is a reminder from God about how big He is! What part of creation do you find most amazing? How do you see God's hand in making it? God is the creator of everything, and creation shouts His praise.

EXPLORE MORE: Look up Luke 19:37–40. What did Jesus say would happen if His disciples kept quiet?

Creation speaks about God.

DID YOU KNOW?
There are two parks in Pennsylvania and Montana that contain ringing rocks. When the rocks are hit with a hammer, they ring or chime.

Pour Out Your Heart to God

My God, my God, why have you left me alone? You are too far away to save me. You are too far away to hear my moans. —Psalm 22:1 ICB

Have you ever felt alone when you were going through a hard time? Sometimes when bad things happen, we can feel so alone that even God seems far away. King David felt like that. And do you know what he did? He talked to God about it.

In some versions of the Bible, Psalm 22 is called "The Prayer of a Suffering Man." We can tell King David wrote it during a very hard time. David starts his prayer by telling God how he feels. David says he feels so alone that when he cries out, it seems like God isn't answering. And then David remembers. He thinks back to all the ways the Israelites trusted God in the past and how God helped them. He remembers that God has been with him, too, and asks God to stay close to him.

As David keeps praying, he uses big examples to tell God how he feels. He says his strength has left him like water poured out on the ground, and his heart is so discouraged, it's like melted wax. David is completely honest with God about how hard things are.

Have you ever prayed like that to God? God deserves our respect because He is holy. But that doesn't mean we can't be honest with Him and tell Him how we feel, even if we feel angry. God already knows what's in our hearts. When we share our feelings with Him, it helps us stay close to Him. He doesn't always take away the hard things in our lives or tell us why certain things happen. But He wants to hear everything we have to say and promises to be with us through it all.

TALK TO GOD
What are you feeling today? Tell God all about it.

DID YOU KNOW?
When Jesus was dying on the cross, He cried out in Aramaic, *Eloi, Eloi, lema sabachthani?* which means "My God, my God, why have you left me alone?"

EXPLORE MORE: Read Psalm 22:29–31. How does David end his prayer?

God wants me to tell Him how I feel.

The Good Shepherd

The Lord is my shepherd. He gives me everything I need.
—Psalm 23:1 NIrV

A shepherd's job is to take care of sheep. Shepherds make sure their sheep have everything they need. They give the sheep food and water. They watch over the sheep while they sleep to make sure nothing happens to them. They show the sheep the right way to go and bring them back if they go the wrong way. When sheep travel through dangerous areas where they might get hurt or another animal might attack them, the shepherd keeps them safe.

King David knew all about a shepherd's job because he was a shepherd when he was young. Before he became king, David watched over his father's sheep in Bethlehem. Later on, he wrote Psalm 23, which is one of the most famous passages in the Bible. It is also called "The Shepherd's Psalm." In Psalm 23 David writes about a good shepherd who takes care of his sheep. He says, "The Lord is my shepherd. He gives me everything I need." In his poem, the Good Shepherd is Jesus.

TALK TO GOD
Thank Jesus for taking care of you like a good shepherd.

As David thought about taking care of sheep, he realized that God takes care of His people the same way. Like a shepherd, Jesus provides for us. He gives our souls peace, like a lamb lying down in the grass. He shows us the right things to do, like a herd of sheep walking on the safe path away from danger. Even when we go through hard times, we don't have to be afraid because Jesus is with us. He is like a shepherd with a staff that will keep us safe. Jesus is the kindest shepherd, and He loves us like shepherds love their sheep.

EXPLORE MORE: What does Jesus say about himself in John 10:11?

Jesus is the Good Shepherd.

DID YOU KNOW?
The first shepherd in the Bible was Abel, Adam and Eve's son.

Who Owns the World?

The earth is the Lord's, and everything in it. The world and all its people belong to him. —Psalm 24:1 NLT

Does your backpack have your name or initials in it in case it gets lost? Maybe you have a sticker on your water bottle with your name, so everyone knows it's yours. Have you ever seen a suitcase with someone's name and phone number on it? It's important to know what things belong to whom. When we own something, it means it's ours and we are in charge of it.

Have you ever wondered who's in charge of the world or who owns it? The Bible tells us that the earth belongs to God. And not just the planet, but everything in it and all the people who live in it. Do you know why everything on earth belongs to God? Because He created it all! Psalm 24 says God founded the earth on the seas and established it on the waters. That's a fancy way of saying God formed the world and made it for people to use in a certain way.

TALK TO GOD
Thank God that the earth belongs to Him and so do you.

It's important for us to remember that God owns the world. No matter how powerful leaders on earth may be, they are not as powerful as God. They will never oversee all of creation. They did not create the earth or stars or animals or people. No one can have as much power as God. And even though God rules galaxies bigger than we can even imagine, He cares enough to notice the tiniest parts of His creation. From the smallest bug to the tallest mountain, everything belongs to Him. If we could put a sticker on the earth, it would say Property of God.

EXPLORE MORE: What does God say He owns in Psalm 50:10–11?

DID YOU KNOW?
Kids in Japan carry leather backpacks called randoseru. Boys usually have black packs, and girls usually have red.

The earth belongs to God.

One Thing

I ask only one thing from the Lord. This is what I want most: Let me live in the Lord's house all my life, enjoying the Lord's beauty and spending time in his palace. —Psalm 27:4 ERV

If you could ask God for one thing, what would it be? Would it be a new toy you'd love to have? Would it be happiness or the health of someone in your family? Would it be a pet? In Psalm 27, King David wrote about one thing he wanted to ask God for.

David didn't ask for money or for God to keep him safe from his enemies. He didn't ask for good health or a lot of friends. Instead of asking for one of those things, he asked God for the very best thing. David asked to live in God's house for his whole life so he could enjoy God's beauty and spend time with Him. He would rather live in the tabernacle surrounded by God's presence than live in the palace as a king. David believed the greatest thing he could do was fill his mind and heart with the goodness of God.

TALK TO GOD
Pray the words from today's verse, Psalm 27:4. Ask God to give you the desire to be close to Him more than anything else.

We can learn from David and the words he shared in Psalm 27. When we fill our thoughts with God and think about how wonderful He is, it changes our hearts and helps us love Him more than anything else. When we seek God, we get to know Him and understand Him in deeper ways. God is so great and wonderful that we can spend all our lives learning about Him and still have more to discover.

One day God will bring His kingdom to earth, and we will worship Him forever. We will enjoy His beauty and spend time with Him. We will never run out of things to praise Him for.

EXPLORE MORE: Read Revelation 21:3–5 to find out what God's new kingdom will be like.

Being in God's presence is the best thing.

DID YOU KNOW?
In the United States, the most common thing people pray for is their families, followed by thanking God. People also pray for healing and for their friends.

The Voice of the Lord

The voice of the Lord is powerful; the voice of the Lord is majestic.
—Psalm 29:4 NLT

Did you know babies can recognize their mothers' voices before they're even born? All our voices sound different, and our brains can tell who someone is just by hearing their voice. It can be hard to understand what God's voice is like since we don't hear Him talk to us like our friends and family. But God still speaks through His Word, the Holy Spirit, and creation. What do you think God's voice is like?

In Psalm 29, "the voice of the Lord" is mentioned seven times. In this song of praise, God's voice is described as powerful and majestic. God's voice is strong like a storm over the ocean. It says, "The Lord thunders over the mighty sea." While sometimes we think of thunderstorms as scary, thinking of God's voice like thunder shows us how great He is. It means His voice is so strong and powerful, it can roar over the sea. But God's voice can also calm the wind and waves to make a wild storm stop. God rules over all creation and everything obeys His voice.

TALK TO GOD
Thank God for speaking so powerfully and ask Him to help you hear His voice.

Psalm 29 says God's voice strikes like lightning. If you have ever seen lightning strike something, it's an amazing thing to see. God's voice is like that—but even more amazing!

No matter what we compare God's voice to, when He speaks it's awesome! If you pay attention, you will notice when He's speaking even if there aren't any words. The next time you hear thunder crack or see lightning light up the sky, remember how great God's voice is!

DID YOU KNOW?
Sound is measured in decibels. A clap of thunder is usually about 120 decibels, which is ten times louder than a garbage truck.

EXPLORE MORE: Read 2 Samuel 22:14. How did King David describe God's voice in this song?

God's voice is powerful.

Help for Broken Hearts

The Lord is close to the brokenhearted. He saves those whose spirits have been crushed. —Psalm 34:18 ICB

If you go to a playground, you might see kids climbing on bars, swinging on swings, spinning on a merry-go-round, or zooming down a slippery slide. Playing outdoors is super fun—unless you get hurt! If you've ever scraped your knee, twisted an ankle, or broken a bone, you know how bad that feels.

God made our bodies in a wonderful way! The scrape on your knee will get better. A twisted ankle will be strong again, and a broken bone can heal. But when we get hurt on the inside, it's a different kind of hurt.

TALK TO GOD
Ask God to heal people who have broken hearts.

When people hurt on the inside, we often say they have a broken heart. That doesn't mean there's anything wrong with their heart that pumps blood through their body. It means they are sad because they are going through a hard time. People get broken hearts when someone they love is sick or dying. Other times, their hearts hurt when someone is mean to them. People also get broken hearts when something they were looking forward to doesn't happen, or when someone breaks a promise. But just like skinned knees, twisted ankles, and broken bones, broken hearts can heal too.

Psalm 147:3 says that God heals broken hearts and bandages our wounds. God knows when you are hurting, and He wants you to tell Him how you feel. He wants you to remember that Jesus died on the cross so you can be God's child. When you hurt on the inside, let God's love fill you up. God's love is like having a big bandage around your heart.

EXPLORE MORE: What does Psalm 73:26 tell us about God?

God heals broken hearts.

DID YOU KNOW?
The heart is a muscular organ about the size of your fist. It is located behind the breastbone and pumps blood through arteries and veins in your body.

Walking with God

The Lord makes secure the footsteps of the person who delights in him. Even if that person trips, he won't fall. The Lord's hand takes good care of him. —Psalm 37:23–24 NIrV

When young children go for a walk with grown-ups, they often hold hands because it keeps them safe. Holding hands keeps a child from running into a street or running too far ahead. When children hold a grown-up's hand, they won't fall down if they trip over a bump because the grown-up helps keep the child up.

Have you ever heard someone say it's important to walk with God? The Bible helps us understand what that means. Walking with God means we keep learning more about Him and how He wants us to live. God gives us many wise instructions in the Bible, and when we follow them, we will walk in the way He wants us to go.

When Jesus lived on earth, people walked with Him and followed Him. Many people knew Jesus was sent from God because they saw His miracles and listened to His teaching. Jesus taught people how to walk with God by loving Him and loving others. And when people walked with Jesus, they were also walking with God.

TALK TO GOD
Ask God to help you learn how to walk with Him.

When you walk with God, you can tell Him about your problems and ask Him to help you. None of your problems are too big or too small for Him. If you have an important choice to make, you can ask God for wisdom to make the best choice. You can also ask Him to watch over you and give you what you need. Even though you cannot see God, He is with you all the time. God wants you to walk with Him by believing and trusting in Him every day. When you do, it's like holding His hand.

EXPLORE MORE: Read Psalm 37:3–6. What are some of the blessings of walking with God?

DID YOU KNOW?
Walking for exercise gives you more energy and helps to strengthen your muscles, bones, and heart.

God wants me to walk with Him.

Thirsty like a Deer

A deer thirsts for a stream of water. In the same way,
I thirst for you, God. —Psalm 42:1 ICB

When you are thirsty, your body is telling you it's time to get a drink. People need to drink water every day to stay healthy. When we don't drink enough, we feel thirsty. You know what it means to be thirsty for water. You want it badly! And when you finally get some water, you drink until you are satisfied.

In Psalm 42, the psalmist talks about being thirsty for God. He compares his thirst for God to a deer that thirsts for water. The psalmist wants to be near God just like a deer wants to be near water. The psalmist thirsts for God when he is sad and lonely. And when he is near to God, he feels satisfied because he remembers God's love and kindness. Some people try to search for God. God is everywhere so it's not hard to find Him! We can see God in His wonderful creation. We can listen to birds as they sing His praises. We can read thousands of His promises in the Bible. And we can talk to Him anytime, no matter where we are.

TALK TO GOD
Thank God that He is always near to fill your heart with His love.

Like a deer that lives near a large body of water, you are always near to God. You can feel close to God by thinking about His love and kindness. Like the birds, you can sing praises to Him. You can read your favorite verses in the Bible, and you can thank God for being your friend. When you spend time with God, you will feel close to Him and not be thirsty.

EXPLORE MORE: How did God turn bitter water into fresh water for the Israelites at Marah? Read Exodus 15:22–25 to see if you remember.

I want to be close to God.

DID YOU KNOW?
Some deer can drink up to five gallons (18.9 liters) of water per day. That's about eighty glasses of water.

A Safe Place

God is our place of safety. He gives us strength. He is always there to help us in times of trouble. —Psalm 46:1 NIrV

Everyone likes to feel safe. If it's cold or stormy outside, we feel safe when we are in our homes. When it's time to go to bed, kids feel safe when a parent or another grown-up is with them. And sometimes, in a game of tag, there's a space called the safety zone. When kids are inside the safety zone, they are safe from being tagged.

Psalm 46 says that God is our place of safety. When you are sad, afraid, or have a problem, you can feel safe when you talk to God because He loves you and cares about you so much. He wants to help you with any troubles or fears you might have.

TALK TO GOD
Tell God that you know you're always safe with Him.

In verse 7 of Psalm 46 it says, "The Lord who rules over all is with us. The God of Jacob is like a fort to us." That means the God who rules over the entire universe is with you! The one and only true God who protected Abraham, Isaac, and Jacob is the same God who protects you. Those exact words are repeated in verse 11, so it's a message God wants you to know.

Some people think that a big house or lots of money will keep them safe. Some people feel safe if they have a good job. Others feel safe if they have a lot of friends. Those are not bad things, but they cannot keep you safe because they don't always last. God is the only one who can keep you safe all the time, forever and ever. He is the safest place there is!

DID YOU KNOW?
A playground safety zone is the area under and around the playground equipment. It is filled with a softer surface to keep children from getting hurt if they fall.

EXPLORE MORE: Read from another psalm in your Bible—Psalm 4:8. How can the words from that verse help you feel safe at night?

God is my safe place.

Praise the King

God is the King of the whole earth. Sing a psalm of praise to him.
—Psalm 47:7 NIrV

We have many reasons to praise God. We praise Him because He is our creator, helper, and friend. He is our counselor, teacher, and father. We also praise God for His greatness, power, and love. And in Psalm 47, the verses remind us to praise God because He is our King.

Cities, states, provinces, countries, and nations all have rulers. From mayors, governors, and prime ministers to kings, queens, and presidents, the world is filled with many different kinds of rulers. But only God rules over everyone and everything.

Psalm 47:1 says, "Clap your hands, all you nations. Shout to God with cries of joy. Do this because the Lord Most High is wonderful. He is the great King over the whole earth." That means *everyone*, *everywhere* can praise God for being their King. If you live in a big city, small town, or tiny village, God is your King. If you are a young child, teenager, or grown-up, God is your King and worthy of your praise.

Do you know how to praise God? You can praise God with a prayer by telling Him how great and wonderful He is. You can sing a song that praises God for His goodness and love. And like Psalm 47 says, you can clap your hands to praise Him!

When you praise God, you give honor to Him, and it shows God how much you love Him. And do you know what? It isn't possible to praise God with a grumpy frown on your face. Praising God will fill your heart with joy and make you smile. So clap your hands, be happy, and praise the King.

TALK TO GOD
Use some of your own words to praise God, the King of the whole earth.

EXPLORE MORE: Read the words that King David used to praise God in Psalm 9:1–2.

I will praise God for being my King.

DID YOU KNOW?
Zamar is the Hebrew word for praising God with musical instruments and singing. The word is usually translated to "sing praises."

No More Fear

When I'm afraid, I put my trust in you. —Psalm 56:3 NIrV

When we looked at some of the chapters in the book of 1 Samuel, we learned that David did a lot of running and hiding from King Saul. David was going to be the next king of Israel, and King Saul was not happy about that!

David wrote many of the psalms that are in the Bible. He wrote some when he was a shepherd out in the fields. He wrote some when he was the captain of King Saul's army, and he wrote more psalms when he was the king of Israel.

Psalm 56 was most likely written when he was trying to get away from King Saul. In the first verse David writes, "Help me, God. Men are chasing me." David knew that calling out to God was the best thing he could do to stay safe. There must have been times when he was afraid since Saul was trying so hard to find him.

TALK TO GOD
Tell God about something that makes you afraid and ask Him to help you trust Him.

We may not have people chasing us or wanting to hurt us, but there are other things that can make us afraid. Some kids are afraid to try out for a team or go to a new school. Maybe you're afraid to talk to someone you want to be friends with. And maybe that big test you have to take makes you nervous!

In verse 10 of Psalm 56, David writes, "I trust in God. I praise his word." David believed God would take care of him because of God's promises in His Word. Like David, you can turn to God when you are afraid. The promises in His Word are for you too!

DID YOU KNOW?
We don't know exactly how long David had to run from King Saul, but it may have been about seven years.

EXPLORE MORE: Do you remember what God told Joshua before he led the Israelites across the Jordan River? Read Joshua 1:9 to find out if you're right.

I will trust God when I am afraid.

Praising God Then and Now

Everyone on earth is amazed at the wonderful things you have done. What you do makes people from one end of the earth to the other sing for joy. —Psalm 65:8 NIrV

Psalm 65 is another psalm that David wrote. In this psalm, David praises God as he thinks about wonderful things that God has done and continues to do. First, David praises God for listening to His people, answering their prayers, and forgiving their sins. Can you see how God does the same thing for His people today? These words were true when David wrote them, and they are still true for us because the Bible is for all people and every generation.

TALK TO GOD
Praise God for something that He does for you.

David then praises God for His creation. In verse 6 David writes, "You formed the mountains by your power. You showed how strong you are." David knew that only a strong and powerful God could create the mountains. We can also praise God for those mountains because they are still standing today!

In the next verses, David praises God for how He cares for His creation by watering the land and making crops grow to provide food for people. In verse 10 David writes, "You water its rows. You smooth out its bumps. You soften it with showers. And you bless its crops." God still cares for His creation today. Farmers work hard to prepare the soil and plant seeds, but God created the land and only He can send rain to make the crops grow.

David was amazed by what God could do. He thought of specific things to praise God for in this psalm. Are you amazed at the wonderful things God does? Then praise God like David did! You can even write your own psalm of praise to share someday with your children and grandchildren. Your words of praise will still be true.

EXPLORE MORE: Read more of David's praises to God in Psalm 65:11–13.

I can praise God for many things.

DID YOU KNOW?
Psalms is the longest book in the Bible. There are 150 individual psalms (songs) in the book, which are divided into five smaller books. David wrote almost half of them.

Asaph the Musician

*God, your ways are holy. . . . You are the God who did miracles.
You showed people your power. —Psalm 77:13–14 ICB*

As you read through the book of Psalms, you will notice that a man named Asaph wrote twelve of the psalms. Asaph was a Levite who was a singer and composer. In 1 Chronicles 6:39, Asaph is listed as one of the temple musicians. The psalms he wrote were songs that were sung with musical instruments.

In Psalm 77, Asaph cries out to God, searching for comfort. Then he remembers how God brought the Israelites out of Egypt. In verses 11 and 12 he writes, "I remember what the Lord did. I remember the miracles you did long ago. I think about all the things you did. I think about what you have done."

The Israelites crossed through the Red Sea before Asaph was born, but he knew how God had parted the waters to make a path through the sea. The story had been passed down from one generation to another and was written in the Book of Moses. The Holy Spirit guided Asaph's thoughts as he imagined what that night was like. In verses 16–18, he writes, "God, the waters saw you . . . and became afraid. The deep waters shook with fear. The clouds poured down their rain. The sky thundered. Your lightning flashed back and forth. Your thunder sounded in the whirlwind. Lightning lit up the world. The earth trembled and shook."

TALK TO GOD
Thank God that He has the power to perform miracles.

God wants us to remember the things He has done for us and the way He cares for us. Memories of God's miracles and of His goodness can bring us comfort when we are going through a hard time. What has God done for you that you want to remember forever?

EXPLORE MORE: What does Asaph's song say that God does in Psalm 50:1–2?

DID YOU KNOW?
Asaph was from a very musical family! Many of his ancestors were musicians and so were many of his descendants.

I will remember the great things God does.

Tell Your Children

We won't hide them from our children. We will tell them to those who live after us. We will tell them what the Lord has done that is worthy of praise. We will talk about his power and the wonderful things he has done. —Psalm 78:4 NIrV

People enjoy listening to stories. Some stories are fiction, which means they didn't really happen but are fun to hear. Nonfiction stories are stories that actually happened. Some nonfiction stories happened a long time ago, like how the automobile was invented.

Before there were history books, Bible storybooks, or books of devotions, parents and grandparents told stories to their children. When the children became adults, they would tell those same stories to their children and grandchildren. Way back in the book of Deuteronomy, Moses told the people what God had told him—that He was the one and only true God, and they were to love Him with all their heart, soul, mind, and strength. God told Moses to instruct the people to teach their children about Him. This message needed to be passed down from one generation to the next.

The Israelites had many experiences that God wanted their children to know and remember. The parents told stories of Abraham, Isaac, and Jacob. Their children learned how God brought the Israelites to Egypt during a famine, and many years later He brought them out of Egypt through the Red Sea. The children heard stories of manna in the wilderness. They learned how God stopped the Jordan River and brought them into the promised land with Joshua as their leader.

TALK TO GOD
Thank God that we can read wonderful stories in the Bible that happened long ago.

God wanted every generation to know these stories so they would not forget Him and they would continue to follow Him. Today you can read all these stories in the Bible. You can learn them now, and someday you can read them to your children and grandchildren.

EXPLORE MORE: Read Psalm 78:5–7. Why did God want parents to tell their children about Him?

It's good to know God's stories.

The House of the Lord

Blessed are those who live in your house. They are always praising you. —Psalm 84:4 NIrV

In the book of Exodus, we read how the Israelites built the tabernacle when they were in the wilderness. Some Bible versions call it the Holy Tent. This is where the people would go when they wanted to meet with God. As they moved from one place to another, they would pack up the tabernacle, carry it with them, and set it up again.

When Solomon was king, he was in charge of building the temple in Jerusalem. This became the place where people would go to worship God and bring their offerings. In Psalm 84, the psalmist talks about how beautiful the temple was. He says, "I can't wait to be in the courtyards of the Lord's temple. I really want to be there.... Even the sparrow has found a home near your altar."

TALK TO GOD
Thank God that you have many places where you can go to worship with others.

Today we have churches where we can go to meet with other families. We sing songs, pray, and listen to pastors give messages from the Bible. But in Bible times, they didn't have churches in different places like we do, so the tabernacle and temple were very special to the people.

Even though we can meet with God wherever we are, meeting with others at church helps us learn more about God. We also grow closer to other Christians and help each other in good times and hard times.

Are you excited when you go to church? Are you happy when you can sing and pray with others? Everyone can find a place in the house of the Lord, even a little sparrow.

EXPLORE MORE: What does Hebrews 10:24–25 tell us to do?

DID YOU KNOW?
Some of the most famous churches in the world are La Sagrada Família in Spain, St. Basil's Cathedral in Russia, and Notre-Dame Cathedral in France.

I want to go to church to worship God.

David's Prayer

Teach me your way, Lord, that I may rely on your faithfulness; give me an undivided heart, that I may fear your name. —Psalm 86:11 NIV

In 1 Samuel 16, we read the story of Samuel going to Jesse's home to anoint one of his sons to be the next king of Israel. God chose David because God saw what was in David's heart. God told Samuel, "The Lord does not look at the things people look at. People look at the outside of a person. But the Lord looks at what is in the heart."

In Psalm 86, we can read one of David's prayers to God. In this prayer he asks God to teach him His ways. David loved God and wanted to do what was right. David praises God for being good and forgiving. He praises God for being the only true God who does great things. David knew he needed to keep following God to lead Israel on the right path. He asks God to give him an undivided heart so that he would trust God completely.

TALK TO GOD
Ask God to give you an undivided heart.

To have an undivided heart means to love God more than anything else. It means that God is the only God you worship and believe in. It means that you will follow God instead of following people or things that may turn you away from Him.

David wanted to follow God because he knew how much God loved him, and he prayed to God from deep inside his heart. His prayer gives us an example of how we can talk to God in the same way. We can thank God for loving us. We can praise Him for His greatness. And we can ask God to give us an undivided heart so we will always follow Him.

EXPLORE MORE: What are some reasons David gives in Psalm 86:8-10 that show us why God is the one and only true God?

I want to pray like David did.

DID YOU KNOW?
The heart symbol is one of the most popular symbols in the world. It's a short way to say, "I love you."

A Song for the Sabbath Day

It is good to give thanks to the Lord, to sing praises to the Most High.
—Psalm 92:1 NLT

In many translations of the Bible, Psalm 92 is titled, "A Song to be Sung on the Sabbath Day." In the Old Testament, the Sabbath was a day of rest when people didn't do any work. It was also a day when the people would come together to sing and praise God. The Sabbath was a happy day filled with joy and thanksgiving.

Psalm 92 begins with the words, "It is good to give thanks to the Lord," and there are many reasons why that's true. It's good to thank God because He is our creator. It's good to thank God because He gives us many promises in His Word. It's good to thank God for blessing us and loving us. And it's good to thank God because it helps us to think about all the wonderful things God does for us.

In the second verse it says, "It is good to proclaim your unfailing love in the morning, your faithfulness in the evening." The entire day—from morning till night—was a special day to praise and worship God.

TALK TO GOD
Give thanks to God for three things He's done for you today.

In verses 4–5 of the psalm, it says, "I sing for joy because of what you have done. O Lord, what great works you do! And how deep are your thoughts." Like the psalmist, we can sing for joy because of the great things God does for us. He cares for us and provides for us. He thinks about us because we are His children. And He gives us a way to be part of His family by believing in Jesus. How can you thank God today?

EXPLORE MORE: What does Ephesians 5:19–20 tell us to do?

DID YOU KNOW?
Psalm 92 is the only psalm in the Bible that says it should be sung on the Sabbath.

It is good to give thanks to God.

Great Is the Lord

Great is the Lord! He is most worthy of praise! He is to
be feared above all gods. —Psalm 96:4 NLT

Many Bible teachers believe that King David wrote Psalm 96 because the words of this psalm are also found in 1 Chronicles 16 when the ark of the covenant was brought to the tabernacle. When the ark was in place, David gave offerings to God, then blessed the people. After the blessing, David gave bread, meat, and raisin cakes to the Israelites. He asked some of the Levites to praise and thank God. Then the musicians played stringed instruments, harps, and cymbals, and the priests blew the trumpets before the ark of the Lord.

TALK TO GOD
Praise God for
something that gives
you joy.

In David's song of thanksgiving, he begins with the words, "Let the whole earth sing praise to the Lord." First, he invites the Israelites to sing a new song to the Lord. Then David tells all the nations of the world to worship God because no other gods are real, and God is the one who made the heavens.

Finally, David speaks to God's creation by telling the heavens to be glad and the earth to rejoice. He tells the sea and everything in it to praise God. He tells the fields with their crops to burst with joy, and says, "Let the trees of the forest sing for joy." David wanted every person from every nation and all of creation to praise our great God because He is worthy of our praise.

In the last verse of Psalm 96, David explains that someday Jesus is coming to bring His truth to the world and make everything right. Knowing that should fill our hearts with hope and joy and make us want to sing!

EXPLORE MORE: Read Revelation 4:11. What does this verse say about God being worthy of our praise?

The Lord is worthy of my praise.

DID YOU KNOW?
Even though there are different types of psalms in the Bible, in the Hebrew Bible (Old Testament) the entire book is named "Psalms of Praise."

Thanksgiving and Praise

Enter his gates with thanksgiving; go into his courts with praise.
Give thanks to him and praise his name.
—Psalm 100:4 NLT

Do you ever wonder what words to use when you want to pray to God? There's no right or wrong way to pray when you pray from your heart, and you can talk to God just like you talk to a friend. But if you ever need some help, the words in Psalm 100:4 show us a good way to begin our prayers.

The Israelites went to the temple to worship God. The temple was surrounded by gates, and a courtyard was inside the gates. People had to enter the gates and walk through the courtyard to get to the temple. In Psalm 100, the psalmist says to enter God's gates with thanksgiving, and His courts with praise.

When we begin our prayers by thanking God for His love, protection, and blessings, it helps our hearts and minds to be grateful for everything God does for us. When we follow our thanksgiving with praise, we focus on God's greatness. We can praise God for His holiness and majesty. We can praise God for being our Creator, King, and Savior. And by the time we finish thanking and praising God, we will feel so close to Him, that we can easily tell Him anything else we want to say.

TALK TO GOD
Thank God for psalms that help us know how to pray.

You don't need to go to a temple to meet with God. You can talk to God wherever you are because He is always with you. But the next time you're not sure how to pray, you can start by thanking and praising God. Then you will have a special talk with God. You just might want to talk for a long time.

EXPLORE MORE: Read Psalm 100:1–2. What are other ways this psalm tells us to worship God?

DID YOU KNOW?
The outer courtyard that surrounded Solomon's Temple was where people gathered to worship. The inner courtyard was where the priests would offer sacrifices for the people.

I will offer God my praise and thanksgiving.

God's Great Love

His love is as high as the heavens are above the earth.
—Psalm 103:11 NIrV

Psalm 103 is another psalm that David wrote. In this psalm, David praises God with his whole heart. He praises God because He is holy, kind, and full of compassion. David says, "I never want to forget the good things God does for me."

David also praises God for doing what is right and fair. He explains that God is slow to get angry and He doesn't punish us for our sins the way we deserve to be punished. In verse 12 he says, God removes our sins from us "as far as the east is from the west." Did you know the distance from east to west is something you cannot measure? If you keep traveling north, you will eventually be traveling south. But if you travel east, you will always be going east, and if you travel west, you will always be going west.

TALK TO GOD
Thank God for His love.

Another distance that you cannot measure is how high the heavens are above the earth, and that's how David describes God's love. Like the sky has no limit, God's love for us has no limit either. And in verse 13, David says God loves us like a father loves his children.

Sometimes it's hard for us to understand how much God loves us. That's why it's important to read the Bible. The stories in the Bible show how God loves and cares for His people, and many of the psalms describe God's great and never-ending love. If you ever wonder how much God loves you, look into the sky and see how high it is. God's love is greater and higher than that!

EXPLORE MORE: How long does God's love last? Read Psalm 103:17–18.

DID YOU KNOW?
Our atmosphere (the gasses that surround our planet and make up the sky) continues upward for around 6,200 miles (10,000 kilometers). After that, the atmosphere of earth blends into outer space.

God's love is higher than the heavens.

The Creation Psalm

Lord, you have made many things. With your wisdom you made them all. The earth is full of your riches. —Psalm 104:24 ICB

Psalm 104 has been called "The Creation Psalm" because many of the verses praise God for His creation. The psalm begins by describing God as being wrapped in light like a robe. In the New Testament, 1 John 1:5 says, "God is light, and in him there is no darkness at all." God, who created light on the first day of creation, is light himself. And in John 8:12, Jesus says, "I am the light of the world," showing us that Jesus is also God.

The next few verses are filled with beautiful poetic words to describe our God in the heavens who spreads out the sky like a tent and builds His home there. The clouds are God's chariot, and He rides on the wings of the wind.

In verse 6 of this psalm, it talks about God covering the earth with water as high as the mountains. Do you remember when that happened? That was when God sent the great flood to wash everything away and start over. Verses 8 and 9 talk about what happened after the flood. "The water went to the places you made for it. You set borders for the seas that they cannot cross. The water will never cover the earth again."

TALK TO GOD
Thank God for creating the sun and moon to give day and night and seasons.

Other verses in the psalm talk about how God created the moon to give us different seasons, and how the sun gives daytime for people to work and night-time for animals to roam. Throughout this psalm, the Holy Spirit guided the writer to praise God for creating the heavens and earth and for taking care of His wonderful, amazing creation.

EXPLORE MORE: Read Psalm 104:24–28 to find out some of the ways God takes care of His creatures.

DID YOU KNOW?
Mount Everest is the highest mountain above sea level and is more than 29,000 feet (about 8,839 meters) tall. The Mauna Kea volcano is the tallest mountain from base to peak and is around 33,000 feet (10,058 meters) tall, but half of it is below sea level.

God is in control of all His creation.

Walking in Wisdom

Whoever is wise will remember these things and begin to understand the Lord's faithful love. —Psalm 107:43 ERV

Have you ever heard someone say, "That was a wise thing to do"? Or have you heard your parents say someone made a wise decision? In the Bible we read a lot about wisdom—like Solomon, the wisest king who ever lived. And we learn what happened to God's people when they made wise choices and unwise choices. Did you know you don't have to wait until you grow up to be wise? No matter how old you are, you can start learning to be wise.

TALK TO GOD
Ask God to help you be wise and to understand how great His love is.

Psalm 107 tells how we can become wise. In the first few verses, the psalm talks about how God's faithful love will last forever. The song of praise goes on to list the times God saved His people out of trouble and rescued them from danger. Even when the Israelites got into trouble because they made bad choices, God saved them when they called to Him for help. And do you know how Psalm 107 ends? It says that people who love God will see these things and be happy. The last line says, "Whoever is wise will remember these things and begin to understand the Lord's faithful love."

One way you can start becoming wise today is by learning the history of God's people in the Bible and then remembering all the great and mighty things God did. As you keep thinking about God's kindness and how He always helped His people when they needed Him, you will start to understand how great His faithful love is. When you understand God's love, you will be wise—no matter how many candles are on your birthday cake!

EXPLORE MORE: Read James 3:17. What is the wisdom of God like?

I can be wise and understand God's love.

DID YOU KNOW?
The word *wisdom* appears in the Bible more than two hundred times.

A Different Kind of Priest

The Lord has made a promise. He will not change his mind. He has said, "You are a priest forever, just like Melchizedek." —Psalm 110:4 NIrV

Have you ever heard of a man named Melchizedek in the Bible? You might be thinking, *Melchiz-a-who?* His name is first mentioned in the book of Genesis when Abraham rescued Lot after being captured during a war. When Abraham returned home, he was blessed by Melchizedek who was called "priest of God Most High."

Melchizedek was a priest, and he was also a king. In the Old Testament, someone was either a priest or a king but not both. Melchizedek doesn't stand out as an important character in the Bible until we start reading about Jesus. In Psalm 110, David remembered God's promise to always let his family rule. Jesus came to earth through David's line and is a King and Priest, similar to Melchizedek. Let's find out what that means for us today!

In the Old Testament, we read about the high priests who came from the family of Aaron and the tribe of Levi. Their job was to talk to God for the people and to offer sacrifices so God would forgive their sins. But Melchizedek was born hundreds of years before Aaron, which means he was another kind of priest. He was a king and priest of a higher order than other priests. Jesus is not like the other priests either. Jesus was made Priest by God's power, and He will be a Priest and King forever.

God sent Jesus to sacrifice himself for our sins. That's why we don't need to make sacrifices anymore to be forgiven. Being a high priest like Melchizedek means Jesus is our King and High Priest forever, and He never changes. What a great High Priest!

EXPLORE MORE: Read Hebrews 7:1–3 to find out more about Melchizedek. How is he like Jesus?

> **TALK TO GOD**
> Praise Jesus for being the greatest High Priest, and for being alive in heaven to talk to God for you.

> **DID YOU KNOW?**
> Some of the hardest names to pronounce in the Bible are Maher-Shalal-Hash-Baz (found in Isaiah 8), Zaphenath-Paneah (found in Genesis 41), and Cushan-Rishathaim (found in Judges 3).

Jesus is the greatest High Priest.

God Gets the Glory

Lord, you should receive the honor, not us. The honor belongs to you because of your faithful love and loyalty. —Psalm 115:1 ERV

Sometimes when people do something amazing, they give credit to others. That means they point out that other people have helped them accomplish the big things they've done. When football players score touchdowns, they give high fives to their teammates or point to the player who passed them the ball. When actors receive big awards, they thank their family and friends and the people who worked on their project with them. Have you ever noticed when someone gave credit to God after doing something amazing? Maybe a football player pointed to the sky to thank God after a big play. Or maybe you've heard people thank God when they received an award.

The beginning of Psalm 115 reminds us that God should receive all the honor in our lives when big things happen. It says that honor belongs to God because of His faithful love and loyalty. God is the one who gives us talents and abilities to do amazing things. Jesus told us in the New Testament that apart from Him, we can do nothing.

It can be tempting to take all the honor and credit for ourselves when we do something awesome. We work hard to achieve our goals, and it takes a lot of effort to reach our accomplishments. But giving honor to God in the big and small things helps us stay humble and remember we can only do things through His power in us. It's also a way we can share our faith with others.

One day God will receive all the honor and glory from every person He has created. But we don't have to wait until then to praise Him for His greatness!

EXPLORE MORE: Look up 1 Chronicles 29:11. What belongs to God?

TALK TO GOD
Think of one good thing you've done lately. Thank God for helping you do that.

God is worthy of all the glory.

DID YOU KNOW?
Some of the most famous awards with the highest honors in the world are the Nobel Prize, the Academy Award, the Pulitzer Prize, the Fields Medal, and the Grammy Award.

Short and Sweet

Praise the Lord, all you nations. Praise him, all you people
of the earth. —Psalm 117:1 NLT

Did you know that Psalm 117 is the shortest psalm? In fact, it is the shortest chapter in the whole Bible! It is only two verses long. It says, "Praise the Lord, all you nations. Praise him, all you people of the earth. For his unfailing love for us is powerful; the Lord's faithfulness endures forever."

In just three sentences, the writer of this psalm says a whole lot! He calls on all the people of the earth to praise God. Then he announces how powerful God's love is and that God's faithfulness will never end.

Do you ever feel like you need to use big fancy words and pray long prayers for God to hear you? Psalm 117 reminds us that we don't need to use a lot of words to talk to God. What God cares about is that we pray from our hearts. When we are honest with our words, we honor God. When we praise Him in our souls, we honor God. When we talk to God like a friend, we honor Him. It doesn't matter how many words we use, if we are praying with the right heart.

TALK TO GOD
Talk to God by finishing this prayer: I love you, God. You are so _____.

When Jesus showed His disciples how to pray, He prayed a prayer that was only four sentences long. He taught His disciples to honor God's name and to ask for God's will to be done, for God to give them what they needed, for forgiveness, and for protection from temptation. Our prayers don't have to be long to be powerful.

EXPLORE MORE: In Matthew 6:7–8, how did Jesus say we should pray?

DID YOU KNOW?
Psalm 119 is the longest psalm in the Bible.

Sometimes the best kinds of prayers are short and sweet.

The Best Flashlight

Your word is like a lamp for my feet and a light for my way.
—Psalm 119:105 ICB

Have you ever gotten up during the night and stubbed your toe on something in the dark? Or maybe your blanket fell on the floor, and it was hard to find it because you couldn't see very well. Do you have a nightlight in your house that helps you see where to walk during the night? Or have you ever used a flashlight when you needed to make your way through a dark room if the lights go out? Light changes everything in a dark place.

TALK TO GOD
Ask God to shine the light of His Word when you go through hard times.

The writer of Psalm 119 describes a hard time he was going through. We don't know exactly what he was dealing with, but he says things like, "I am sad and tired," and, "People have made up lies about me." But in the middle of all his sadness and suffering, he keeps talking about God's law and His Word. About halfway through the psalm, he says, "Your word is like a lamp for my feet and a light for my way."

Have you ever felt sad and tired when you've gone through a hard time? It's like trying to walk in a dark room without a light. Sometimes it feels lonely and scary. Sometimes you're not sure what to do. But God's Word is like turning on a flashlight in those hard times. It's like a nightlight that stays with you. Reading God's Word encourages our hearts when we are sad and discouraged. It also helps us know what to do when things are hard. No matter how dark your problems may feel, the light of God's Word changes everything.

EXPLORE MORE: What does John 1:4–5 say about Jesus?

DID YOU KNOW?
Light is measured in units called *lumens*. An outdoor flashlight is about 150 lumens. An indoor lamp is about 800 to 1,000 lumens.

God's Word is a light in the darkness.

The Maker of the Mountains

I lift up my eyes to the mountains—where does my help come from?
My help comes from the Lord, the Maker of heaven and earth.
—Psalm 121:1–2 NIV

Psalm 121 is called "A Song of Ascents." There are fifteen songs of ascents in the book of Psalms. You might be wondering, *What is a song of ascents?* An *ascent* is a climb or going up. Three times a year the Israelites would go on a journey to the city of Jerusalem to celebrate special festivals. The people would travel uphill to get to Jerusalem, which was located in the mountains. As the people walked miles and miles, they would sing songs of ascents, or songs for going up.

In Psalm 121, the words of the song even begin with looking up to the mountains. The song continues by asking, "Where does my help come from?" Then it gives the answer, "My help comes from the Lord, the Maker of heaven and earth."

TALK TO GOD
Thank God that He is always with you, and that His Holy Spirit lives inside those who love Him.

One way we can understand this song is by thinking about how the Israelites worshiped at the temple in ancient times. When people sang this song, they remembered that even though they were far away from the temple, God was still with them. They didn't have to be in Jerusalem for God to watch over them and protect them. The temple in the mountains wasn't their helper, but God, who made the mountains, was their helper.

Today we can remember the words of this song in our own lives. It doesn't matter where we go or how far away we are from the churches where we worship God. He is always with us. When we look at creation, we can remember that the Maker of heaven and earth is watching over us all the time.

EXPLORE MORE: Solomon, who built the first temple, wrote a song of ascent in Psalm 127. Read his words in your Bible.

DID YOU KNOW?
The three festivals the Israelites celebrated in Jerusalem were Passover, the Festival of Weeks, and the Festival of Shelters. Many Jews still celebrate these festivals today.

The Maker of heaven and earth watches over me.

Live in Unity

How good and pleasant it is when God's people live together in unity! —Psalm 133:1 NIV

Unity is a word you might hear people talk about after an election. They might say people need to come together in unity to support their new leaders. You also might hear someone talk about unity when different groups of people join together to achieve a goal or change a bad situation. *Unity* means to come together as one or work as a team. It means there is peace between people.

In Psalm 133 we read that it is good and pleasant when God's people live together in unity. A lot of times we don't see unity in the world. People disagree easily and become very upset when others don't see things their way. These disagreements make people do and say unkind things. But as Christians, one of the best ways we can show our love for God is by loving others, especially people in God's family.

It's not always easy for people in churches or groups of Christians to get along. We might not like every Christian we meet. But that doesn't mean we can't have unity. When we remember that each person is loved by God and used for His glory, we can find ways to agree and be unified.

TALK TO GOD
Ask God to bring unity to your own church and churches around the world.

You might not always get along with your brothers or sisters, but you still love them because you're a part of the same family. When we say yes to following Jesus, we become a part of God's big family, and that means there's a whole lot of new people to love. We don't have to look the same, talk the same, or agree on everything to be united in worshiping the one true God.

EXPLORE MORE: What did Peter write in 1 Peter 3:8–9 to encourage Christians?

It is good for God's people to live in unity.

DID YOU KNOW?
The United Kingdom is a group of four countries united together under a king or queen and a prime minister. The countries include England, Scotland, Wales, and Northern Ireland.

A Special Psalm

Give thanks to the Lord, because he is good. His faithful love continues forever. —Psalm 136:1 NIrV

Have you ever noticed in some songs certain lines are repeated over and over? When you hear the same phrase over and over, it gets stuck in your head and becomes the part of the song you remember most.

Psalm 136 is just like one of those songs. In all twenty-six verses, the same words are used: *His faithful love continues forever.* Why does this psalm say the same thing twenty-six times? This phrase is used in other parts of the Old Testament, and it seems the people would sing this to reply to the Levites leading worship. You can almost hear the Israelites singing back to the leaders when you read these words:

> Give thanks to the Lord, because he is good.
> *His faithful love continues forever.*
>
> Give thanks to the greatest God of all.
> *His faithful love continues forever.*
>
> Give thanks to the most powerful Lord of all.
> *His faithful love continues forever.* (vv. 1–3)

Of all the words the writer of this psalm could have chosen to repeat over and over, aren't you glad he chose these? Knowing that God's love never ends is a wonderful thought to have stuck in your head! The Hebrew word used for "faithful love" in this psalm is *hesed.* You can understand the word *hesed* as God's grace, His loyal love, and His covenant or promise to His people. It's almost as if the writer of this song is reminding us that we can't sing about God's love enough. The next time you feel God's love in your heart, you can sing with joy, "His faithful love continues forever!"

EXPLORE MORE: What did the people sing when they rebuilt the temple after leaving Babylon? Read Ezra 3:10–11 to find out.

TALK TO GOD
Take a moment to think about something wonderful in your life. Then praise God with all your heart and tell Him, "Your faithful love continues forever!"

DID YOU KNOW?
Psalm 136 has been called the Great Hallel, or the Great Psalm of Praise.

It's wonderful to sing about God's love.

Wonderfully Made

I praise you because you made me in an amazing and wonderful way. What you have done is wonderful. I know this very well.
—Psalm 139:14 ICB

Did you know it takes about nine months for babies to grow inside their mothers' tummies? It takes four to five months for other people to be able to see that a mom has a baby in her belly. But do you know who sees the baby growing the whole time? God does! And God doesn't just *see* the baby growing, the Bible tells us He's the one who makes the baby grow. Psalm 139:13 says, "You made my whole being. You formed me in my mother's body.

TALK TO GOD
Tell God some of the things you love about how He made you, and thank Him for creating you.

God is the one who created you. He had the idea of you before you were even born. God knows everything about you. There's nothing about yourself that you can hide from God. There's nothing about you that surprises Him. He knows what you're afraid of and what makes you smile. He knows if your right foot is slightly bigger than your left foot and how many freckles you have on your nose. He knows if talking in front of people makes you nervous and if you love math or art.

It's incredible to think about how well God knows us. And it's also really wonderful! There may be times when you feel like no one understands you, but God does. There may be times when everything feels hard, and you wonder if you're good at anything. But God created you for a certain reason, and He gave you unique gifts and talents.

God makes every one of us on purpose. He closely watches over us as He creates us with love and care. Let's praise God for making us in such an amazing and wonderful way!

EXPLORE MORE: What did God tell the prophet Jeremiah? Read Jeremiah 1:5 to find out.

God made me.

DID YOU KNOW?
Babies start out about the size of a poppy seed. By the time they are ready to be born, they are the size of a watermelon!

God's Greatness Is Unfathomable

Great is the Lord and most worthy of praise; his greatness no one can fathom. —Psalm 145:3 NIV

Unfathomable is a difficult word to spell, and it's also tough to say! It's a bit of a tongue twister—just try saying it three times! *Unfathomable* is one of those words that we don't use much anymore, but it has an important meaning. To fathom something means that you can understand it. You can fathom (or understand) that if you put a cup of water in the freezer, it will turn to ice. You can fathom that when you mix blue and yellow paint, the paint will turn green. You can fathom that when you wash dirt off your hands with soap and water, your hands will be clean.

Unfathomable means the opposite. It means that something is beyond what our minds can understand. The Bible says that God's greatness is unfathomable. He is greater than we can understand or imagine. He is great enough to create the world with His words and keep it going. God's wisdom is unfathomable. He knows everything there is to know and is wiser than the wisest man who ever lived. God's love is unfathomable. He loves you enough to send His son, Jesus, to die for you. No one loves you more than God does. His forgiveness is unfathomable too. No matter what we do wrong, and no matter how many times we sin, He will keep forgiving us.

TALK TO GOD
Thank God that He loves you more than you can even understand.

God created us with minds that can understand many things. But there are some things about God that are unfathomable. When we can't understand everything there is to know about God, all we need to do is believe it's true. God's greatness is so great because it is unfathomable.

EXPLORE MORE: According to 1 Chronicles 29:11, why is God great? And according to Hebrews 11:3, what helps us to understand that God created the world with His words?

DID YOU KNOW?
The three hardest subjects for people to understand are quantum physics, thermodynamics, and rocket science.

I believe in God's greatness.

Naming the Stars

He counts the stars and calls them all by name. —Psalm 147:4 NLT

On the fourth day of creation, God set two great lights in the heavens to shine down on the earth and separate the light from the darkness. He made the sun to rule over the day and the moon to rule over the night. In Genesis 1:16 it says, "He also made the stars."

Psalm 147 speaks of God's power and control over nature. God covers the heavens with clouds and sends rain to the earth. He makes green grass grow on the mountains. He sends snow like white wool and scatters frost over the ground like ashes. He rains hail down from heaven like stones, and parts of earth freeze over with ice and snow. But then—at God's command—the snow melts and warm winds thaw the ice.

> **TALK TO GOD**
> Ask God to help you shine like a star to bring glory to Him.

Psalm 147 has many great verses about God and nature, but one that stands out is today's Bible verse, "He counts the stars and calls them all by name." We learn in Genesis that God created the stars, and this verse tells us more. Since there are billions and billions of stars, it would be impossible for us to count them. But it's not impossible for God. He not only counts the stars, He gives every star a name.

God must love the stars to count them and name them all. But He loves you even more. God created the stars so we can look into the nighttime sky and enjoy their twinkling lights as we think about His greatness. Every star that God created reflects His glory and majesty. Every person was created by God, too. And that includes *you*! Since God made you in His image with a soul to worship Him, you can shine with His glory just by being you.

EXPLORE MORE: What does 1 Corinthians 15:41 say about the sun, moon, and stars?

God's glory shines in the stars.

> **DID YOU KNOW?**
> The hottest stars look white or blue. Cooler stars look red or orange.

Praise the Lord with Music

Let everything that breathes praise the Lord. Praise the Lord!
—Psalm 150:6 ICB

Psalm 150 is the last chapter in the book of Psalms. The first verse tells us to praise God in His Temple and in His mighty heavens—which is a way of saying we can praise God anywhere. The second verse tells us to praise God because He is strong and great. The rest of the psalm lists different instruments we can use to praise God. From trumpets and harps to tambourines and flutes, the instruments the Israelites used to make music are listed as ways to praise God.

For thousands of years, praising God with musical instruments has helped people enjoy worshiping God. Music makes us feel happy and energetic. When people hear music, it's hard to sit still. Some people clap their hands, tap their feet, or get up and dance. Music made with instruments like a violin or harp can be soft and smooth. But music from trumpet blasts and crashing cymbals is loud and strong.

TALK TO GOD
Sing a song to God to worship Him.

This psalm shows us that God loves hearing our worship with all kinds of instruments. Do you like to bang on drums, blow a horn, or strum a guitar? Maybe you like shaking a tambourine or playing the piano. Whatever way you enjoy making music, your instruments create a beautiful melody for God.

If you don't play an instrument, you can use the one God gave you—your voice! And whether you sing in tune or a little bit off key, it's still music to God's ears. The last verse in this psalm says, "Let everything that breathes praise the Lord." If you have breath in your lungs, you can praise the Lord today!

EXPLORE MORE: Read 2 Chronicles 5:13–14 to find out what instruments were played when the ark of the Lord was brought to the temple.

DID YOU KNOW?
Until the 1800s, the pipe organ was the only musical instrument allowed in churches.

I will praise God with music.

Get Wisdom

If you really want to gain knowledge, you must begin by having respect for the Lord. But foolish people hate wisdom and instruction. —Proverbs 1:7 NIrV

Do grown-ups ever remind you to make wise choices? You've probably heard that many times! It's important to make wise choices because they can keep you from making a mistake that might hurt you or someone else. Wise choices can help you live a safer and happier life. Unwise choices can bring problems and sadness.

No one is perfect, and everyone will make an unwise choice now and then—even grown-ups! But it's important to gain wisdom and understanding so we can make better choices at home, at school, or wherever we are.

Do you remember the stories you read about King Solomon? He asked God for wisdom, and God answered his prayer. Solomon knew that having wisdom would help him to be a good king. Solomon wrote many chapters in the book of Proverbs, which is often called "the book of wisdom."

In the first chapter of Proverbs, the verses explain why the book was written. The purpose of Proverbs is to help people gain wisdom, knowledge, and understanding so they can make good choices and do what is right and fair. Some of the verses warn against listening to people who want you to do something you know is wrong. Following them will only bring trouble.

Proverbs 1:7 says loving and respecting God is the beginning of knowledge. When we love and respect God, we will want to learn more about Him and how He wants us to live. The more we learn about God, the wiser we will be. Foolish people don't care about knowing God or having wisdom, but wise people do. Which do you think is best?

TALK TO GOD
Ask God to give you lots of wisdom so you can make good choices.

EXPLORE MORE: What good advice can you find in Proverbs 1:8–9?

DID YOU KNOW?
The book of Proverbs has thirty-one chapters, and some people like to read one a day for a whole month.

Knowing God makes me wise.

Looking for Treasure

Look for wisdom like silver. Search for it like hidden treasure. If you do this, you will understand what it means to respect the Lord, and you will come to know God. —Proverbs 2:4–5 ERV

Kids enjoy hunting for treasures. Whether it's a fun game at a birthday party, looking for a four-leaf clover, or searching for cool seashells on the beach, it's exciting to look until you find something special. A treasure is something we value because it is important to us. It's something we may want to keep for a long time. The Bible says that wisdom is a treasure. That's because wisdom is important and it has great value.

Proverbs 2:4 says to look for wisdom like you would look for silver, and to search for it like it's a hidden treasure. Do you know what it means to search for wisdom? It means that you spend time learning more about God by reading the Bible and praying. You can read books of devotions or Bible storybooks that help you know more about how God wants us to live. And when you go to a church that teaches from the Bible, you will also get to know God better.

TALK TO GOD
Thank God for giving you the treasure of wisdom.

You don't have to search long and hard to find wisdom. Proverbs 2:6 says, "The Lord gives wisdom; from his mouth come knowledge and understanding." Do you want more wisdom? Then just do like King Solomon did and ask God to give it to you. Having wisdom will help you live the way God wants you to live. And once you start gaining wisdom, you can keep asking and looking for more!

EXPLORE MORE: How did David describe God's Word in Psalm 12:6?

DID YOU KNOW?
Some people, called metal detectorists, like hunting for treasures with their own metal detectors. They find coins and other valuable items at beaches, outdoor markets, parks, and stadiums.

Wisdom from God is a valuable treasure you will want to find and keep forever.

Straight Paths

Trust in the Lord with all your heart. Do not depend on your own understanding. In all your ways obey him. Then he will make your paths smooth and straight. —Proverbs 3:5–6 NIrV

Have you ever gone hiking on a trail that had lots of twists and turns? Maybe it was bumpy with tree roots and rocks. It can be very challenging to hike on a trail like that! Do you think it would be easier to walk along a path that was smooth and straight? The answer, of course, is yes!

Some people compare the way you live your life to walking on a path. You might hear phrases such as, "life is like a journey" or "the path of life." When someone talks about life's path, it can be about the choices you make or the dreams and goals you have. Are you on the path to becoming a good scientist, nurse, or mathematician? Maybe your path is taking you on a musical or artistic journey. Do you have sports on your path of life? Or maybe your path is leading you to help people with special needs. These are all good things, but no matter what path or journey you are on, it's important to ask God to guide you and lead the way.

TALK TO GOD
Ask God to help you stay on the smooth and straight path for your life.

Kids have many years to decide what they want to do or where they want to go. It's okay if you change your mind many times and try different things along the way. The important thing is to keep trusting God and asking Him to lead you on the right path. When we choose to do things our own way, we can get on a bumpy and twisted path. But when we follow God's way, He will make our paths smooth and straight.

EXPLORE MORE: What promise does God give us in Psalm 32:8?

I will trust God to lead me.

DID YOU KNOW?
Lumpy Bumpy is the name of a trail in Allamuchy Mountain North State Park in New Jersey. The trail is popular with bikers and hikers and gets more difficult the farther you go.

Gentle Words

A gentle answer turns anger away. But mean words stir up anger.
—Proverbs 15:1 NIrV

Has someone ever told you to be gentle? Being gentle means you are careful in the way you handle something. If you're petting a puppy, holding a baby, or planting a flower, it's important to be gentle. You wouldn't want to hurt the puppy or baby by being too rough. And if you're not gentle with a flower, it could break in half.

Did you know you can be gentle with your words? The way we talk to others can help them or hurt them. When you're gentle with your words, you can help someone who's having a hard day and make them feel better. But when you are rough with your words, you can hurt them and make them feel sad.

TALK TO GOD
Ask God to help you speak gentle words.

Proverbs 15 talks about how we use our words. The first verse says when someone is angry, we can encourage them to be calm by saying something kind. But if we say something mean, it just makes that person angrier. Another verse says that wise people speak words that are good, but unwise people speak words that are foolish.

In verse 4, it compares gentle words to a tree that gives life. Did you know that trees help us to live? Trees give us oxygen and help clean the air. They give us shade to keep us cool on a hot day, and they give us oranges, apples, and pears for a healthy snack.

Our gentle words are like that. We won't grow fruit or give shade with our words, but our words can make others have a happy heart and put a smile on their face. And that makes them feel full of life!

EXPLORE MORE: What does Proverbs 12:18 say about our words?

DID YOU KNOW?
Some of the gentlest animals are doves, sheep, dolphins, and giant pandas.

My gentle words can help others.

Peace at the Table

It is better to eat a dry crust of bread in peace and quiet than to eat a big dinner in a house full of fighting. —Proverbs 17:1 NIrV

In some homes, families sit around a table to eat dinner. It's an important time to connect with each other and talk about what happened during the day. Some families go around the table and give each person a chance to talk. They might share something fun or exciting that happened that day. Some families play a game called "sweet and sour" where they share one good thing and one not-so-good thing.

Talking about your day helps everyone know how to support and encourage each other. If you find out your brother or sister got a good grade on a test you can say, "Good job!" If someone had a bad day, you could give them a hug.

Talking about your day at dinner can be really fun, but it's not fun when there's arguing and fighting at the table. Brothers and sisters don't always get along, and adults can have disagreements too. When this happens, you may not even feel like eating. Today's Bible verse from Proverbs talks about that. You wouldn't want to eat dry bread for dinner, but this verse says that it's better to eat a dry crust of bread in peace than to eat a big dinner where people are fighting.

TALK TO GOD
Ask God to help your family have happy and peaceful meals together.

It's hard to know what to do if people in your family are not being kind to each other, but you can ask God to help you be a good example and not be the one who starts a quarrel. You can ask your brother or sister about their day or thank the person who made dinner for you. And if you see delicious food on the table you can say, "Pass the potatoes, please!"

EXPLORE MORE: What does Proverbs 17:14 say about starting a quarrel?

I will be kind at the dinner table.

DID YOU KNOW?
Studies have shown that kids who eat meals with their family are happier and get better grades in school.

Be Good to Yourself

The person who gets wisdom is good to himself. And the one who has understanding will succeed. —Proverbs 19:8 ICB

It's good to be good to others because it's a way we can share God's love. You can donate groceries to a food shelter so hungry people can get food. You can give your too-tight shoes to a kid with smaller feet. But did you know you can be good to yourself too? The Bible says when you gain wisdom, you are good to yourself. That may sound like you're being selfish, but when it comes to getting wisdom, it's good to get as much as you can!

Getting wisdom from God's Word is a way that you can be good to yourself. Wisdom from the Bible will help you be a better, happier person and live the way God wants you to live. Wisdom helps you make good choices, and good choices are good for you and everyone around you.

Today's verse from Proverbs 19 also says that people who have understanding will succeed—so you want to get some of that understanding for yourself too! If you understand how to be kind to others, it can make others happy. If you understand how to be patient, it will help when you have to wait for something. And if you understand that God listens to your prayers, you will pray more often. But the best understanding you can get is to understand how much God loves you!

Getting wisdom and understanding doesn't happen all at once. Just as it takes time to grow up, it takes time to learn about how God wants us to live. As you grow and learn, be good to yourself and get all the wisdom and understanding you can!

TALK TO GOD
Ask God to help you learn more about Him and to give you wisdom and understanding.

EXPLORE MORE: Proverbs 16:16 says wisdom and understanding are better than something very valuable. Open your Bible to find out what it is.

DID YOU KNOW?
Maya Angelou, an American author, once said, "Do the best you can until you know better. Then when you know better, do better."

I will be good to myself.

A Good Name

It is better to be respected than to be rich. A good name is worth more than silver or gold. —Proverbs 22:1 ERV

What is your name? Were you named after someone in your family, like a parent or grandparent? Maybe your parents chose your name because they like what it means. Some kids have names that are more common, and some have unique names, but everyone has a name because your name lets others know who you are.

Today's Bible verse says that it's better to have a good name than to be rich. The "good name" in this verse is not about having a name that sounds nice. It's about having a good reputation. That means people respect the kind of person you are.

TALK TO GOD
Ask God to help you have a good name by the way you treat others.

Kids who are bullies do not have a good reputation, and other kids do not respect them. When someone hears their name, they think of how that person is mean. But when someone is kind and caring, that person has a good name because others think about their kindness when they hear their name.

No one can be perfect all the time, and sometimes you might say or do something that hurts someone else. When that happens, you can say you're sorry and ask them to forgive you. Doing the right thing when you make a mistake gives you a good name too.

Whether your name is popular or one that's not very common, you can ask God to help you treat others with kindness. And besides the name you were given when you were born, you can also have another name. When you believe in Jesus as your Savior, you have the name "Christian." That's not just a good name, it's the best name you can have!

EXPLORE MORE: How could following the instructions in Romans 12:9–13 help you to have a good name?

I want to have a good name.

DID YOU KNOW?
Some people have the same first and last name. Some of the most common are: Thomas Thomas, James James, Santiago Santiago, Rose Rose, Ruth Ruth, and Grace Grace.

Small and Wise

There are four things on the earth that are small but very wise.
—Proverbs 30:24 ERV

We don't know much about Agur, the son of Jakeh, but his words in Proverbs 30 show that he was amazed by God's power over creation. He knew he could never understand how great God is. In verse 4 he asks, "Who has ever gone up to heaven and come back down? Who gathered the winds in his hand? Who can gather up all the water in his lap? Who set the limits for the world?" He knew only God can do that!

Agur was also amazed at how God created animals to have habits and abilities to help them survive. In verses 24-28 he lists four animals that are small but wise. The first one is the ant. Ants are tiny, yet they are able to store up food for the winter. The next animal is the badger that makes its home in the rocks to be sheltered from wind, rain, and other animals. Then he mentions the locusts. They have no king but march like an army and work together. The fourth animal is the lizard. Lizards are small enough to catch with your hands, but they can be found in a king's palace. The more Agur looked at everything God created, the more amazed he was.

The wonders of God's creation are all around us. Like Agur, we can be amazed at the earth, the sky, and the waters God put into place. We can watch bees buzzing between flowers, squirrels gathering acorns, and robins carrying twigs to build a nest—small and wise—just the way God made them. All of God's creation shows how great He is. Aren't you amazed?

EXPLORE MORE: Read Proverbs 30:29-31. What four things walk with pride?

TALK TO GOD
Tell God something about His creation that amazes you.

DID YOU KNOW?
Rock badgers (also called hyraxes) are small, but they have big appetites and gobble up plant food very quickly. They also have excellent vision that helps them see birds or animals in the distance.

I am amazed at God's creation.

A Time for Everything

For everything there is a season, a time for every activity under heaven. —Ecclesiastes 3:1 NLT

Do your parents ever tell you it's time to get up and eat breakfast? If you're tired, you'd probably rather stay under the covers. And then when it's time for bed, most kids wish they could stay up longer, but they need to sleep so they will have energy for the next day. Many of our activities are based on time, which is why we have clocks and watches. Even our phones tell us what time it is.

King Solomon talks about time in Ecclesiastes 3. He says there is a time for everything like being born, planting crops, crying, laughing, and hugging. He says there is a time to speak and a time to be quiet. Most of us go about our day looking at the clock now and then to see what time it is. But the verses in this chapter are not talking about when it's time to eat breakfast or go to bed. The verses in this chapter remind us that God is in control of our lives, and everything happens according to His time.

TALK TO GOD
Ask God to help you be patient and wait for His perfect timing.

Waiting for God's timing can be hard—especially when you're a kid. Maybe you're waiting to grow a few more inches or waiting for the day when you can drive a car, go to college, or choose a career. But while you're waiting to grow up, God has good things for you to enjoy right now. Now is the time for you to enjoy being part of your family. It's time for you to learn new things in school. And it's always the right time to learn more about God and how much He loves you.

EXPLORE MORE: What can you learn about God from Ecclesiastes 3:11?

DID YOU KNOW?
Watches were invented in the late 1400s and were usually worn on a chain around a person's neck. In the 1600s, pocket watches became popular with men, and wristwatches were invented around 1812.

God's timing is always right.

Two Are Better than One

Two people are better than one. They get more done by working together. —Ecclesiastes 4:9 ICB

When God created Adam, He said it was not good for him to be alone, so God created Eve to be his helper. When God sent Moses to Egypt to free the Israelites, God chose Aaron to go with him. When God told King Solomon it was time to build the temple, it took thousands of people more than forty years to build it. The Bible is full of stories that show how people lived and worked together because it's God's idea.

It would be boring and lonely to live without your family, friends, and neighbors. We need other people to play with, to work with, and to help us. Today's Bible verse says that two people are better than one, and it takes two people to do many things. It takes two people to sing a duet. It takes two people to play a game of checkers. And if you want to give someone a hug, you can't just hug the air!

God created you to be part of a family, and your family is part of a community. Have you noticed that when you work on something with other people, the job gets finished sooner and it's also more fun? If you help your parents plant flowers, they might have time to play a game with you. If your family cleans the house together, it won't take as long. And when it comes to setting the table, the more people who help, the sooner you can eat!

Working alone is not always fun. But working with others can be fun while you get the job done!

EXPLORE MORE: What does Romans 12:4–5 say about how we all work together?

TALK TO GOD
Think of someone who helps you work or play, and thank God for that person.

DID YOU KNOW?
Checkers is one of the oldest two-player games. In Europe the game is called draughts (pronounced *drafts*). In 1847, the first Checkers Champion Award was given.

Working together is better than working alone.

Enjoy Every Day

It is good to be alive to enjoy the light of day.
—Ecclesiastes 11:7 ICB

Is morning your favorite time of day? For many people, it is. Watching the sunrise and seeing light shine through your window is a great way to start your day. In many places around the world, every new day begins with light, and light makes people happy. When it's light you can go outside to play. You can watch birds flying through the air, or giggle at squirrels chasing each other up a tree. Light helps you see the world around you and enjoy God's beautiful creation.

King Solomon reminds us in today's Bible verse that it's good to be alive and we should enjoy every day. It's true that some days are better than others. It can be hard to enjoy a day if you're not feeling well. And if you're having a problem with a friend, that can be hard too. It's important to remember that not every day is going to be a great day. What's important is to look for something good in each day and thank God that He has given you another day of life. That's how we find joy no matter what's going on.

TALK TO GOD
Think of something you are enjoying today, and thank God for that.

In verse 9 of this chapter, Solomon tells young people to enjoy every minute of being young. You won't be young forever, so enjoy being a kid while you're still a kid! Build towers with blocks, play in the sand, and tell silly jokes. Every day is a gift from God, and He makes each day for you to enjoy. No matter what kind of day you are having today, try to enjoy it—even just for a moment!

EXPLORE MORE: Read Psalm 118:24. Why is this a good verse to read every morning?

Every day is a gift from God.

DID YOU KNOW?
Some cities in Alaska get between nineteen and twenty-two hours of daylight in the summer and only two to five hours of daylight in the winter.

Sing in the Spring

Look, winter is past, the rains have come and gone. The flowers are blooming in the fields. It's time to sing! Listen, the doves have returned. —Song of Solomon 2:11–12 ERV

In many parts of the world, people look forward to the spring season. If they live in places where winters are long and cold, signs of spring make them happy. When snow begins to melt and singing birds return from warmer places, it means that spring will soon arrive.

Warmer weather, sunshine, and spring rains make flowers pop out of the ground and dot the land with bright colors. Animals that spent the long winter months hibernating come out of their burrows and run around the earth. Green leaves fill the bare trees, and everything comes back to life. It's no wonder that people love spring!

When God created the world, He created the sun and moon to give us days and months and seasons. He is a God of order, and we can be sure that spring will always follow winter. Springtime brings new life, and that gives hope and joy to the world—just like Jesus does.

God sent Jesus to the world to give a new life to everyone who believes in Him. When we believe in Jesus as our Savior, we become children of God. We get a new life on earth filled with the Holy Spirit, and we have a life that will last forever in heaven. Sometimes things in this world are hard and sad. But with Jesus, we can always have hope and joy for better days ahead. And just as the doves sing their songs in the spring, we can sing with joy every season of the year because of the new life we have in Jesus.

TALK TO GOD
Thank God for springtime that brings new life on earth, and for Jesus who gives us eternal life in heaven.

DID YOU KNOW?
In North America the spring months are March, April, and May, but in Australia they are September, October, and November.

EXPLORE MORE: Read Zechariah 10:1. What can we ask God for in the spring season?

Jesus gives new life.

As White as Snow

"Even though your sins are bright red, they will be as white as snow. Even though they are deep red, they will be white like wool."
—Isaiah 1:18 NIrV

Isaiah was a prophet to the people of Judah for more than fifty years. We can read his writings in the book of Isaiah, which is one of the longest books in the Bible. The name Isaiah means "the Lord saves." Isaiah brought messages from God to the people of Judah so they would be sorry for their sins and follow God.

TALK TO GOD
Ask God to help you follow Him, and thank Him for forgiving your sins.

God told Isaiah He was angry that the people of Judah no longer obeyed Him. They pretended to serve Him by celebrating festivals and making sacrifices, but God could see that their hearts were far from Him. Isaiah gave the people strong warnings about what would happen if they continued to sin against God.

Even though God was angry with their sinful ways, He was always willing to forgive them. Their sins were like a deep red stain, but God said He would remove their sins if they agreed to follow and obey Him. God promised to make their hearts pure and clean. He would wash the stains of their sin and make them as white as freshly fallen snow or like white wool.

God wants us to follow and obey Him, just like He wanted the people of Judah to follow Him. Turning away from God leads us away from Him and the good plans He has for us. But when we follow God, He will shower His love on us and give us the blessings that come with being close to Him. If you love and follow God, He will forgive your sins. And no matter how big the stain is, He can make it as white as snow.

EXPLORE MORE: What did God tell the people to do in Isaiah 1:16–17?

God will wash away my sins and make me clean.

DID YOU KNOW?
Isaiah's words are quoted in the New Testament more than any other prophet. Many of his messages are about Jesus, the Messiah.

God Calls Isaiah

Then I heard the Lord asking, "Whom should I send as a messenger to this people? Who will go for us?" I said, "Here I am. Send me."
—Isaiah 6:8 NLT

In Isaiah 6, Isaiah describes a vision of seeing the Lord sitting on a high throne. His robe filled the temple, and heavenly creatures with six wings hovered above Him. The creatures covered their faces and feet as they flew around the throne singing, "Holy, holy, holy is the Lord God Almighty." Their singing shook the doorframes, and the temple filled with smoke.

Isaiah was frightened because he knew he was a sinful man in the presence of Almighty God. Then one of the creatures flew over to the altar and picked up a burning coal. He touched the coal to Isaiah's lips and said, "This coal has touched your lips. Now your guilt is removed, and your sins are forgiven."

TALK TO GOD
Ask God to help you tell others about Him.

The Lord spoke to Isaiah and said, "Whom should I send as a messenger to this people? Who will go?"

Isaiah answered, "Here I am. Send me."

God had a special purpose for Isaiah's life. God called him to be a messenger, and Isaiah said yes. Isaiah knew he was not a perfect person, and he was not holy like God. But when people are willing to say yes to God and serve Him, God will give them the power to do what He wants them to do.

We are all called to be God's messengers and share His love with the people in our lives. Telling someone that God loves them is the best message we can give. It's not always easy to tell someone about God, but if you ask God, He will give you the right words at the right time.

DID YOU KNOW?

The heavenly creatures mentioned in Isaiah 6 are also known as seraphim. They are angels who worship God all the time.

EXPLORE MORE: What did God say to Moses when he was afraid to deliver a message to his people in Egypt? Read Exodus 4:10–12 for the answer.

I can be God's messenger.

Many Names for Jesus

This will happen when the special child is born. God will give us a son who will be responsible for leading the people. —Isaiah 9:6 ERV

Isaiah lived about seven hundred years before Jesus was born, but God gave him messages that came true when He sent Jesus to earth. Isaiah shared this message: "The Lord will still show you this sign: The young woman is pregnant and will give birth to a son. She will name him Immanuel" (Isaiah 7:14).

Do you know who God was talking about in this message? The young woman was Mary, and the Son was Jesus. The name Immanuel means, "God with us." It was an important name given to Jesus because when Jesus lived on earth, He was God in a human body.

TALK TO GOD
Thank God that the Bible tells us what Jesus was going to be like before He was even born.

Isaiah wrote about other names Jesus would have too. His name would be Wonderful Counselor because He would be kind and loving and teach people about God. He would be called Powerful God because He would heal people who were sick, cast out evil spirits, and raise people from the dead. He would be called Father Who Lives Forever, because He would be a Father to all who believe in Him. And His name would be Prince of Peace because He would bring peace to the world (Isaiah 9:6).

Isaiah said God's Son would rule with love and fairness forever. When Jesus was on earth, He loved everyone and taught them how to love others. Now He rules from heaven, and someday He will come back to rule on earth—forever. God gave these messages to Isaiah, who gave them to the people. They were written down so that hundreds of years later, when Jesus was born, people would know He was the Messiah. Today we can read these messages in the Bible and believe that Jesus is the Son God promised to send.

EXPLORE MORE: Read Luke 1:30–33 to learn of another name Jesus would be called.

Jesus's names tell us who He is.

DID YOU KNOW?
There are more than fifty different names for Jesus in the Bible.

God's Spirit Is in Jesus

A branch will grow from a stump of a tree that was cut down. So a new king will come from the family of Jesse. —Isaiah 11:1 ICB

Many verses in the book of Isaiah talk about Jesus. We know from other Bible passages that Jesus would be born into the family of David, and today's verse from Isaiah 11 says it again. The "branch" from the family of Jesse, David's father, is Jesus, and He would bring new life to a dying kingdom.

In this chapter, the verses tell us how Jesus would have God's Spirit in Him and be filled with wisdom. When Jesus was on earth, He spoke with wisdom and had the right answer for everything. We can learn from His wise words in the Bible and ask Him to give us wisdom as we live and learn.

Jesus was also filled with understanding. He understood the needs of people who followed Him, and He understands our needs too. Jesus wants us to come to Him with our problems because He understands how we feel and has the power to help us.

TALK TO GOD
Ask God to give you wisdom as you read the Bible to learn more about Jesus.

Verse 3 says that Jesus would not judge people by the way they look. He would find joy in obeying God and always do what was right and fair. When Jesus was on earth, He was kind to the poor and loved everyone. He healed people who couldn't walk. He placed His hands on people with skin diseases to make them better. He helped a blind beggar to see, and let little children come to Him. Jesus still loves people today and wants us to follow Him just as we are.

God gave Isaiah these words to write so people would know that Jesus is the Son of God, filled with the Holy Spirit, who came to save us from sin and teach us how to live.

DID YOU KNOW?
A tree stump can grow back to a full-size tree if the roots are still alive. If there are enough nutrients left in the roots, a sprout will grow from the stump.

EXPLORE MORE: What does Luke 2:39–40 tell us about Jesus when He was a young boy?

Jesus is filled with God's Spirit.

My Strength and My Song

Sing to the Lord, for he has done wonderful things. Make known his praise around the world. —Isaiah 12:5 NLT

The Israelites sang a song of praise to God after they fled from Egypt and crossed the Red Sea. They were filled with joy to see God's power as He parted the waters and led them safely through the sea on dry ground. In Exodus 15:2, Moses and the people sang, "The Lord is my strength and my song; he has given me victory."

> **TALK TO GOD**
> Praise God for something great that He does for you.

When Hezekiah was the king of Judah, Isaiah told him that the Babylonians would come to take some of the people with all their treasures and bring them to Babylon. They would live in Babylon for seventy years, then God would allow them to return to their homeland. The years in Babylon would be long and hard. But when they returned back to Judah, they would praise God with a song of praise just like their ancestors had done. Someday they would sing almost the same words, "The Lord God is my strength and my song; he has given me victory" (Isaiah 12:2).

We don't have to wait to praise God until He does something great in our lives, because He already has. We have many reasons to sing songs to God, just like the Israelites did. God promises to love us and bless us. He protects us from evil. He is always with us. He gives us wisdom and understanding. And He gives us salvation through Jesus His Son. If God is your strength and your song, then do what today's Bible verse reminds us to do—praise the Lord for the wonderful things He does and let the whole world know.

EXPLORE MORE: Read Psalm 95:1-2. What name for God is given in verse 1?

God is my strength and my song.

DID YOU KNOW?
The people of Judah returned home from Babylon about nine hundred years after their ancestors crossed the Red Sea.

Trust in the Lord

But the people who trust the Lord will become strong again. They will be able to rise up as an eagle in the sky. They will run without needing rest. They will walk without becoming tired. —Isaiah 40:31 ICB

Isaiah wrote the verses in Isaiah 40 to remind the people of Judah how great and powerful God is. He is like a shepherd who cares for His people. He created the whole world and everything in it. He measures the ocean with His hand and stretches out the sky like a tent. He knows how much the mountains weigh. He leads out the stars and calls them by name, so not one star is missing.

Isaiah told the people that God is greater than any ruler, and no one can understand how wise He is. He never gets tired or weak, and He will live forever. So if God is greater and more powerful than anyone can understand, then He could surely help them with their problems.

TALK TO GOD
Think of a problem you have and ask God to give you strength to work it out.

The words God gave Isaiah to write were not only for the people of Judah. God's Word is for everyone. Today's Bible verse says to trust the Lord, so we can find new strength and soar like eagles. That doesn't mean we'll be able to fly, but it means we can trust God to help us with our problems, so we don't need to worry. Sometimes life can be hard, and things happen that we don't understand. Problems and worries can make us tired and weak, and sometimes they make us sad. But when we talk to God about our problems and ask Him to help us, He will make us feel strong.

Do you want to have the strength of an eagle? Then give your worries to God and flex your muscles! God will give you hope and joy for the days ahead.

EXPLORE MORE: What does Isaiah 40:28–29 tell us about God?

DID YOU KNOW?
There are more than sixty species of eagles. The bald eagle is native to North America, and many other species can be found in Asia and Africa.

I will trust in God to give me strength.

Called by Name

Now this is what the Lord says. He created you, people of Jacob. He formed you, people of Israel. He says, "Don't be afraid, because I have saved you. I have called you by name, and you are mine." —Isaiah 43:1 ICB

Have you ever gotten separated from your parents in a crowd? Maybe you looked around trying to find them and felt scared and worried. Then you heard someone call your name above the noise. And as soon as you heard your name, you knew it was one of your parents and you were safe, and everything was okay.

When someone calls you by name, it's because they know who you are. That's the picture Isaiah gives us in chapter 43. God called the Israelites by their name because they belonged to Him.

Isaiah said God would get the Israelites through hard times like crossing through deep waters and rivers without drowning. When Isaiah said this, the Israelites remembered God parting the Red Sea when the Egyptians chased their ancestors hundreds of years before, and stopping the waters of the Jordan River so they could enter the promised land. Isaiah also said God would get the Israelites through hard times like walking through fire without getting burned. As we will see later in the book of Daniel, this story would become part of the Israelites' history when three men survived being thrown into a fiery furnace.

TALK TO GOD
Ask God to be with you when you go through hard times, and thank Him that He knows your name.

If God can protect His people from deep waters and scorching flames, then He can help us with our problems too. He is our Father in heaven, and we are His children. He knows us better than we know ourselves. We belong to Him, and He calls us by name. When you feel afraid and things around you seem too big to handle, look for God by talking to Him and reading His Word. He will be there!

EXPLORE MORE: What promise does God give us in Psalm 91:14–16?

God calls me by name.

DID YOU KNOW?
Dale Carnegie, an American writer and speaker, said, "Remember that a person's name is to that person the sweetest and most important sound in any language."

A Light for the Nations

And now he says, "You are a very important servant to me. You must bring back to me the tribes of Jacob. You must bring back the people of Israel who are still alive. But I have something else for you to do that is even more important: I will make you a light for the other nations. You will show people all over the world the way to be saved." —Isaiah 49:6 ERV

One of the most amazing things about the Bible is that it is one big story. It's not a bunch of separate stories bound together in the same book. The things that happen in the Old Testament are part of the story of the New Testament, and the other way around. Isaiah 49 is one of the places where we see a connection between the Old and New Testaments in the big story of God's Word.

In this part of Isaiah, God is talking about the Messiah who would come to save Israel. And God tells us that He had an even bigger plan than that. The Savior of the Israelites would be the Savior of the entire world! God said, "You will show people all over the world the way to be saved."

TALK TO GOD
Thank God for sending Jesus to save you and people from all over the world.

By reading stories in the New Testament, we learn the Messiah is Jesus. And we know that Jesus didn't just come to save the descendants of Israel—He came to save all of us. As we go through more of the Bible, we will see the ways Jesus reached out to people who weren't Israelites and how He helped His disciples get ready to tell people all over the world about Him.

From the beginning, God's plan was for Jesus to save people from every part of the world. God said Jesus is a light to all the nations. Aren't you glad that Jesus is shining His light in your life? We all get to be a part of God's big plan by believing in Jesus as the Savior of the world.

DID YOU KNOW?
The Bible is the most widely read book all around the world. It has been translated into more than seven hundred languages.

EXPLORE MORE: What did Jesus tell His disciples in John 14:6?

Jesus came to save people all over the world.

The Suffering Servant

After his suffering he will see the light, and he will be satisfied with what he experienced. The Lord says, "My servant, who always does what is right, will make his people right with me; he will take away their sins." —Isaiah 53:11 ERV

A prophecy is when God tells someone about something that will happen in the future. God told Isaiah many prophecies to write down. Some of the prophecies in the book of Isaiah are about what would happen to the Israelites for disobeying God. And some prophecies describe what Jesus would be like and what He would do when He came to earth.

Isaiah 53 is one of the chapters that is all about Jesus. All twelve verses tell us about Jesus hundreds of years before He was born. God told Isaiah that there would be nothing special about the way Jesus looked to make us notice Him. He said that people would make fun of Him, and they wouldn't accept Him. He would also know what it was like to go through pain and sadness.

TALK TO GOD
Thank God for His plan to send Jesus to save you. And thank Jesus for loving you so much that He died for you.

And then God told Isaiah exactly why Jesus was coming and what would happen to Him. Isaiah said, "But he was being punished for what we did. He was crushed because of our guilt. He took the punishment we deserved, and this brought us peace. We were healed because of his pain."

God said His Servant, Jesus, would take away our sins by giving His life for us.

Jesus was willing to go through all that pain and suffering because He loves you. It was worth it to Him to be mistreated and hurt because it would give all of us the chance to be made right with God. It's amazing that God told us about that before it even happened. And it's beautiful that Jesus loves us so much!

EXPLORE MORE: What did Jesus say about giving His life for us in John 10:17–18?

Jesus makes me right with God.

DID YOU KNOW?
Some people who study the Bible believe there are more than three hundred prophecies about Jesus in the Old Testament.

Higher Thoughts

"For just as the heavens are higher than the earth, so my ways are higher than your ways and my thoughts higher than your thoughts." —Isaiah 55:9 NLT

There are some things that are hard for us to understand. Like the Milky Way galaxy is about 100,000 light years from one end to the other. Or that scientists still don't know exactly why we yawn and why yawns are contagious. Our human brains just can't understand certain things. But do you know who understands everything? God does! That's because He is the one who created it all and decided how things should work. God's mind is much bigger and more powerful than ours will ever be. That's why He's in control of the universe and we aren't.

Just like there are things in the world we don't understand, there may be times when things happen in your life that you don't understand either. Like when someone you love gets sick or when you have to move to a new place away from all your friends. And that's when it's important to remember how big God's thoughts are. He doesn't see things the way we do. In Isaiah 55 He tells us, "My ways are higher than your ways and my thoughts higher than your thoughts."

TALK TO GOD
Thank God that He is such a big God and that His ways are higher than your ways.

The best part is that God's ways and thoughts are always good. When God spoke today's verse to Isaiah, He was talking about how He would generously forgive people who come to Him. Sometimes here on earth it can be hard to see how God's plans are good—especially if we don't understand them or like them right away. But we can trust that God sees something we don't. Just like He told Isaiah, His ways are far beyond anything we could imagine!

EXPLORE MORE: What does Psalm 40:5 say about the wonderful things God has planned for us?

DID YOU KNOW?
A human's yawn can be contagious to chimpanzees. They will yawn if they see a person yawn.

God's ways are beyond my understanding.

Words like Rain

"The words I speak are like that. They will not return to me without producing results. They will accomplish what I want them to. They will do exactly what I sent them to do." —Isaiah 55:11 NIrV

If you live near farmland that's used for crops, or if you have a garden in your backyard, you know how important water is. The rain and snow God sends bring water to the ground which helps crops to grow and produce food for us to eat. Then the water evaporates into the atmosphere, and after it cools and forms clouds, it returns to earth again. Isaiah 55:10–11 says God's words are like that. Every word that comes out of His mouth has a purpose and will not return to Him until it does exactly what He wants it to do.

TALK TO GOD
Thank God that you can always trust His Word.

When the Israelites were living in Babylon, a day was coming when they would be free. Isaiah 55:12 says, "My people, you will go out of Babylon with joy. You will be led out of it in peace. The mountains and hills will burst into song as you go. And all the trees in the fields will clap their hands." This was God's word to His people, and it would happen just like He said it would.

In the New Testament book of John, Jesus is called the Word. Jesus was the Word who came down from heaven and did not return to heaven until He did exactly what God wanted Him to do—which was die on the cross for our sins. And someday He will return to earth again to rule forever.

Like the Israelites who were set free, we are set free from sin when we believe in Jesus. Then we can live in peace, burst into song, and clap our hands with the trees.

EXPLORE MORE: Read 1 Chronicles 16:31–33. What parts of creation praise God in these verses?

God's Word always does what He wants it to do.

DID YOU KNOW?
Trees make noises as they grow, and healthy trees sound different than unhealthy trees. Trees that need water form air bubbles that make a crackling or popping sound.

No More Bad Memories

"I am creating a new heaven and a new earth. The troubles of the past will be forgotten. No one will remember them." —Isaiah 65:17 ERV

Have you ever done something you wish you could forget? Maybe you said something unkind to your sister or you disobeyed your mom and dad when they told you to clean your room. Because there is sin in the world, we all do things we shouldn't sometimes. Even when we say we're sorry for the wrong things we do, it can be hard to forget about them. Wouldn't it be nice if we got to live in a perfect world one day and not remember all the bad things that have happened?

That's exactly what God has planned! One day God will make a new heaven and a new earth, and it will be perfect without sin and bad things. He tells us in Isaiah 65, "The troubles of the past will be forgotten. No one will remember them."

One day, God wants us to live in a perfect world with Him, just like He created in the beginning. It will be a world where God will rejoice and be happy with His people. There will be no crying or sadness. God even says it will be a place that is full of joy and will make the people who live there happy. No one will hurt anyone else, and things will be done fairly. Doesn't that sound like the kind of place you'd like to live?

We don't know exactly when God will create a new heaven and a new earth, but we know it will be worth the wait. Until then, we can ask for forgiveness when we make mistakes and look forward to the wonderful things God has planned.

TALK TO GOD
Ask God to forgive you for the mistakes you make, and thank Him that one day everything bad will be wiped away.

EXPLORE MORE: Look up Isaiah 65:25. What will animals be like in the new earth?

DID YOU KNOW?

Bees have the worst memories of animals studied. They can only remember something for 2.5 seconds!

God will make a new heaven and earth.

A Prophet Who Spoke for God

Then the Lord reached out and touched my mouth and said, "Look, I have put my words in your mouth!" —Jeremiah 1:9 NLT

Have you ever had to say something that was hard to say? Maybe you had to tell your brother that you broke his toy, or you had to tell your parents that you lied. Maybe you had to tell your teacher you didn't do your homework. Some conversations can be hard and make us afraid.

Jeremiah was a prophet called by God to say some difficult things to the people of Judah and their kings. Even though his job was challenging, it was very important. The Bible tells us that before Jeremiah was even born, God chose him to be a prophet to the nations.

Jeremiah felt afraid to say the things God wanted him to say. When God first told Jeremiah what He wanted him to do, Jeremiah said, "I can't speak for you! I'm too young!" But God replied, "Don't say, 'I'm too young,' for you must go wherever I send you and say whatever I tell you. And don't be afraid of the people. I will be with you and will protect you." The Bible tells us that God put His words in Jeremiah's mouth. From that moment on, Jeremiah prophesied the things God told him.

TALK TO GOD
Ask God to help you do the things He wants you to do.

Sometimes it's hard to do the things God wants us to do. We might be afraid of what people will do or say, like Jeremiah was. As we look at more chapters in Jeremiah, we will see that Jeremiah didn't have the easiest life doing God's work.

But he never stopped loving and trusting God. God used Jeremiah in big ways for His kingdom. God will use us when we obey and trust Him too.

EXPLORE MORE: What promise did God make to Jeremiah in Jeremiah 1:18–19?

I can obey God, even when I'm afraid.

DID YOU KNOW?
Jeremiah was the son of Hilkiah, who was a priest. Jeremiah began prophesying when Josiah was king.

Jeremiah Buys a Field

"Lord and King, you have reached out your great and powerful arm. You have made the heavens and the earth. Nothing is too hard for you. You show your love to thousands of people. But you cause the sins of parents to affect even their children. Great and powerful God, your name is the Lord Who Rules Over All." —Jeremiah 32:17–18 NIrV

Jeremiah was thrown in prison because the officials didn't trust him or like what he was saying. Jeremiah told the people that kingdoms from the north would defeat Judah because of their sin.

While Jeremiah was in prison, God told him to buy a field from his cousin, Hanamel. Jeremiah bought the field and signed the papers to show he owned the land. Jeremiah had a scribe named Baruch who wrote things down for him. After Jeremiah signed the papers, he told Baruch that God said to put the papers in a clay jar so they would be protected. Jeremiah told Baruch and a group of men, "[The Lord] says, 'Houses, fields and vineyards will again be bought in this land.'" Then Jeremiah praised God for how great He is.

There were two parts to Jeremiah's message from God. The first part was that the people of Judah would be punished for disobeying God and not loving Him with all their hearts. But the second part was that God would bring them back to their home after their punishment was over. God told Jeremiah, "I have brought all this horrible trouble on these people. But now I will give them all the good things I have promised them. Once more fields will be bought in this land."

TALK TO GOD
Praise God like Jeremiah did, and tell Him how loving and powerful He is.

Because God is holy, He deserves our respect and love. When we don't honor Him, we suffer the consequences of disobeying Him. Because God is loving, He always forgives us and makes things right when we come to Him. God's love and forgiveness are greater than the consequences of our sin.

DID YOU KNOW?
Jeremiah bought his cousin's field for seventeen pieces of silver. That many silver coins weighed seven ounces or about 198 grams.

EXPLORE MORE: How does Romans 5:8 say God showed His love for us in our sin?

God's love is greater than our sin.

The Good Branch

"In those days and at that time, I will make a righteous branch sprout from David's family. He will do what is fair and right in the land. At this time Judah will be saved. The people of Jerusalem will live in safety. The branch will be named: The Lord Does What Is Right." —Jeremiah 33:15—16 ICB

As you've seen in other books of the Bible, Jesus shows up everywhere! The book of Jeremiah is no different. In Jeremiah 33, God tells us a little more about the promised Messiah, Jesus. God told Jeremiah, "The time is coming when I will do the things I promised. I made a special promise to the people of Israel and Judah." And then God starts talking about a righteous branch that would grow from David's family. God told Isaiah about this branch too. God said this "branch" would do what is fair and right. The people of Judah would be saved by this branch, and the people of Jerusalem would live in safety. The branch would be named The Lord Does What Is Right.

TALK TO GOD
Thank God that He always keeps His promises and that you can trust Him to do what He says.

God was not talking about an actual branch from a real tree. But have you ever heard of a family tree? It's a graph that shows how people are related to each other. God was saying that Jesus would be a part of King David's family tree. That's important because it shows He is part of a royal family, which means He is a King. And it shows that He was born into a human family, which means He was a real person in addition to being God.

God promised that all this would happen. He said it was as sure as how day and night always come at the right time. Then the Lord told Jeremiah, "Someone from David's family will always sit on the throne and rule the family of Israel." That person is Jesus, the King who will rule forever!

EXPLORE MORE: What did Jesus call himself in John 15:5?

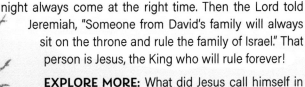

Jesus is the righteous branch.

A Muddy Well and a Good Friend

Ebed-Melek was an official in the royal palace. He was from the land of Cush. He heard that Jeremiah had been put into the well.
—Jeremiah 38:7 NIrV

Jeremiah told the people of Judah they would be captured by Babylon. This message didn't make Jeremiah very popular. Some officials heard Jeremiah's message and got angry. They went to King Zedekiah and said Jeremiah should be punished. King Zedekiah answered, "He's in your hands. I can't do anything to stop you." So the officials took Jeremiah and put him in an empty well. They lowered him down with ropes into the mud at the bottom.

There was another official in the palace named Ebed-Melek. When he heard what happened to Jeremiah, he talked to King Zedekiah. Ebed-Melek said, "My king, everything these men have done to Jeremiah is evil. They have thrown him into an empty well. Soon there won't be any more bread in the city, and he'll starve to death."

Zedekiah replied, "Take thirty men with you and lift Jeremiah out of the well before he dies."

Ebed-Melek took the men with him, and they pulled Jeremiah up with ropes. Then Jeremiah stayed in the courtyard of the guard as a prisoner.

When Ebed-Melek saw that Jeremiah was being mistreated, he spoke up. He helped Jeremiah because it was the right thing to do. It took a lot of courage for him to talk to the king and go against the other officials, but he did what was right. We don't know if Ebed-Melek and Jeremiah knew each other well, but Ebed-Melek treated Jeremiah like a true friend. We can do the same thing for the people God puts in our lives. If we see someone being mistreated, we can ask God to help us stand up for what is right.

EXPLORE MORE: Look up Matthew 22:36–40. What did Jesus say is the most important commandment?

TALK TO GOD
Ask God to help you see those who are being mistreated around you and give you courage to help them.

DID YOU KNOW?
Ebed-Melek got rags and worn-out clothes from the palace to pad the ropes for Jeremiah. That way when they pulled Jeremiah out, it didn't hurt his armpits.

I will stand up for others.

Keep Hoping

I say to myself, "The Lord is everything I will ever need. So I will put my hope in him." —Lamentations 3:24 NIrV

Did you know that Jeremiah is called the weeping prophet? That's because the message he had to tell the people of Judah was very sad. He also watched the people get captured by the Babylonians and taken away from their home. Jeremiah's job was hard, and his heart was broken for his people.

Besides writing the book of Jeremiah in the Bible, Jeremiah also wrote the book of Lamentations. The word *lament* means to cry or be sad about something. The book of Lamentations is a collection of sad songs about Judah being captured by Babylon. But in the middle of Lamentations, there is a set of verses that show us how Jeremiah never gave up hope.

Lamentations 3:22–24 says:

> The Lord loves us very much.
>> So we haven't been completely destroyed.
>> His loving concern never fails.
>
> His great love is new every morning.
>> Lord, how faithful you are!
>
> I say to myself, "The Lord is everything I will ever need.
>> So I will put my hope in him."

When you go through hard times, it's easy to feel discouraged. Sometimes you may feel just like Jeremiah—that nothing is going right and everything around you is sad. It's okay for us to be sad and for our hearts to hurt when bad things happen. But we can still have hope even in sad times. God takes care of us in good times and in bad times. His love never changes. He will always keep His promises to us, and He will never leave us. No matter how sad things get, we can always hope in Him.

EXPLORE MORE: What does Romans 5:3–5 tell us about hard times and hope?

TALK TO GOD
Thank God that we always have hope because of His good plans for us.

DID YOU KNOW?
Convoy of Hope is an organization that offers help and hope to communities around the world. They help feed kids, reach out to hurting communities, and help affected areas after natural disasters.

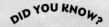

I always have hope because of God.

Ezekiel Has a Vision

From the center of the cloud came four living beings that looked
human, except that each had four faces and four wings.
—Ezekiel 1:5–6 NLT

Have you ever read something in the Bible that didn't make sense? There are some things in the Bible that are hard for us to understand—especially some of the visions God gave to prophets.

Ezekiel was a priest in Jerusalem and became a prophet to Judah while they were captives in Babylon. God gave Ezekiel visions about what would happen to Israel. A vision is like a dream God used to tell prophets what was going to happen. Some visions in the Bible use symbols, which means the things the prophet saw represent something else.

In Ezekiel 1, Ezekiel describes seeing four creatures that looked like humans, but they had four faces and four wings. One of their faces was a human face, and the others were a lion, an ox, and an eagle. Later, Ezekiel calls these creatures "cherubim." Cherubim are angels who serve God and do His work on earth. Above these creatures Ezekiel saw a man with the brightness of fire sitting on a throne. Ezekiel said, "This is what the glory of the Lord looked like to me."

TALK TO GOD
Ask God to help you see His glory in every story of the Bible.

Reading these verses may be confusing. We may not always understand everything we read in the Bible, and that's okay. We can ask the Holy Spirit to help us learn and understand more. But we know from Ezekiel that his vision showed him God's glory, and we can look for God's glory too. That's what the whole Bible is about! The next time you have a hard time understanding a Bible story, ask God to show you His glory in that story. He wants you to see it.

DID YOU KNOW?
After Adam and Eve left the garden of Eden, God used cherubim with flaming swords to guard the entrance.

EXPLORE MORE: Read Ezekiel 1:13–14 to learn more about these four creatures in Ezekiel's vision.

The Bible tells me about God's glory.

Receive and Share

Then he added, "Son of man, let all my words sink deep into your own heart first. Listen to them carefully for yourself." —Ezekiel 3:10 NLT

God came to Ezekiel and called him to be a prophet to Israel in Babylon. God told Ezekiel the people would get upset about the things Ezekiel would say, but Ezekiel didn't need to be afraid. God said, "You must give them my messages whether they listen or not." Then God filled Ezekiel's mouth with the words He wanted Ezekiel to say.

Before Ezekiel delivered God's words to the people, God told him to do something very important. He said, "Let all my words sink deep into your own heart first. Listen to them carefully for yourself. Then go to your people." Why do you think God told Ezekiel to do that?

TALK TO GOD
Ask God to help you understand and receive the message of Jesus.

In order for Ezekiel to do the work God gave him, he needed to be filled with God's Word first. He needed to accept what God said in his own heart before he told everyone else about it. Then he would be ready to share God's message with the people in captivity.

Like Ezekiel, the most important job we have as Christians is to share God's message with others. The message God wants us to share is that He loves them so much He sent Jesus to die on the cross for their sins and make them right with God. This message is called the gospel, which means "good news." But before we can share the good news with others, we need to first accept it for ourselves. We need to listen closely to what the Bible tells us about Jesus and let it sink deep into our own hearts. When we have received that message in our hearts, we will be ready to go out and share the good news with those around us.

EXPLORE MORE: What does Paul say about sharing the good news of the gospel in 1 Corinthians 15:1–5?

God wants me to accept His message in my own heart first.

DID YOU KNOW?
When God put His words in Ezekiel's mouth, Ezekiel had a vision of eating a scroll. He said it tasted as sweet as honey.

Old Bones Find New Life

So I prophesied just as the Lord commanded me to. As I was prophesying, I heard a noise. It was a rattling sound. The bones came together. One bone connected itself to another. —Ezekiel 37:7 NIrV

God gave Ezekiel some very interesting and powerful visions. We can read one of the most important visions in Ezekiel 37. Ezekiel tells us God's Spirit put him down in the middle of a valley. The valley was full of very dry bones. God asked Ezekiel, "Can these bones live?"

Ezekiel answered, "Lord and King, you are the only one who knows."

Then God told Ezekiel, "Tell the dry bones, 'The Lord will put breath in you. Then you will come to life again. Then you will know that He is the Lord.'" Ezekiel did what God said, and he began to hear a rattling sound. The bones came together and connected to each other. Tendons and flesh appeared on the bones, and skin covered them. And just as God commanded, breath entered the bones, and they came to life again.

TALK TO GOD
Thank God that He can make all things new.

God told Ezekiel the meaning of this vision. "Tell the people that I am going to take them back to the land of Israel. Then they will know that I am the Lord. I will put my Spirit in them, and they will live again."

God showed Ezekiel He can do all things. He can give us new life, just like Ezekiel saw the dry bones come alive. God gives us new life when we become a part of His family by believing in Jesus. And once we are a part of God's family, He continues to make things new in our hearts and lives. When things seem dark and hopeless, God can make them brand new. Nothing is too bad or broken or old for Him to fix.

DID YOU KNOW?
A grown adult has 206 bones, and 27 bones are found in each hand.

EXPLORE MORE: What does 2 Corinthians 5:17 say about people who belong to Jesus?

God gives new life.

One Nation and One King

"I will live with them. I will be their God. And they
will be my people." —Ezekiel 37:27 NIrV

After Ezekiel saw the valley of dry bones, the next thing God told him to do was gather two sticks together. On one stick, God told Ezekiel to write, "Belonging to the tribe of Judah and the Israelites who are connected with it." On the other stick, God told him to write, "Ephraim's stick. Belonging to the tribes of Joseph and all the Israelites connected with them." Then God told Ezekiel to join them together into one stick in his hand.

TALK TO GOD
Thank God that someday Jesus will be the ruler over all.

God said, "I am going to join Ephraim's stick to Judah's stick. I will make them a single stick of wood in my hand." He told Ezekiel, "Tell the people, the Lord says, 'I will take the Israelites out of the nations where they have gone. I will gather them back together and bring them back to their own land. They will never be separated into two kingdoms again.'" And the best promise God gave Ezekiel was, "I will live with them. I will be their God. And they will be my people."

God doesn't want His people to be separated. Israel's sin divided them into two kingdoms. That wasn't God's best plan for them. They turned away from following Him and that led to division and destruction. Until Jesus returns, we will have many nations and many different rulers. But someday, when Jesus comes back, all God's people will be one nation in one faith with Jesus as their Lord and King. God's promise to Ezekiel is also His promise to us: "I will live with them. I will be their God. And they will be my people."

EXPLORE MORE: What did God tell Ezekiel in Ezekiel 37:28?

God's people will become one.

DID YOU KNOW?
In the early 1950s, the Knights of Columbus added the phrase, "under God" to the words "one nation" in the pledge of allegiance. In 1954 the United States Congress made the change official.

Four Smart Men

God gave knowledge and understanding to these four young men.
So they understood all kinds of writings and subjects. And Daniel
could understand all kinds of visions and dreams. —Daniel 1:17 NIrV

The book of Daniel was written while the people of Judah lived in Babylon. Reading this book helps us learn about things that happened while God's people were living in a land that was not their home as a part of their punishment. King Nebuchadnezzar wanted some young men to serve in the palace. He told his officer, "Choose strong, healthy, handsome young men who are smart, and train them for three years to be my advisers." Daniel, Hananiah, Mishael, and Azariah were four men who were chosen from the tribe of Judah to serve the king.

When the men began their training, Daniel and his friends didn't want to eat the food that the king required them to eat because the food had been offered to the Babylonian idols. They told the officer they only wanted to eat vegetables and drink water. The officer didn't like their idea. He was concerned the men would become pale and thin, and then the king would be angry with him. But Daniel said, "Test us for ten days and compare us with the other men who eat the king's rich food." The officer agreed. At the end of ten days, Daniel and his friends looked healthier than the other men, so they were allowed to eat the food they wanted to eat.

TALK TO GOD
Thank God for giving you food to eat, and thank Him for your favorite vegetables.

After three years of training, the king saw that Daniel and his friends were smarter and wiser than any of the magicians in his kingdom. That's because God gave knowledge and understanding to them so they could speak about anything. God also gave Daniel wisdom to understand visions and dreams. The king was impressed with all four men, and he would soon learn that their wisdom came from God.

DID YOU KNOW?
The word *phytonutrient* means "nutrition from plants." Vegetables such as spinach, broccoli, kale, sweet potatoes, and carrots are rich in phytonutrients.

EXPLORE MORE: Read Daniel 1:6–7 to learn the Babylonian names that were given to the four young men.

God makes us wise.

The King's Dream

Daniel asked his friends to pray to the God of heaven. Daniel asked them to pray that God would show them mercy and help them understand this secret. —Daniel 2:18 ICB

King Nebuchadnezzar woke up from a strange dream. He was confused and troubled and wanted to know what his dream meant. He called for his magicians and wise men and asked them to tell him the meaning of his dream. But it was impossible because he would not tell them what he dreamed. They begged him to tell them his dream, but the king refused. "If I tell you my dream, you will just make something up and trick me," he said.

One of the wise men said to the king, "There isn't a man alive who can tell the king your dream and what it means. That is impossible! Only the gods can do that!"

When Daniel heard about the king having a dream, he asked his friends to pray with him. They asked God to tell them the king's dream and the meaning of the dream. God answered their prayers and told Daniel everything he needed to know.

TALK TO GOD
Ask God to help you know and understand the things He wants you to know.

Daniel went to see King Nebuchadnezzar. He told him that God helped him figure out and understand the dream. "In your dream you saw a big, shiny statue that got smashed to pieces by a rock. This means that weaker kingdoms will follow yours. Then God will set up another kingdom that will continue forever. This kingdom will crush all the other kingdoms and will bring them to an end. This kingdom can never be destroyed."

The wise man was right when he said no man could tell the king his dream. But he was wrong to think that "the gods" could do it. Only the one true God has the power to know all things.

EXPLORE MORE: Read Daniel's prayer of thanks in Daniel 2:19–23.

God is the only one who knows everything.

DID YOU KNOW?
Our brains are active all night long. Most adults and children dream nearly two hours every night, and some people even dream in color!

The God of All Gods

Then the king said to Daniel, "I know for sure your God is the God over all gods and the Lord over all kings. He tells people about things they cannot know. I know this is true because you were able to tell these secret things to me." —Daniel 2:47 ERV

Daniel was the only person who could tell King Nebuchadnezzar his dream and what it meant. But Daniel never took credit for knowing about the dream. He made sure the king knew God was the one who had told him everything.

Daniel was living in a land where people did not worship God. They worshiped false gods made from gold and silver, or wood and stone. Can a piece of silver speak? Does a chunk of stone know how to explain a dream? Of course not! That's why the king's wise men were not able to give the king the answers he wanted. When Daniel explained the dream, King Nebuchadnezzar knew Daniel's God was greater than all the false gods in Babylon.

Even though Daniel was far from home, he was never far from God. God is not made from metal or stone, so He is everywhere all the time. Daniel continued to love and worship God even though many people around him did not know God. From refusing to eat the king's food, to being able to explain a dream, Daniel trusted God to take care of him and help him be a good leader.

TALK TO GOD
Thank God that you can talk to Him no matter where you are.

King Nebuchadnezzar gave Daniel expensive gifts and made him ruler over all of Babylon. He even put Daniel in charge of the king's wise men. Daniel asked the king to make his friends important rulers too. So, Shadrach, Meshach, and Abednego became leaders in Babylon with Daniel.

No matter where we are, God is with us. He will help us when we love and follow Him because He is a true and living God.

DID YOU KNOW?
Babylon was the capital city of Babylonia. Today there is almost nothing left of the old city. What is still remaining can be found about 60 miles (96.5 kilometers) south of Baghdad, Iraq.

EXPLORE MORE: Read Genesis 41:37–40 to help you remember how Pharaoh treated Joseph after he explained the meaning of Pharaoh's dream. How is this similar to today's story of Daniel and King Nebuchadnezzar?

There is no other god like our God.

A Gold Statue and a Hot Furnace

"But even if God does not save us, we want you, our king, to know this: We will not serve your gods. We will not worship the gold statue you have set up." —Daniel 3:18 ICB

King Nebuchadnezzar knew Daniel's God was greater than all other gods. But sadly, the king turned away from the one true God and made a gold statue that was 9 feet (2.7 meters) wide and 90 feet (27.4 meters) tall. When the statue was finished, the king asked the important leaders of Babylon to come to a special meeting to honor it. Royal rulers, judges, and important officers came and stood in front of the gold statue.

The king's messenger gave this order, "You will hear the sound of the horns, flutes, lyres, zithers, harps, pipes and all the other musical instruments. When this happens, you must bow down and worship the gold statue." Then he added, "Anyone who doesn't will be quickly thrown into a blazing furnace."

When the music sounded, Shadrach, Meshach, and Abednego refused to worship the gold statue. Nebuchadnezzar was angry, but he gave them one more chance. The three men said they would never worship the gold statue, even if they were punished. Then the king was even more angry. "Tie them up and throw them into the furnace and make it seven times hotter!" he said.

After the men were thrown in the furnace, Nebuchadnezzar looked inside and was surprised to see not three, but four men walking around. The fourth man looked like an angel. They were not tied up anymore, and they were not burned. The king called for them to come out. Once again, Nebuchadnezzar was amazed at God's power and protection. Then he commanded that no one was allowed to speak a word against the God of Shadrach, Meshach, and Abednego, who were servants of the Most High God.

TALK TO GOD
Thank God that He is great enough to protect us no matter where we are.

EXPLORE MORE: Daniel 3:27 describes how the three friends looked when they came out of the furnace. Read the verse to see what it says.

DID YOU KNOW?
The color of flames depends on temperature. Red flames are the coolest and range from 1,112 to 1,800° Fahrenheit (600–800° Celsius). Blue flames are the hottest and range from 2,600 to 3,000° Fahrenheit (1400–1650° Celsius).

God's power can even amaze kings.

The Fourth Man in the Fire

The king said, "Look! I see four men. They are walking around in the fire. They are not tied up, and they are not burned. The fourth man looks like a son of the gods." —Daniel 3:25 ICB

The story of Shadrach, Meshach, and Abednego is an exciting story that many kids learn about at church or by reading Bible storybooks. It's an amazing story of God's power and protection for His people.

Nebuchadnezzar wasn't sure who the fourth person in the fire was. At first, he called him a son of the gods. Then he said, "God sent His angel to rescue His servants who trusted Him."

Do you remember that Isaiah talked about this story around a hundred years before it happened? In Isaiah 43:2, it says, "When you pass through the waters, I will be with you. When you cross rivers, you will not drown. When you walk through fire, you will not be burned. The flames will not hurt you."

The Israelites had already passed through the waters of the Red Sea and Jordan River. Now, in today's story, we see how God could help His children pass through the fire and not get burned. That's exactly what happened to Shadrach, Meshach, and Abednego. An important part of the verse in Isaiah is, "I will be with you." Do you know who "I" is? It's God, who promised to be with His people when they faced hard times.

God is always with His people, and sometimes He sends an angel to deliver a message or protect His people. When Nebuchadnezzar described the fourth person as a son of the gods, he didn't know about Jesus, God's Son, but that's who some Bible teachers say the fourth man may have been. God's promise to the Israelites is also for us. When we have problems, God will be with us no matter what we have to walk through.

TALK TO GOD
Think of a problem you have and ask God to walk you through it.

DID YOU KNOW?
The Fourth Man in the Fire is the name of a pizza restaurant in Toronto, Ontario. The owner, Shant Mardirosian, attended Bible college and likes to weave Bible themes into his businesses.

EXPLORE MORE: How did King Nebuchadnezzar treat Shadrach, Meshach, and Abednego after they came out of the fire? Read Daniel 3:30 to find out.

God walks through hard times with me.

Another Bad Dream

"Seven periods of time will pass while you live this way, until you learn that the Most High rules over the kingdoms of the world and gives them to anyone he chooses." —Daniel 4:25 NLT

King Nebuchadnezzar had another dream that he didn't understand. In this dream he saw a tall tree that reached to the sky. It had fresh leaves and fruit that fed the whole world. Wild animals came to rest in the shade, and birds made nests in the branches. Then an angel from heaven said, "Cut down the tree and lop off its branches! Shake off its leaves and scatter its fruit! Chase the wild animals from its shade and the birds from its branches. But leave the stump and the roots in the ground."

TALK TO GOD
Ask God to help you remember that He will always be greater than anyone.

Once again, the king's wise men were not able to tell the king what his dream meant. And once again, God told Daniel the meaning of the dream so he could explain it to Nebuchadnezzar. Daniel told the king, "You are strong and great like the tall tree, but you will lose your kingdom. You will become like a wild animal and eat grass like a cow. After seven years, you will know that God rules over all the kingdoms on earth, and you will become king again."

One year later, Nebuchadnezzar was walking on the flat roof of his palace. He looked over the city and said, "Look at this beautiful city I have built by my own mighty power. It shows how great I am."

Just then a voice from heaven called down and said, "King Nebuchadnezzar, you are no longer ruler of the kingdom!" Then Nebuchadnezzar lived like a wild animal for seven years until God restored him. When Nebuchadnezzar became king again, he praised and worshiped God. He learned that God is the greatest King who will rule forever.

EXPLORE MORE: Read what Nebuchadnezzar said in Daniel 4:37.

No king will ever be as great as God.

DID YOU KNOW?
The roofs in Babylon were flat to provide extra living space. Some people slept or cooked on their roofs.

Words on a Wall

Then Daniel answered the king, "King Belshazzar, you can keep your gifts for yourself, or you can give them to someone else. But I will still read the writing on the wall for you and explain what it means." —Daniel 5:17 ERV

Belshazzar was Nebuchadnezzar's grandson who became the next king of Babylon. One night he was having a feast with a thousand guests. While they were eating and drinking, he told his servants to bring the gold and silver cups that Nebuchadnezzar had taken from the temple. His guests drank from the cups while they praised their false gods.

All of a sudden, Belshazzar saw a hand with fingers writing words on the palace wall. He became pale from fear and his knees knocked together. His legs were so weak that he couldn't walk. He called for his wise men and promised to give a reward to anyone who could understand the words. "I will give him purple robes to wear and will put a gold chain around his neck. I will make him the third highest ruler in the kingdom," he said.

The king's wise men could not tell Belshazzar what the words meant. Then the king's mother told him how Daniel had great wisdom and understanding to explain dreams for King Nebuchadnezzar. So Belshazzar called for Daniel and asked him to explain the message. Daniel agreed but said he didn't want a reward. He knew that God gave him the ability to understand things that no one else could.

TALK TO GOD
Begin your prayer by telling God He is a holy God, and then pray whatever is on your mind today.

Daniel told Belshazzar he would lose his kingdom because he dishonored God when he used the cups from the temple. He said the Babylonian kingdom would be divided and given to the Medes and Persians. And that very night, Darius the Mede took over the kingdom.

When people don't honor God as holy, God will not honor them.

DID YOU KNOW?
"The writing is on the wall" is a phrase that comes from today's story. It means that something bad or unpleasant is going to happen soon.

EXPLORE MORE: The message on the wall is explained in Daniel 5:25–28. Look it up to read what it says.

I will honor our holy God.

A Night with the Lions

"My God sent his angel. And his angel shut the mouths of the lions. They haven't hurt me at all. That's because I haven't done anything wrong in God's sight. I've never done anything wrong to you either, Your Majesty." —Daniel 6:22 NIrV

When Darius became king, he divided the Babylonian kingdom into 120 territories and chose a ruler for each section. He made Daniel and two other men supervisors over the other rulers to make sure they were honest. Darius liked Daniel and wanted to put him in charge of the whole kingdom. The other rulers weren't happy about this idea.

The jealous rulers tried to catch Daniel doing something wrong, but they couldn't. Daniel 6:4 says, "He could always be trusted. He never did anything wrong. And he always did what he was supposed to."

The men knew Daniel prayed to God three times a day, so they came up with a plan.

They told the king to make a new law. "Don't let any of your people pray to any god or human being except to you. If they do, throw them into the lions' den."

The king was foolish and signed the law, but it didn't stop Daniel from praying. As soon as the rulers caught Daniel praying, they reported it. Darius was upset that he had made this law. He looked for ways to protect Daniel, but he finally had to send him to the lions' den. "You always serve your God faithfully. So may He save you!" Darius said.

The next morning King Darius called out to Daniel, "Was the God you serve able to save you?"

Daniel said, "My God sent His angel. And His angel shut the mouths of the lions." The king was overjoyed and got Daniel out of the den.

Daniel was faithful to God, and God was faithful to Daniel. Praying to God is always the right thing to do—no matter what!

EXPLORE MORE: Read Daniel 6:25–27 to learn about a new decree King Darius made.

TALK TO GOD
Thank God that we always can pray to Him.

No one can stop me from praying to God.

DID YOU KNOW?
Lions are known for being beautiful, strong, powerful, and fearless. They are often called the king of beasts. In the Bible Jesus is called the Lion of Judah.

Pray like Daniel

Three times each day Daniel got down on his knees and prayed. He prayed and thanked God, just as he always had done. —Daniel 6:10 ICB

Daniel prayed to God even when it went against the king's law. He knew he would be punished, but like his three friends who walked around in a hot furnace, Daniel loved God and refused to worship anyone or anything besides Him.

Many people live in places where they can pray whenever they want to. But lots of other people live in places where they might be in danger if someone sees them praying. Because God is everywhere, we can pray to Him wherever we are. We don't worship an idol made from gold, wood, or stone. We don't have to bow down to a statue or stand high on a mountain to say our prayers.

TALK TO GOD
Thank God that you can pray to Him whenever you want to.

Prayer is talking to God—out loud, in a soft whisper, or in your thoughts. You can kneel, sit, or stand, and you can pray while you are lying in bed at night. You can pray with your friends and family, or you can pray by yourself.

Think of all the times that you can pray. When you get up in the morning, you can thank God for a new day and ask God to bless your family. Throughout the day you can pray for your friends or teachers. You can ask God to help you with a problem or thank Him for the sandwich in your lunch box.

No matter where you are or what you are doing, you can talk to God. And like Daniel, you can pray even if someone says you can't. Only God knows your thoughts, so you can talk to Him even if no one else can hear you. How cool is that!

EXPLORE MORE: What does Colossians 4:2 tell us about praying to God?

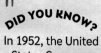

DID YOU KNOW?
In 1952, the United States Congress established the National Day of Prayer to be held on the first Thursday of May. All Americans are asked to pray to God on that day.

I can pray anytime and anywhere.

God Sends Hosea to Judah

"Let's learn about the Lord. Let's try hard to know who he is. He will come to us as surely as the dawn comes. The Lord will come to us like the rain, like the spring rain that waters the ground." —Hosea 6:3 ICB

The book of Hosea comes after the book of Daniel in the Bible, but Hosea was a prophet to the Israelites more than one hundred years before they went to Babylon. God sent Hosea to the Israelites for two reasons: to warn the Israelites to turn back to Him, and to be an example of how much God loved His people.

God told Hosea to marry a woman who would not be a good wife. She would turn away from Hosea and would not honor him as her husband. He would even have to buy her out of slavery when she got into trouble! But God told Hosea to love her and treat her with kindness. Hosea's wife was like the Israelites who did not honor God, and Hosea was like God who kept loving them anyway.

Hosea warned the Israelites that they would be punished for turning away from God. In today's Bible verse, we read how Hosea begged the people to love God and receive His blessings. But the people continued to do whatever they wanted to. As we learned from some of the Old Testament books we read, the Israelites who were living in Judah while Jehoiakim was king were taken to Babylon. After seventy years, God delivered His people and brought them home.

God wants all people to love Him and be faithful to Him, but none of us can live a perfect life. Like Hosea who bought his wife out of slavery, God sent Jesus to pay for our sins. When we believe in Jesus, we are no longer slaves to sin. We can love God and receive His blessings.

EXPLORE MORE: What message does God give in Hosea 14:8–9?

TALK TO GOD
Thank God for His never-ending love, and ask Him to help you love Him more each day.

God loves me all the time.

DID YOU KNOW?
The name Hosea means "salvation" or "God's salvation."

An Army of Locusts

Come back to the Lord your God. He is kind and shows mercy.
He doesn't become angry quickly. He has great love. He
would rather forgive than punish. —Joel 2:13 ICB

Bible teachers think Joel was a prophet to Judah during the reign of King Joash. A swarm of locusts had come to the land like a powerful army of soldiers. They ate and destroyed all the fields of grain, the fruit trees, and the grapevines. The barns and storerooms for grain were empty, and the animals walked around hungry and confused because they couldn't find food or pastures.

Joel told the people their punishment would be worse than the swarm of locusts if they didn't turn back to worshiping God. God didn't want to punish them. He wanted to forgive them and bless them. Joel said that God wanted them to return to Him with broken hearts, being sorry for their sins. He told them to blow the trumpets and call for a special meeting with all the people.

TALK TO GOD
Thank God for
His mercy and
forgiveness.

God promised to give back everything the locusts had taken from them. God said He would send new grain and oil. The trees would grow fruit, and the pastures would grow green grass for the animals. The fig trees and the grapevines would be full, and He would send rain in the spring and the fall. God also promised to pour out His Spirit upon His people. This promise was fulfilled in the New Testament after Jesus went back to heaven.

It breaks God's heart when people turn away from Him. But God is full of love and waits for people to come to Him. He is full of mercy and forgives people who are sorry for their sins. And He is full of grace and gives salvation to everyone who believes in Jesus.

DID YOU KNOW?
A large swarm of
locusts can have
billions of locusts
and cover an area
as big as 620 square
miles (1,000 square
kilometers).

EXPLORE MORE: Look up Acts 2:17–21 to read the words the apostle Peter quoted from Joel 2:28–32.

God is full of love and forgiveness.

Amos the Shepherd

"Try to do good, not evil. Then you will live. And the Lord God of heaven's armies will be with you just as you say he is." —Amos 5:14 ICB

Amos was a shepherd in Judah during the reign of King Uzziah in Judah and King Jeroboam II in Israel. Being a shepherd meant other people didn't think of him as important. He wasn't a leader or a priest, but God sent Amos visions so he would warn Judah, Israel, and the surrounding nations to turn from their sin and follow God.

The people in the Northern Kingdom of Israel were enjoying a time of power and wealth, but they were greedy and selfish. They didn't take care of the poor the way God wanted them to. God didn't accept their offerings and celebrations because their hearts were far from Him.

Amos obeyed God and delivered the messages God gave him. Some of the priests in Israel didn't like his messages and told him to leave. But Amos replied, "The Lord took me away from tending the sheep. He said to me, 'Go, prophesy to my people, the Israelites.'"

TALK TO GOD
Thank God that following Him leads to a life of closeness to God and His goodness.

The messages in the book of Amos are similar to those written by other prophets. If the people continued rejecting God, they would face the punishment they deserved. But if they turned back to God, He would forgive them and bless them. And like the other prophets, Amos gives a message of hope. The day would come when God would bring the people home and bless their land.

The book of Amos was written to warn people thousands of years ago, but the messages are for everyone. Turning away from God brings hardship and pain, but loving God leads to a close relationship with Him, filled with His blessings. We have the power to choose which way we want to live.

EXPLORE MORE: What does Amos say about God in Amos 5:8?

I can choose to live a life that follows God.

DID YOU KNOW?
Amos lived with a group of shepherds in Tekoa, a small town near Jerusalem. Besides being a shepherd, he also took care of fig trees.

Jonah Runs Away

But Jonah tried to run away from the Lord. He went to Joppa and found a boat that was going to the faraway city of Tarshish. —Jonah 1:3 ERV

Jonah was a prophet who received a message from God. God said to Jonah, "Nineveh is a big city. I have heard about the many evil things the people are doing there. So go there and tell them to stop doing such evil things."

God wanted the people of Nineveh to stop doing bad things because He loved them. That's why He wanted Jonah to go and tell them to change their ways. But Jonah didn't want to go. Instead of traveling to Nineveh, he went in the opposite direction to a seaport in Joppa. He bought a ticket and got on a ship. Jonah tried to run away from God, but that is impossible!

Jonah rode on the ship as it was sailing along. Suddenly, a powerful wind blew across the sea, and a fierce storm rocked the boat. The sailors were afraid the boat would sink and they would drown. They cried out to their gods and threw the cargo overboard to lighten the ship. And do you know what Jonah was doing while they tried to save the boat? He was sleeping!

TALK TO GOD
Ask God to help you do what He wants you to do.

The sailors found Jonah and said, "Pray to your god! Maybe your god will hear your prayer and save us!" Jonah told them he was running away from God, and the storm was his fault.

"Throw me into the sea, and the sea will become calm," he said.

The sailors tried to row back to shore, but the winds and waves were too strong. They finally threw Jonah into the sea, and the storm stopped immediately. The sailors were amazed at God's power—and Jonah's journey was just beginning!

EXPLORE MORE: Read Jonah 1:8–10 to see what questions the sailors asked Jonah and how he answered them.

DID YOU KNOW?
The ship Jonah got on was sailing to Tarshish, a city on the Mediterranean Sea where some of the largest ships would sail. It was known for having a great supply of metals, especially silver.

It's impossible to run away from God.

Three Days inside a Fish

When Jonah fell into the sea, the Lord chose a very big fish to swallow Jonah. He was in the stomach of the fish for three days and three nights. —Jonah 1:17 ERV

When the sailors threw Jonah into the sea, he sank to the bottom. Seaweed wrapped around his head, and he was sure that he would die. But God was not finished with Jonah and wanted to give him a second chance. God sent a big fish to swallow Jonah, and Jonah quickly learned that he could not run away from God.

When Jonah found himself inside the belly of a giant fish, he cried out to God. He finally made a promise to God and said, "I will give sacrifices to you, and I will praise and thank you. I will make special promises to you, and I will do what I promise. Salvation only comes from the Lord!"

Jonah was inside the fish for three days and three nights. Then God told the fish to spit out Jonah onto the shore, and it did. The Lord spoke to Jonah again and said, "Go to that big city Nineveh and say what I tell you." This time Jonah obeyed and went to Nineveh.

TALK TO GOD
Thank God for second chances, and ask God to help you listen to Him.

Many of the stories in the Old Testament point to Jesus, and this is one of them. Matthew 12:40 says, "Jonah was in the stomach of the big fish for three days and three nights. In the same way, the Son of Man will be in the grave three days and three nights." When Jesus died on the cross, His body was placed in a tomb. But three days later He came back to life to show that He has power over sin and death. And like Jonah said, "Salvation only comes from the Lord!"

EXPLORE MORE: Read part of Jonah's prayer in Jonah 2:5-7.

God gives us many chances to obey Him.

DID YOU KNOW?
Great white sharks, groupers, and sperm whales are large enough to swallow a human. The largest fish known is the whale shark, which could swallow a human too.

Jonah Goes to Nineveh

So Jonah obeyed the Lord and went to Nineveh. It was a very large city. A person had to walk for three days to travel through it. —Jonah 3:3 ERV

Jonah finally went to the city of Nineveh like God told him to. He was probably happy to be walking through the city instead of sitting inside the belly of a stinky fish! On the first day that Jonah got there, he shouted, "After forty days, Nineveh will be destroyed!"

Instead of being angry with Jonah's message, the people believed that this was a message from God. They decided to go without food and wear special clothes to show they were sorry. When the king heard Jonah's message, he got down from his throne and took off his royal robe. He put on special clothes like the other people were wearing to show he was sad. He even sat on a heap of ashes. Then the king sent out a command telling everyone in Nineveh to continue their fasting from food, and to call out to God. He told everyone to change their lives and stop doing what was wrong. Then he said, "Who knows? Maybe God will stop being angry and change his mind, and we will not be punished." God saw that the people were sorry for their sins and wanted to change their ways. Because of His love and mercy, He did not punish them. You would think Jonah would be happy that the people listened to the message God gave him, but he wasn't. He probably thought the people didn't deserve God's forgiveness. But the Bible says that everyone sins, and no one deserves God's forgiveness. That's why Jesus came to pay for our sins so we can be forgiven. When people are sorry for their sins, God will never turn them away.

TALK TO GOD
Thank God that He is always willing to forgive us.

EXPLORE MORE: What can you learn from reading Romans 3:23–24?

DID YOU KNOW?
In Bible times people wore sackcloth and sat in ashes or put ashes on their heads to show they were sad about something or sorry for their sins. Sackcloth was a rough material made from black goat's hair.

God forgives people who are sorry for what they have done.

A Message for the Future

"But you, Bethlehem Ephrathah, are one of the smallest towns in Judah. But from you will come one who will rule Israel for me. He comes from very old times, from days long ago." —Micah 5:2 ICB

Micah was a prophet who received messages from God in the form of visions. He lived around the same time as Isaiah and Hosea, and his messages were for both Israel and Judah. Jerusalem was the capital city of Judah, and Samaria was the capital city of Israel. Micah's messages were the same as the messages from other prophets, "Turn back to God or be captured by your enemies."

The people didn't listen to Micah. Israel was captured by the Assyrians, and Judah was captured by the Babylonians. But like the other prophets, Micah also gave a message that someday God would make everything right.

As you know from other passages, many stories and verses in the Old Testament point to Jesus. In the book of Micah, about seven hundred years before the birth of Jesus, we learn that Jesus would be born in Bethlehem.

Bethlehem was a small, unimportant town in Judah. It was also known as the City of David because that's where King David was from. Many verses in the Old Testament tell us the Messiah would be born into the family of David, and Micah is the first to tell us exactly where that would be. The ruler born in Bethlehem would be Jesus, the King over all the earth, and His kingdom would never end.

TALK TO GOD
Thank God that you can learn many great things by reading every chapter of the Bible.

Some people may want to skip over a few chapters in the Old Testament. The books from the prophets seem like they are filled with harsh messages that can be hard to understand. But some exciting verses are tucked in between the warnings to God's people, and today's Bible verse is one of them!

EXPLORE MORE: What does Micah 5:4 tell us about Jesus?

The Messiah would be born in Bethlehem.

DID YOU KNOW?
The name Bethlehem means "house of bread," and Jesus calls himself the Bread of Life.

Three Good Things

The Lord has told you what is good. He has told you what he wants from you: Do what is right to other people. Love being kind to others. And live humbly, trusting your God. —Micah 6:8 ICB

God used prophets like Micah to deliver messages to His people. In Micah 6, Micah reminds the Israelites how God had cared for their ancestors many years earlier. He brought them out of slavery in Egypt. He sent Moses, Aaron, and Miriam to help them. He made Balaam bless them instead of curse them. And He brought them safely from one camp to another by helping them cross the Jordan River.

The Israelites asked Micah, "What can we bring as an offering to the Lord? Should we bring calves, thousands of sheep, or rivers of olive oil?" But God was not interested in their offerings. Instead, He wanted their lives to be full of goodness.

Micah told the people three good things God wanted them to do—and these messages are also for us. First, God wants us to do what is right. That means being honest, fair, and obedient. The more we learn about God and His words in the Bible, the more we will know how to do what is right. The second good thing is to be kind to others. That means we must treat everyone with love and respect. It means that we should care about others and help someone who may need it. The third good thing is to be humble before God. We need to remember that God is greater than we are, and if we do something great, it's because God gave us the ability to do it.

TALK TO GOD
Ask God to help you do what's right and to be kind and humble.

It can be hard to do all these good things, but with God's help, we can do our best to live in a way that honors Him.

EXPLORE MORE: Read Micah 7:18–19. What does God do with our sins?

DID YOU KNOW?
The name Micah is from the name Micaiah, and it means, "Who is like God?"

God tells us how we can live to honor Him.

Be Totally Amazed

"Look at the nations. Watch them. Be totally amazed at what you see. I am going to do something in your days that you would never believe. You would not believe it even if someone told you about it." —Habakkuk 1:5 NIrV

Habakkuk was a prophet to the people of Judah shortly before the Babylonians came to capture them. He was overwhelmed and discouraged because God's people were arguing and fighting and living lives that went against God's Word. Habakkuk called out to God and said, "How long do I have to cry out for help? Why do you put up with the wrong things the people are doing?"

God told Habakkuk the Babylonians would become a strong power and take over the world. Then Habakkuk was even more upset. He asked God why He would use a nation that worshiped false gods to capture God's people. Habakkuk waited for God to answer him.

God said to Habakkuk, "Write down the message I am giving you. Write it clearly on the tablets you use. Then a messenger can read it and run to announce it."

TALK TO GOD
Ask God to help you trust Him even when you don't understand what's happening.

God said that everything would happen when the time was right, and the Babylonian kingdom would not last. Their man-made idols of wood and stone would not be able to save them. God told Habakkuk to trust Him to do amazing things and that He would take care of His people.

Sometimes it's hard for us to understand why God allows certain things to happen. Good things can happen to bad people, and bad things can happen to good people. But we need to remember that God is in control, and He knows the future. Even when we can't see it, God is working in ways that will amaze us. When we believe in our hearts that God loves us and He is good, then we can trust Him in the good times and bad times.

EXPLORE MORE: How can Psalm 46:10–11 help us when we don't understand God's ways?

I can trust God even when I don't understand.

DID YOU KNOW?
In the Bible, the name Habakkuk only appears in the book he wrote (Habakkuk 1:1 and Habakkuk 3:1). He is called a prophet, but there is no mention of where he was from or who his parents were.

Habakkuk's Prayer

But I will still be glad in the Lord and rejoice in God my Savior.
—Habakkuk 3:18 ERV

The book of Habakkuk has three chapters. In the first two chapters we learn about the questions Habakkuk asked God and the answers God gave him. In the third chapter we can read Habakkuk's prayer, which is actually a song.

Even though Habakkuk didn't understand why God was going to allow His people to be captured by the Babylonians, he trusted that God knew what was best. He knew the land of Judah would lose its crops, fields, and cattle. In verses 17–18 he says, "Figs might not grow on the fig trees, and grapes might not grow on the vines. Olives might not grow on the olive trees, and food might not grow in the fields. There might not be any sheep in the pens or cattle in the barns. But I will still be glad in the Lord and rejoice in God my Savior."

Habakkuk didn't want to see God's people lose everything they had, but he believed that God had a purpose for what was going to happen. Because of his faith and trust in God, Habakkuk could praise God with joy even though things would not be good.

TALK TO GOD
Praise God for being able to trust Him in good times and bad times.

It's easy to praise God when everything is great. You can praise God for helping you to get a good grade on a test. You can praise God for a new place to live. And you can be full of joy if you get a new brother or sister. But it's harder to praise God when great things don't happen. What we learn from the prophet Habakkuk is to trust God completely. Even in hard times we can praise God, our Savior, with joyful hearts.

EXPLORE MORE: Read Habakkuk 3:19 to find out what Habakkuk says in the last verse of his song.

DID YOU KNOW?
Since Habakkuk's prayer is also a song, it is possible that he was from the tribe of Levi. The Levites served as musicians in Solomon's Temple.

Even in hard times I can praise God.

God Sings

"For the Lord your God is living among you. He is a mighty savior. He will take delight in you with gladness. With his love, he will calm all your fears. He will rejoice over you with joyful songs." —Zephaniah 3:17 NLT

What is your favorite song to sing? When it pops in your head or you hear it playing, do you sing it at the top of your lungs? Singing happy songs makes us feel happy. And singing is also a great way to show our happiness.

Have you ever wondered if God sings? The Bible tells us in Zephaniah 3 that God does sing! And the verse even tells us what kind of songs God sings. He sings joyful songs to show His happiness. What makes Him so happy that He sings? The Bible tells us it's His people!

Zephaniah 3:17 helps us understand how God feels about His people. If you love and follow God, you are one of His people. There may be times you wonder if God is upset or frustrated with you. Sometimes you might wonder if God likes you. Today's Bible verse answers all those questions. God is our mighty Savior. He delights in us with gladness. He calms all our fears with His love. And He sings over us with joyful songs.

Any time you feel afraid or unsure, ask God to help you remember He is singing over you. Even though you can't hear His beautiful songs with your ears, you can feel His love in your heart. You can go outside and listen to the happy songs of the birds and remember that they are singing to the God who sings for you. You can turn on a song that makes you feel happy and think about how you make God happy. One day we will hear God's joyful song in heaven, and it will be the most beautiful music we've ever heard.

EXPLORE MORE: What part of creation is singing in Job 38:6–7?

TALK TO GOD
Tell God how happy it makes you that He sings for you, and then sing a song of joy back to Him.

God sings over me with joy.

DID YOU KNOW?
A song that gets stuck in your head is called an earworm. Psychologists have discovered that earworms are usually faster songs with a melody that's easy to remember.

Return to God

And now he says to us, "Return to me. Then I will return to you," announces the Lord. —Zechariah 1:3 NIrV

The prophet Zechariah served God in the years after the people of Judah returned from Babylon to their homeland. Zechariah brought a message of hope to the people. He encouraged them to turn away from their sin and come back to God with all their hearts.

In the beginning of the book of Zechariah, he tells the people the message God gave him, "Return to me. Then I will return to you." When the people of Judah came back to their land, they were discouraged and felt like God was far away. It was hard to rebuild their homeland. They didn't have a lot of money, and they had a hard time getting crops to grow. Their life seemed easier in Babylon. They had experienced the consequences of turning away from God, and now it was hard to get back to their normal life.

But God invited the people to come back to Him by loving Him and following Him. He didn't force them—He wanted them to come back on their own because they were sorry for what they had done. God promised that if they returned to Him, He would be close to them again.

God wants us to come back to Him after we do the wrong thing. He will always forgive us and make things right. All we have to do is return to Him by telling Him we're sorry. When we spend time talking to God in prayer and reading His Word, it shows our love for Him and helps us come back to Him too. And the best way we can stay close to God is by doing the things He wants us to do.

EXPLORE MORE: According to Isaiah 55:6–7, what will God do for people who turn to Him and seek Him?

TALK TO GOD
Ask God to show you if there is anything you need to tell Him you're sorry for. Then return to Him by telling Him you're sorry and you love Him.

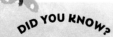

DID YOU KNOW?
Mother sea turtles return to the place they were born to lay their eggs for their baby sea turtles to be born. Some mother turtles on the coast of Brazil will travel more than a thousand miles (1,609 kilometers).

God will always take me back.

The King Is Coming

Rejoice, people of Jerusalem. Shout for joy, people of Jerusalem. Your king is coming to you. He does what is right, and he saves. He is gentle and riding on a donkey. He is on the colt of a donkey. —Zechariah 9:9 ICB

The book of Zechariah is another book in the Old Testament where we can read future prophecies about Jesus. If you've ever celebrated Palm Sunday, you've probably heard the story of Jesus riding on a donkey into Jerusalem while people waved palm branches and shouted, "Hosanna!" But did you know Zechariah said that was going to happen more than five hundred years before Jesus was born? Zechariah even told the people to shout for joy when they saw their King riding on a donkey. Isn't that amazing?

TALK TO GOD
Thank God that His words are always true and that Jesus is coming back someday.

In today's verse, Zechariah told the Israelites what Jesus the Messiah would be like. He said Jesus would be their King, and He would be the one who will rule forever. Jesus would always do what is right. Jesus would also be their Savior and take away their sins. And Jesus would be gentle and humble—that's why He would ride on a donkey, which was a lowly animal and symbol of peace.

When we read the New Testament, we see that everything Zechariah said about Jesus was true. And what's even more wonderful is that Jesus, our King, is coming again! He will still do what is right. He will continue to be our Savior, and He will bring peace to the whole world. But this time, He will create His kingdom that will last forever. We know it's going to happen because God tells us in the Bible that it will, just like He told the prophet Zechariah many, many years ago. And when the King comes back, we can shout for joy just like the Israelites.

EXPLORE MORE: When Jesus comes back, what animal will He ride? Read Revelation 19:11 to find out.

Jesus is the King who is coming.

DID YOU KNOW?
A colt is a young male donkey that is less than four years old. A young female donkey less than four years old is called a filly.

Shine On

On that day the Lord their God will rescue his people, just as a shepherd rescues his sheep. They will sparkle in his land like jewels in a crown. —Zechariah 9:16 NLT

Have you ever seen a diamond or another type of expensive jewel? Jewels are also called gemstones or precious stones, and they can be found in rocks and minerals, which God created. Jewels and gemstones are valuable because some are very rare and hard to find. They are known for their beauty because of the way they sparkle and shine.

The books in the Old Testament that were written by the prophets warned the Israelites of the seriousness of turning away from God. The people of Judah would be captured and taken to Babylon for seventy years. But God gave them a promise that He would bring them back to their homeland and bless them.

In today's Bible verse, the prophet Zechariah gives a beautiful picture of what would happen to God's people. He says God would rescue them, and then they would sparkle in the land like jewels in a crown. God's people were His precious jewels, and He loved them very much.

Did you know you are God's precious jewel too? You are more valuable to Him than the most expensive jewel on earth. And do you know how you can show your love for God? You can sparkle and shine!

TALK TO GOD
Ask God to help you sparkle for Him.

Being kind to others with your words and actions is one way you can sparkle. You can also sparkle when you help out someone who needs a little extra help. And you can sparkle by telling others that God loves them. Knowing that you are precious and valuable to God can fill your heart with so much joy that it sparkles on the outside!

EXPLORE MORE: Read Matthew 5:16. What happens when others see us shine for God?

DID YOU KNOW?
Queen Elizabeth, who ruled the United Kingdom for sixty-nine years, wore the Imperial State Crown for her coronation in 1953. The crown had so many jewels that it weighed more than 4 pounds (1.8 kilograms) and could only be worn for a short time.

I can sparkle for God.

No Holding Back

"Bring all the tithes into the storehouse so there will be enough food in my Temple. If you do," says the Lord of Heaven's Armies, "I will open the windows of heaven for you. I will pour out a blessing so great you won't have enough room to take it in! Try it! Put me to the test!" —Malachi 3:10 NLT

Have you ever heard someone say, "Put it to the test"? People say this when they want to see how good or strong something is. If you put something in a "test" situation, you'll see how well it holds up. You can put a thing to the test—like driving a remote-control car over a speed bump you made. You can also put yourself to a test—like seeing if you can do ten push-ups. In the book of Malachi, God told the Israelites to put Him to the test. There isn't another verse in the Bible where God commands His people to test Him. What did He mean?

In Malachi 3, we learn that the Israelites weren't giving all their tithes to God like they should. They disobeyed God's rules about giving ten percent of their food to take care of the priests. The Israelites held back some things for themselves. God saw their selfish hearts, and through the prophet Malachi, He told the Israelites, "Bring all the tithes into the store-house so there will be enough food in my Temple." Then He gave them a challenge: "If you do, I will pour out a blessing so great you won't have enough room to take it in! Try it! Put me to the test!"

God promises to provide for His people and protect them when they obey and give with a grateful heart. No matter how much we give, we can never give more than God. Everything we have comes from Him. He wants us to love Him more than the gifts He gives us. When we love God more than anything else, we can give without holding back.

TALK TO GOD
Ask God to help you love Him more than anything else.

EXPLORE MORE: What does 2 Corinthians 9:6–8 say about giving to others?

I will give without holding back.

DID YOU KNOW?
December is the most popular month for giving to charity.

The Rising Sun

"But here is what will happen for you who have respect for me. The sun that brings life will rise. Its rays will bring healing to my people. You will go out and leap for joy like calves that have just been fed."
—Malachi 4:2 NIrV

The last chapter of Malachi is the shortest chapter in the book. It's only six verses long, but in the second verse, God gives us a beautiful picture of what Jesus is like. Jesus is called "the sun that brings life."

The sun rises every day. It shines rays of warm light that cover the earth. Jesus is like a sun that rises, and His rays of light bring healing to our hearts. He gives us joy and makes us whole. Have you ever noticed that when it's sunny, you don't need any other light? That's how it is with Jesus. We don't need anything else to help us have the right kind of life. He gives us everything we need. When the sun rises in the morning, we all notice it. There is nowhere the light doesn't reach. And that's how Jesus shines His light into our lives too. His love touches every part of our hearts and makes us completely alive in Him.

TALK TO GOD
Ask Jesus to shine His healing light in your life.

Today's verse also says we will go out and leap with joy like a baby cow that has just eaten. When morning comes and the sun rises, calves are let out of the barn and go out in the green grass to enjoy the day. When Jesus shines His love on us, we are free to enjoy the wonderful life He gives us.

The next time you see a happy calf munching grass in a pasture, you can think of this verse. And when you feel the warm sun on your face, close your eyes and remember that Jesus brings you life.

EXPLORE MORE: What two things does Psalm 84:11 say God is like?

Jesus shines like the sun.

DID YOU KNOW?
Some places, like the Sahara Desert, receive more than four thousand hours of sunlight per year. Other places, like Scotland and Iceland, receive only two thousand hours of sunlight per year.

Jesus's Special Family

This is the written story of the family line of Jesus the Messiah. He is the son of David. He is also the son of Abraham. —Matthew 1:1 NIrV

As we've been going through the stories of the Old Testament, we've seen how Jesus is everywhere in the Bible! Today is a special day because we get to start the New Testament. We will begin learning about what Jesus did when He lived on earth and how His disciples started the church after He went back to heaven. There are four books of the Bible that tell us all about Jesus's life. Those books are called *the Gospels*. They are the books of Matthew, Mark, Luke, and John.

Matthew was a tax collector before he became one of Jesus's twelve disciples. His gospel starts with the family line of Jesus. From the very beginning, Matthew calls Jesus the Messiah, which means He was the Savior God promised to send. Then Matthew tells us that Jesus was the Son of David and the Son of Abraham, which means He was a part of their families. Because Jesus was the Son of David, it means He came from the family of kings in the Old Testament. It also means He fulfilled the prophecy that the Messiah would be a part of David's family.

Matthew also connects Jesus to Abraham, which shows how God kept His promise to Abraham that everyone would be blessed through him. David and Abraham were two of the most important men in the Israelites' history. Since Jesus was a part of their family, it showed how important He was.

Jesus's family was perfectly planned by God. From the beginning, He knew exactly how He would accomplish His plan to send Jesus into the world. God always finishes what He starts.

TALK TO GOD
Thank God for the perfect way He planned Jesus's family and birth, and for keeping all His promises.

EXPLORE MORE: Who are the two women mentioned in Jesus's family line in Matthew 1:5?

DID YOU KNOW?
There were fourteen generations from Abraham to David, fourteen generations from David until the Israelites went to Babylon, and fourteen generations from that time until Jesus was born.

God planned Jesus's birth from the beginning.

An Unbelievable Promise

But the angel said to him, "Zechariah, don't be afraid. Your prayer has been heard by God. Your wife, Elizabeth, will give birth to a son. You will name him John." —Luke 1:13 ICB

During the time Herod ruled in Judea, a priest named Zechariah had a wife whose name was Elizabeth. Zechariah and Elizabeth followed God's law and obeyed Him. They didn't have any children because Elizabeth couldn't have a baby.

When Zechariah and Elizabeth were old, Zechariah was burning incense in the temple. Suddenly, an angel appeared next to the incense table. How do you think Zechariah felt when he saw the angel? The Bible says he was confused and afraid, but the angel told him the most wonderful news. "Zechariah, don't be afraid," he said. "Your prayer has been heard by God. Your wife, Elizabeth, will give birth to a son. You will name him John. You will be very happy." Then the angel said something more amazing, "Even at the time John is born, he will be filled with the Holy Spirit. He will help many people of Israel return to the Lord their God. . . . He will make people ready for the coming of the Lord."

TALK TO GOD
Thank God that His promises always come true.

Zechariah had a hard time believing this news. He told the angel, "I am an old man, and my wife is old, too."

The angel answered, "God sent me to talk to you and to tell you this good news. Now, listen! You will not be able to talk until the day these things happen. You will lose your speech because you did not believe what I told you. But these things will really happen."

Sometimes God's promises are so amazing, it's hard to believe they are true. But just like everything happened exactly the way the angel told Zechariah, all God's promises will come true one day.

DID YOU KNOW?
The angel who visited Zechariah was named Gabriel. The angel Gabriel also visited Daniel to explain one of his visions in Daniel 8–9.

EXPLORE MORE: Find out how Zechariah was able to speak again by reading Luke 1:59-64.

God's promises always come true.

Mary Trusts God's Plan

"You will become pregnant and give birth to a son. You must call him Jesus. He will be great and will be called the Son of the Most High God." —Luke 1:31–32 NIrV

The angel Gabriel had a lot of important announcements to make. Shortly after telling Zechariah that Elizabeth would have a baby, Gabriel visited a young girl named Mary in the town of Nazareth. Mary was engaged to a man named Joseph, who was from King David's family line. When Gabriel greeted Mary he said, "The Lord has blessed you in a special way. He is with you" (Luke 1:28). Mary was upset by what the angel said because she didn't understand what he meant. But Gabriel said, "Do not be afraid, Mary. God is very pleased with you. You will become pregnant and give birth to a son. You must call him Jesus." Then Gabriel told Mary that her baby boy would be the Son of God and would rule forever.

Mary didn't understand how she could have a baby when she wasn't married yet. Gabriel explained, "The Holy Spirit will come to you. The power of the Most High God will cover you." Gabriel told Mary that Elizabeth, her cousin, was having a baby even in her old age. "What God says always comes true," Gabriel said.

Mary replied, "I serve the Lord. May it happen to me just as you said it would."

TALK TO GOD
Tell God that you are willing to obey His plans for you.

Even though Mary didn't understand God's plans for her right away, she trusted that His plans were good. She did what God told her to do because she loved Him. There may be times when we don't understand the plans God has for us too. But we can remember that God loves us and wants what's best for us. And we can serve God with a willing heart just like Mary did.

EXPLORE MORE: Which prophecy about the Messiah was fulfilled through Mary? Read Isaiah 7:14 to find out.

I can obey God even when I don't understand.

DID YOU KNOW?
Nazareth is a town in the region of Galilee. Around the time Jesus was born, Nazareth was very small. Some people estimate that it had fewer than 500 people. Today more than 77,000 people live in Nazareth.

Mary Visits Elizabeth

In a loud voice she said to Mary, "God has blessed you more than any other woman. And God has blessed the baby you will have." —Luke 1:42 ERV

As soon as Mary heard Gabriel's surprising news that she was going to have a special baby, she went to visit Elizabeth. Mary went inside Zechariah and Elizabeth's house and said hello to Elizabeth. When Elizabeth heard Mary's voice, the baby inside her jumped for joy. She was filled with the Holy Spirit and said, "God has blessed you more than any other woman. And God has blessed the baby you will have. You are the mother of my Lord, and you have come to me!" (Luke 1:42–43).

Elizabeth told Mary what happened. "When I heard your voice, the baby inside me jumped with joy. Great blessings are yours because you believed what the Lord said to you! You believed this would happen."

It must have been encouraging for Mary to hear Elizabeth's words. Everything Elizabeth said agreed with Gabriel's message to Mary. Elizabeth was loving and kind to Mary as she went through something very unusual and hard to understand. Mary had felt afraid and confused, but Elizabeth's words must have comforted and assured her that God's plans were good.

When God asks us to do something, He will help and encourage us along the way. At times He may tell us the same message more than once through His Word, through prayer, and through the words of others to help us be sure about what He wants us to do. He may send a friend to encourage us as we obey Him, like Elizabeth encouraged Mary. And God will always, always be with us and give us the strength to do what He asks us to do.

EXPLORE MORE: After hearing Elizabeth's words, Mary replied with a song of praise. Some versions of the Bible call this song the Magnificat. Read it in your Bible in Luke 1:46–55.

TALK TO GOD
Ask God to show you His plans and give you a willing heart.

DID YOU KNOW?
The distance from Nazareth, where Mary lived, to Hebron, where Elizabeth lived, is about 81 miles (131 kilometers). Depending on how fast Mary walked, it would have taken her somewhere between twenty and twenty-six hours to get there.

God provides what we need to do His work.

Joseph Listens to God

While Joseph thought about this, an angel of the Lord came to him in a dream. The angel said, "Joseph, descendant of David, don't be afraid to take Mary as your wife. The baby in her is from the Holy Spirit." —Matthew 1:20 ICB

Mary was engaged to marry a man named Joseph. The news of Mary's special baby must have been a big shock to Joseph since he and Mary weren't married yet. He must have had a lot of concerns and questions, and it was probably hard for him to understand what Mary told him about the angel's message.

The Bible says that Joseph was a good man and wanted to protect Mary. He decided not to marry her since he thought that was the right thing to do. He planned on breaking their engagement quietly. But then an angel visited Joseph in a dream. The angel said, "Don't be afraid to take Mary as your wife. The baby in her is from the Holy Spirit." The angel explained to Joseph God's wonderful and amazing plan. "You will name the son Jesus. Give him that name because he will save his people from their sins."

TALK TO GOD
Ask God to show you the right thing to do with a hard situation in your life.

When Joseph woke up, he did what the angel said and agreed to become Mary's husband. He followed God's plan and did what was right, even if it was very hard to understand.

Sometimes it can be hard to know the right thing to do. There isn't always a clear right or wrong way. But when we don't know what to do, we need to listen to what God says—by reading the Bible and talking to Him in prayer. Even though other people might have good advice, what God wants us to do is the most important thing. He always wants us to come to Him when we don't know what to do.

EXPLORE MORE: What can we do to find God's path? Look up Proverbs 3:5–6 to find out.

God tells me the right thing to do.

DID YOU KNOW?
Joseph was a carpenter, which means he built things. In Matthew 13, some people called Jesus "the son of the carpenter."

God with Us

"The virgin is going to have a baby. She will give birth to a son. And he will be called Immanuel." The name Immanuel means "God with us." —Matthew 1:23 NIrV

Have you ever heard people call Jesus "Immanuel"? We often hear this name for Jesus around Christmastime. You may have heard the Christmas song, "O Come, O Come Emmanuel." This name can be spelled with an *I*, from the Hebrew version, or an *E* from the Greek version. But do you know why Jesus is called "Immanuel"?

Matthew 1:23 tells us the name Immanuel means "God with us." It means that when Jesus was born, He was God in a human body, right here on earth, living with His people. And what's really special about this name is that the prophet Isaiah told us Jesus would be called Immanuel hundreds of years before He was born.

Isaiah said, "The Lord himself will give you a sign. The virgin is going to have a baby. She will give birth to a son. And he will be called Immanuel" (Isaiah 7:14). Matthew tells us everything that happened with Mary and Joseph, and the birth of Jesus fulfilled what God said in Isaiah. How wonderful is that!

Even though Jesus isn't living on earth today, He is still God with us. He understands exactly how we feel and what it's like to be us because He lived a human life. He didn't just try to help us from far away, He came down to where we live and became one of us so He could save us. He is always with us through the Holy Spirit in our hearts. He is always listening when we need someone to talk to. And one day we will see Him face to face and live with Him forever. Jesus truly is Immanuel!

TALK TO GOD
Tell Jesus how thankful you are that He came down to earth and lived a life just like you.

EXPLORE MORE: Read Hebrews 4:14-16. According to these verses, how was Jesus like us?

DID YOU KNOW?
The song "O Come, O Come Emmanuel" comes from a poem written in the eighth century. It was translated into English by J. M. Neale in 1851.

Jesus is God with us.

Jesus Is Born

*While Joseph and Mary were there, the time came for
the child to be born.* —Luke 2:6 NIrV

Caesar Augustus was the first emperor of Rome. He wanted to count the people in the whole Roman empire. He ordered everyone to go to their family's hometown to be counted in a census. Since Joseph was from David's family, he had to travel to Bethlehem with Mary, who would soon be having a baby. It may have taken five or six days for them to travel from Nazareth to Bethlehem, and it was not an easy trip! The winding mountain trails were dusty and bumpy, and some were not very safe.

When they finally reached Bethlehem, the small town was crowded with many travelers who had come for the census. While they were there, the time came for Jesus to be born. Mary wrapped Him in strips of cloth and placed Him in a manger because there was no room for them in the inn.

TALK TO GOD
Thank God for sending Jesus into the world so He could be our Lord and Savior.

We don't know for sure where Joseph and Mary stayed. It might have been a stable, or maybe an open space on the bottom floor of a house where families kept their animals. What we do know is that Jesus left His beautiful home in heaven so He could come to earth to save us.

He was born to be a King, but His first bed was a manger—a stone box that was used for feeding animals.

Jesus, the Messiah, was born in Bethlehem, just like the prophet Micah had foretold nearly seven hundred years earlier. This story shows us again how the Old Testament and New Testament fit together and how God makes all His words come true.

EXPLORE MORE: Read John 18:37. What is the reason Jesus gave for being born?

God planned that Jesus would be born in Bethlehem.

DID YOU KNOW?
It's about 70 miles (112 kilometers) from Nazareth to Bethlehem. The road is often referred to as the Nativity Trail.

Shepherds and Angels

Today in the town of David a Savior has been born to you.
He is the Messiah, the Lord. —Luke 2:11 NIrV

On the night Jesus was born, some shepherds were watching their sheep in a field near Bethlehem. This was something they did every night, but this night was different from all the other nights. While the shepherds were caring for their sheep, a bright angel suddenly appeared. The shepherds were terrified! But the angel said, "Do not be afraid. I bring you good news. It will bring great joy for all the people" (Luke 2:10).

The good news was that the Messiah had been born! The angel told the shepherds to go to Bethlehem and they would find the baby wrapped in strips of cloth and lying in a manger. Then an army of angels filled the sky, praising God and saying, "May glory be given to God in the highest heaven! And may peace be given to those He is pleased with on earth."

TALK TO GOD
Thank God for the gift of Jesus. Ask Him to help you share the good news with others.

When the angels went back to heaven, the shepherds said, "Let's go to Bethlehem. Let's see this thing that has happened, which the Lord has told us about." So, they hurried to Bethlehem and found the baby lying in the manger. Everything was just like the angel had said it would be.

DID YOU KNOW?
Lambs that were brought to the temple for sacrifice were often wrapped in strips of cloth. When the shepherds saw Jesus wrapped in strips of cloth, they were looking at the Lamb of God, who would sacrifice himself for us.

Some people wonder why God sent the angel to share the news of Jesus's birth with shepherds instead of an important king or ruler. During Bible times, people looked down on shepherds. They were often dirty and smelly from living out in the fields. But Jesus came to earth to save everyone who believed in Him—from royal kings to lowly shepherds. God loves everyone and wants all people to believe in Jesus.

EXPLORE MORE: Read Luke 2:17–20. What did the shepherds do after they saw Jesus? What did Mary do?

Jesus came for everyone.

Simeon and Anna Meet Jesus

"I have seen with my own eyes how you will save your people. Now all people can see your plan." —Luke 2:30–31 ERV

When Jesus was forty days old, Mary and Joseph brought Him to the temple to present Him to the Lord. This was a special rule from the Law of Moses. A man named Simeon, who lived in Jerusalem, loved God very much. The Holy Spirit had told Simeon that he would live to see the Messiah. The Holy Spirit led Simeon to the temple on the day Mary and Joseph were there with Jesus.

When Simeon saw the baby, he took Jesus in his arms and praised God. He said, "I have seen with my own eyes how you will save your people. Now all people can see your plan.

He is a light to show your way to the other nations. And he will bring honor to your people Israel."

There was also a woman at the temple named Anna. She was a prophetess and a widow. Anna never left the temple but stayed there to pray and worship God. When Anna saw Jesus, she gave thanks to God. Many people were waiting for God to send the Messiah, and Anna told them He had come.

TALK TO GOD
Thank Jesus for being the promised Messiah.

After meeting Jesus, Simeon and Anna thanked and praised God. Then they told others about Him. Today, we don't have to look for Jesus in a manger or a temple. You can meet Jesus right where you are. You can believe in your heart that He is God's Son, and you can ask Him to be your Savior.

When you get to know Jesus, you can praise and thank God like Simeon and Anna did. Then you can tell everyone you know about Jesus, so others can get to know Him too.

EXPLORE MORE: Read Luke 2:33 to learn how Joseph and Mary felt about what Simeon said.

I can get to know Jesus wherever I am.

DID YOU KNOW?
The Law of Moses required every firstborn male child to be dedicated to the Lord. The parents also had to offer a sacrifice of two doves or two young pigeons.

The Christmas Star

"Where is the child who has been born to be the king of the Jews? We saw the star that shows he was born. We saw it rise in the sky in the east and have come to worship him." —Matthew 2:2 ERV

In a city far from Jerusalem, some wise men saw a bright star in the sky and wondered what it meant. They remembered that the prophet Daniel had talked about signs in the sky, announcing the birth of a Savior. The wise men decided to follow the star, believing it would lead them to Jesus.

We don't know how long it took the wise men to get to Jerusalem, but it may have been many weeks or months. The roads through the desert were rough and dangerous, and they had to travel a long way.

When the wise men got to Jerusalem, they asked, "Where is the child who has been born to be the king of the Jews? We saw His star and have come to worship Him." King Herod was upset when he heard this because he didn't want anyone else to be king. He asked the priests and teachers where the Messiah would be born. They read the words from Micah 5:2, which said He would be born in Bethlehem. Herod told the wise men to go to Bethlehem and report back to him so he could worship Jesus too. But that's not really what he planned to do.

TALK TO GOD
Thank God for the Christmas star that led people to Jesus.

The wise men followed the star until it stopped above the house where Jesus was living with Mary and Joseph. When they finally found Jesus, they were overjoyed! They bowed down to worship Him and gave Him expensive gifts of gold, frankincense, and myrrh.

God placed a special star in the sky so all the world would know the Messiah He promised to send had come to earth.

EXPLORE MORE: Read Matthew 2:12 to find out why the wise men went home a different way.

DID YOU KNOW?
Frankincense is an oil that comes from the Boswellia trees found in the Middle East and Africa. The Israelites poured the oil on their offerings at the temple, and they also used it as perfume.

God wanted the world to know that Jesus had been born.

Three Dreams

After they left, an angel of the Lord came to Joseph in a dream. The angel said, "Get up! Take the child and his mother and escape to Egypt." —Matthew 2:13 ICB

Herod was upset when the wise men left Jerusalem without coming to see him. He wanted to find Jesus, too, but it wasn't so he could worship Him. Herod was a mean and jealous king who wanted to kill Jesus.

An angel of the Lord warned Joseph in a dream to take Mary and Jesus to Egypt where they would be safe. Joseph listened to God. He got up in the middle of the night and traveled with Mary and Jesus to Egypt. They lived there until Herod died.

Then Joseph had another dream. This time the angel of the Lord told him they could go back to Israel. So, Joseph brought Mary and Jesus home to Israel. When Joseph heard that Herod's son was the new king of Judea, he was afraid to go to Bethlehem. Joseph was warned in a third dream and took Mary and Jesus to live in Nazareth, a town in Galilee.

TALK TO GOD
Thank God that we can learn so much about Jesus by reading the Bible.

The dreams God gave Joseph kept Jesus safe from an evil king, but that's not the only reason God sent them. When Joseph left Egypt with Mary and Jesus, it fulfilled what God had said through Hosea the prophet. Hosea 11:1 says, "When Israel was a child, I loved him. And I called my son out of Egypt." And in Matthew 2:23 it says, "What God had said through the prophets came true: 'He will be called a Nazarene.'" Jesus grew up in Nazareth and many people called Him "Jesus of Nazareth."

God gave the prophets messages to help people know that Jesus was the Messiah. And He gave dreams to Joseph to make His messages come true.

EXPLORE MORE: Read John 1:45–46. What question did Nathaniel ask Jesus's disciple?

God's words always come true.

DID YOU KNOW?
Nazareth was a small town about 55 miles (88.5 kilometers) north of Jerusalem. The people from Nazareth were looked down upon by Judeans.

Jesus Amazes the Teachers

Everyone who heard him was amazed at how much he understood. They also were amazed at his answers. —Luke 2:47 NIrV

When Jesus was twelve years old, He went to Jerusalem with His parents to celebrate the Passover. The Jewish people celebrated this festival every year to remember how God delivered their ancestors from Egypt. Jesus and His family traveled for several days with many other people until they finally reached Jerusalem. The Passover lasted seven days. During that time, they ate special meals and offered sacrifices to God at the temple.

As Joseph and Mary traveled home, they thought Jesus was with their friends or relatives, but when they looked for Him, they couldn't find Him. They finally went back to the temple and found Jesus with the teachers of the law, listening and asking questions. The teachers were amazed at how much Jesus knew and understood. Joseph and Mary told Jesus they had been very worried. But Jesus said, "Why were you looking for me? Didn't you know I had to be in my Father's house?" (Luke 2:49). They didn't understand what Jesus meant, but Mary remembered what He said and kept it like a treasure in her heart.

TALK TO GOD
Ask Jesus to teach you with His great wisdom.

Jesus went back to Nazareth with His parents and obeyed them. This is the only Bible story about Jesus as a boy. But in Luke 2:52 ERV it says, "As Jesus grew taller, he continued to grow in wisdom. God was pleased with him and so were the people who knew him."

Jesus had to grow up, just like you do, and He understands what it's like to be a kid. Whenever you need to talk to Him, He will listen—just like He listened to the teachers at the temple.

DID YOU KNOW?
From age six to age ten, a child can grow as much as ten inches.

EXPLORE MORE: How did the people respond to Jesus when He first began His ministry? Read Mark 1:21–22 to find out.

Jesus will listen to me.

A Preacher in the Desert

When it was the right time, John the Baptizer began telling people a message from God. This was out in the desert area of Judea.
—Matthew 3:1 ERV

Mary's relative Elizabeth had a baby boy a few months before Jesus was born. His name was John, and God had important work for him to do. God chose John to prepare the way for Jesus's ministry on earth. He lived in the desert and ate locusts

and wild honey. He wore clothes made from camel's hair and tied a leather belt around his waist.

John was a preacher in the desert of Judea. Many people from all over Judea came to see him. His message was, "Change your hearts and lives, because God's kingdom is now very near" (Matthew 3:2). When the people said they were sorry for their sins, John baptized them in the Jordan River.

TALK TO GOD
Ask God to help you do important things for Him.

The prophet Isaiah had prophesied about John. In Isaiah 40:3 it says, "Listen, there is someone shouting: 'Prepare a way in the desert for the Lord. Make a straight road there for our God.'"

John told his followers that someone greater and more powerful was coming soon. John was talking about Jesus. John said that he baptized with water, but Jesus would baptize with the Holy Spirit.

Even though many people followed John the Baptist, he never thought he was important. In verses 28 and 30 of John chapter 3, he said, "'I am not the Messiah. I am only the one God sent to prepare the way for him. . . . He must become more and more important, and I must become less important.'"

Many people have important jobs, and we all have important things to do. But no one is more important than Jesus, and nothing is more important than telling others about Him.

EXPLORE MORE: Read what John said about Jesus in Mark 1:7.

Jesus is more important than anyone.

DID YOU KNOW?

Locusts belong to the grasshopper family, and people in many countries eat them. They are packed with protein and can be smoked, fried, or roasted until they are crunchy.

Jesus Is Baptized

A voice from heaven said, "This is my Son, and I love him. I am very pleased with him." —Matthew 3:17 NIrV

One day Jesus came from Galilee and saw John the Baptist at the Jordan River. Jesus asked John to baptize Him. At first John was confused and said that Jesus should baptize him instead. But Jesus said, "Let it be this way for now. It is right for us to do this. It carries out God's holy plan." So John agreed to baptize Jesus.

When Jesus came up out of the water, the heavens opened, and God's Spirit came down in the form of a dove and rested on Him. Then a voice from heaven said, "This is my Son, and I love him. I am very pleased with him."

The voice from heaven was the voice of God. He sent Jesus to earth to save the world from sin and show us how much God loves us. And Jesus also came to earth to teach people how to love God and how to love each other.

John baptized people after they turned away from their sin. Their baptism was a sign that they were choosing to follow God and have their sins washed away. Even though Jesus never sinned, He was baptized to show that He was obedient to following God's plan for His life on earth.

TALK TO GOD
Ask God to help you follow His plan for your life like Jesus did.

Jesus is our greatest example of how to live. Like Jesus, we can choose to follow God's plan for our lives and be obedient to Him. Even though we will never be able to live a life without sin, we can have our sins washed away by believing in Jesus. Jesus lived a perfect life for us, so we don't have to.

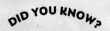

DID YOU KNOW?
Nearly a million visitors every year go to see where John baptized Jesus in the Jordan River, and many choose to get baptized there too.

EXPLORE MORE: What did John say about Jesus in John 1:14–15?

Believing in Jesus washes my sins away.

Jesus Is Tempted

Jesus said to the devil, "Go away from me, Satan! It is written in the Scriptures, 'You must worship the Lord your God. Serve only him!'"
—Matthew 4:10 ICB

After Jesus was baptized, the Holy Spirit led Him into the wilderness to be alone. He didn't eat for forty days and was very hungry. The devil, who is also called Satan, is God's enemy. He came to Jesus to make Him sin. First, he told Jesus to turn stones into bread. But Jesus spoke the words from Deuteronomy 8:3. "It is written in the Scriptures, 'A person does not live only by eating bread. But a person lives by everything the Lord says'" (Matthew 4:4).

Then Satan led Jesus to a high place on the temple and told Jesus to jump off. He said God's angels would catch Him. But Jesus answered with words from Deuteronomy 6:16, "Do not test the Lord your God."

Satan tried one more time. He took Jesus to a high mountain and showed Him all the kingdoms of the world. He said, "If you will bow down and worship me, I will give you all these things." Jesus said to him, "Go away from me, Satan! It is written in the Scriptures, 'You must worship the Lord your God. Serve only him!'" Then Satan went away, and angels came to be with Jesus.

The devil tempted Jesus because he wanted Jesus to sin against God. But Jesus didn't listen to him. Jesus spoke words from Scripture to help Him stay strong against temptation. Satan wants us to sin too, and Jesus is our example of what to do when we're tempted. You can think about Bible verses you know. You can remember that obeying God is always right. And you can ask God to help you be strong. Temptation can be strong, but God is stronger.

EXPLORE MORE: What does 1 Corinthians 10:13 say about temptation?

TALK TO GOD
Ask God to help you be strong when you are tempted.

Jesus is my example of how to face temptation.

DID YOU KNOW?
The highest point of the temple was called the pinnacle, and it was located at the southeast corner of the building.

Jesus Goes to Capernaum

[Jesus] left Nazareth and went and lived in Capernaum, a town near Lake Galilee. Capernaum is in the area near Zebulun and Naphtali.
—Matthew 4:13 ICB

We know from reading the Bible that Jesus moved from one place to another. He was born in Bethlehem, and then lived in Egypt where God kept Him safe from King Herod. After that, Jesus grew up in Nazareth in the region of Galilee. All these places fulfilled what the Old Testament prophets said about the Messiah.

In Matthew 4, we learn that Jesus left Nazareth and began His teaching ministry in Capernaum, in the area of Zebulun and Naphtali by the Sea of Galilee. And do you know what? This fulfilled an Old Testament prophecy too!

In Isaiah 9, the prophet Isaiah said the land of Zebulun and Naphtali would be made great. This land stretched along the Mediterranean Sea to the land along the Jordan River. It continued north to Galilee where the people who were not Israelites lived. Isaiah 9:2 says, "Now those people live in darkness. But they will see a great light. They live in a place that is very dark. But a light will shine on them." That light is Jesus.

TALK TO GOD
Thank God for all the verses in the Bible that point to Jesus.

God sent Jesus to be a light to the world—to the Jewish people and also to people who are not Jewish, called gentiles. Most of His time was spent in the region of Galilee, but news about Jesus spread all over the world.

The prophets of the Old Testament and disciples of the New Testament wrote down the words God gave them. Because they did, the whole world can know that Jesus is the Son of God who came to save us. He is a light in the darkness to shine for all to see.

EXPLORE MORE: According to Isaiah 9:3, what would happen to the people living in Zebulun and Naphtali?

DID YOU KNOW?
Zebulun and Naphtali were two of Jacob's sons. Their descendants became two of the tribes that settled in the northern area of the promised land.

Jesus is a light in the darkness.

Jesus Finds His First Followers

"Come and follow me," Jesus said. "I will send you out to fish for people." —Matthew 4:19 NIrV

As Jesus walked along the Sea of Galilee, He saw two fishermen throwing nets into the water. One was Simon, who was also called Peter, and the other was his brother, Andrew. Jesus called to them, "Come and follow me! I will send you out to fish for people." Do you know what Simon and Andrew did? They left their nets right there and followed Jesus.

Farther along the shore, Jesus saw two more fishermen who were also brothers. Their names were James and John, and they were fixing their nets with their father, Zebedee. Jesus said, "Come and follow me!" Do you know what they did? They left everything and followed Jesus!

A man named Philip also agreed to follow Jesus. Then Philip told his friend Nathanael about Jesus. He said, "We have found the one whom Moses wrote about in the Law. The prophets also wrote about him. He is Jesus of Nazareth, the son of Joseph."

At first, Nathanael doubted. "Can anything good come from Nazareth?" he asked.

But when Jesus saw Nathanael He said, "He is a true Israelite. Nothing about him is false."

Nathanael was surprised. "How do you know me?" he asked. Jesus said, "I saw you under the fig tree, before Philip told you about me." Then Nathanael knew Jesus was the Son of God, and he followed Jesus too.

These men learned from John the Baptist that the Messiah was coming soon. They also knew what the Old Testament prophets had written. Their hearts were ready to meet Jesus and follow Him. When people's hearts are ready to follow Jesus, they will know and believe that He is the Messiah.

EXPLORE MORE: Read Mark 3:17 to find out the name Jesus gave to James and John.

TALK TO GOD
Ask God to help you follow Jesus every day.

My heart is ready to follow Jesus.

DID YOU KNOW?
In Bible times, fishing with nets was usually done at night so the fish couldn't see the nets. Otherwise they would swim around the nets and not get caught.

Jesus's First Miracle

This was the first of all the miraculous signs Jesus did. He did it in the town of Cana in Galilee. By this he showed his divine greatness, and his followers believed in him. —John 2:11 ERV

Jesus was invited to a wedding in Cana, which was in Galilee. He went with His mother, Mary, and some of His followers. In Bible times weddings were big celebrations and lasted for several days. Jesus's mother came to Him and said, "They have no more wine."

Mary must have known that Jesus could help. He hadn't done any miracles yet, but she knew that God's power was in Him. Maybe she remembered the words the angel Gabriel had said—that Jesus would be great and would be the Son of the Most High. Maybe she remembered the words of Simeon who said, "I have seen with my own eyes how God will save His people." Mary treasured many things in her heart, so somehow, she knew Jesus could help. Mary said to the wedding servants, "Do whatever He tells you to do."

TALK TO GOD
Say thank you to Jesus that He has power to do miracles.

Jesus saw six stone water jars that the Jewish people used for their washing ceremonies. He told the servants to fill them with water, so they did. Then Jesus said, "Dip out some water and take it to the man in charge of the feast."

When the man in charge tasted the water, it had turned into wine. He didn't know where the new wine came from, but the servants and Jesus's followers knew. The man said to the bridegroom, "People serve the best wine first, but you have saved the best for now."

That was the first miracle Jesus did on earth to show He was the Son of God. His followers were amazed and put their faith in Him. And they would continue to be amazed as they kept following Him.

EXPLORE MORE: Read Acts 2:22 to see what Peter said about Jesus.

DID YOU KNOW?
The Wedding Feast at Cana is a famous oil painting by Paolo Veronese painted in 1563. Until 1700, the painting hung in the San Giorgio Monastery in Venice, Italy. It now hangs in the Louvre Museum in Paris, France.

Jesus's power is amazing.

Jesus Shows His Power

The people were amazed. They asked each other, "What is happening here? This man is teaching something new. And he teaches with authority. He even gives commands to evil spirits, and they obey him." —Mark 1:27 ICB

Jesus was in Capernaum on the Sabbath day. He went into the synagogue, which is like a temple, and began to teach. The people who listened to Him were amazed that Jesus spoke with more authority than the teachers of the law.

While Jesus was teaching, a man came into the synagogue who had an evil spirit in him. The evil spirit cried out, "Jesus of Nazareth! What do you want with us? Did you come to destroy us? I know who you are—God's Holy One!" (Mark 1:24).

Then Jesus commanded, "Be quiet! Come out of the man!" The man began to shake, and the spirit gave a loud cry and came out of him.

The people were stunned. They saw with their own eyes and heard with their own ears everything that happened. They said, "What is happening? Even the evil spirits obey Him!"

This miracle showed that Jesus has power over Satan. No power in heaven or earth is greater than God's power. And since Jesus is the Son of God, He has God's power within Him.

TALK TO GOD
Thank Jesus that He cares about people and can help them.

The news about Jesus spread quickly through Galilee. Many more people began following Jesus to listen to Him teach and watch His miracles. People who were sick came to Jesus to be healed, and many believed in Him.

You can follow Jesus too by reading these amazing stories in your Bible and learning more about His earthly ministry. You can ask Jesus to help you with any problems you have. And you can thank Him that He cares for you just like He cared for people long ago.

EXPLORE MORE: Who did Jesus heal in Mark 1:29–31?

Jesus's power is the greatest of all.

DID YOU KNOW?
A synagogue is a place of worship for Jewish people. It is believed that synagogues were first used by the Israelites when they were in Babylon.

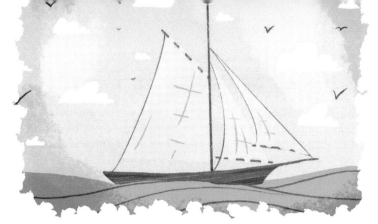

A Net Full of Fish

When Jesus finished speaking, he said to Simon, "Take the boat into the deep water. If all of you will put your nets into the water, you will catch some fish." —Luke 5:4 ERV

As Jesus stood by the Sea of Galilee, people tried to get closer to Him. Jesus got in Simon Peter's boat and told Him to push it out into the water. Then He sat in the boat and taught the people who were on shore.

When Jesus finished teaching, He told Simon to go out into the deep water and let down the nets. Since they had just washed their nets, they were probably tired and not happy about going back out on the lake. Simon told Jesus, "Master, we worked hard all night trying to catch fish and caught nothing. But you say I should put the nets into the water, so I will" (Luke 5:5).

The fishermen did what Jesus told them to do. They caught so many fish their nets began to break. They hollered out to their friends in another boat to come and help them. Both of the boats were so full of fish they began to sink! When Simon saw this, he bowed before Jesus and said, "Go away from me, Lord. I am a sinful man!"

TALK TO GOD
Thank Jesus that you can be part of His kingdom.

But Jesus said to Simon, "Don't be afraid. From now on your work will be to bring in people, not fish!"

James and John were with Simon too. They were Jesus's first disciples. Now they knew for sure that Jesus was the Messiah, and they would work with Him to bring people into God's kingdom. Just like there were too many fish to count, the people who would come to follow Jesus would also be too many to count. Even today, more and more people are added to God's kingdom by believing in Jesus.

DID YOU KNOW?
The Sea of Galilee is the largest freshwater lake in Israel and is popular with people who like to fish. Thousands of fish are caught every year including tilapia, sardine, and catfish.

EXPLORE MORE: Read James 2:5. Who can be included in God's kingdom?

God's kingdom has many people.

Jesus Heals a Humble Man

Jesus reached out his hand and touched the man. "I am willing to do it," he said. "Be 'clean'!" —Luke 5:13 NIrV

Jesus was walking through a town when a man with a bad skin disease came to Him. The man fell face down to the ground when he saw Jesus. The man begged Jesus, "Lord, if you are willing to make me 'clean,' you can do it."

Jesus had compassion for the man. He reached out His hand and touched the man. "I am willing to do it," he said. "Be 'clean'!" And just like that, the man was completely healed of His skin disease.

TALK TO GOD
Thank Jesus that He has the power to heal.

The man's skin disease was called leprosy, and it was common in Jesus's day. One person could catch it easily from someone who had it, and it was very serious. People who had it needed to live by themselves or with other lepers. If people with leprosy went out to be around other people, they would shout, "Unclean, unclean," to warn others to stay away from them.

The man with leprosy must have heard about Jesus's miracles and how He could heal people. He believed that Jesus could make him well, so he went out to find Him. The way he talked to Jesus showed that he was a humble man. He didn't demand that Jesus heal him. He said, "Lord, if you are willing."

Jesus reached out and touched the man to heal him. This was not something anyone else would have done. People were afraid to get close to someone with leprosy because they didn't want to get the disease. By touching the man, Jesus showed His love. By healing the man, Jesus showed His power. The news about Jesus continued to spread, and crowds of people followed Jesus wherever He went.

EXPLORE MORE: What did Jesus tell the man to do after He healed his skin disease? Luke 5:14 will give you the answer.

Jesus is willing to heal people.

DID YOU KNOW?
Leprosy is also known as Hansen's disease. It can now be cured with a combination of antibiotics. The World Health Organization provides free treatment for people with leprosy.

Faithful Friends

When Jesus saw that they had faith, he spoke to the man. He said, "Friend, your sins are forgiven." —Luke 5:20 NIrV

One day Jesus was at a home, teaching and healing people. The Pharisees and teachers of the law were there too. They had heard about Jesus and wanted to see for themselves what He was doing.

A man who couldn't walk had some friends who carried him on a mat. They wanted Jesus to heal him, but the house was too crowded for them to get in. They carried the man on his mat to the top of the roof. Then they cut a hole in the roof and lowered him down in front of Jesus.

Jesus saw that the man's friends had faith in Him. Jesus said to the man, "Friend, your sins are forgiven."

The Pharisees and teachers of the law were angry. They thought to themselves, "How does this man dare to say such things? Only God can forgive sins!"

Jesus knew what they were thinking. "Why are you thinking these things?" He asked. "Is it easier to say, 'Your sins are forgiven,' or 'get up and walk'? The Son of Man has authority on earth to forgive sins." Then Jesus said to the man, "Get up! Take your mat and go home!"

The man stood up, picked up His mat, and walked home praising God. Everyone in the house was able to see that Jesus had the power to heal. The teachers of the law and the Pharisees saw what Jesus did too, but they did not put their faith in Him. They were not happy that so many people were following Jesus. But as Jesus continued to heal and perform miracles, the crowds that followed Jesus grew bigger every day.

EXPLORE MORE: Read Luke 5:26. How did the people respond when they saw the man get up and walk?

TALK TO GOD
Ask God to help you be a faithful friend, like the friends in this story.

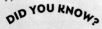

DID YOU KNOW?
In Bible times, some homes had an outdoor stairway that led to a flat roof that was made of sticks and clay.

Jesus sees our faith.

Matthew Follows Jesus

Jesus heard the Pharisees ask this. So he said, "Healthy people don't need a doctor. Only the sick need a doctor." —Matthew 9:12 ICB

As Jesus walked through the town of Capernaum, he saw a man named Matthew, who was also called Levi. Matthew was sitting in a booth where he collected taxes from the Jewish people. Even though Matthew was Jewish, he worked for the Roman government.

The Jewish people did not like tax collectors. The Roman leaders asked for too much money from the Jews, and many of the tax collectors were not honest. Sometimes they would take extra money from the people and keep it for themselves.

Jesus looked at Matthew in his booth. "Follow me," He said. So Matthew left his booth and followed Jesus.

Matthew invited Jesus to his house for dinner. He invited other people too, including more tax collectors. When the Pharisees saw Jesus at Matthew's house, they asked His disciples, "Why does your teacher eat with tax collectors and 'sinners'?"

When Jesus heard what they said He replied, "Healthy people don't need a doctor. Only the sick need a doctor." Then He told them to learn what this means: "I want faithful love more than I want animal sacrifices." Those are words from the prophet Hosea (Hosea 6:6).

Jesus wants all people to follow Him, no matter how good or bad they seem. He wants to give us a new life that only He can give. But Jesus wants people to follow Him because they love Him. He doesn't care about traditions and sacrifices and offerings if people's hearts are not right with God.

Jesus reached out to sinful people because they needed a Savior. And He still reaches out to people today—because everyone still needs a Savior.

TALK TO GOD
Thank Jesus that He invites everyone to follow Him.

EXPLORE MORE: Read Mark 3:16–19 to learn the names of the twelve disciples who followed Jesus.

Jesus wants all people to follow Him.

DID YOU KNOW?
The book of Matthew includes nine references to Old Testament prophecies that Jesus fulfilled. Matthew refers to more verses from the Old Testament than any other New Testament book.

Jesus and Nicodemus

God so loved the world that he gave his one and only Son. Anyone who believes in him will not die but will have eternal life. —John 3:16 NIrV

Nicodemus was an important Jewish ruler who wanted to talk to Jesus, so he met with Jesus at night. Maybe he didn't want other Jewish rulers to see him talking to Jesus. They didn't want anything to do with Jesus, but Nicodemus knew there was something special about Him.

Nicodemus had seen Jesus heal people. He said to Jesus, "We know that God is with you. If he weren't, you couldn't do the signs you are doing."

Jesus told Nicodemus, "What I'm about to tell you is true. No one can see God's kingdom unless they are born again."

Nicodemus was confused. He didn't understand how someone can be born a second time. But Jesus wasn't talking about being born again as a baby. Jesus meant that by believing in Him, people can have a new life on earth and a home in heaven that lasts forever. It's a person's spirit that gets born again, not their body.

TALK TO GOD
Thank God for sending Jesus to die on the cross so that everyone who believes in Him can have eternal life, including you!

Today's Bible verse, John 3:16, is like putting the whole message of the Bible into one verse. God sent Jesus to earth because He loves us so much and wants us to live with Him forever. God is holy, and we are not. That's why God sent His Son to die on the cross to pay for our sins, so we can be made holy. God didn't send Jesus to earth to tell us how bad we are. God sent Jesus to save us.

Being born again is not about obeying rules. It's believing that Jesus is the Son of God and asking Him to be our Savior. Then we can follow Jesus and love Him back.

EXPLORE MORE: Read John 19:38–40 to find out something Nicodemus did after Jesus died.

DID YOU KNOW?

For a football game in 2009, Tim Tebow wrote John 3:16 in black under his eye. That day, 90 million people googled the Bible verse to see what it says.

God sent Jesus because He loves me.

A Samaritan Woman Meets Jesus

"But those who drink the water I give will never be thirsty again. It becomes a fresh, bubbling spring within them, giving them eternal life." —John 4:14 NLT

As Jesus traveled from Judea to Galilee, He stopped at Jacob's well in Samaria. A woman came to draw water from the well, so Jesus asked her for a drink. She was surprised because Jews didn't like Samaritans. The woman said to Jesus, "You are a Jew, and I am a Samaritan woman. Why are you asking me for a drink?"

Jesus answered, "If you only knew the gift God has for you and who you are speaking to, you would ask me, and I would give you living water."

The woman was confused. Living water was the fresh water that flowed at the very bottom of the well, and Jesus didn't even have a bucket or rope to get the water. "Do you think you're greater than our ancestor Jacob, who gave us this well?" she asked. "How can you offer better water?"

Jesus said, "Those who drink the water I give will never be thirsty again."

TALK TO GOD
Ask Jesus to fill you up with living water.

"Please, sir," she said, "give me this water! Then I'll never be thirsty again, and I won't have to come here to get water."

Jesus was talking about water for our souls. Just like people get thirsty for a drink of water, our souls are thirsty for God. Believing in Jesus is like water for our souls. It fills us with God's love and keeps filling us up as we follow Him.

As Jesus talked with the woman, He told her all about her past. She said, "I know the Messiah is coming—the one who is called Christ. When he comes, he will explain everything to us."

Then Jesus said, "I AM the Messiah!"

The woman was so excited, she dropped her water jars and ran to tell everyone about the man who told her everything she ever did.

EXPLORE MORE: What did the Samaritans do when the woman from the well told them about Jesus? Read John 4:39–42 to find out.

Jesus gives us living water.

DID YOU KNOW?
Jacob's Well Natural Area in Wimberly, Texas, is a free-flowing spring that releases thousands of gallons of water a day. It is the second largest submerged cave in Texas.

Jesus Tells Us How to Live

One day as he saw the crowds gathering, Jesus went up on the mountainside and sat down. His disciples gathered around him, and he began to teach them. —Matthew 5:1—2 NLT

As more people heard about Jesus, large crowds followed Him wherever He went. One day when He saw a crowd gathering, He went up on the side of a mountain to teach everyone who came to see Him. This teaching is called the Sermon on the Mount. In the sermon, Jesus taught eight blessings called the Beatitudes.

This is what Jesus said:

God blesses those who are poor and realize their need for him,
> for the Kingdom of Heaven is theirs.

God blesses those who mourn,
> for they will be comforted.

God blesses those who are humble,
> for they will inherit the whole earth.

God blesses those who hunger and thirst for justice,
> for they will be satisfied.

God blesses those who are merciful,
> for they will be shown mercy.

God blesses those whose hearts are pure,
> for they will see God.

God blesses those who work for peace,
> for they will be called the children of God.

God blesses those who are persecuted for doing right,
> for the Kingdom of Heaven is theirs. (Matthew 5:3–10 NLT)

TALK TO GOD
Ask God to help you receive the blessings of the Beatitudes by living like Him.

With these words, Jesus told everyone what His kingdom is all about. When we become a part of God's family through believing in Jesus, the Beatitudes are like a map for us. They show us how to live out our love for God every day. The map takes us on a path of recognizing we need God, we need to be humble and merciful, and we should work to get along with others.

And then we use our map to help others. We tell our friends and family what Jesus said. He loves us and wants us to live in a way that keeps us close to Him and brings us the most happiness.

EXPLORE MORE: What does God do when people make fun of us for following Jesus? Look up Matthew 5:11–12 to find out.

DID YOU KNOW?
The Mount of Beatitudes is a hill in northern Israel located on the Korazim Plateau. It is believed that Jesus preached the Sermon on the Mount on this hill.

The Beatitudes tell us what Jesus's kingdom is about.

Salty and Bright

"You are the light that shines for the world to see. You are like a city built on a hill that cannot be hidden." —Matthew 5:14 ERV

After Jesus finished preaching the Beatitudes, He taught His followers another lesson. Jesus said they were like salt and light. It might sound strange, but those were two important things during Bible times.

First Jesus said, "You are the salt of the earth. But suppose the salt loses its saltiness. How can it be made salty again? It is no longer good for anything." During the time Jesus lived, salt was worth a lot of money. Jesus was saying His followers are precious to God. Salt was also used to add flavor and keep meat from going bad. Jesus wanted His followers to bring flavor to the world through their joy. He wanted them to keep themselves and the world from "going bad" by guarding against sin.

TALK TO GOD
Ask God to help you shine brightly for Him and to add His flavor wherever you go.

Next Jesus said, "You are the light that shines for the world to see. . . . People don't hide a lamp under a bowl. They put it on a lampstand. Then the light shines for everyone in the house." We don't turn on a light and hide it. In the same way, Jesus wanted His followers to be a light for other people. He wanted them to live so others would see the good things they did and praise God.

Even though Jesus spoke these words thousands of years ago, He still wants His followers to be salt and light. We are precious to God, and we can give people a taste of what God is like by loving them the way He does. Jesus is like a bright light that shines into our hearts. We can shine His light by caring for others and showing the love and peace of Jesus. We can be salty and bright!

EXPLORE MORE: What did Jesus say about himself in John 8:12?

I am salt and light.

DID YOU KNOW?
Salt used to be so valuable that it was used as money for trade. This is where the phrase "worth his salt" comes from.

Teach Us to Pray

One day Jesus was praying in a certain place. When he finished, one of his disciples spoke to him. "Lord," he said, "teach us to pray, just as John taught his disciples." —Luke 11:1 NIrV

Jesus often went to quiet places to pray. Sometimes He went by himself, and sometimes His disciples went with Him. One day when He was praying, one of His disciples said, "Lord, teach us to pray."

Jesus said, "When you pray, this is what you should say. 'Father, may your name be honored. May your kingdom come. Give us each day our daily bread. Forgive us our sins, as we also forgive everyone who sins against us. Keep us from falling into sin when we are tempted.'"

This special prayer became known as the Lord's Prayer, and many Christians have learned it over the years. Groups of Christians will often say this prayer at church or other special services. Have you ever heard these words before? Whether or not you know this prayer, you can pray the way Jesus taught His disciples. You can start by telling God how wonderful His name is and ask that it be treated as holy. Then you can ask God to bring His kingdom to earth—by having His way each day and having Jesus return to build His kingdom.

> **TALK TO GOD**
> Pray the words of the Lord's Prayer found in Matthew 6:9–13.

Next you can ask God for what you need today. Nothing is too big or small to ask for. Then, ask God to forgive your sins and help you forgive others when they do something wrong to you. Finally, you can end your prayer by asking God to keep you from doing the wrong thing when you are tempted.

The Lord's Prayer is a great way to pray, and there are many other ways to pray too. Any time we pray with an open heart, God will listen to us.

EXPLORE MORE: Read Romans 8:26–27. What does the Holy Spirit do for us when we don't know what to pray?

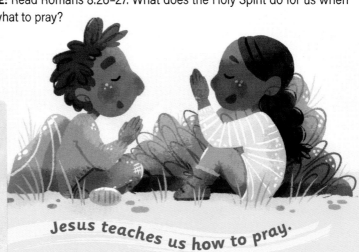

> **DID YOU KNOW?**
> Other names for the Lord's Prayer are the Our Father, Oratio Dominica (which means "Lord's Prayer" in Latin), and the Pater Noster (which means "Our Father" in Latin).

Jesus teaches us how to pray.

Ask, Seek, and Knock

"And so I tell you, keep on asking, and you will receive what you ask for. Keep on seeking, and you will find. Keep on knocking, and the door will be opened to you." —Luke 11:9 NLT

When you get hungry, what happens when you ask your parents for something to eat? Do they give you a dog bone? Do they pick up a stick from the ground and put it in a hotdog bun with ketchup? No, your parents give you real food! Seeing those silly things on your plate might make you giggle, but your parents don't give them to you when you're hungry because they aren't good for you to eat.

> **TALK TO GOD**
> Ask God to help you learn more about Him and grow closer to Him every day.

Your parents give you what you need when you ask, and so does God. Jesus told His followers, "Keep on asking, and you will receive what you ask for. Keep on seeking, and you will find. Keep on knocking, and the door will be opened to you. For everyone who asks, receives. Everyone who seeks, finds. And to everyone who knocks, the door will be opened."

Sometimes when we ask God for something, He might not give it to us right away. And other times, He might say no. But we know that He wants the very best for us, so when He says no, it's because He loves us—just like when our parents say no to keep us safe or to do what's best for us. The Bible tells us in 1 John 5:14 that whenever we ask for something that goes along with God's best plan, He hears us and gives us what we ask for. We can always be sure God's answer to our prayers is loving and part of His plan.

The best thing we can pray for is to know more about God and grow closer to Him. That's what asking, seeking, and knocking are all about.

EXPLORE MORE: Read Luke 11:11–13. What is the good gift God gives to those who ask Him?

God answers my prayers.

DID YOU KNOW?
In France, people eat pigeon dinners at fancy restaurants. Pigeon is considered an elegant meal and can be an expensive item on the menu.

Don't Worry

"The thing you should want most is God's kingdom and doing what God wants. Then all these other things you need will be given to you." —Matthew 6:33 ICB

Have you ever seen a bird going shopping at the grocery store? Or have you ever seen a flower making a beautiful dress to wear? Of course not! That would be so silly! Birds find their food outside each day as they fly around. And flowers don't need to create fancy clothes because their petals are so beautiful. God gives the birds what they need to eat each day, and God makes the flowers of the fields look more beautiful than the fanciest dress.

That's exactly what Jesus taught His followers on the mountainside. He said that when we see birds, we can remember God feeds them every day. And when we look at flowers growing in a field, we can remember God dresses them in beautiful colors. Jesus told the people that God would take care of them too: "And you know that you are worth much more than the birds," He said. "God clothes the grass in the field . . . so you can be even more sure that God will clothe you."

Jesus wants us to know God will always give us what we need, just like He told His followers long ago. Instead of worrying about what to eat or what to wear, Jesus wants us to spend our time thinking about God's kingdom and what God wants us to do. God already knows what we need and how He will give it to us. Whether we have a lot or a little, He promises to always watch over us, so we can think about more important things like loving and serving Him.

EXPLORE MORE: Jesus said the flowers were dressed fancier than one of the richest kings in history. Read Matthew 6:29 to find out who it was.

TALK TO GOD
Ask God to give you what you need today and thank Him for always taking care of you.

DID YOU KNOW?
The type of food birds eat depends on their species and the time of year. During the spring and summer, songbirds eat insects and spiders. In the winter, birds that don't migrate eat fruit and seeds.

God gives me what I need.

Solid Rock

"Anyone who listens to my teaching and follows it is wise, like a person who builds a house on solid rock." —Matthew 7:24 NLT

When construction workers start building a house, one of the first things they do is make a foundation. The foundation is usually something hard and sturdy—like concrete or stone. It's like a base that the rest of the house is built on. The job of a foundation is to hold up the weight of the house and keep water and wet soil from getting in. The foundation is the most important part of the house.

TALK TO GOD
Ask God to help you build your life on Jesus.

Jesus told His followers that we all have the choice to build on a good foundation. But He wasn't talking about building a house. He was talking about following His teaching in our lives. When we hear Jesus's words and do what He says, we become like a wise person who builds a house on solid rock. When bad things happen, Jesus told us we will be like a strong house in a big storm: "Though the rain comes in torrents and the floodwaters rise and the winds beat against that house, it won't collapse because it is built on bedrock."

Jesus also told us what happens when people hear His words and don't follow Him. He said, "But anyone who hears my teaching and doesn't obey it is foolish, like a person who builds a house on sand. When the rains and floods come and the winds beat against that house, it will collapse with a mighty crash."

What we choose to build our lives on is the most important decision we make. We can choose to build our lives on doing things our own way like sinking sand, or the solid rock of Jesus's perfect teaching.

EXPLORE MORE: What is God called in Deuteronomy 32:4?

Jesus is the solid rock.

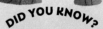

DID YOU KNOW?

Reinforced concrete is used to create foundations for many new houses. Builders make wooden forms and then put steel reinforcing bars in between the forms. The forms are filled with poured concrete to finish the foundation.

A Roman Officer's Faith

The officer answered, "Lord, I am not good enough for you to come into my house. All you need to do is command that my servant be healed, and he will be healed." —Matthew 8:8 ICB

In the Old Testament, God promised the Messiah would come for everyone—not just the Israelites. In Matthew 8 we read one of the first stories about a man who believed in Jesus who was not an Israelite. That man was an officer in the Roman army.

As Jesus went into Capernaum, the officer came to Jesus and begged Him for help. He said, "Lord, my servant is at home in bed. He can't move his body and is in much pain."

Jesus answered, "I will go and heal him."

Instead of bringing Jesus to the servant, the Roman officer said something surprising. "Lord, I am not good enough for you to come into my house. All you need to do is command that my servant be healed, and he will be healed. I myself am a man under the authority of other men. And I have soldiers under my command. I tell one soldier, 'Go,' and he goes. I tell another soldier, 'Come,' and he comes." Jesus was amazed by these words. He told the people around Him, "This man has more faith than any other person I have found, even in Israel." Then Jesus told the Roman soldier, "Go home. Your servant will be healed just as you believed he would." At that moment, the servant was healed.

We don't have to be born into a certain family or country to have faith. All we need to do is believe Jesus is the Messiah and believe in His power, just like the Roman soldier did.

EXPLORE MORE: What did the apostle Paul say about the gospel in Romans 1:15–17?

TALK TO GOD
Ask God to help you have a strong faith in Jesus and His power.

DID YOU KNOW?
The Roman soldier in today's story is also called a centurion. A centurion was the commander of a century, which was a group of one hundred soldiers.

Anyone can have faith in Jesus.

The Farmer and His Seeds

"Still other seed fell on good soil. It grew up and produced a crop 30, 60, or even 100 times more than the farmer planted."
—Mark 4:8 NIrV

As Jesus began teaching by the Sea of Galilee, people crowded around Him. So, Jesus sat in a boat and taught those who were on shore. Jesus told a parable, which is a story to help people understand the truth of God's Word.

Jesus said, "A farmer went out to plant seeds and scattered them on the ground. Some seeds fell on a hard path, but the birds came and ate them. Some seeds fell in rocky places where there wasn't enough soil. The plants grew quickly but dried up from the sun because they had no roots. Other seeds landed among thorns, which crowded out the plants when they started to grow. But the seeds that fell on good soil produced a crop of thirty, sixty, or one hundred times more than the farmer planted."

> **TALK TO GOD**
> Ask God to help you have a heart that's always open to learning more about Him.

When the disciples were alone with Jesus, they asked Him the meaning of the parable. Jesus explained that the seed is like God's message and the soil is like the hearts of people who hear it. Some people hear God's message but don't believe it because their hearts are like the hard path. Other people believe for a while but then turn away because their hearts are like the rocky soil. Some people love the things of the world, which are like thorns that keep them from loving God. But people who hear God's message and believe it are like the good soil. Their hearts are ready to follow Jesus and share God's message with others.

Today, people's hearts are still like that. Some believe God's message, and some don't. You can ask God to help your heart be like good soil so you can keep growing and loving Him.

EXPLORE MORE: Read John 1:12–13. What right do people have when they believe in Jesus?

I want to keep learning and growing.

DID YOU KNOW?
Bible teachers agree that there are close to forty parables of Jesus in the Gospels.

The Storm Obeys

Jesus stood up and gave a command to the wind and the water. He said, "Quiet! Be still!" Then the wind stopped, and the lake became calm. —Mark 4:39 ERV

One evening, after Jesus finished teaching a crowd, He asked His disciples to go with Him across the lake. They got into the boat and began to cross the lake when a strong wind came. The waves grew bigger until they splashed over the sides of the boat and started filling the bottom with water.

While all this happened, Jesus was sleeping. The disciples woke Him up. "Teacher," they said, "don't you care about us? We are going to drown!"

Jesus stood up and spoke to the wind and waves. "Quiet! Be still!" He said. The wind stopped, and the water in the lake became calm. He said to His disciples, "Why are you afraid? Do you still have no faith?"

The disciples were scared and asked each other, "What kind of man is this? Even the wind and the water obey him!"

In the beginning of Genesis, we read that God created the sky and seas. The gospel of John tells us Jesus was with God at creation, and everything was created through Him. Jesus was not afraid of the storm because He knew creation would obey Him. But Jesus was surprised by the way His disciples acted. Jesus understood why the storm frightened them, but He was with them. They had everything they needed to get through the storm safely. He would protect them.

Sometimes we act like the disciples and forget that Jesus is always with us through the Holy Spirit in our hearts. No matter what scary things we face, Jesus promises He will never leave us. We don't have to be afraid because He is bigger than all our fears.

EXPLORE MORE: Read John 1:1–5 to see that Jesus (the Word) was with God at creation.

TALK TO GOD
Thank Jesus that He is with you even when you feel afraid.

DID YOU KNOW?
The lake Jesus and the disciples crossed was the Sea of Galilee. It is also known as Lake Tiberias and is the lowest freshwater lake on earth. It is about 686 feet (209 meters) below sea level.

Jesus is in control.

The Best Healer of All

**When Jesus went back to Galilee, the people welcomed him.
Everyone was waiting for him. —Luke 8:40 ERV**

As news about Jesus spread, many people came to Him to be healed. Some were blind, some couldn't walk, and some brought friends and family who were sick. A man name Jairus was a leader in Galilee. His daughter was very sick. Jairus begged Jesus to come to his house.

While Jesus was going with Jairus, a woman came behind Jesus hoping she wouldn't be seen. She had a sickness that made her bleed for twelve years. She spent all her money on doctors, but no one could heal her. She touched the bottom of Jesus's coat. Jesus said, "Who touched me?"

Peter answered, "Master, people are all around you, pushing against you."

Jesus replied, "Someone touched me. I felt power go out from me."

The woman bowed before Jesus. She said she was healed the moment she touched Jesus's coat.

Jesus said to her, "My daughter, you are made well because you believed. Go in peace." Just then someone came from Jairus's house and told him his daughter had died. Jesus told Jairus, "Don't be afraid! Just believe and your daughter will be well." Jesus went into the house with Peter, James, John, and the girl's parents. Jesus said, "Don't cry. She is not dead. She is only sleeping." Jesus took her hand and said, "Little girl, stand up!" Her spirit came back, and she stood up.

Jesus has the power to make people well, and He has the power to raise people from the dead. One day He will heal all our sickness and hurts and give us a forever life with Him. We can have faith to believe just like the woman and Jairus.

TALK TO GOD
Pray for someone you know who needs Jesus's healing.

EXPLORE MORE: Read Psalm 103:1–3. Why should we praise God?

Jesus is my healer.

DID YOU KNOW?
The woman who was bleeding was considered unclean by Jewish law. She tried to touch Jesus's robe in secret because she could have been punished for touching someone while she was sick.

Two Blind Men Have Faith

They went right into the house where he was staying, and Jesus asked them, "Do you believe I can make you see?" "Yes, Lord," they told him, "we do." —Matthew 9:28 NLT

After Jesus healed Jairus's daughter, two blind men followed Him. They shouted, "Son of David, have mercy on us!" They followed Jesus right into the house where He was staying.

He asked them, "Do you believe I can make you see?"

They answered, "Yes, Lord, we do." Jesus touched their eyes and said, "Because of your faith, it will happen." They could see immediately! Jesus warned them "Don't tell anyone about this." But they told people about Him all over the area.

After this, another man was brought to Jesus. He was being controlled by a demon and could not speak. Jesus commanded the demon to come out of the man, and then the man was able to talk. The crowds were amazed to see such a powerful thing happen. They said, "Nothing like this has ever happened in Israel!"

Jesus loved all the people who came to Him for healing. It must have hurt His heart to see their sicknesses and disabilities. We know Jesus wanted them to get better because He healed them. But even more than that, Jesus cared about what they believed. He wanted them to be spiritually healthy too. That's why Jesus often pointed out people's faith or asked if they believed—like the woman who had been bleeding and the blind men who came into His house.

TALK TO GOD
Ask Jesus to help you believe in Him more each day.

Jesus wants the same thing for us today. He wants us to love Him and believe in His power as the Son of God. We can always ask Jesus for what we need. His love is the greatest thing we can ever receive from Him.

EXPLORE MORE: What did Jesus do after these miracles? Read Matthew 9:35–38 to find out.

DID YOU KNOW?
There are at least eight stories in the Gospels where Jesus healed blind people. He healed them in different ways. Sometimes He spoke, one time He spit on a man's eyes, and another time He used clay.

Jesus cares about our faith.

Disciples on a Mission

"As you go, preach this message, 'The kingdom of heaven has come near.' Heal those who are sick. Bring those who are dead back to life. Make those who have skin diseases 'clean' again. Drive out demons. You have received freely, so give freely." —Matthew 10:7–8 NIrV

Jesus called His twelve disciples together to give them a special gift and an important mission. First, He gave them power to heal every sickness and drive out evil spirits that were hurting people. Then Jesus told them their special mission was to tell the good news about God's kingdom to the people of Israel. He said, "They are like sheep that have become lost. As you go, preach this message, 'The kingdom of heaven has come near.'" As part of their mission, Jesus told the disciples to heal people. Jesus had been kind to the disciples, and He wanted them to show the same kindness to others.

TALK TO GOD
Ask the Holy Spirit to give you the right words to tell others about God's kingdom.

Jesus told the disciples some people would be happy to hear the good news they shared, but others would get angry. He told them to greet people as they traveled on their mission, but if people didn't welcome them, they should leave and move on.

Jesus let the disciples know their mission wouldn't be easy. He said some of them would be punished by leaders for what they were doing. But Jesus promised, "When they arrest you, don't worry about what you will say or how you will say it. At that time you will be given the right words to say. . . . The Spirit of your Father will be speaking through you."

Just like the disciples, Jesus has given us a mission to tell people about God's kingdom. It may not be easy for us either, but we have the same Holy Spirit that the disciples had. When we accept Jesus's mission for our life, God will help us and speak through us to tell others how much He loves them.

EXPLORE MORE: What animals did Jesus tell the disciples to be like? Read Matthew 10:16 to find out.

I'm on a mission for Jesus.

DID YOU KNOW?
The book of Acts tells the stories of the disciples traveling around Israel and preaching the good news about Jesus. Many of the stories show how the disciples healed people with the power Jesus gave them.

John the Baptist Feels Forgotten

John the Baptist, who was in prison, heard about all the things the Messiah was doing. So he sent his disciples to ask Jesus, "Are you the Messiah we've been expecting, or should we keep looking for someone else?" —Matthew 11:2–3 NLT

Have you ever felt disappointed or confused when things turned out differently than you expected? Maybe your best friend couldn't come to your birthday party. Or maybe you didn't get the role you wanted in a play. It's hard when we feel overlooked.

That's exactly how John the Baptist felt. He was in prison because Herod's wife didn't like the things he was saying. From prison, John heard about all the things Jesus was doing. He sent his followers to ask Jesus, "Are you the Messiah we've been expecting, or should we keep looking for someone else?"

Jesus told them, "Go back to John and tell him what you have heard and seen—the blind see, the lame walk, those with leprosy are cured, the deaf hear, the dead are raised to life, and the Good News is being preached to the poor. . . . God blesses those who do not fall away because of me."

John probably felt like Jesus had forgotten about him. Many of the Israelites believed that when the Messiah came, He would rescue them from the leaders ruling over them. But Jesus encouraged John and his followers that He was the Messiah they had been waiting for, even if His kingdom looked different than they expected. Jesus wanted John to stay strong when he was facing hard times because it would honor God's plan.

There may be many times when things happen that don't make sense as you follow Jesus. That's when it's important to remember He doesn't always do things the way we do. When we feel hurt or confused, we can still follow Jesus because He is trustworthy. And that is when we show our love for Him the most.

TALK TO GOD
Tell God you want to keep following Jesus, even when things are hard.

EXPLORE MORE: What did Jesus say to the crowds about John the Baptist after John's followers left? Look up Matthew 11:7–15 to see that Jesus had not forgotten about John.

DID YOU KNOW?
Mark 6:20 says that Herod knew John the Baptist was a righteous and holy man. Even though he didn't understand his teaching, Herod liked to listen to him.

I can keep following Jesus when life is hard.

Jesus Heals on the Sabbath Day

"Surely a man is more important than a sheep. So the law of Moses allows people to do good things on the Sabbath day."
—Matthew 12:12 ICB

We know from the book of Genesis that God created the world in six days and rested on the seventh day. Genesis 2:3 says, "God blessed the seventh day and made it holy." Then in Exodus 20, God gave Moses the Ten Commandments. These commandments, or rules, were to help the Israelites know how to love God and love others. The fourth commandment is, "Remember the Sabbath day by keeping it holy." The Sabbath was a day of rest for God's people. They were not supposed to work on that day.

One Sabbath day, Jesus and His disciples were walking through a field. They were hungry, so they picked some grain and ate it. The Pharisees saw this and were upset. They said it went against their Jewish laws of resting on the Sabbath. But Jesus knew they were just trying to catch Him doing something wrong.

TALK TO GOD
Thank Jesus for being the Lord of the Sabbath and teaching us how to be kind to others.

Later that day, Jesus went to the synagogue. A man was there with a crippled hand. Some people asked, "Is it right to heal on the Sabbath?" Jesus said, "If a sheep falls into a ditch on the Sabbath day, you will help the sheep out of the ditch. A man is more important than a sheep. The law of Moses allows us to do good things on the Sabbath." Jesus asked the man with the crippled hand to stretch out his hand. When he did, his hand became well.

Being kind and helping others is never wrong no matter what day it is. Matthew 12:8 says, "The Son of Man is Lord of the Sabbath." Who is the Son of Man? Jesus!

EXPLORE MORE: When Jesus talked to the Pharisees, He quoted a verse from Hosea 6:6. Look it up to see what it says.

Jesus is Lord of the Sabbath day.

DID YOU KNOW?
Jews still recognize the Sabbath today. The Sabbath begins at sunset on Friday and ends at sunset on Saturday. The Hebrew word for Sabbath is *Shabbat*.

God's Chosen Servant

"Here is my servant, the one I have chosen. He is the one I love, and I am very pleased with him." —Matthew 12:18 ERV

Many verses in the Old Testament point to Jesus. Some verses tell us where He would be born and the good names He would be called. God also gave the prophets messages to tell the people about the Messiah. God promised to send a Savior for the people and us.

In Matthew 12:18–21, Matthew shares verses about Jesus that were written by the prophet Isaiah more than seven hundred years earlier. In these verses, God tells us Jesus is the one God chose to save His people. God says, "Here is my servant, the one I have chosen. He is the one I love, and I am very pleased with Him." God said He would put His Spirit on Jesus, and many people would find their hope in Him.

Did you know you are also one of God's chosen servants? If you believe in Jesus, then you are a child of God. You are chosen to serve Him. It might seem hard to know how to serve God while you are young, but the more you learn about God, the more you will understand how you can serve Him.

TALK TO GOD
Ask God to show you how you can serve Him.

For example, you can serve God by serving others—like helping your brother or sister find their shoes or calling your grandma or grandpa just to say hi. You can serve God by being kind and playing with someone who is playing alone. If someone drops their markers, you can help pick them up. If you like to sing or play an instrument, you can serve God by praising Him.

It's impossible to list all the ways you can serve God, but you can ask Him to show you how. And as you serve God, you can thank Him for loving and choosing you.

EXPLORE MORE: What does Mark 10:45 tell us about Jesus?

DID YOU KNOW?

Studies have shown that serving others can make us happier and more confident.

I am one of God's chosen servants.

Mustard Seeds and Yeast

Jesus spoke all these things to the crowd using stories. He did not say anything to them without telling a story. —Matthew 13:34 NIrV

Did you know mustard seeds are super tiny? They're about the size of a pinhead. What's so amazing is when farmers plant these tiny seeds, they grow into a huge plant. Mustard plants can grow 20 to 30 feet high (6 to 9 meters). The plants grow branches with leaves and golden flowers, and every plant produces thousands of seeds.

When Jesus taught, He often told stories, called parables. One day He told a parable about a mustard seed. He said, "The kingdom of heaven is like a mustard seed. Someone took the seed and planted it in a field. It is the smallest of all seeds. But when it grows, it is the largest of all garden plants. It becomes a tree. Birds come and rest in its branches."

TALK TO GOD
Ask God to give you opportunities to tell others about Jesus.

Jesus meant that people are like tiny mustard seeds. When they become Christians, they become part of God's kingdom, which keeps growing and growing. Jesus also compared His kingdom to yeast. When yeast is added to bread dough, the dough expands and becomes much bigger.

Jesus told these parables to help people understand how God's kingdom would grow. When God's people tell others about Jesus, and those people tell more people about Jesus, the kingdom of God just keeps growing and growing. And do you know what? God's kingdom is still growing and getting bigger every day!

If you are part of God's kingdom, you are like the mustard seed. You are also like yeast. When you tell people about Jesus, you can help God's kingdom grow. There's always room for more people in the kingdom of God.

EXPLORE MORE: Read Psalm 78:1–2. How did Jesus fulfill these words?

I can help God's kingdom grow.

DID YOU KNOW?
Mustard is an important spice in many recipes. The yellow mustard you spread on a sandwich is made by grinding and mixing mustard seeds with water, vinegar, and other liquids.

Jesus Feeds a Hungry Crowd

Jesus looked up and saw a large crowd coming toward him. He said to Philip, "Where can we buy bread for all these people to eat?" —John 6:5 ICB

Wherever Jesus went, large crowds followed Him. Many people had seen Jesus do miracles, like make sick people better. The crowds of people wanted to know more about Jesus and see what He would do next. One day Jesus walked up a hill and sat down with His disciples. He looked at the crowd and knew they were hungry. He asked His disciple, Philip, "Where can we buy bread for all these people to eat?" Jesus already knew what He was going to do, but He said this to see what Philip would say.

Philip knew it would be impossible to feed so many people. He said, "Someone would have to work almost a year to buy enough bread for each person here to have only a little piece."

Then Andrew said, "Here is a boy with five loaves of bread and two little fish. But that is not enough for so many people."

TALK TO GOD
Thank God for giving you what you need each day.

Jesus told the disciples to have the people sit down on the grass. Jesus took the bread and thanked God for it. Then He broke the bread and passed it around to all the people. He did the same thing with the fish. When everyone had finished eating, Jesus told His disciples to gather the leftover food.

The food they picked up was enough to fill twelve extra baskets.

Whenever Jesus performed a miracle, it was to show that He was God's Son—the One whom the prophets said would come. But He also did miracles to help people because He loved them. More than five thousand hungry people had enough to eat that day. The disciples didn't need to go into town to buy food, and they didn't need any money. In the same way, Jesus can give us what we need, and it's always enough.

DID YOU KNOW?
On November 13, 2008, Joaquim Goncalves of Brazil made the largest loaf of bread in history to celebrate Guinness World Records Day. The loaf weighed 3,463.46 pounds (1,571 kilograms).

EXPLORE MORE: Read John 6:14 to find out what the people said about Jesus when they saw this miracle.

Jesus gives me what I need.

Jesus Is the Living Bread

"I am the living bread that came down from heaven. Anyone who eats this bread will live forever; and this bread, which I will offer so the world may live, is my flesh." —John 6:51 NLT

People all over the world have been making and eating bread since the beginning of time. Did you know bread is often called the "staff of life" because for many people it's part of their daily meals? In Bible times, bread was usually made from wheat or barley because those were common grains in Israel. Today bread is also made from different flours like rice, potato, and almond.

We can read many stories about bread in the Bible. When the Israelites were in the wilderness, God sent manna, a type of bread, from heaven, so they could eat this special bread every day. When God told Elijah to hide out by the Kerith Ravine, God sent ravens to feed him with bread and meat. The prophet Elisha fed one hundred men with only twenty loaves of bread, and they even had some left over.

TALK TO GOD
Thank God for bread to eat and for eternal life from Jesus.

Bread was also used in the tabernacle and the temple. In Leviticus 24:5–9, God tells the people to bake twelve loaves of bread and set them in two stacks on the table of gold before the Lord. This bread needed to be baked every week, since the loaves provided food for the priests. The bread was a sign of the covenant agreement between God and His people.

John 6:33 says, "The true bread of God is the one who comes down from heaven and gives life to the world." The one who came down from heaven is Jesus. Just as bread gives us food for our daily lives, Jesus gives eternal life to those who believe and follow Him. Bread gives us food for our bodies, and Jesus gives us food for our souls.

EXPLORE MORE: Read what Jesus said in John 6:47–51.

Jesus is the bread that gives eternal life.

DID YOU KNOW?
Baking bread takes a lot of time, so many bread companies make enough to last for about a week. The color of the twist ties used to close the bags lets grocery store workers know which day of the week the bread was baked.

Jesus Walks on Water

Then those in the boat worshiped Jesus. They said, "You really are the Son of God!" —Matthew 14:33 NIrV

Jesus told His disciples to go ahead of Him across the Sea of Galilee. He sent the crowds who were following Him away, then went to a mountainside where He could pray by himself. The disciples were far from shore when the wind and the waves began to rock their boat.

While it was still dark, Jesus went to see His disciples. He didn't use a boat to find them, and He didn't swim. Jesus walked on top of the water! When they saw Him, they cried out in fear, "It's a ghost!"

But Jesus called out, "Be brave! It is I. Don't be afraid."

Peter said, "Lord is it you? If it is, tell me to come to you on the water."

Jesus said one word: "Come."

Peter bravely walked on the water toward Jesus. But when he saw the wind, he got scared and began to sink. "Lord! Save me!" he cried. Jesus reached out and caught him. As soon as they climbed into the boat, the wind calmed down. The disciples were amazed and said, "You really are the Son of God!"

The disciples had seen Jesus heal sick people. They had watched Him feed a big crowd of hungry people with a bit of food. And now they had seen Him walk on the water. Their faith was growing and helping them to believe that Jesus truly was God's Son.

Even though we can't be with Jesus like the disciples were, we can read about His life and miracles in the Bible to help our faith in Him to grow. And just like Jesus called Peter to come to Him, He is calling you to come to Him too.

TALK TO GOD
Thank God for stories in the Bible that show us how Jesus is the Son of God.

EXPLORE MORE: Read Matthew 14:34–36 to find out what happened when Jesus and His disciples reached the shore.

DID YOU KNOW?
With long toes and fringes of skin between their toes, the basilisk lizard, also known as the Jesus lizard, can run across the water's surface.

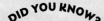
Jesus wants me to come to Him.

Jesus Heals a Blind Man

Jesus and his followers came to Bethsaida. Some people brought a blind man to him and begged him to touch the man. —Mark 8:22 ERV

One day Jesus and His followers came to Bethsaida, a small village near the Sea of Galilee.

Wherever Jesus went, crowds followed Him and tried to get close to Him. Many of them wanted healing. Some people wanted healing for themselves, and others wanted healing for their friends or family.

While Jesus was there, some people brought a blind man to Him. They begged Jesus to touch the man and heal Him. The people must have heard how Jesus could heal people just by touching them. Other people had seen Him perform miracles right before their eyes. The news about Jesus had spread far, but many people in Bethsaida did not believe that Jesus was the Son of God.

Jesus took the blind man by the hand and led him out of the village. Then He spit on the man's eyes and put His hands on him. "Can you see now?" Jesus asked.

The man looked up. "Yes, I see people, but they look like trees walking around."

Jesus put his hands on the man's eyes again. When the man opened his eyes, he could see everything clearly, and his blindness was healed.

TALK TO GOD
Ask God to show himself to people who need Him.

Some people wonder why Jesus healed the man in this unusual way. Jesus could have healed him just by saying the words. But Jesus always has a reason for doing things a certain way, even if we don't understand it. Jesus wanted to heal the man so he could see, but He also wanted to give the man spiritual healing. The Bible doesn't tell us if the man became a follower of Jesus, but Jesus surely changed his life that day.

EXPLORE MORE: Which of the disciples were from Bethsaida? Read John 1:44 to find out.

Jesus opens our eyes so we can see Him.

DID YOU KNOW?

Pliny the Elder, a Roman author who lived from AD 23–79, wrote about injuries and diseases that can be cured with saliva in his natural history book.

The Most Important Question

Then Jesus asked, "And who do you say I am? —Luke 9:20 ICB

People were amazed as Jesus taught the crowds and healed those who were sick, blind, deaf, or couldn't walk. Some wondered how Jesus could teach with so much wisdom. Others knew He had to have God's power to heal people from their diseases and disabilities. Others didn't believe He was the Son of God and wanted Him to go away.

One day as Jesus was alone praying, His disciples came to be with Him. Jesus asked them an important question: "Who do people say I am?"

"Some say you are John the Baptist," they replied. "Others say you are Elijah. And others say you are one of the prophets from long ago who has come back to life."

"And who do you say I am?" Jesus asked.

Peter was the first to answer Jesus's question. He said, "You are the Christ from God." Peter had seen Jesus do many miracles and heal lots of people. He had followed Jesus long enough to know that no one but God's Son could do the things that Jesus did.

TALK TO GOD
If you believe that Jesus is the Son of God, tell Him in your prayer, and ask Him to help you follow Him every day.

Did you know that many people today are like the people in the Bible? Some people think Jesus was a prophet. Some say He was a great teacher. Others say He was a good man. Jesus was all of those things, but He was and still is so much more.

Every person needs to answer the most important question, "Who is Jesus?" Peter gave the right answer. Jesus is the Christ, the Son of God. If you believe that, then you are a follower of Jesus.

DID YOU KNOW?
Some of the most common questions people ask are "How are you?" "What's your name?" and "Where are you from?"

EXPLORE MORE: What did the people in Jesus's hometown think about Him? Read Mark 6:1–3 to find out. The answer may surprise you!

Jesus is the Christ, the Son of God.

Glory on the Mountain

A voice from the cloud said, "This is my Son, and I love him. I am very pleased with him. Listen to him!" —Matthew 17:5 NIrV

Jesus took Peter, James, and John up a high mountain to pray. When they reached the top, Jesus's clothes became very bright, and His face shone like the sun. Suddenly, Moses and Elijah were standing before them and talking with Jesus.

Peter was happy to be there and wanted to stay. He even wanted to build three tents for Jesus, Moses, and Elijah. But while Peter was talking, a bright cloud came over them. God's voice came from the cloud and said, "This is my Son, and I love him. I am very pleased with him. Listen to him!"

The disciples were afraid and fell to the ground when they heard God's voice. Jesus put His hands on them and said, "Get up. Don't be afraid." Then, when the disciples looked up, they only saw Jesus; Moses and Elijah were no longer there.

As Jesus led the disciples back down the mountain, He said to them, "Don't tell anyone what you have seen. Wait until the Son of Man has been raised from the dead."

This must have been an awesome experience for Peter, James, and John! They had been following Jesus for a while and had seen Him do amazing things. But until this moment, they had only seen Jesus as a man. On the mountain that day, they saw God's glory shine through Him and heard God's voice.

The Bible doesn't tell us why Jesus brought the disciples to the mountain top, but it may have been to prepare them for the time when He would die on the cross and come back to life. After Jesus went to heaven, these disciples would have powerful stories to share with others.

EXPLORE MORE: Peter shares this experience in 2 Peter 1:16–18. Read the verses to see what he says.

TALK TO GOD
Thank God for stories in the Bible that show us His glory in Jesus.

Jesus reflects the glory of God.

DID YOU KNOW?
Today's Bible story is called the Transfiguration. "Transfiguration" means a complete change in the way something looks. Jesus's body was transformed to show God's glory.

A Blind Man Tells His Story

"Ever since the world began, no one has been able to open the eyes of someone born blind. If this man were not from God, he couldn't have done it." —John 9:32–33 NLT

Jesus and His disciples were walking along the road when they saw a man who was born blind. The disciples asked Jesus, "Why was this man born blind? Was it because of his own sins or the sins of his parents?"

Jesus explained that the man's blindness had nothing to do with sin. He said, "This happened so the power of God could be seen in him."

Jesus spit on the ground and made some mud. Then He spread the mud over the man's eyes. "Go wash yourself in the pool of Siloam," Jesus said. The man did what Jesus told him to do. When he came back, he could see!

The people who knew the man were confused. "Isn't this the blind man who used to sit and beg?" they asked. "Who healed you? How did this happen?"

TALK TO GOD
Ask Jesus to open the eyes of people who are spiritually blind.

The man told his story. "Jesus spread mud over my eyes and told me to wash in the pool of Siloam. So I did, and now I can see."

The Pharisees asked the man many questions. They said Jesus wasn't from God because He healed on the Sabbath.

But the man said, "This I know: I was blind, and now I can see. He healed my eyes, and you don't know where He comes from? Ever since the world began, no one has been able to open the eyes of someone born blind. If this man were not from God, He couldn't have done it."

The Pharisees could clearly see with their eyes what Jesus had done, but they were living in spiritual darkness, which made them blind. Their hearts were unable to see Jesus as the Son of God.

EXPLORE MORE: Read John 9:18–23. What did the blind man's parents say to the Pharisees who questioned them about their son?

DID YOU KNOW?

Siloam was a stone pool built while King Hezekiah ruled in Judah. In 2004, while workers were digging for a new sewer line, they uncovered stone steps that they believe were part of the pool.

Jesus is from God.

Tell What Jesus Has Done

At once the man was able to see, and he followed Jesus, thanking God. All the people who saw this praised God. —Luke 18:43 ICB

We don't know exactly how many blind people Jesus healed, but we know there were many! When Jesus made blind people able to see, the people who saw what happened were amazed, surprised, and confused. Many of Jesus's miracles were hard to explain and understand. Sometimes the only explanation was, "Jesus must be from God. That's why He can heal the blind!"

TALK TO GOD
Think of something Jesus has done for you, and say a prayer to thank Him.

Jesus's miracles showed His power over sickness, disease, disabilities, and even nature. And when people saw His miracles, they could not be quiet! News about Jesus's miracles spread quickly. When people heard these stories, they praised God. Many came to believe that Jesus truly was God's Son.

Even though Jesus isn't walking the earth today, He is still doing amazing things for us. He blesses families with children and grandchildren. He gives us wisdom to make good choices. He provides sunshine and rain for crops to grow, so we have good food to eat. And He promises a forever home in heaven to everyone who believes in Him.

Jesus does many wonderful things for us. The way to say "thank you" is to praise Him and tell others about Him. When you invite people to your home for dinner, you can say a prayer and ask God to bless your food. If you get a new brother or sister, you can tell others that God blessed your family with another child. You can also play music and sing songs that praise Jesus for His goodness and love. And on top of telling others about the wonderful things He has done for you, you can tell Jesus how much you appreciate all that He's done too.

EXPLORE MORE: After Jesus healed a man who was filled with demons, He told the man to do something. Read Luke 8:38–39 to see what it was.

I will tell others what Jesus does for me.

DID YOU KNOW?
Writing in a journal is a good way to remember what God does for you. Journaling helps your mind be more creative, and studies show that journaling at night helps you clear your mind and sleep better.

Who Is the Greatest?

"The one among you who is the most humble—this is the one who is great." —Luke 9:48 ERV

Everyone enjoys being good at something, but some people think they have to be the best to be important. Some kids think they have to get all As in order to be smart. Some athletes think winning a championship is what matters. Artists and musicians might feel they have to become famous to be successful. There's nothing wrong with working hard and doing your best—those are ways we can honor God. But what honors God the most is when we make loving and serving Him the most important thing.

One day, Jesus's disciples were arguing about who was the greatest. Jesus knew what they were thinking. Do you know what He did? He took a young child and had the child stand beside Him. Then Jesus said, "Whoever accepts a little child like this in my name is accepting me. And anyone who accepts me is also accepting the one who sent me. The one among you who is the most humble—this is the one who is great."

TALK TO GOD
Ask God to help you care about others and serve them the way Jesus did.

Jesus used the child as an example of people who are humble. Humble people aren't worried about being the greatest. They care more about others than themselves, just like Jesus did. And when we care about others, we show the love that's in our hearts.

It's good to work hard and do your best. If you get all the answers right on a test or hit a home run, thank God for giving you the ability to do it. And when you have the heart of a servant and share God's love with others, that's when you are really great!

EXPLORE MORE: According to Philippians 2:3–4, how should we think about others?

DID YOU KNOW?

Ricardo Kaká is a former soccer star from Brazil who is known for his charity work and his faith. In 2004 he was the youngest person to be named a UN World Food Programme Ambassador.

It's great to be humble.

Who Is My Neighbor?

But the man wanted to show that the way he was living was right. So he said to Jesus, "And who is my neighbor?" —Luke 10:29 ICB

The Jewish teachers often tried to trick Jesus by asking Him questions. They knew the commandments God had given to Moses because they studied the law. Jesus taught that the law was about loving God and loving our neighbors. One day as Jesus was teaching, one of the teachers asked, "Who is my neighbor?"

Jesus answered by telling a story, called a parable.

"A Jewish man was traveling from Jerusalem to Jericho when some robbers attacked him. They took his clothes, hurt him badly, and left him on the road to die. After a while a Jewish priest came by and saw the man, but the priest crossed the road and walked by on the other side. Then a Levite from the temple came by. He saw the man lying in the road, but the Levite walked by on the other side too. Finally, a Samaritan came by and saw the man. The Samaritan felt sorry for him, so the Samaritan stopped to help the hurt man. The helpful Samaritan poured medicine on the man's wounds and placed the injured man on his own donkey. He brought the man to an inn and paid the innkeeper to take care of him. Now, which one of these men was a neighbor to the man who was hurt?"

"The one who helped him," the teacher of the law replied.

"Then go and do the same thing he did!" Jesus said. The teacher thought he deserved eternal life by obeying lots of rules, but that's not what Jesus taught. Eternal life comes by believing in Jesus, who wants us to love God more than anything else and to love others like we love ourselves.

EXPLORE MORE: Read Romans 5:8. How did God show His love for us?

Everyone is my neighbor.

TALK TO GOD
Ask God to help you learn how to be a good neighbor to others.

DID YOU KNOW?
The parable that Jesus told is called the Good Samaritan. A law in the United States called the Good Samaritan Law protects people from being sued if they stop to help someone who is injured and they accidentally injure that person further in the process.

Two Sisters Welcome Jesus

"Only one thing is important. Mary has made the right choice, and it will never be taken away from her." —Luke 10:42 ERV

Jesus and His disciples traveled through a village where a woman named Martha invited Him to stay at her house. Martha had a sister named Mary who sat on the floor at Jesus's feet. Mary wanted to listen to everything Jesus had to say.

The Bible doesn't tell us exactly what Martha was doing, but it says that Martha was busy with work that needed to be done. Maybe she was cooking a big meal for Jesus and His disciples or preparing a comfortable room where Jesus could rest. What we do know is that Martha was upset because Mary wasn't helping her.

Martha said to Jesus, "Lord, don't you care that my sister has left me to do all the work by myself? Tell her to help me!"

Jesus's answer was not what Martha was expecting. "Martha, Martha, you are getting worried and upset about too many things. Only one thing is important. Mary has made the right choice and it will never be taken away from her."

TALK TO GOD
Think of something you want to tell Jesus, and talk about it in your prayer.

It's good to welcome people into your home and give them a meal and a place to rest. Serving others is a kind and generous thing to do. But Mary knew how special it was to have Jesus in her home. She wanted to spend every minute with Him and learn from Him.

Sometimes we get so busy that we forget to spend time with Jesus. But nothing is more important than learning from Him. No matter how busy you are today, take time to talk to Jesus and listen to His words in the Bible. It's always the best way to spend our time.

DID YOU KNOW?
Mary and Martha lived with their brother, Lazarus, in Bethany, which was a small town in Judea, near Jerusalem.

EXPLORE MORE: What did Jesus take time to do even when He was very busy? Read Luke 5:15–16 to find out.

I will take time to be with Jesus.

The Story of the Lost Sheep

"When he finds it, he will joyfully put it on his shoulders and go home." —Luke 15:5–6 NIrV

As people gathered around Jesus to listen to Him, the Jewish leaders and teachers of the law whispered among themselves. They criticized Jesus for spending time with tax collectors and people they thought of as sinners. Jesus knew what they were thinking, so He told a story.

"If a shepherd has one hundred sheep, and one sheep gets lost, won't he leave the ninety-nine sheep and go out to search for the one lost sheep? The shepherd will be so happy when he finds the sheep that he will carry it home on his shoulders. Then he will call his friends and neighbors and say, 'Be happy with me! I have found my lost sheep!'"

Then Jesus explained the meaning of His story. He said, "It will be the same in heaven. There will be great joy when one sinner turns away from sin."

TALK TO GOD
Tell Jesus you are happy that He is your Shepherd.

Just like the shepherd in Jesus's story searched for his lost sheep, Jesus searches for people who are spiritually lost. Being spiritually lost means someone doesn't believe that Jesus is God's Son and hasn't started following Him yet. When people decide to follow Jesus, they are no longer lost. This story shows us there is great joy in heaven if even one person becomes a Christian.

Every person is important to Jesus. He doesn't want anyone to be lost. Jesus is the Good Shepherd who gave His life for us, so we can be saved by believing in Him. If you believe in Jesus, then you are one of His sheep. And you can be happy every time one more lost sheep is found.

EXPLORE MORE: Isaiah 40:11 points to Jesus. How is this verse like today's story?

Jesus searches for people who are spiritually lost.

DID YOU KNOW?
When a sheep gets lost, it cannot find its way back home like some other animals can. That's why the shepherd needs to go out and find it.

A Happy Father

"While the son was still a long way off, his father saw him coming and felt sorry for him. So he ran to him and hugged and kissed him." —Luke 15:20 ERV

Jesus told His disciples a parable about a father who had two sons. The younger son decided to leave home, so he asked his father for the money that would be his when he got older. The son left home and quickly spent all of his money on foolish things. When he had no more money, he worked for a farmer who hired him to feed his pigs. The son became so hungry that even the pigs' food looked good to him to eat.

The son realized he had made some bad choices and was sorry for the way he had been living. He decided to go home and offer to be a servant for his father. But while he was still far from home, his father saw him coming. The father ran to him and hugged him and kissed him. When they got home, the father gave his son new clothes to wear and put a ring on his finger. Then he asked his servants to prepare a big party with food and music.

The older son was out in the field when he heard the music. He was upset when he found out the party was for his brother. But the father said, "Everything I have is always yours. But your brother was gone, and now we must celebrate because he is home."

This parable is known as the Prodigal Son. Jesus told this story to help the disciples understand how God is a Father who loves His children and gives them many blessings. When someone who has turned away from God comes back to Him, God welcomes that person with open arms.

TALK TO GOD
Thank God for being your Father and giving you everything you need.

EXPLORE MORE: Read Ephesians 1:3 to learn why we should praise God.

DID YOU KNOW?
Pigs are omnivores. That means they can eat many different things like fruit, vegetables, meat, and even bugs.

God is my Father who loves me.

Filled with Praise

He came into a small town, and ten men met him there. They did not come close to him, because they all had leprosy. But the men shouted, "Jesus! Master! Please help us!" —Luke 17:12–13 ERV

Another story of Jesus's healing power took place in a small village near Samaria and Galilee. This time it wasn't just one sick person who came to Jesus—it was ten men with leprosy. The men didn't dare come close to Jesus since people thought of them as being "unclean." But they shouted out to Him, "Jesus! Master! Please help us!"

When Jesus saw the men, He said, "Go and show yourselves to the priests." This is what people with leprosy had to do when they got better, so they could be around other people again. As the ten men went on their way, they were all healed. One of them, a Samaritan, looked at his skin and saw the amazing thing Jesus had done. He went back to Jesus and praised God with a loud voice. He bowed down before Jesus and thanked Him.

TALK TO GOD
Ask God to help you have a heart of thankfulness that praises Him.

Jesus said, "This man is not even one of our people. Is he the only one who came back to give praise to God?" Then Jesus told the man, "Stand up! You can go. You were healed because you believed."

All of the men did what Jesus told them to do and were healed, but only one was thankful enough to come back.

What can we do when Jesus does wonderful things for us and answers our prayers? We can be like the Samaritan in this story and let our hearts fill up with true praise. We can pray to Jesus or sing a song to tell Him how much we love Him and thank Him for being so kind.

EXPLORE MORE: Read Psalm 146:1–2. How long should we praise God?

I will be filled with praise.

DID YOU KNOW?
Samaritans were people who lived in Samaria. They were related to the Israelites, but the Jewish people didn't respect them like Jesus did.

The Resurrection and the Life

Jesus told her, "I am the resurrection and the life. Anyone who believes in me will live, even after dying." —John 11:25 NLT

Lazarus was the brother of Mary and Martha, and he was very sick. His sisters sent Jesus a message that Lazarus was not doing well. Jesus stayed where He was for two days and then traveled to Bethany to see them. When Jesus got there, someone told Him Lazarus had died and was buried four days earlier

Martha came to Jesus and said, "Lord, if only you had been here, my brother would not have died. But even now, I know that God will give you whatever you ask." Jesus told her, "Your brother will rise again." Martha answered, "Yes, he will rise when everyone else rises, at the last day." Then Jesus said something amazing: "I am the resurrection and the life. Anyone who believes in me will live, even after dying. Do you believe this, Martha?" Martha said she did because she believed that Jesus was the Messiah.

When Jesus saw Martha and Lazarus's friends crying, He was sad and cried too. He asked to see where Lazarus was buried. When He got to the tomb, He told the people to roll away the stone that covered the entrance. Jesus looked up to heaven and prayed out loud, so everyone could hear Him. Jesus shouted, "Lazarus, come out!" Then Lazarus walked out of the tomb, wrapped in graveclothes!

TALK TO GOD
Tell Jesus how powerful He is to conquer death and thank Him for being the Resurrection and the Life.

Jesus has power over death. What He did for Lazarus was incredible! What's even more wonderful is what He told Martha. Jesus promises that those who trust in Him will live with Him forever someday. He will raise our bodies from death just like He did for Lazarus, and we will never die again. Only Jesus can make that happen!

DID YOU KNOW?
Bethany comes from the word *bethel*, which means House of God. Today the city of Bethany is called Al Eizariya, which means Place of Lazarus.

EXPLORE MORE: 1 Corinthians 15:51–52 says something amazing will happen to everyone who is a part of God's family. What is it?

Jesus has power over death.

Jesus Loves the Little Children

Jesus saw what happened. He did not like his followers telling the children not to come. So he said to them, "Let the little children come to me. Don't stop them, because God's kingdom belongs to people who are like these little children." —Mark 10:14 ERV

Has anyone ever made you feel small because you're a kid? That's what happened to some kids in the Bible. Their parents brought them to Jesus so He could bless them. But the disciples told them to stop bringing their children to Jesus. Maybe they thought Jesus was too busy to spend time with kids.

Jesus saw what His disciples did, and He did not like it. He told His disciples, "Let the little children come to me. Don't stop them, because God's kingdom belongs to people who are like these little children." Then Jesus held the children in His arms and blessed them.

TALK TO GOD
Tell Jesus what you're feeling today. He wants to hear it!

Jesus told His followers that if they wanted to be a part of God's family, they needed to accept His kingdom the way kids accept things. That means trusting God the way kids trust their parents. Kids are happy to receive gifts and help from adults who love them. They don't feel like they have to earn everything on their own. That's how God's kingdom is. Jesus wants us to be happy to receive the gift He gives us by taking away our sins. He wants us to know it's something He did for us because He loves us. We can't earn this gift.

Just like the children in this story, you are important to Jesus. He loves you, and He wants you to come to Him. You can tell Him when you're feeling sad or when you're excited about something. And you can thank Him for the wonderful gifts He gives you. When grown-ups see you loving Jesus, it will teach them how to follow Him too.

EXPLORE MORE: What advice does 1 Timothy 4:12 have for kids?

I am important to Jesus.

DID YOU KNOW?

The song "Jesus Loves the Little Children" was written more than one hundred years ago. George Frederick Root composed the tune for another song, and later his friend, Clare Herbert Woolston, wrote the words. Woolston was inspired by today's story when he wrote the song.

The Loving Savior

Then Jesus talked to the 12 apostles alone. He said to them, "Listen! We are going to Jerusalem. Everything that God told the prophets to write about the Son of Man will happen!" —Luke 18:31 ICB

From the beginning, God's plan was to send Jesus to take away our sins. Even the prophets in the Old Testament told the people of Israel that it would happen. Because the sin of everyone in the world is so ugly and serious, God made a way for our sins to be forgiven through Jesus. Jesus knew the reason God sent Him to earth, and He was willing to die for us. Jesus knew what was going to happen to Him and when it would happen. He even told His disciples about it ahead of time. Jesus told them that He would be turned over to the Romans, and they would make fun of Him, spit on Him, and laugh at Him. They would even beat Him and kill Him. But Jesus also shared the wonderful part of His mission from God— He would rise from the dead three days later.

Even though the disciples heard everything Jesus said, they didn't understand what His mission was all about. They wouldn't be able to understand it until God gave them the ability to do so. God would help the disciples understand everything about Jesus's mission on earth after Jesus died.

TALK TO GOD
Tell Jesus how grateful you are that He was willing to be made fun of and die to take away your sins.

Jesus wasn't surprised by the way He was treated or what happened to Him when He died. He knew all along that it was part of God's special plan to show His love to all of us. Jesus loves you enough that He was willing to die because it would bring you back to God. He is a kind and selfless Savior.

EXPLORE MORE: Read Genesis 3:15 to see that God already planned for Jesus to defeat Satan when Adam and Eve first sinned.

DID YOU KNOW?
There are passages that talk about Jesus's death in Psalms, Isaiah, and Zechariah. Some of these passages were written more than six hundred years before Jesus was born.

Jesus came to die for the sins of the world.

Zacchaeus Wants to See Jesus

When Jesus came to where Zacchaeus was, he looked up and saw him in the tree. Jesus said, "Zacchaeus, hurry! Come down! I must stay at your house today." —Luke 19:5 ERV

Jesus was traveling through the city of Jericho. A tax collector named Zacchaeus lived there. You may remember that the Jewish people didn't like tax collectors because they often stole money from the taxes they took. Zacchaeus was a rich and important tax collector. He wanted to see Jesus, so he ran to a place where Jesus would pass by. But Zacchaeus was short and couldn't see over the crowds of people who also wanted to see Jesus, so Zacchaeus climbed a sycamore tree to get a good view.

When Jesus came to where Zacchaeus was, He saw Zacchaeus in the tree. Jesus called to him, "Zacchaeus, hurry! Come down! I must stay at your house today." Zacchaeus quickly came down the tree. He was happy for Jesus to stay at his house. Everyone who saw what was happening started to complain. "Look at the kind of man Jesus is staying with. Zacchaeus is a sinner!" they said.

Zacchaeus told Jesus, "I want to do good. I will give half of my money to the poor. If I have cheated anyone, I will pay them back four times more." Jesus answered, "Today is the day for this family to be saved from sin. Yes, even this tax collector is one of God's chosen people. The Son of Man came to find lost people and save them."

TALK TO GOD
Ask God to help you see people the way He sees them.

Even though other people judged Zacchaeus, Jesus knew that Zacchaeus wanted to know Him and was willing to change. Jesus didn't come for the people who think they are good enough to be saved, He came for everyone who wants to know and follow Him.

EXPLORE MORE: Do you remember the name of another tax collector who followed Jesus? Read Matthew 9:9 to see if you're right.

Jesus sees those who want to know Him.

DID YOU KNOW?
Sycamore trees are the largest deciduous trees in the United States. Deciduous trees shed their leaves yearly. Sycamore trees can grow 75 to 100 feet (23 to 30 meters) tall.

The Shepherd and the Gate

"I'm like a gate. Anyone who enters through me will be saved."
—John 10:9 NIrV

Back in Exodus, God told Moses His name was "I AM." Jesus also used this name to tell others that He was God's Son and part of the three persons of God—the Trinity. In the gospel of John, there are seven "I am" sayings from Jesus. One of them is: "I am the gate."

King David thought of God like a shepherd when he wrote Psalm 23. He even began with the words, "The Lord is my shepherd . . ." Jesus used the same example one day when He was talking with a group of Pharisees. He said that only the shepherd of a flock of sheep enters through the gate of a sheep pen. The sheep listen to the shepherd's voice. The shepherd calls every sheep by name and leads them out. Jesus said He was the Good Shepherd. Then Jesus said, "I am like a gate for the sheep. . . . Anyone who enters through me will be saved."

> **TALK TO GOD**
> Thank Jesus for making a way for us to get back to God.

When Jesus said this, He was explaining that He was the only way to God. Then He said, "I give my life for the sheep." This meant that He was going to die to save them. He also explained that there would be "one flock" and "one shepherd" in God's family, which means that everyone would be united in Jesus, no matter where they came from.

Jesus loves His people, and He knows them, just like a shepherd knows every sheep in his flock. Jesus came to take care of us, to lead us, and to protect us. Most of all, Jesus came so He could open the gate for all His followers to be made right with God. Jesus is the best shepherd we could ever have.

EXPLORE MORE: What did Jesus say in John 10:27–30?

DID YOU KNOW?

The seven "I am" sayings of Jesus are I am the bread of life; I am the light of the world; I am the gate of the sheep; I am the resurrection and the life; I am the good shepherd; I am the way, the truth, and the life; and I am the true vine.

Jesus is the gate for His people.

An Expensive Bottle of Perfume

Mary brought in a pint of very expensive perfume made from pure nard. She poured the perfume on Jesus' feet, and then she wiped his feet with her hair. And the sweet smell from the perfume filled the whole house. —John 12:3 ICB

Jesus and His followers were traveling to Jerusalem where Jesus would die on a cross. On their way, they had a special dinner with Mary, Martha, and Lazarus in Bethany. Martha served the food while Lazarus ate with Jesus. Then Mary did something unexpected.

Mary had a jar of expensive perfume called nard. She poured the perfume on Jesus's feet and wiped His feet with her hair. The sweet-smelling perfume filled the whole house. Judas, the disciple who would turn against Jesus, saw what Mary did and was angry. "This perfume was worth an entire year's wages," he said. "It should have been sold and the money given to the poor." But Judas didn't really care about helping the poor. He was in charge of the money bag and would steal money from it.

Jesus said to Judas, "It was right for her to save this perfume for today—the day for me to be prepared for burial." In Bible times when someone died, family members would pour oil and spices on the body and wrap it with special cloths. When Mary poured perfume on Jesus's feet, she showed that He was getting ready to die for us. What Mary did was beautiful, and Jesus said this story would be shared everywhere the gospel is told.

Mary honored Jesus by wiping His feet. She had learned from Him and followed Him. She gave what she had to show her love for Jesus. We honor Jesus when we worship Him too, and we can show how thankful we are for His love by telling other people what He did. When we praise and honor God, it's like sweet-smelling perfume filling our lives.

EXPLORE MORE: Another woman also poured perfume on Jesus's feet. You can read about her in Luke 7:36–38.

TALK TO GOD
Ask God to help you be like sweet-smelling perfume as you worship Him.

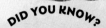

DID YOU KNOW?
Nard comes from a flowering plant in the honeysuckle family. It is also called spikenard, nardin, and muskroot, and it grows in the Himalayan Mountains, China, and India.

I can honor Jesus for all that He's done.

Jesus Rides into Jerusalem

On the way to Jerusalem, many people spread their coats on the road for Jesus. Others cut branches from the trees and spread them on the road. —Matthew 21:8 ERV

As Jesus and His followers continued their trip to Jerusalem, they stopped at the Mount of Olives. Jesus sent two of His followers into town. He told them, "You will find a donkey with her colt. Untie them both and bring them to me. If anyone asks you why you are taking the donkeys, tell them 'The Master needs them.'"

His followers did what Jesus said. They brought the mother donkey and her colt back to Jesus. They covered the donkeys with their coats, and Jesus sat on them. As they traveled to Jerusalem, crowds of people spread their coats on the road to honor Him as a King. They shouted, "Praise to the Son of David! Welcome! God bless the one who comes in the name of the Lord! Praise to God in heaven!" Some of the Pharisees saw what was happening, and they told Jesus, "Teacher, tell your followers not to say these things." But Jesus answered, "I tell you, if my followers didn't say them, these stones would shout them." No one could hold back the royal praise that Jesus deserved.

Back in the Old Testament, Jesus's entrance into Jerusalem was described exactly like this by the prophet Zechariah. He told the Israelites their king would come humble and riding on a donkey. Jesus didn't come as a warrior on a horse, trying to take over the world by fighting wars. He came as a servant out of love to make us right with God and show us how He wants us to live. He is the perfect King and worthy of all of our praise.

TALK TO GOD
Thank Jesus for coming as a humble King who showed love to the world.

EXPLORE MORE: Go back and read the prophecy of Jesus entering Jerusalem in Zechariah 9:9.

DID YOU KNOW?
In some translations of the Bible, the word *Hosanna* is used in today's story. *Hosanna* is a Hebrew word that the Israelites shouted to praise Jesus as He entered Jerusalem. It means "joy," "adoration," or "praise" and was also used in praying to God for help.

Jesus, the humble King, deserves all our praise.

Love God, Love People

One of them, an expert in religious law, tried to trap him with this question: "Teacher, which is the most important commandment in the law of Moses?" —Matthew 22:35–36 NLT

Do you remember all the commandments that God gave to Moses? There were ten of them. They were important rules for the Israelites to follow to be respectful to each other and to show their obedience to God. A Pharisee who was an expert in the law of Moses asked Jesus a question one day: "Teacher, which is the most important commandment in the law of Moses?" When the Pharisee asked this question, he was hoping to trap Jesus. If Jesus said one part of the law was more important, that meant other parts were less important, which would not be true and would not honor God's words. But Jesus didn't fall for the trick.

Jesus answered, "'You must love the Lord your God with all your heart, all your soul, and all your mind.' This is the first and greatest commandment." Then He added, "A second is equally important: 'Love your neighbor as yourself.'" Jesus knew exactly what the Pharisee was trying to do. He finished His answer by saying, "The entire law and all the demands of the prophets are based on these two commandments."

Jesus knew that all of God's commandments were important, and the most important thing is what's in a person's heart. Following God isn't about checking off a list of doing the right things; it's about loving God and loving others. When we love God with all of our heart, soul, and mind, we will honor the commandments that put God first. When we love others as ourselves, we will treat them with kindness and respect. The religious leaders tried to make following God confusing and hard, but Jesus made it simple: love God and love others.

EXPLORE MORE: Read Deuteronomy 6:4–6 and Leviticus 19:18 to see the words Jesus quoted from the law when He answered the Pharisee's question.

TALK TO GOD
Ask God to help you love Him and love others.

DID YOU KNOW?
The Pharisee in today's story is also called a lawyer. Lawyers in Bible times were not like lawyers today who help people in court. Instead, they were experts who studied the law of Moses. They were similar to scribes who copied Scripture.

God's rules are about love.

A Very Special Supper

When the time came, Jesus and the apostles were sitting at the table. He said to them, "I wanted very much to eat this Passover meal with you before I die." —Luke 22:14–15 ICB

After Jesus and His disciples arrived in Jerusalem, it was time to celebrate the Day of Unleavened Bread. On this day Passover lambs were sacrificed, and the people remembered what God did for their ancestors in Egypt at the first Passover. Jesus told Peter and John, "Go and prepare the Passover meal for us." They asked, "Where do you want us to prepare it?" Jesus said they would see a man carrying a jar of water. When they followed him to a house, the owner would show them a room. Peter and John left, and everything happened the way Jesus said it would.

At dinner, Jesus sat with His twelve disciples. He said, "I wanted very much to eat this Passover meal with you before I die." Then Jesus took some bread and thanked God for it. He broke it, gave it to His disciples, and said, "This bread is my body that I am giving for you. Do this to remember me." After dinner, Jesus took a cup and said that God was making a new agreement with His people. "This new agreement begins with my blood which is poured out for you."

The special meal Jesus ate with His disciples is called the Last Supper. It was the last time He ate with them before He died. The bread and cup were symbols that showed Jesus was going to give His life for all who believed in Him. This Passover meal was also special because Jesus is the Lamb of God. His blood saves us from punishment, like the lamb's blood saved the Israelites in Egypt. Jesus is a kind and loving Savior.

EXPLORE MORE: Read Joshua 5:10 to see what Joshua and the Israelites did after crossing the Jordan River.

TALK TO GOD
Thank Jesus for giving His life for yours.

DID YOU KNOW?
Today people remember the Last Supper when they take communion or the Lord's Supper at church. They break bread or crackers and drink juice or wine to remember what Jesus told His followers on that special night.

Jesus is the Lamb of God.

An Unexpected Foot Bath

So while they were eating, Jesus stood up and took off his robe. He got a towel and wrapped it around his waist. —John 13:4 ERV

After Jesus and His followers entered Jerusalem, Jesus knew the time had come for Him to leave the world and go back to the Father. He ate a special dinner with His followers, and while they were eating, He stood up and poured water into a bowl. Then He began to wash their feet. When Jesus got to Peter, Peter said, "Lord, you should not wash my feet." Jesus answered, "If I don't wash your feet, you are not one of my people."

When Jesus finished washing His disciples' feet, He went back to the table and asked them, "Do you understand what I did for you? You call me 'Teacher.' And you call me 'Lord.' And this is right, because that is what I am. But I washed your feet. So you also should wash each other's feet. You should serve each other just as I served you."

TALK TO GOD
Ask God to show you how to be a servant like Jesus.

The disciples were probably surprised by what Jesus did. Washing someone's feet was the job of the least important servant in the house. Jesus told His disciples to serve others and to not think of themselves as better than others. Jesus was different from what most people expected the Messiah to be like. Instead of coming into the world as a powerful king in a fancy palace, He was a humble servant who cared about people that others looked down on.

When we believe in Jesus, He washes our sins away, just like how He washed the disciples' feet. When our hearts are changed by Jesus's love, we take His love and share it with others by serving them with kindness.

EXPLORE MORE: Read John 13:1 to find out what Jesus did until the very end of His life on earth.

Jesus shows me how to be a servant.

DID YOU KNOW?

People had to wash their feet a lot in Bible times because they wore sandals and walked on dusty roads. A servant or the wife of the host usually washed guests' feet when they came over for dinner.

The Only Way

Thomas said to Jesus, "Lord, we don't know where you are going. So how can we know the way?" Jesus answered, "I am the way. And I am the truth and the life. The only way to the Father is through me." —John 14:5–6 ICB

As Jesus continued His special dinner with His disciples, He didn't want them to be confused or scared about the things that were going to happen. He wanted them to know He still cared about them. Jesus said, "Don't let your hearts be troubled. Trust in God. And trust in me." Then He told His disciples that He was going to His Father's house to get a place ready for them. He said He would come back and take them to be with Him. Jesus told them, "You know the way to the place where I am going." But Thomas said, "Lord, we don't know where you are going. So how can we know the way?" Jesus replied, "I am the way. And I am the truth and the life. The only way to the Father is through me."

Jesus explained to His disciples His amazing and true plan, even if they didn't understand it right away. He let them know He was going back to heaven to get His kingdom ready. He promised to come back and bring all of His followers to His new kingdom.

TALK TO GOD
Praise Jesus for being the way to God.

Jesus's death on the cross made a way for all sinners to get back to God if they believe in Jesus. He is the only way to be made right with God. When we accept Jesus's free gift of saving us from our sins, it's like He creates a bridge from us to God. This bridge leads us back to God, who created us and loves us.

EXPLORE MORE: What did Peter say to some Jewish leaders after he healed a crippled man? Read Acts 4:12 to find out.

DID YOU KNOW?
The Apostle Islands National Lakeshore on Lake Superior in Wisconsin is named after the twelve disciples, or apostles, and has twenty-one islands. There's only one way to get to the islands and that is by boat.

Jesus is the only way to God.

The Helper

I will ask the Father, and he will give you another Helper to be with you forever. —John 14:16 ERV

Do you wish you had a best friend you could tell everything to? Someone who always understands how you're feeling and always knows just what to say? Do you ever wish there was someone who could help you make good choices or make you feel better when you're sad? That's the kind of friend Jesus promised to give His disciples.

As Jesus encouraged the disciples on the night of the Last Supper, He told them, "I will ask the Father, and he will give you another Helper to be with you forever. The Helper is the Spirit of truth . . . you know him. He lives with you, and he will be in you." The Helper and Spirit of truth was the Holy Spirit, the third person of the Trinity.

Jesus explained that people who didn't love Him couldn't accept the Holy Spirit. Their hearts were far from God. But the Holy Spirit knew Jesus's disciples and would be with them because they loved Jesus. There was another important thing the Holy Spirit would do for the disciples. Jesus said, "The Helper will teach you everything and cause you to remember all that I told you."

TALK TO GOD
Thank God for the gift of the Holy Spirit, and ask Him to help you.

The same Holy Spirit that God sent to the disciples is also for us! He is the best friend we could ever have. He teaches us and helps us know the right thing to do. He comforts us and always understands what we're going through, even if we don't know how to explain it to others. The Holy Spirit is a wonderful gift from God. It's the part of Him that is with us forever. What a perfect friend!

EXPLORE MORE: Read John 16:13–15. What does the Holy Spirit do for us?

The Holy Spirit is my Helper.

DID YOU KNOW?
The Greek word for the Holy Spirit is *paraclete*, which means "advocate" or "helper."

Growing Grapes

"I am the vine. You are the branches. If you remain joined to me, and I to you, you will bear a lot of fruit. You can't do anything without me." —John 15:5 NIrV

Did you know grapevines were everywhere in Israel? Lots of grapes grew in vineyards, and vines were a symbol of God's people in the Old Testament. There was even a large golden vine on the front of the temple.

One day Jesus taught a parable about a vineyard. Jesus used the symbol of a vine to teach His disciples. He said, "I am the vine. You are the branches. If you remain joined to me, and I to you, you will bear a lot of fruit. You can't do anything without me. . . . When you bear a lot of fruit, it brings glory to my Father."

Did Jesus mean that His followers would have grapes hanging off their arms? That would definitely be something everyone would remember! But that's not what Jesus meant. As we've seen in other stories, Jesus liked to use symbols to teach people. The symbol of fruit was the work of Jesus in the disciples' hearts showing on the outside—things like being patient, kind, gentle and loving, and having joy, peace, and self-control. All of Jesus's followers grow this fruit when they stay close to Him.

TALK TO GOD
Tell Jesus you want to stay close to Him and ask Him to grow His fruit in your life.

When we don't stay close to Jesus, we can't grow His fruit, just like a branch that falls off a tree can't grow leaves. That's what Jesus meant when He said we can't do anything without Him. God doesn't expect us to do all the work on our own. He wants to help us and has given us everything we need through the Holy Spirit. When we stay close to Him and that fruit shows up in our lives, it gives all the glory back to God. What delicious fruit!

EXPLORE MORE: Read John 15:1. If Jesus is the vine, who is the gardener?

DID YOU KNOW?
Israel is only the size of New Jersey, but there are hundreds of vineyards in Israel today. There are 70 vineyards that produce 50 tons (45,359 kilograms or 100,000 pounds) of grapes in a year.

Jesus is the vine.

The Savior's Prayer

After Jesus said these things he looked toward heaven. Jesus prayed, "Father, the time has come. Give glory to your Son so that the Son can give glory to you." —John 17:1 ICB

Jesus went to a garden to pray. He told Peter, James, and John that His heart was breaking with sadness. He knew He was about to die on the cross for the sins of the world. But even with everything Jesus was going through, do you know what He prayed for? He prayed for His disciples, and He prayed for *you*. That's right—Jesus was thinking of you on that quiet night in the garden thousands of years ago.

First Jesus prayed for the twelve disciples who had followed Him. He said, "I want them to have all of my joy. I have given them your teaching." Then He asked God to keep them safe from the Evil One and to make them ready to serve and teach God's truth.

Then Jesus prayed for people who would believe in Him. If you know Jesus, that's you! He asked God, "Father, I pray that all people who believe in me can be one . . . I pray that these people can also be one in us, so that the world will believe that you sent me." Jesus also said, "I want them to see my glory . . . I showed them what you are like . . . they will have the same love that you have for me, and I will live in them."

TALK TO GOD
Tell Jesus how thankful you are that He prayed for you, and ask Him to help you honor His name.

How amazing that Jesus thought of us the night before He died! And it's wonderful to see Jesus's prayers have been answered. We see Jesus's glory in the world He made, in His Spirit living inside of us, and in the way He hears our prayers and changes our hearts. The best way we can keep shining Jesus's glory is by loving each other with God's love.

EXPLORE MORE: What does Hebrews 7:25 tell us about Jesus?

DID YOU KNOW?
The garden where Jesus prayed was called Gethsemane, which means "oil press" in Hebrew. It was probably a grove of olive trees with an oil press in it for making olive oil.

Jesus prayed for me.

Another Prayer in the Garden

Jesus and his followers went to a place called Gethsemane. He said to his followers, "Sit here while I pray." —Mark 14:32 ICB

Jesus brought His disciples to a garden by the Mount of Olives in Jerusalem. The garden was filled with olive trees. The place was called Gethsemane. Jesus told the disciples to sit and wait while He went by himself to pray. He walked a little farther with Peter, James, and John, then told them to watch and pray. When Jesus was alone, He dropped to the ground. His heart was sad as He talked to God. He prayed, "Abba, Father! You can do all things. Let me not have this cup of suffering. But do what you want, not what I want."

Jesus got up and walked back to the disciples and found them sleeping. He woke them up and told them again to watch and pray. Jesus went back to pray by himself. When He returned to the disciples, they were sleeping. This happened a third time too. Then a group of men came to the garden. They were the Roman soldiers who had come to arrest Jesus and take Him away. Judas, who was one of Jesus's disciples, kissed Jesus on the cheek. This was a sign to the soldiers that Jesus was the man they were looking for.

TALK TO GOD
Thank Jesus for obeying God's will, so you can be saved from your sins.

The soldiers were sent by the Jewish chief priests and teachers of the law. They were armed with swords and clubs, but they didn't have to use them. Jesus didn't put up a fight or perform a miracle to escape. He went along willingly because He knew this was God's plan.

Jesus knew the days ahead would be filled with pain and suffering, but He wanted to do God's will and make a way for us to be saved.

EXPLORE MORE: What happened to Jesus as He was praying? Read Luke 22:43–44 to find out.

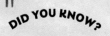

DID YOU KNOW?

According to a 2012 study by the Italian National Research Council, three of the olive trees in Gethsemane are among the oldest trees in the world.

Jesus did what God wanted Him to do.

Jesus and Pilate

Jesus answered, "You are right to say that I am a king. I was born for this: to tell people about the truth. That is why I came into the world. And everyone who belongs to the truth listens to me." —John 18:37 ERV

The Roman guards took Jesus to the governor's palace. His name was Pilate. Some Jewish leaders went with Jesus but stayed outside. Pilate went out and asked the leaders, "What has this man done wrong?"

"He's a bad man," they said. "That's why we brought Him to you."

Pilate took Jesus into the palace and asked Him some questions. "Are you the king of the Jews?" he asked. "Your people and their leaders brought you to me. What have you done wrong?"

"My kingdom does not belong to this world," Jesus said. "If it did, my servants would fight so that I would not be handed over to the Jewish leaders. My kingdom is not an earthly one."

"So you are a king," Pilate said.

"You are right to say that I am a king," Jesus replied. "I was born for this: to tell people about the truth. That is why I came into the world. And everyone who belongs to the truth listens to me."

TALK TO GOD
Ask Jesus to help you stand up for Him no matter what.

Pilate could not find a reason to punish Jesus. He asked the people if they wanted him to let Jesus go free or to let a criminal named Barabbas go free. The Jews chose Barabbas.

Pilate knew Jesus hadn't done anything wrong, but he was afraid of the crowd. Instead of standing up for Jesus, Pilate handed Jesus over to be crucified.

We should be willing to stand up for Jesus no matter what others say or do. It might be hard, and others might even laugh at us. But standing up for Jesus is always the right thing to do because Jesus always stands up for us.

EXPLORE MORE: Read Matthew 27:19 to find out what Pilate's wife said to him.

I will stand up for Jesus.

DID YOU KNOW?
"Stand Up, Stand Up for Jesus" is a hymn that was written in 1858 by a Presbyterian minister named George Duffield. He was inspired to write the song when a preacher named Dudley Tyng said in a sermon, "Let us stand up for Jesus."

Jesus Is Crucified

They put a sign above Jesus' head with the charge against him
written on it. The sign read: "THIS IS JESUS THE KING OF THE JEWS."
—Matthew 27:37 ICB

After Pilate handed Jesus over to the Roman soldiers, they put a robe on Him and made a crown of thorns for His head. They put a staff in His hand and got down on their knees. "Hail, king of the Jews," they said as they made fun of Him. They spit on Jesus and hit Him with the staff. Then they led Him away to be crucified.

The soldiers took Jesus to a place outside the city gates of Jerusalem called Golgotha. They met a man named Simon from Cyrene and made him carry Jesus's cross. Then the soldiers nailed Jesus's hands and feet to the cross and stood it up on a hill. Two criminals were crucified next to Jesus, one on each side.

As people walked by, they yelled mean things at Jesus. "Come down from the cross if you're really the Son of God!" they said. "He saved others, but He can't save himself! If He's the King of Israel, let Him come down from the cross and we will believe in Him!"

> **TALK TO GOD**
> Thank God for sending Jesus to die for our sins and take our place.

Jesus had the power to come down from the cross at any time. He could have performed a thousand miracles to prove that He was the Son of God. But that was not God's plan. Jesus had to die on the cross because He is the Lamb of God who sacrificed His life for ours. God showed His greatest love for us by sending Jesus to die for our sins. We deserve to be punished for our sins, but we are set free because Jesus took our place.

EXPLORE MORE: Read Luke 23:39–43 to find out what the criminals said as they hung on a cross next to Jesus.

> **DID YOU KNOW?**
> Golgotha means "The Place of the Skull." Jerusalem was considered a holy city, so Golgotha was a place where they crucified criminals. It's also where they brought the remains of animals that were sacrificed.

Jesus was crucified for me.

Jesus Dies

When Jesus died, the curtain in the Temple was torn into two pieces. The tear started at the top and tore all the way to the bottom. Also, the earth shook and rocks were broken.
—Matthew 27:51 ERV

As Jesus hung on the cross, the sky became dark for three hours. Jesus said He was thirsty, so the soldiers soaked a sponge in vinegar and lifted it to His lips. Then He cried out, "My God, my God, why have you forsaken me?" When Jesus cried out these words, He took our sins upon himself and showed how sin separates us from God.

Jesus's last words on the cross were, "It is finished." Then Jesus died. At that moment the curtain in the temple was torn in two from top to bottom. This showed that our sin no longer separates us from God. Because of Jesus's death on the cross, we can be in God's presence. Jesus's death on the cross made a way for people to be cleansed from their sins.

When Jesus died, the earth shook, and rocks split apart. Some of the tombs opened up, and people who had died came out. The guards who saw what happened were terrified. They said, "He really was the Son of God!"

A rich man named Joseph was a follower of Jesus. He was from the town of Arimathea. He asked Pilate for Jesus's body, and Pilate agreed. Joseph wrapped Jesus's body in new linen cloths and placed Him in a tomb that he had dug in a wall of rock. He put a large stone over the opening of the tomb.

TALK TO GOD
Thank God that everything that happened to Jesus was part of His plan.

The Jewish leaders remembered how Jesus said He would rise from the dead on the third day, so they told Pilate to make sure the tomb was sealed and guarded. But the people would soon find out that nothing can stop God's plan.

EXPLORE MORE: Who were some other followers watching Jesus that day? Read Matthew 27:55–56 to find out.

Jesus really is the Son of God.

DID YOU KNOW?
Joseph of Arimathea was a Jewish leader. He is only mentioned in this story, but Matthew, Mark, Luke, and John all include him in their gospels.

He Isn't Here!

"He isn't here! He is risen from the dead, just as he said would happen. Come, see where his body was lying." —Matthew 28:6 NLT

Early on Sunday morning, Mary Magdalene and Mary the mother of James went to the tomb where Jesus was buried. They wanted to put spices on Jesus's body but wondered how they would move the heavy stone. Suddenly, the earth shook, and an angel came down from heaven and rolled the stone away from the tomb. The angel's face and clothing were as bright as lightning. The guards standing watch at the tomb were so frightened they fell to the ground.

The angel said to the women, "Don't be afraid. I know you are looking for Jesus, who was crucified. He is not here. He has risen just like He said. Come and see where His body was lying. Then go tell His disciples, 'Jesus has risen from the dead.'"

The women were frightened but filled with joy! They ran to tell the disciples what the angel had said, and on their way, they met Jesus. He said to them, "Don't be afraid. Tell my brothers to go to Galilee, and I will see them there."

When the guards realized what had happened, they went to Jerusalem and told the Jewish leaders. The leaders had a meeting and decided to pay the guards a lot of money to lie. They told the soldiers, "Tell everyone Jesus's disciples came during the night and stole His body while you were sleeping." The guards agreed and took the money.

TALK TO GOD
Ask God to help you believe the truth that is in the Bible.

The people who didn't believe that Jesus was God's Son had to make up lies because they didn't want to accept the truth. Jesus's followers believed that Jesus was the Son of God, and now they would believe that He had come back to life.

EXPLORE MORE: What did the disciples think when the women told them about the empty tomb? Read Luke 24:9–12 to find out.

DID YOU KNOW?

During the time of Jesus, the stones that were used to seal a tomb were about 4 to 6 feet (1.2 to 1.8 meters) tall and weighed 1.5 to 2 tons (1,361 to 1,814 kilograms). It was very hard to roll the stone away because it sat in a groove in the ground.

Jesus came back to life, just like He said He would.

Jesus Walks with Two Men

"He explained to us what the Scriptures meant. Weren't we excited as he talked with us on the road?" —Luke 24:32 NIrV

On the day Jesus rose from the dead, two men were walking from Jerusalem to a village called Emmaus. They were talking about everything that had happened. Jesus came next to them and asked what they were talking about. One of the men, Cleopas, was surprised and thought Jesus must be a visitor. "Don't you know about the things that have happened in the last few days?" he asked.

"What things?" Jesus replied.

The men told Him everything that had happened—how Jesus was a powerful prophet from Nazareth. They said the chief priests and rulers handed Him over to be crucified, and how that very morning, the women saw an angel and the tomb was empty. Then Jesus said, "Didn't the Messiah have to suffer these things and then receive His glory?" Jesus went on to explain everything that Moses and the prophets had said about Him.

When they got to the village, the men asked Jesus to stay with them. Jesus sat with them at the table. He took the bread and gave thanks. Then He broke it and gave it to them. At that moment they realized they were with Jesus, and He had taught them the meaning of the Scriptures. After Jesus left them, they returned to Jerusalem and were excited to tell the disciples they had seen Jesus.

It must have been amazing for these men to listen to Jesus explain the words that the prophets had said about Him. Jesus helped them understand everything clearly. And when they finally sat down with Him, they saw with their own eyes that Jesus was alive.

TALK TO GOD
Ask Jesus to help you clearly understand His words in the Bible.

EXPLORE MORE: Read Luke 24:28–29. Why did the men tell Jesus He should stay with them?

Jesus can help me understand God's Word.

DID YOU KNOW?
Emmaus, Pennsylvania, a township in the Lehigh Valley region of the United States, gets its name from the village of Emmaus in the Bible. It has been listed as one of the top 100 "Best Places to Live" in the United States.

No More Doubts

Then Jesus told him, "You believe because you have seen me. Blessed are those who believe without seeing me." —John 20:29 NLT

Even though Jesus had told His disciples He would rise from the dead on the third day, they were still confused. Not all of them believed that Jesus was alive. In the evening they were meeting together with the doors locked because they were afraid of the Jewish leaders. Suddenly, Jesus stood before them. "Peace be with you!" He said. Jesus showed them the wounds in His hands and feet. The disciples were filled with joy when they saw Him. They no longer doubted that Jesus was alive.

Thomas, one of Jesus's twelve disciples, was not with them. When the disciples told them they saw Jesus, He didn't believe them. Thomas said, "I won't believe it unless I see the nail wounds in His hands, put my fingers into them, and place my hand into the wound in His side."

Eight days later the disciples were meeting again with the doors locked, and Thomas was with them. Suddenly, Jesus stood before them, just like before. "Peace be with you," He said. Then He said to Thomas, "Put your finger here, and look at my hands. Put your hand into the wound in my side. Don't doubt anymore. Just believe!"

TALK TO GOD
Thank God that we never have to doubt the words in the Bible because we know they are true.

Thomas didn't need any more proof. He said out loud, "My Lord and my God!" He saw with his own eyes that Jesus was alive. Jesus said, "You believe because you have seen me. Blessed are those who believe without seeing me."

We cannot see Jesus right now, but someday we will see Him face to face. The Bible tells us it's true, so we don't have to doubt. We can just believe!

EXPLORE MORE: What does John tell us in John 20:31?

DID YOU KNOW?
Thomas also went by the name Didymus, which is a Greek name that means "the twin," but the Bible doesn't tell us whether or not Thomas was a twin.

I believe I will see Jesus.

Breakfast on the Beach

Jesus said to them, "Come and have breakfast." None of the disciples dared to ask him, "Who are you?" They knew it was the Lord. —John 21:12 NIrV

One night after Jesus's resurrection, Peter and Thomas decided to go fishing. Some of the other disciples went with them. They fished all night and didn't catch anything. Early in the morning, a man was standing on shore. He called out, "Friends, don't you have any fish?"

"No," they answered. The disciples didn't realize the man was Jesus.

"Throw your net on the right side of the boat," He said. "There you will find some fish."

When they did, their net was bursting with fish. "It's the Lord!" John said. Peter jumped in the water while the other disciples followed in the boat, towing the net full of fish.

When they reached the shore, they saw fish cooking over a fire of burning coals and some bread. Jesus told them to bring some of the fish they had caught, so Peter went to the boat and dragged the net to shore. Jesus said, "Come and have breakfast." He took the fish and bread and gave it to the disciples to eat.

Even though Jesus had finished what God sent Him to do, He wanted to encourage His followers and serve them. He even called them His friends. Soon, He would no longer be with them in person, but He would always be with them in spirit. More than anything else, Jesus loved His followers and wanted them to tell the world about Him—the Son of God they had come to know.

Jesus is your friend too. The more time you spend with Him, the more you will get to know Him. And you can even talk to Him when you eat your breakfast!

TALK TO GOD
Ask God to help you learn more about Him every day.

EXPLORE MORE: Read John 21:11 to find out how many fish were in the disciples' net.

I want to know Jesus more.

DID YOU KNOW?
Israeli breakfasts are considered one of the healthiest breakfasts in the world. In Israel people eat eggs, fruits, vegetables, salads, breads, fish, and cheese for breakfast.

So Much More

Jesus also did many other things. What if every one of them were written down? I suppose that even the whole world would not have room for the books that would be written. —John 21:25 NIrV

Matthew, Mark, Luke, and John are four books in the Bible called the Gospels. They talk about the birth and life of Jesus when He was on the earth. They tell us about Jesus's travels through different towns and villages and how He taught and healed many people. These books include about thirty-seven miracles that Jesus performed and forty-three parables that He shared. He also taught many sermons and prayed many prayers. All of this took place in about three and a half years.

John, who was one of Jesus's disciples, wrote the gospel of John in the Bible. In the last verse of the last chapter, he writes something that's pretty amazing. John 21:25 says, "Jesus also did many other things. What if every one of them were written down? I suppose that even the whole world would not have room for the books that would be written."

John is saying that it's impossible to keep a record of everything Jesus did because He did so many things. The Holy Spirit guided the writers to write down the things God wanted us to know. When we read about Jesus's miracles and parables and the things He taught His followers, we can be amazed at everything He did. And He did so much more!

John was there when Jesus showed love and compassion for others. He saw Jesus walk on water and calm the storms. He watched Jesus use His power to heal the sick and raise people from the dead. John listened to Jesus's parables and followed Him everywhere. John knew how great Jesus is, and he wanted everyone else to know it too, including you!

TALK TO GOD
Thank God for the Gospels, so we can learn about Jesus's life on earth.

EXPLORE MORE: Why can we believe what John said about Jesus? You can find the answer in John 21:24.

DID YOU KNOW?

With more than 167 million items, the Library of Congress in Washington, DC, is the largest library in the world. It opened on April 24, 1800.

Jesus did too many things to write in books.

Go and Make Disciples

So you must go and make disciples of all nations. Baptize them in
the name of the Father and of the Son and of the Holy Spirit.
—Matthew 28:19 NIrV

The disciples went to Galilee to meet Jesus at a mountain where He gave them an important message. First, He said, "All authority in heaven and earth has been given to me." That means Jesus has power and control over everything, and He can use His power to help His followers do great things.

Then Jesus said, "Go and make disciples of all nations." The gospel message was first given to the Jews, but even during Jesus's time on earth, people from other nations were given the chance to believe in Him. Jesus wanted His disciples to bring the message of salvation to *all* people *everywhere*.

TALK TO GOD
Ask God to help you
spread His message
of love and salvation
wherever you go.

Then Jesus said, "Baptize them in the name of the Father and of the Son and of the Holy Spirit." Baptism is a sign that people choose to follow Jesus and have asked Him to forgive their sins. Their old life is in the past, and they have a new life as they follow Jesus.

The next thing Jesus said was, "Teach them to obey every-thing I have commanded you." Jesus taught His disciples how to love God and others. Now He wanted them to teach others everything that He taught them.

Jesus ended His message with an important promise. "And you can be sure that I am always with you, to the very end." Jesus was going back to heaven, but He would not leave them alone. He promised to send the Holy Spirit to give them the courage to teach and the right words to say.

Jesus's message is also for us. Anyone who believes in Jesus is His disciple, and He wants us to make more disciples wherever we go.

EXPLORE MORE: Some of Jesus's last words are also found in Acts 1:8. Read it to see what Jesus said.

Jesus wants me to make disciples.

DID YOU KNOW?
The verses in Matthew 28:18–20 are called "The Great Commission." This was the last command Jesus gave His disciples before He went to heaven. A commission is a special duty given to a group of people.

Jesus Goes to Heaven

After Jesus said this, he was lifted up into the sky. While they were watching, he went into a cloud, and they could not see him. —Acts 1:9 ERV

After Jesus came back to life, He lived on earth for forty days. He appeared to His disciples many times to prove that He had risen from the dead. When it was time for Jesus to leave for heaven, He gave His followers special directions. It was time for them to do the work Jesus had started.

After He told His disciples what to do, Jesus rose into the sky. A cloud covered Jesus, and the disciples could no longer see Him. As they kept looking into the sky, two men wearing white clothes came and spoke to them. "Men from Galilee," they said, "why are you standing here looking into the sky? You saw Jesus carried away from you into heaven. He will come back in the same way you saw him go." From that day on—even until today—Jesus's followers have important directions to follow. We are called to share God's love with others everywhere. We can follow Jesus's example of being kind and helping our friends, neighbors, and other people we meet. We can invite people to church, give them a Bible, or tell them the story of Jesus. We can spread the news that Jesus is our Savior—the Messiah that God promised to send. And everyone who believes in Jesus will have a forever life with Him.

TALK TO GOD
Thank Jesus that He is coming back someday. Ask Him to help you follow Him now.

Jesus came to earth so He could sacrifice His life for our sins. He went back to heaven, but that is not the end of the story. Jesus will come again someday to be the King over all the earth.

EXPLORE MORE: What did the disciples do after Jesus went to heaven? Read Luke 24:50–53 to find the answer.

DID YOU KNOW?
The day Jesus went to heaven is called Ascension Day. It is still celebrated around the world, forty days after the celebration of Jesus's resurrection. In many countries it is a public holiday.

Jesus is coming back someday.

The Holy Spirit Comes

They were all filled with the Holy Spirit, and they began to speak different languages. The Holy Spirit was giving them the power to do this. —Acts 2:4 ERV

One day as Jesus's followers were meeting together several weeks after Jesus ascended to heaven, a noise filled the house. It sounded like a strong wind blowing. Then small flames of fire appeared and stood above everyone there. The believers were filled with the Holy Spirit and began speaking in languages they did not know. The Holy Spirit gave them the power to do this amazing thing.

Jewish people from every country were staying in Jerusalem at that time. Many of them came to the house where Jesus's followers were because they had heard the sound of wind and wanted to see what was happening. They were surprised when they heard the disciples speaking in different languages. Everyone heard someone speaking their own language, and they didn't know how that was possible. "These men are from Galilee," they said. "How can they be speaking our languages? We can all understand the great things they are saying about God!"

Once Jesus's followers had received the Holy Spirit, they had the power to spread the gospel throughout the whole world. The Holy Spirit would also fill them with wisdom and truth. The Holy Spirit would give them patience, peace, and comfort as they faced many challenges. Jesus had promised the Holy Spirit would come, and His promises are true.

Everyone who believes in Jesus as their Savior receives the gift of the Holy Spirit. The Holy Spirit helps us know what God wants us to do and gives us the wisdom and strength to do it. He comforts us when we are sad and guides us as we live. Jesus doesn't want us to be alone, so He sent the Holy Spirit to be with us.

EXPLORE MORE: Look up Acts 2:9-11 to read a list of all the different places the people were from who heard the disciples speaking their own languages.

TALK TO GOD
Thank God for the gift of the Holy Spirit, who is our helper, teacher, and comforter.

Jesus gives the Holy Spirit to everyone who believes in Him.

DID YOU KNOW?
The day the Holy Spirit came is known as Pentecost. It comes from the Greek word *pentekoste* which means "fiftieth." Pentecost is celebrated fifty days after Easter.

The Believers Share

The believers met together in the Temple every day. They all
had the same purpose. They broke bread in their homes, happy
to share their food with joyful hearts. —Acts 2:46 ICB

Jesus's disciples were also called apostles. When they were disciples, they followed Jesus and learned from Him because He was their teacher. Now they were apostles, which means they were messengers and teachers who taught others what they had learned from Jesus.

With the power of the Holy Spirit, the apostles began doing miracles and signs that showed that God had sent them to tell the world about Jesus. The believers met together every day at the temple. They shared everything they had. They even sold their land and gave their money to people who needed it. They shared meals together and were filled with joy. They praised God as many more people were being added to their group.

This is the beginning of what we call "the church." Sometimes they met at the temple, and other times they met in people's homes. The reason God created the church is for believers to meet together to worship God and learn from a pastor or teacher who has studied the Bible. It's also a place where people can serve each other and share God's blessings. People in the church can care for someone who is sick or comfort someone who is sad. The people in the church are like a big family that loves God and loves each other.

Today there are many different places people meet for church. Some are really big, others are small, and some people still meet in homes. It doesn't matter what size the building is. What matters is that people come together to learn more about God and share His love with everyone.

TALK TO GOD
Thank God that we have many places where we can meet with other Christians.

DID YOU KNOW?

The Dura-Europos Church in Syria was one of the first Christian churches. It was built in 233 and may have been someone's home before it was used as a church building. Today only broken pieces are left.

EXPLORE MORE: What did Jesus say in Matthew 18:20?

It's good for believers to meet together.

Better than Money

But Peter said, "I don't have any silver or gold, but I do have something else I can give you." —Acts 3:6 ICB

One afternoon, Peter and John went to the temple for the daily prayer service. They passed by a man who had been unable to walk since the day he was born. Every day someone brought him to the temple gate to beg for money. The temple gate was called the Beautiful Gate.

TALK TO GOD
Ask God to help you see the power of Jesus in your life.

When the man saw Peter and John, he asked them for money. They told him, "Look at us!" The man looked at them because he thought they were going to give him some money. Then Peter said, "I don't have any silver or gold or money, but I do have something else I can give you: by the power of Jesus Christ from Nazareth—stand up and walk!"

The man's feet and ankles became strong as Peter lifted the man up. The man jumped up and began to walk! Then he went into the temple, praising God for healing him.

When the people saw the man walking and praising God, they were amazed. They knew he was the man who sat by the gate every day begging for money. They did not understand how he was able to walk.

Just as the crowds had followed Jesus, many people were now following the apostles. As stories about them spread, people brought the sick to be healed. They even laid sick people on their mats in the streets, hoping they would be healed by Peter's shadow as he walked by.

The healing power of Jesus was now given to the apostles through the Holy Spirit. As they continued to show God's power, more people were being saved every day.

EXPLORE MORE: How did Peter explain this miracle in Acts 3:16?

The power of Jesus goes on and on.

DID YOU KNOW?
The Beautiful Gate at the temple was bigger than most of the other temple gates. It was 70 feet (nearly 23 meters) high. It was so heavy it took twenty men to move it.

Questions for Peter and John

"You can't be saved by believing in anyone else. God has given people no other name under heaven that will save them." —Acts 4:12 NIrV

The Jewish leaders were upset when they heard Peter and John had healed the man who couldn't walk. They put them in prison until the next day, but they couldn't stop everyone from talking about what had happened.

More and more people were believing in Jesus every day. The number of believers had grown to about five thousand. Do you remember the parable Jesus told about the mustard seed? He said that God's kingdom was like the tiny seed that could produce giant plants and that every plant would produce thousands of seeds. That's exactly what was happening! God's kingdom was growing, and the Jewish rulers couldn't stop it.

When the rulers and teachers let Peter and John out of prison, they had some questions for them. "By what power do you do this?" they asked. "And through whose name?"

The Holy Spirit gave Peter courage to speak. "Do you want to know why we were kind to a man who couldn't walk?" he asked. "Are you asking how he was healed? You nailed Jesus Christ of Nazareth to the cross, but God raised him from the dead. It is through Jesus's name that this man stands healed in front of you."

TALK TO GOD
Ask God to give you courage to be able to speak about Him to others.

The leaders were surprised that Peter and John were so bold because they were ordinary men with little education. The leaders realized that following Jesus is what made them brave and powerful. The man who had been healed stood near them as they talked, so they knew the story was true. The leaders ordered Peter and John to stop talking about Jesus. But the apostles would never stop telling everyone about Jesus, no matter what the leaders tried to do.

EXPLORE MORE: Read what else Peter and John said to the rulers in Acts 4:19–20.

DID YOU KNOW?

In Acts 4, Peter quoted a verse from Psalm 118:22 NIrV: "The stone you builders did not accept. But it has become the most important stone of all." Peter explained that the "stone" is Jesus.

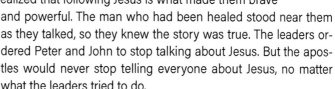

Never stop talking about Jesus.

Seven More Apostles

So, brothers, choose seven of your own men. They must be men who are good. They must be full of wisdom and full of the Spirit. We will put them in charge of this work. —Acts 6:3 ICB

After Jesus went back to heaven, the apostles chose a man named Matthias to replace Judas. The twelve apostles worked hard telling others about Jesus and bringing more believers into God's kingdom. When they found out that some of the Jewish widows were not getting their fair share of food each day, the twelve apostles chose seven more men to be apostles. The new apostles were full of wisdom from the Holy Spirit and were put in charge of caring for the widows. The twelve apostles prayed with the new apostles and laid hands on them to give them God's blessing.

TALK TO GOD
Pray for people whose lives are in danger for telling others about Jesus.

One of the men was Stephen. Acts 6:5 says that Stephen was a man of great faith, filled with the Holy Spirit. As more apostles taught about Jesus, God's message was reaching more people. The group of Jesus's followers was growing, and some Jewish priests believed in Jesus too.

But some of the Jewish leaders were still trying to stop the apostles. When they found out Stephen had power to do miracles, they arrested him. The leaders tried to argue with Stephen, but he spoke with so much wisdom, they didn't know what to say. They asked people to lie about Stephen to get him in trouble.

As the Jewish leaders looked at Stephen, his face looked like the face of an angel. Stephen told them stories of Abraham, Joseph, and Moses. He told the leaders they had the law of Moses but didn't obey it. This made them angry, so they took Stephen out to stone him. Stephen became the first martyr, which means he was willing to die for believing in Jesus—the Savior who died for him.

EXPLORE MORE: Read Acts 7:55–56 to see what Stephen said as he looked up to heaven.

The apostles loved Jesus with all they had.

DID YOU KNOW?
The name Stephen comes from the Greek name *Stephanos*, which means crown of honor. What a good name for someone who loved Jesus so much!

Philip Shares God's Message

So Philip ran up to the chariot. He heard the man reading Isaiah the prophet. "Do you understand what you're reading?" Philip asked.
—Acts 8:30 NIrV

The Jews who didn't believe in Jesus began to put Jesus's followers in prison. This made many Christians leave Jerusalem and scatter throughout Judea and Samaria. The Jewish leaders probably thought this would slow down the spread of the gospel message, but it only made the message of Jesus spread farther!

The apostle Philip went to a city in Samaria where he preached about Jesus and did many miracles. An angel told Philip to go to a desert road that went from Gaza to Jerusalem. On the road, Philip saw a man from Ethiopia who was an important official for the queen. The man was on his way home from worshiping God in Jerusalem. He was sitting in a chariot reading from the scroll of Isaiah. The Holy Spirit led Philip to the chariot. "Do you understand what you are reading?" Philip asked the man.

"I need someone to explain it to me," he said.

The man was reading Isaiah 53:7-8: "He was led like a sheep to be killed. Just as lambs are silent while their wool is being cut off, he did not open his mouth. When he was treated badly, he was refused a fair trial." The man asked Philip, "Please tell me, who is the prophet talking about?" Philip told him about Jesus and all He had done to save us from our sins. When Philip and the man rode by some water, the man asked Philip to baptize him. The man became a believer.

TALK TO GOD
Ask God to lead you to people who you can tell about Jesus.

Just like the Holy Spirit led Philip to the Ethiopian to tell him about Jesus, the Holy Spirit can lead us to people who need to hear about Jesus. And when the Holy Spirit leads you to someone, He will also help you know what to say.

EXPLORE MORE: Read Matthew 27:12-14. How did Jesus fulfill the words that the Ethiopian read in Isaiah 53:7?

DID YOU KNOW?
During the time of the apostles, an entire scroll of Isaiah would have been big and expensive. The man may have bought the big scroll for his synagogue, or he may have been reading a smaller section of the scroll.

The Holy Spirit leads us to people who want to know Jesus.

Saul Meets Jesus

But the Lord said to Ananias, "Go! I have chosen this man to work for me. He will announce my name to the Gentiles and to their kings. He will also announce my name to the people of Israel." —Acts 9:15 NIrV

Saul was a Jewish leader who wanted to destroy the church by putting believers in prison. One day as he was on his way to Damascus to capture more Christians, a light from heaven flashed around him. Saul fell down as a voice called out, "Saul, Saul, why are you doing things against me?"

"Who are you, Lord?" Saul asked.

"I am Jesus," the voice replied. "I am the One you are trying to hurt. Get up now, and go into the city. Someone there will tell you what you must do." Saul opened his eyes but could not see anything. The men who were with him led him to Damascus.

A man named Ananias was one of Jesus's followers. Jesus told him in a vision, "Go to the house of Judas on Straight Street. Ask for a man from Tarsus named Saul. He is praying."

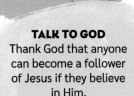

Ananias had heard bad things about Saul, so he wasn't happy about going to see him. But Jesus told Ananias, "He has seen a vision of you laying hands on him so he can see again. I have chosen this man to work for me."

Ananias found Saul and placed his hands on him. Something like scales fell from Saul's eyes, and he could see. When Saul believed in Jesus, he was baptized, and people started calling him by his Roman name, Paul. Then he spent the rest of his life traveling around telling everyone he met about Jesus.

When people come to believe in Jesus, they are not the same anymore. They have a brand-new life filled with the Holy Spirit, and they become part of God's family. Jesus can change anyone's life, no matter who they are, when they believe in Him.

TALK TO GOD
Thank God that anyone can become a follower of Jesus if they believe in Him.

EXPLORE MORE: Who became Saul's friend when he went back to Jerusalem? See Acts 9:26–28 for the answer.

Jesus can change people's lives.

DID YOU KNOW?
Damascus, Syria, is also called the city of Jasmine. It is the oldest city in the world where people still live and has a population of more than two million.

Prison Break

Suddenly an angel of the Lord appeared. A light shone in the prison cell. The angel struck Peter on his side. Peter woke up. "Quick!" the angel said. "Get up!" The chains fell off Peter's wrists. —Acts 12:7 NIrV

The Jewish leaders didn't want the disciples preaching about Jesus and performing miracles, so Peter ended up in prison again. This time he was guarded by four soldiers. Sometimes prisoners would be handcuffed to one soldier so they couldn't escape, but Peter was handcuffed to two soldiers because the king knew the disciples were mysteriously escaping from prison. While Peter was in prison, the church prayed for him.

One night as Peter was sleeping between two soldiers, two more soldiers stood guard at the entrance. Suddenly, an angel appeared with a bright light. The angel woke Peter up. "Quick!" the angel said. "Get up!" The chains fell off Peter's wrists. The angel told Peter, "Put on your clothes and sandals. Put on your coat. Follow me." Peter did what the angel said and followed him out the door. Peter thought he was having a vision. The angel led Peter to the city and walked down a street. Suddenly, the angel left, and Peter realized it was real!

Peter went to Mary's house. She was the mother of John Mark, who helped the apostle Paul and Barnabas on their missionary trips. He knocked on the door. A servant ran to tell everyone in the house, but no one believed her until they saw Peter. In the morning the soldiers at the prison were so confused! They couldn't figure out what happened.

TALK TO GOD
Bring your biggest cares to God, and thank Him that He answers prayers.

Have you ever wondered if God hears your prayers? Maybe you've wondered if praying really makes a difference. What happened to Peter shows how powerful prayer is. When we pray, we connect with God. The Holy Spirit helps us talk to God and gives us strength for the things we face. God heard the church's prayers for Peter, and God hears your prayers too.

EXPLORE MORE: What does Micah 7:7 say about God?

DID YOU KNOW?
The name of the servant who heard Peter knock was Rhoda. She was so excited when she heard Peter's voice that she ran to tell everyone and forgot to open the door to let Peter in!

God answers prayer.

Lydia Meets Paul

Lydia was listening to Paul, and the Lord opened her heart to accept what Paul was saying. —Acts 16:14 ERV

Saul of Tarsus, who met Jesus on the way to Damascus, traveled around and started telling everyone the good news. He was also called Paul by many of the people he met. Paul traveled with two men named Silas and Timothy. As they sailed around, they went to Philippi. On the Sabbath day they went to a river outside the city gate to find a special place to pray. A group of women was meeting there, and Paul and his friends talked with them.

One of the women was named Lydia. Her job was selling purple cloth, and she was a worshiper of God. As she listened to Paul, God opened her heart to accept what he said. Then she was baptized and so was everyone who lived in her house. Lydia invited Paul, Timothy, and Silas to stay at her house. She said, "If you think I am a true believer in the Lord Jesus, come stay in my house." The three men went and stayed with her.

TALK TO GOD
Ask God to bring people to you that need to hear about Jesus.

Paul and his friends were always ready to tell people about Jesus wherever they went. Even in this story, they were looking for a place to pray and found a chance to share Jesus instead! It's important for us to tell everyone about Jesus. Lydia was from a completely different place than Paul, and they may not have had a lot in common, but God used Paul to teach her. The gospel is for everyone. We have the special job of telling people about it. We can be ready to share Jesus's love everywhere we go.

EXPLORE MORE: What does 2 Timothy 4:2 tell us to do?

I can spread the gospel.

DID YOU KNOW?
Lydia is believed to be the first person to become a Christian in Europe. She was a business woman who sold cloth dyed in purple to people who could afford expensive clothes.

The Power of Praise

About midnight Paul and Silas were praying and singing songs to God. The other prisoners were listening to them. —Acts 16:25 ICB

What do you do when you're having a hard day? Do you get in bed and pull the covers over your head? Do you talk to your parents or a friend? Paul and Silas were having a bad day, and they did something unexpected. They prayed and sang songs to God.

Paul had performed a miracle by commanding an evil spirit to come out of a servant girl. Her owners were angry because they used the servant girl to make money by having her make prophecies. Her owners brought Paul and Silas to the Roman rulers. "These Jewish men are making trouble in our city," they said. The Roman officers threw Paul and Silas in jail.

Around midnight Paul and Silas were praying and singing songs to God. The other prisoners listened. Suddenly, there was a strong earthquake. It shook the jail so hard that all the doors broke open, and the prisoners' chains fell off! The jailer woke up and was afraid the prisoners had escaped. But Paul shouted, "We're all here!" When the jailer saw that no one had left, he was so amazed. He asked Paul and Silas, "What must I do to be saved?" They told him to believe in the Lord Jesus. That night the jailer and his family were baptized. They were very happy because they had become believers in Jesus.

No matter where we are, we can praise God. We can praise Him in church, we can praise Him in bed at night, and we can even praise Him in hard situations like Paul and Silas did. Praise is one of the most powerful tools we have. It's mighty enough to shake the ground and bring a jailer into the family of God! Let's use the power of praise.

EXPLORE MORE: Read Psalm 63:4. How long did David say he would praise God?

DID YOU KNOW?
Paul and Silas were Roman citizens and were not supposed to be punished. When the Roman leaders found this out, they apologized to Paul and Silas and let them leave.

TALK TO GOD
Praise God for something right here and now.

I can praise God anywhere.

Paul Stays Faithful to God

I try to find common ground with everyone, doing everything
I can to save some. —1 Corinthians 9:22 NLT

Paul's journeys took him many places besides Philippi. He traveled all around the Roman Empire telling everyone he met about Jesus. He even shared the gospel with people who were not Jews. These people were called gentiles, and they became Christians when they believed in Jesus. As Paul traveled, he started many churches. He also wrote letters to the people he met along the way. Many of those letters became part of the New Testament, and you can read them in your Bible.

TALK TO GOD
Thank God for the first Christians, like Paul, who spread the gospel, so we could know Jesus today.

Even though Paul spent the rest of his life telling people about Jesus, he went through many hard times. He was put in jail more than once. He was shipwrecked three times. He was whipped and beaten and was often in danger. But he never stopped obeying God, and he kept taking the message of Jesus to everyone he could. He always tried to find something in common with the people he met so he could talk to them about Jesus.

Paul's life shows us that being a Christian can be hard sometimes. But because of Paul's work, many people heard about Jesus, and Christianity spread all over the world. Paul loved God so much that he was willing to keep obeying Him through hard times. There are still times when Christians are treated badly today. Sometimes people make fun of Christians or say unkind things about what Christians believe. But we can keep spreading the gospel like Paul did because we know that's what God wants us to do. It may not always be easy to follow Jesus, but it's always worth it.

EXPLORE MORE: Paul wrote Philippians while he was in prison. What does he say in Philippians 1:18–20?

I will stay faithful to God.

DID YOU KNOW?
It's estimated that Paul traveled about 10,000 miles (16,000 kilometers) across the Roman Empire telling people about Jesus.

Faith in the Storm

"Men, continue to be brave. I have faith in God. It will happen just as he told me." —Acts 27:25 NIrV

Paul was put in prison again for preaching about Jesus. He was guarded by a Roman commander named Julius. Paul was sent with other prisoners to see the Roman emperor for judgment. As they sailed to Italy, strong winds made sailing the ship difficult. Paul warned the sailors, "I can see that our trip is going to be dangerous. The ship and everything in it will be lost. Our own lives will be in danger also."

The commander of the ship didn't listen to Paul. As they continued their journey, wind blew across the island with the force of a hurricane. The ship was caught in the storm, and the crew had to throw everything overboard to keep from sinking.

Things were so bad, everyone on the ship gave up hope of being saved. But Paul stood up and said, "Men, I beg you to be brave. Not one of you will die. Only the ship will be destroyed."

Why was Paul sure everyone would survive? Because an angel of the Lord had visited him the night before. He told Paul "Do not be afraid. You must go on trial in front of Caesar. God has shown his grace by sparing the lives of all of those sailing with you." Paul had faith everything would happen the way God told him.

TALK TO GOD
Ask God to give you faith to believe what He says.

Nothing can get in the way of God's plans. No matter what unexpected things happen, God is still in control. Paul believed that with all of his heart. We can believe everything God tells us too. The words of the Bible will always be true. We can have faith that things will happen the way God told us because He is in control.

EXPLORE MORE: What does Proverbs 19:21 tell us about God's plans?

DID YOU KNOW?
The strong wind that came when Paul was sailing was called a northeaster. In some translations it is also called *Euroclydon*. It's a stormy wind that comes from the northeast in the Mediterranean, usually during autumn and winter.

God is always in control.

True Wisdom

God has shown these things to us through his Spirit. The Spirit understands all things. He understands even the deep things of God. —1 Corinthians 2:10 NIrV

You might remember that the book of Proverbs tells us a lot about wisdom. In Proverbs we read that we can get wisdom by listening to good advice and accepting instruction from teachers, parents, and other adults we trust. But sometimes you might hear something that isn't very wise, even if others think it is. With so many different opinions, it can be hard to know what is *truly* wise—especially when people don't always agree on the right thing to do.

TALK TO GOD
Ask the Holy Spirit to give you God's wisdom.

So, how can we get wisdom to know what is wise and true? In 1 Corinthians 2, Paul told the Corinthian church that the words he spoke were wise. How did he know that was true? He said, "Our words are different from the wisdom of this world . . . we announce God's wisdom." Then Paul said, "God has shown these things to us through his Spirit."

The Holy Spirit is the only one who can understand the deep things of God because He is God. The Bible tells us that the spirit of the world is not the Holy Spirit. But we have the Holy Spirit in us when we are followers of Jesus. The Holy Spirit helps us understand the things God wants us to know and shows us what is true and good and right. First, the Holy Spirit helps us understand the message of the gospel and receive it in our hearts. Then the Holy Spirit continues to give us wisdom as we seek God and ask for His help. When we listen to God's wisdom, we can be sure that it's true wisdom!

EXPLORE MORE: What does 1 Corinthians 2:14–16 say about the Holy Spirit?

DID YOU KNOW?
The Greek word for wisdom used in the New Testament is *sophia.* It means full of intelligence. Sophia is currently one of the most popular names for baby girls born around the world.

The Holy Spirit gives us wisdom.

One Body

The human body has many parts, but the many parts make up one whole body. So it is with the body of Christ. —1 Corinthians 12:12 NLT

Did you know that scientists have determined the human body has nine different sections and that a person has seventy-eight different organs? Your body has many different parts that do different things. Your eyes see. Your ears hear. Your heart pumps blood. Your toes help you balance. Each part of your body has its own job, and all those parts work together to keep your body moving and working.

In his first letter to the Corinthians, Paul said the same thing about the church. Paul called the church the body of Christ. The church isn't just a building where we worship God; it is the entire group of Christians around the world who believe in Jesus. And Paul said no matter where we come from or who we are, we are all united in the Spirit. The Holy Spirit gives all of us gifts and talents that help us serve each other and grow God's kingdom.

The gifts that the Holy Spirit gives you may look different than the gifts someone else has, but that doesn't mean your gifts aren't important. Some people have the gift of teaching while others have the gift of helping. Paul said, "If the whole body were an eye, how would you hear? Or if your whole body were an ear, how would you smell anything?" God put each part of our body just where He wants it. It's the same with the church—He gave each of us the gifts and talents He wants us to use. When we each do our part, we can work together as one body because we all belong to Jesus.

EXPLORE MORE: Read 1 Corinthians 12:27–28 to see a list of gifts that God gives people for the church.

TALK TO GOD
Ask God to show you the spiritual gifts He has given you and how He wants you to use them.

DID YOU KNOW?

The human body can be divided into nine major parts. They are the head, neck, chest, abdomen, pelvis, back, hip, limbs, and trunk. All the parts are connected, and they all work together.

I can do my part in the body of Christ.

The Secret Ingredient

If I don't have love, I get nothing at all.
—1 Corinthians 13:3 NIrV

If you've ever helped cook something, you know that many ingredients go into a recipe. Sometimes a chef will add a secret ingredient to make a dish extra tasty. Did you know there's a "secret ingredient" when it comes to serving others? No matter what gifts the Holy Spirit gives us, there's a way to serve God that's better than all other ways. Do you know what that secret ingredient is? The Bible says it's love!

First Corinthians 13 is often called the "love chapter" of the Bible. In this passage, Paul talks about what real love looks like. He says, "Love is patient. Love is kind. It does not want what belongs to others. It does not brag. It is not proud. It does not dishonor other people. It does not look out for its own interests. It does not easily become angry. It does not keep track of other people's wrongs. Love is not happy with evil. But it is full of joy when the truth is spoken. It always protects. It always trusts. It always hopes. It never gives up."

> **TALK TO GOD**
> Ask God to fill you with the love of Jesus.

If we try to serve others and share the gospel by doing good things but we don't show them this kind of love, it doesn't do any good. Even if we understood everything about God or had faith to move mountains, it would mean nothing without love. Love is the secret ingredient that shows our hearts have been changed by God, and our love shows God's love to others. What matters most to God is what's in our hearts. When we are filled with His love, we have all the ingredients we need to create something wonderful.

EXPLORE MORE: Read 1 John 4:19 to find out why we should love others.

Love matters most.

> **DID YOU KNOW?**
> The word used in the Bible to describe God's love is *agape*. Agape love is a sacrificial love that is a part of God's character. This kind of love focuses on what is best for others without expecting anything in return.

The God of Comfort

*He comforts us in all our troubles so that we can comfort others.
When they are troubled, we will be able to give them the same
comfort God has given us.* —2 Corinthians 1:4 NLT

Have you ever scraped your knee or elbow while you were playing outdoors? Maybe you bumped your toe on a chair. Those things can really hurt, but a bandage or warm cloth can make you feel better. Most hurts on our body can heal pretty quickly. But when you are hurting on the inside from problems or sadness, those kinds of hurts are harder to heal.

When someone makes us feel better on the inside by caring about us or helping us, it's called *comfort*. It's like when your mom or dad wraps you up in a big hug when you feel scared or sad.

TALK TO GOD
Thank God for the loving comfort He offers us when we face hard times.

In Paul's second letter to the Corinthian church, he reminds us that comfort comes from God. Paul tells us that God comforts us in all the troubles we face. The amazing thing about God's comfort is that it never runs out. Paul said the more hard times we face as Christians, the more God will shower us with His comfort through Jesus. And there is a special reason God does that. On top of helping us feel better, God comforts us so we can comfort others. When other people face hard times like we have, we will be able to share the comfort with them that God gave to us.

Going through challenges, sadness, or difficult things has a purpose. Even though it's hard, God uses those things to help us grow closer to Him and feel His love. Then we use that love to comfort others who are sad. And maybe we can find a way to cheer them up.

EXPLORE MORE: Read Psalm 119:50. What comforted the writer in his troubles?

DID YOU KNOW?
Studies have shown that giving at least eight hugs a day helps us to be happier.

God is my comforter.

Cheerful Giving

Your gifts meet the needs of the Lord's people. And that's not all. Your gifts also cause many people to thank God. —2 Corinthians 9:12 NIrV

Have you ever given something to someone who needed it? Maybe you gave clothes to someone when you outgrew them or shared a snack with a hungry friend. Giving to others is an important part of following Jesus because God wants us to share what we have. Did you know God cares about our hearts when we give? Paul said, "Each of you should give what you have decided in your heart to give. You shouldn't give if you don't want to. You shouldn't give because you are forced to. God loves a cheerful giver."

In 2 Corinthians 9:10 Paul compares our giving to a farmer planting seeds. He says, "God supplies seed for the person who plants . . . God will also supply and increase the amount of your seed. He will increase the results of your good works." We can expect God to do good things with our gifts, just like a farmer who plants seeds and sees a harvest. As we share with others, God will continue to give us what we need and provide more for us to share.

When we pray and ask God what He wants us to give, we can give with a cheerful heart because we know we are obeying Him.

God will take care of us when we give the way He wants us to. Paul said, "In all things and at all times, you will have everything you need." The good gifts we give help those who receive them and cause them to thank God. When you share with others, it shows you believe the good news about Jesus—and that's something to be cheerful about!

TALK TO GOD
Ask God what you can give to someone in need.

EXPLORE MORE: Who are we really serving when we give to others? Look up Matthew 25:37–40 to find out.

God uses what I have to help others.

DID YOU KNOW?
The Salvation Army is an organization that receives gifts to help people in need. It was founded in 1865 by William Booth in London, England. Now, it is one of the largest charity organizations in the United States.

One True Gospel

There is no other message that is the Good News, but some people are confusing you. They want to change the Good News about Christ. —Galatians 1:7 ERV

The word *gospel* means "good news." As you read through the Bible, you can see why it's such good news that Jesus came to save us from our sins. And that's why Paul and the first Christians wanted to spread the gospel message around the world.

Today's Scripture is from a letter to a church in a place called Galatia. The Christians in Galatia tried to follow God, but they believed some confusing messages from false teachers. Paul heard about what was happening and sent a letter to remind them of the truth. The false teachers told the Galatians they had to do certain things to be made right with God. They said they needed to do more than believe in Christ. The false teachers were adding to the gospel of Jesus's death and resurrection. Paul explained that these teachers were trying to change the gospel by telling people they had to do more than believe in Jesus to be saved.

TALK TO GOD
Ask God to help you know His truth by studying His Word.

There are still religions in the world today that change the gospel message. How can we tell which messages are true? By following what the Bible says! The Bible shows us the way to God. It tells us believing in Jesus is the only way to be saved from our sins. Anyone or any religion that says something different isn't the true gospel. There is only one gospel message: Jesus is the Son of God, who came to earth, died on the cross, and was raised again, so we can have eternal life. That's the best news of all!

EXPLORE MORE: Read the gospel message Paul shared in 1 Corinthians 15:1–4.

DID YOU KNOW?
Galatia was an area in the north-central part of modern-day Turkey. It was settled by the Celtic Gauls, which is where the name Galatia comes from.

There is only one true gospel.

Free in Jesus

Christ has set us free to enjoy our freedom. So remain strong in the faith. —Galatians 5:1 NIrV

When you're a kid, there are lots of rules to follow. Your parents have rules about what time you have to go to bed and when you can have screen time. Your teachers have rules at school and tell you when you can talk and when you have to listen. If you play on a sports team, there are rules to play the game. Even though rules keep you safe and help you learn, sometimes they can be hard to follow.

Some people think being a Christian means following a long list of rules. They may not understand what the Bible says. These people think they have to do or not do certain things for God to accept them. Thinking this way goes all the way back to the first Christians Paul taught about Jesus. Paul said to the Galatians, "Some of you are trying to be made right with God by obeying the law. . . . But we long to be made completely holy because of our faith in Christ." Paul explained that Jesus's sacrifice on the cross set us free from having to follow lots of rules like the Israelites in the Old Testament. No one can keep God's law perfectly. Jesus came so we didn't have to keep the law perfectly.

Believing in Jesus's sacrifice for us takes away our sin; it doesn't mean we have to follow a bunch of rules to be good enough. Jesus gave us His goodness instead. When we trust in Him, we are made right with God, and we can enjoy our lives, knowing we are free and right with God.

EXPLORE MORE: What did Paul tell the Galatians to do with their freedom in Galatians 5:13–14?

TALK TO GOD
Thank Jesus that He has given you freedom from sin.

Jesus sets me free.

DID YOU KNOW?
One of the most common rules parents give in the United States is "always say please and thank you." After that it's "always be kind" and "you have to finish your homework before you can play."

Remember Others in Your Prayers

I have not stopped thanking God for you. I always remember you in my prayers. —Ephesians 1:16 NIrV

Today's verse comes from a letter Paul wrote to a group of Christians in a city named Ephesus. The people who lived there were called Ephesians. Paul had heard good things about the Ephesians' faith in Jesus and their love for God's people. He was excited that they were doing their part in God's great work. Paul always remembered them in his prayers.

So, what did Paul pray for the Ephesians? He asked God to keep giving them wisdom and understanding from the Holy Spirit. He prayed for them to know God better. He prayed that they would understand God's Word more clearly and have hope because of God's many promises to them. He also said that he always thanked God for the Ephesians.

TALK TO GOD
Choose someone in your life to pray for today. Pray for God to give them wisdom and understanding.

Who are you thankful for? Do you have a special friend, parent, grandparent, or teacher who encourages you and helps you? Maybe there's someone in your life who has taught you about God and the Bible. That person is special too. When you think about how much those people mean to you, you can thank God for them like Paul did. You can ask God to give them wisdom, and you can pray for them to know God better. You can pray for God to help them understand Him more and know His great power in their lives.

We can show God's love to others when we remember them in our prayers. And when you pray for someone special in your life, you can encourage them by letting them know.

EXPLORE MORE: Read Ephesians 1:17–18 to see some of Paul's prayers for the Ephesians.

DID YOU KNOW?
Ephesus was located on the coast of modern-day Turkey. It was one of the oldest Greek cities on the Aegean Sea. Today it is called Selçuk, and about 36,000 people live there.

I can pray for the special people in my life.

Saved by Grace

God's grace has saved you because of your faith in Christ. Your salvation doesn't come from anything you do. It is God's gift.
—Ephesians 2:8 NIrV

Nothing could stop Paul from telling others about Jesus. Even when he was in prison, he kept preaching about Jesus to the guards and other prisoners. When he was in prison, Paul also wrote letters to Christians in different cities. He wanted the believers to become more like Jesus by showing kindness and love to each other.

In Paul's letter to the Ephesians, he reminded them that because of God's great love, they were saved from sin by His grace. Do you know what grace means? It's getting something wonderful that you don't deserve. It's like getting the best present you've ever received just because someone loves you. Paul wanted Christians to understand that believing in Jesus is what saves them. Salvation from sin is a gift from God, and not something anyone can earn by doing good things. That message is not just for the Ephesians; it's for everyone.

Some people think they have to do good things to go to heaven, but that's not what the Bible tells us. No one is good enough to earn their salvation, which is why God sent Jesus to die for us. Salvation is a gift we don't deserve. But because of God's grace, He gives salvation from sin to everyone who believes in Jesus.

Aren't you glad you don't have to work hard to earn your way to heaven? You can just accept God's gift and enjoy living for Jesus. You can follow Jesus's example of being kind and loving to everyone—and that includes your friends, family, neighbors, and new people you meet. Being kind to others shows the love of Jesus in your heart.

EXPLORE MORE: Read Ephesians 2:7 to learn more about God's grace.

TALK TO GOD
Thank God that we can be saved by believing in Jesus.

DID YOU KNOW?
Ephesians, Philippians, Colossians, and Philemon are four letters Paul wrote while he was in prison that became books of the Bible. For this reason, they are sometimes called the "Prison Epistles," or prison letters.

Jesus saves me by God's grace.

Created for Good Things

We are God's creation. He created us to belong to Christ Jesus. Now we can do good works. Long ago God prepared these works for us to do. —Ephesians 2:10 NIrV

As you read the Bible, you can see how much God loves you. God loves you for thousands of reasons, and most of all He loves you because He created you. He thought about creating you even before you were born. God made only one of you. Even if you have an identical twin, you are still one of a kind!

God created you with special gifts, talents, and abilities, so that you can do good things. When you choose to follow Jesus, you start out on a new path for your life. As you continue to learn more about God and His plan for you, God will help you do whatever He created you to do.

Maybe God's plan is for you to become a music teacher, a minister, or a leader in your church or community someday. Maybe God wants you to help children with special needs or build homes for families. God might give you the ability to learn another language, so you can write stories for kids in other countries or be a missionary who tells others about Jesus.

Do you like science? If so, God might use you to create a medicine to cure a disease. Are you good at engineering? Then maybe you will design machines or robots to help people do their jobs.

No matter what God created you to do, if you keep following Him, He will give you everything you need to serve Him. You don't need to figure it out right now. Just keep loving God and learning more about Him. God created you to do good things, and He will lead you one step at a time.

EXPLORE MORE: Who helps us do what we were created to do? Find the answer in Philippians 2:13.

TALK TO GOD
Ask God to show you the work He wants to do through you.

DID YOU KNOW?
The world's first industrial robot, called Unimate, was installed at a General Motors automobile plant in New Jersey in 1961. The robot took hot metal parts from a casting machine, something that was too dangerous for humans to do.

God created me to do good things.

God's Great Love

Christ's love is greater than anyone can ever know, but I pray that you will be able to know that love. Then you can be filled with everything God has for you. —Ephesians 3:19 ERV

Have you ever looked up at a high mountain and seen its peak reaching into the sky? Have you ever stood on the shore of a lake or ocean that's so wide you can't see the other side? Maybe you've seen pictures of a deep canyon, or maybe you've seen one with your own eyes! Have you ever traveled for hours on a long road that looked like it had no end? The apostle Paul says that's what God's love is like.

In Ephesians 3, Paul prays that Christians would understand God's great love and know how wide, how long, how high, and how deep it is. If we turn back to the book of Psalms, we can find some verses to help us understand the greatness of God's love.

Psalm 36:5 says, "Lord, your faithful love reaches to the sky. Your faithfulness is as high as the clouds" (ERV).

Psalm 36:7 says, "Nothing is more precious than your loving kindness. All people can find protection close to you" (ERV).

Psalm 100:5 says, "The Lord is good! There is no end to his faithful love. We can trust him forever and ever!" (ERV).

And in Psalm 136, there are twenty verses that say, "His faithful love will last forever" (ERV).

Even with all those verses—and there are many more—it isn't possible to fully understand how much God loves us. His love is wider than an ocean, longer than a never-ending road, higher than a mountain, and deeper than a canyon. Even though we can't understand it completely, we can thank God every day for His wide, long, high, deep love that never ends.

TALK TO GOD
Thank God that He loves you so much, and then tell Him you love Him too.

EXPLORE MORE: What did Jesus tell His followers in John 15:12?

God's love is enormous!

DID YOU KNOW?
Mount Everest is the highest mountain on earth. Its peak is 29,032 feet (8,848.9 meters) above sea level. It's part of the Himalayan Mountain Range, located on the border of China and Nepal.

Put Your Armor On

That is why you need to get God's full armor. Then on the day of evil, you will be able to stand strong. And when you have finished the whole fight, you will still be standing. —Ephesian 6:13 ERV

Before you go outside, you need to decide what clothes to wear. If it's cold, you put on a warm jacket. If it's warm, you might wear a T-shirt. And if it's raining, you put on your raincoat and rainboots.

Police officers, firefighters, and soldiers wear uniforms. Their uniforms protect them from danger and help them do their jobs. In Ephesians 6, the apostle Paul talks about a different kind of uniform called the armor of God. The armor of God protects us from our enemy, Satan, who tempts us to do things we shouldn't do. But when we wear the armor of God, it will protect us and help us be strong.

The armor of God has six pieces. When we wear truth like a belt around our waist, it will keep us from telling lies. When we wear the breastplate of righteousness, it protects us from Satan's attacks and helps us make good choices. When we tell others about Jesus, it's like wearing shoes that help us share His love wherever we go. Having faith in Jesus is like using a shield to protect us from enemy attacks. Knowing we are saved is like wearing a helmet that protects our minds from believing Satan's lies. And finally, the sword of the spirit is the Word of God. God's Word is a powerful weapon to help us know what's true and what's false.

When you wear your full armor, you will be able to stand up to anyone who tries to turn you away from God, no matter where you go!

EXPLORE MORE: What else does Paul say to do in Ephesians 6:18?

TALK TO GOD
Ask God to help you put on His armor every day.

DID YOU KNOW?

In medieval times a knight's armor weighed around 45 to 55 pounds (20 to 25 kilograms). Some of the pieces they wore were greaves (leg guards) on their ankles and legs, vambraces (arm guards) that covered their lower arms, breastplates for their chests, and helmets for their heads.

I will put on the full armor of God.

Be Humble like Jesus

In whatever you do, don't let selfishness or pride be your guide. Be humble, and honor others more than yourselves. —Philippians 2:3 ERV

In Paul's letter to the Philippians, he gave the people an important message. He told them to be humble like Jesus was. Even though Jesus was God's Son, He didn't use His power for selfish reasons when He came to earth. Jesus humbled himself by becoming a man. He gave up His beautiful home in heaven to come into a broken world as God's servant.

If we are followers of Jesus, we need to be humble like He was. Jesus cared about everyone. He showed love and kindness to people who came to Him. He was never proud or selfish. Jesus didn't brag about His ability to perform miracles. He did miracles to help people. Jesus put the needs of others before His own.

God has given each of us special talents and abilities. But He didn't give those to us so we can brag about how good we are. God wants us to use what He has given us to serve others. That's what Jesus did.

TALK TO GOD
Ask God to help you be humble and care about others.

Being humble doesn't mean that you think of yourself as unimportant. You are important to your family and friends, and you are very important to God! Being humble means that you think others are just as important as you. It means you want to be more like Jesus in the way you treat other people.

Do you know what happened to Jesus after He went back to heaven? God gave Jesus the most honored place in heaven and made His name more important than any other name. When Jesus returns to earth, everyone who hears His name will humble themselves and bow down to worship Him.

EXPLORE MORE: What did Jesus tell His disciples in Mark 10:43–45?

Jesus honored others more than himself.

DID YOU KNOW?

At state banquets in England, the guest of honor sits to the right of the king or queen. The king or queen speaks to that person during the first course of the dinner. Then the king or queen talks to the person on the left for the next course.

Shine like a Star

Among them you shine like stars in the dark world.
—Philippians 2:15 ICB

Have you ever looked at the stars in the nighttime sky? People notice stars because they are beautiful as they twinkle and glow, and they remind us of God's wonderful creation. And the darker the sky is at night, the brighter they shine. Even though there are millions of stars, each star adds light to the darkness.

In Philippians 2, the apostle Paul compared Christians to stars. He said that God wants His love to shine through us, like stars in the nighttime sky. Just like the sky is dark at night, the world we live in can be a dark place too! Some people in the world live in ways that don't honor God. So when people who follow Jesus are honest and helpful and show their love for others, they shine God's light in a dark world.

When God helps you say kind things instead of complaining or arguing, you shine like a star with your words. When you ask your parents or teacher if you can help put things away, you shine by being helpful. When God gives you comforting words to share with a friend who is sad, you shine by showing you care. When you enjoy time with your grandparents, you shine by being a loving grandchild.

Even though we all make mistakes sometimes, God can still use us to show others His light. We can ask God to help us make good choices and treat others with kindness. With help from the Holy Spirit, you can honor God and shine like a star no matter what time of day it is.

EXPLORE MORE: When the Holy Spirit works in our lives, what does He give us? Read Galatians 5:22–23 to find out.

> **TALK TO GOD**
> Thank God for using you to shine for Him.

> **DID YOU KNOW?**
> A binary star is a system of two stars that orbit around each other. A binary star is also called a "double star." Since the invention of the telescope, astronomers have found many pairs of binary stars.

God helps me shine like a star.

Paul's Instructions for Life

Always be filled with joy in the Lord. I will say it again. Be filled with joy. —Philippians 4:4 ERV

As Paul wrote his letter to the church in Philippi, the Holy Spirit gave him some words of advice. These words are like good instructions that are written for everyone who reads them. First, Paul tells us to be filled with joy. Why should we be filled with joy? Because when we believe in Jesus, He becomes our Savior and friend. He is everything we need, so we can always be joyful!

The next thing Paul tells us is to be gentle and kind, so others can see God's love in us. Then he tells us to stop filling our minds with lots of worries. Instead of worrying, we should pray and ask God for what we need. After that we can think about all the good things God has already given us and thank Him for those blessings.

TALK TO GOD
Think of something good God has given you, and ask Him to fill you with peace and joy.

Another thing Paul tells us is to think about good things. Sometimes our minds can get stuck on scary thoughts or things that aren't good. But God wants you to think about everything that is good and beautiful. Think about your family, friends, and neighbors who are kind, and thank God for them. Thank God for flowers and trees and all the beautiful things you see around you in His creation. And think about how good it is that God loves you!

When you trade fearful thoughts for good thoughts, do you know what happens? God gives you His peace, which is the opposite of worry. When you follow these good instructions for living, God's peace will fill you with so much joy that it will show on your face for everyone to see.

EXPLORE MORE: What does Isaiah 26:3 say about finding peace?

God gives me peace and joy.

DID YOU KNOW?
Manatees, rabbits, sloths, and koalas are considered to be the most peaceful animals because of their personalities and behaviors.

No Matter What

I have learned to be satisfied with the things I have and with everything that happens. —Philippians 4:11 ICB

As Paul traveled around preaching about Jesus, he lived in many different places. Sometimes he lived with people from churches whom he helped, and other times he lived on a ship. For almost five years, Paul lived in prison. In the book of Philippians, he thanked the people who cared about him. He said that he learned how to be satisfied no matter where he was, no matter what he had, and no matter what happened.

Being satisfied means that you feel okay about the way things are. Sometimes Paul didn't have very much, and other times he had more than enough. Sometimes he had plenty to eat, and other times he was hungry. Paul learned to be happy if he had a lot or a little. Do you know why he could be that way? Because he trusted God to give him what he needed. And sometimes what he needed was strength to help him get through hard times. In Philippians 4:13 Paul writes, "I can do all things through Christ because he gives me strength."

TALK TO GOD
Thank God for giving you what you have, and talk to Him about something you need.

Like Paul, we can be satisfied as we trust God to give us what we need. Sometimes you might have everything you need, and other times it may seem like you don't have enough. But no matter what is happening around you, you can trust God to take care of you. If you have a need, talk to God about it. He might answer your prayer in a surprising way. God loves you and will always take care of you, no matter what.

EXPLORE MORE: What does Paul tell us in Philippians 4:19?

I will trust God and be satisfied.

DID YOU KNOW?
The Global FoodBanking Network helps get food to people who don't have enough to eat. They help people in more than 30 countries and have 811 food banks.

The Best Outfit

Therefore, as God's chosen people, holy and dearly loved,
clothe yourselves with compassion, kindness, humility,
gentleness, and patience. —Colossians 3:12 NIV

In Ephesians we learned about the armor of God, and in the book of Colossians, Paul talks about another set of clothes for us to wear. These aren't clothes from a store. They are actions and attitudes we "put on" to help us treat others the way Jesus did.

First, we need to put on compassion. Jesus had compassion as He cared about everyone He met. He fed crowds who were hungry and healed people who were sick. You can wear compassion like a shirt by caring about others and praying for them.

The next piece of clothing is kindness. If we want to be like Jesus, then kindness is part of our outfit. You can put on kindness like jeans and wear kindness every day. Another thing to wear is humility. You can wrap humility around yourself like a belt by showing others they're important. That's what Jesus did.

The next item is gentleness. Being gentle doesn't mean you're weak. Jesus was both strong and gentle. When you're gentle, you can work out your problems in a way that's calm and peaceful rather than angry. Think of gentleness like a hat to top off your outfit.

Patience is also good to wear. It's hard to be patient when you're waiting, but patience helps us wait with a peaceful heart. When you tie your shoes each day, think about being patient with others.

The last thing you need is a coat of love. When you put love over your entire outfit, it makes everything fit together. The best thing about these clothes is you will never outgrow them, and they will never go out of style!

EXPLORE MORE: According to Colossians 3:17, what is the right thing to do in every situation?

TALK TO GOD
Ask Jesus to help you be kind and compassionate like He is.

I want to clothe myself like Jesus.

DID YOU KNOW?
Fashion experts say that jeans, tennis shoes, and hats will never go out of style.

A Guidebook for Christians

Always be full of joy. Never stop praying. Whatever happens, always
be thankful. This is how God wants you to live in Christ Jesus.
—1 Thessalonians 5:16–18 ERV

Do you know what a guidebook is? When people visit a place they've never been before, they can use a guidebook to help them as they travel around. A guidebook gives information about where to stay, things to do, ways to get around a city, and interesting things to see. Visitors can use it to find their way through an unfamiliar place.

Even though we are all born on earth, the Bible tells us that when we become Christians, our real home is in heaven. One day everyone who is a part of God's family will be together in God's kingdom. That means we're kind of like visitors here on earth because we're away from our true home. But Paul gave us some directions that are like a guidebook to help us find our way while we are here. In 1 Thessalonians 5:16–18, Paul tells us exactly how God wants us to live. He says, "Always be full of joy. Never stop praying. Whatever happens, always be thankful."

Our guidebook is easy to remember because it's just three things: be filled with joy, keep praying, and be thankful. No matter what we face while we're on our journey, we can do those three things. We can have joy because God is always with us and promises to work everything out for good. We can keep praying when we're happy, sad, worried, or confused. And no matter what else is going on, we can always be thankful because Jesus loves us and takes away our sins. The Bible is the best guidebook of all. We can follow it every day!

EXPLORE MORE: What does Philippians 3:20–21 say about where we belong?

TALK TO GOD
Ask the Holy Spirit to help you have joy, always pray, and be thankful.

DID YOU KNOW?
Peregrinatio in Terram Sanctam, which means "Pilgrimage to the Holy Land," is said to be the world's first travel guide. It was written by Bernhard von Breydenbach and was published in 1486. The guide had illustrations of Rhodes, Cairo, and Beirut and a pull-out map of Jerusalem.

The Bible tells me how to live.

Be Strong

Brothers and sisters, remain strong in the faith. Hold on to what we taught you. —2 Thessalonians 2:15 NIrV

You've probably never heard of Jón Páll Sigmarsson, but he is one of the strongest men to ever live. Each year the World's Strongest Man competition takes place in a different city around the world. Men from all over compete against each other in events to see who is the strongest. Jón Páll Sigmarsson was the first man to win the competition four times. He was also the first man to squat 804 pounds (364 kilograms). Jón Páll spent his entire life training for the competitions. He knew what it was like to be strong.

The apostle Paul told the church in Thessalonica to be strong. But instead of holding heavy weights, he told them to hold on to the true teaching about Jesus. Paul wasn't talking about being physically strong; he was talking about being spiritually strong. The Thessalonians were being treated badly because of their faith. Their land was taken away, and they weren't allowed to work. Some of their families stopped talking to them, and some of them were hurt because of their beliefs. Paul passed on the teachings of Jesus through his preaching and his letters to the Thessalonians. He told them to stay strong in their faith when they faced hard times.

Just like a bodybuilder uses weights to grow muscles, we can use the Word of God to grow spiritually strong. We can develop "spiritual muscles" to stay joyful and patient in hard times when we train our minds and hearts to know the promises in God's Word. Paul said one day we will share in the glory of Jesus, and that will be better than winning a strong man trophy!

TALK TO GOD
Pray for Christians around the world who are being treated badly because of their faith. Ask God to help them stay strong.

EXPLORE MORE: What does 1 Timothy 4:8 say about training our bodies?

I can stay strong in my faith.

DID YOU KNOW?
Some of the events in the World's Strongest Man competition include pushing a steam train and pulling vehicles like buses and planes.

Set an Example

You are young, but don't let anyone treat you as if you are not important. Be an example to show the believers how they should live. Show them by what you say, by the way you live, by your love, by your faith, and by your pure life. —1 Timothy 4:12 ERV

Do you remember when the disciples tried to keep parents from bringing their children to Jesus? Jesus told them to let the children come and that anyone who wanted to be part of His kingdom needed to have faith like a child. Sometimes the world can make kids feel like they're not as important as adults. But do you know what the Bible says? It says that kids are important, and they can also show older people how to follow God.

Timothy was a young man who joined Paul on a journey to preach and teach people about Jesus. The older Christian men noticed Timothy because he was strong in his faith. Paul loved him and called Timothy his true son in the faith. The books of 1 Timothy and 2 Timothy in the Bible are letters that Paul wrote to Timothy to encourage him and teach him. In his first letter, Paul told Timothy that even though he was young, he should not let others treat him as if he were not important. He also told him to be an example to others by the way he lived.

TALK TO GOD
Ask God to help you be a good example to believers, young and old.

Paul's words to Timothy also apply to kids today. You can use kind words and speak the truth. You can get along with your siblings and your friends. You can show love to others by praying for them and helping them. You can show your faith by reading your Bible, learning about God, and telling others about Jesus. And when you choose to obey God and stay away from sin, you can be a good example to others no matter how old you are.

EXPLORE MORE: Look up Acts 16:1–2 to read about when Paul and Timothy first met.

DID YOU KNOW?
The name Timothy means "honoring God."

I can be an example to older believers.

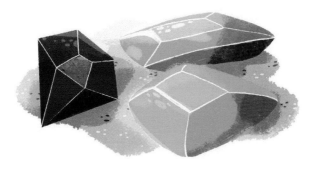

Treasure Hunt

By doing that, they will be saving a treasure for themselves in heaven. That treasure will be a strong foundation. Their future life can be built on that treasure. Then they will be able to have the life that is true life. —1 Timothy 6:19 ICB

Have you ever gone on a treasure hunt? When doing a treasure hunt, you search for special things that are hidden. You follow a trail of clues to find each item. Throughout history, people have searched for treasures to become rich and get a lot of money. Sometimes people are so concerned about getting treasures on earth—like money, big houses, and fancy cars—they make those things the most important things in their lives. Having money or nice things isn't bad. What matters is what we treasure and care about the most.

In 1 Timothy 6, Paul says, "The love of money causes all kinds of evil. Some people have left the true faith because they want to get more and more money." Paul goes on to explain that being rich isn't a bad thing. What God cares about is where people put their hope. Paul said, "Give this command to those who are rich with things of this world. Tell them not to be proud. Tell them to hope in God, not their money."

TALK TO GOD
Ask God to help you want His kind of riches.

God is the one who gives us every good thing to enjoy. The Bible says that it's more important to be rich in doing good things than to be rich with money. The good things we can do to become rich in God's eyes are giving to others and sharing. When we do that, the Bible tells us we will store up true riches. That means God will reward us in heaven one day. God's treasure is better than anything we could ever hunt for here on earth, and it will last forever.

EXPLORE MORE: Where does Jesus say we should store our treasure in Matthew 6:19–20?

I will hunt for God's kind of treasure.

DID YOU KNOW?
One of the biggest treasures ever found was in 2008 near the Channel Islands in the English Channel. Back in 1744 the HMS *Victory* was shipwrecked in that area. The gold and silver that was found on the boat was worth $750 million in US currency.

The Greatest Book of All

All Scripture is inspired by God and is useful to teach us what is true and to make us realize what is wrong in our lives. It corrects us when we are wrong and teaches us to do what is right. —2 Timothy 3:16 NLT

Thousands of years ago the disciples and the apostle Paul wrote down the things Jesus said and did. They also wrote letters to other Christians. What they wrote became the New Testament that we read today. It must have been very special for them to help write God's Word for future Christians to read. How do you think these men felt to have such a big job? Some Bible experts think Paul and Peter knew God was creating the New Testament through their writings. Even though the writers of the New Testament had an important job, God is the true author of the Bible. In his second letter to Timothy, Paul said the Bible comes from God and not from people.

Paul told Timothy why God wrote the Bible. He said, "All Scripture is inspired by God and is useful to teach us what is true and to make us realize what is wrong in our lives. It corrects us when we are wrong and teaches us to do what is right." Maybe you've had a time when you read your Bible, and God reminded you to obey your parents or use kinder words. Or maybe a grownup read you a Bible story, and you learned that it's right to tell the truth and to share what you have with others. That's why God gave us the Bible! First, He wants the Bible to teach us that He is real, that He loves us, and that we need Him. And then He wants to keep using the Bible to show us how to live. The Bible is the most important book we will ever read!

TALK TO GOD
Thank God for the gift of the Bible and for perfectly putting together the Old and New Testaments.

EXPLORE MORE: What does Hebrews 4:12 say about God's Word?

DID YOU KNOW?
The Codex Sinaiticus is a handwritten copy of the Bible in Greek. It was written over 1,600 years ago and contains the oldest full copy of the New Testament.

The Bible teaches me and prepares me for God's work.

Do What Is Good

Remind God's people to obey rulers and authorities. Remind them to be ready to do what is good. —Titus 3:1 NIrV

Have you ever said, "I don't know what to do"? Sometimes you might not know what to do because you're in a hard situation, like when a friend is being unkind. Sometimes you might not know what to do because you have too many choices—like what to eat at a restaurant. Or sometimes you might not know what to do because you're bored and can't think of anything fun. It's hard when you don't know what to do.

Titus was a man who helped Paul spread the gospel in Crete, a large island off the coast of Greece. The book of Titus is a letter that Paul wrote to Titus to teach and encourage him. In this book, Paul gives Titus and all believers some good advice about what they can do no matter what. Paul says we should always be ready to do what is good.

What were the good things Paul wanted the Christians in Crete to do? He told Titus to remind believers to obey their country's leaders. He also said they shouldn't say bad things about other people or get into arguments. Paul said, "Instead, they should be gentle and show true humility to everyone."

You can do these same good things today. You can obey the people God put in charge of you. You can keep your lips from saying bad things about kids at school and disagreeing with your siblings. You can help your parents with chores around the house. And you can put others before yourself, like letting your friend go first when you play a game. The next time you don't know what to do, do something good!

EXPLORE MORE: Why did Paul say we could trust God and do good? Read Titus 3:4–7 to find out.

TALK TO GOD
Ask God to help you to set an example for those around you by doing what is good.

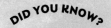

DID YOU KNOW?
Titus was a Gentile (a non-Jew) whom Paul led to faith in Christ. He traveled with Paul on several journeys and is mentioned in the books of Acts, Galatians, 2 Corinthians, and 2 Timothy. Titus also went to serve the church in Corinth and delivered the letter of 2 Corinthians to the church in Corinth.

I will be ready to do what is good.

Paul Makes Peace

If you think of me as your friend, then accept Onesimus back. Welcome him as you would welcome me. —Philemon 17 ICB

Do you remember the Beatitudes? One of the blessings Jesus taught was that people who work for peace will be called children of God. It's good to be a peacemaker. Being a peacemaker means encouraging others to get along and helping them work through problems when they disagree. In the book of Philemon, Paul worked to be a peacemaker.

Can you guess who Paul wrote the letter of Philemon to? A man named Philemon! Paul wrote this note while he was in prison. Bible scholars think that Paul led Philemon to believe in Jesus. While Paul was in Rome, he met Onesimus, who was one of Philemon's servants. Onesimus had escaped from working as a servant for Philemon and ran away. Paul taught Onesimus about Jesus, and Onesimus became a Christian. Onesimus would be in big trouble with Philemon for running away, but Paul wanted them to work through their problem because they were both part of God's family. Paul asked Philemon to forgive Onesimus and be kind to him. He sent Onesimus back to Philemon with his letter to help them work things out.

TALK TO GOD
Ask God to help you be a peacemaker.

We don't know for sure what happened when Onesimus went back to Philemon, but most Bible scholars think Philemon forgave Onesimus. Paul told Philemon that he should think of Onesimus like a brother when he came back because they both loved and served God.

Can you be a peacemaker like Paul? Can you help your friends get along when they disagree about what they want to do? Can you help your siblings when they fight over a toy? When you are a child of God, you have the power to be a peacemaker.

DID YOU KNOW?
The book of Philemon is the third-shortest book in the Bible. It is only one chapter and is just over three hundred words.

EXPLORE MORE: What good advice do we read in Romans 12:18?

It's good to be a peacemaker.

God's Message

And now in these last days God has spoken to us through his Son. God has chosen his Son to own all things. And he made the world through the Son. —Hebrews 1:2 ICB

In the Old Testament we read about prophets God spoke through to carry His message to the Israelites. We also know that God still speaks through the Bible and the Holy Spirit. Did you know there is one more way God spoke? The book of Hebrews tells us it's through His Son, Jesus!

Jesus told us many things that God wanted us to know, but His message from God was more than the words He shared. God sending Jesus to earth was an important message all by itself. There are seven things in Hebrews 1:2–3 that God tells us to help us understand the message of His wonderful Son, Jesus.

First, God chose Jesus to own all things. That means He is the most honored in all of heaven and earth. Second, God created the world through His Son. Next, Jesus reflects God's glory. We see the light of God the Father through Jesus's life on earth. Fourth, Jesus is the exact copy of God's nature. Jesus shows us exactly who God is. Next, He holds the world and everything together with His word. He keeps everyone and everything in its place. He also forgives our sins and wipes them away. No one else can do this for us except Jesus. Finally, He sat down at the right side of God. That means His work of saving us is finished, and He has been given a special seat of honor next to God the Father.

TALK TO GOD
Thank God for speaking through His Son, Jesus.

So, what is the message God spoke through Jesus by showing us all these things? Jesus shows us God's power. Jesus shows us God's glory. And Jesus shows us God's love.

EXPLORE MORE: What does God the Father say about Jesus in Hebrews 1:10–12? Look it up to find out!

Jesus is God's message to us.

DID YOU KNOW?
No one knows who wrote the book of Hebrews. Hebrews was probably written around AD 67–69. There is no mention of the author in the book, but all the focus is on God. And that's perfect!

A Big Family

So now Jesus and the ones he makes holy have the same Father. That is why Jesus is not ashamed to call them his brothers and sisters. —Hebrews 2:11 NLT

How many siblings do you have? Some people come from families with one or two siblings. Some come from families with eight siblings or even more! And some kids are the only children in their families.

No matter how many siblings are in your family, did you know you have a brother when you join God's family? When you decide to follow Jesus, God becomes your Father in heaven. And since Jesus is God's Son, that makes Him your brother in the family of God!

Hebrews 2:11 says, "Jesus and the ones he makes holy have the same Father. That is why Jesus is not ashamed to call them his brothers and sisters." If all the people Jesus makes holy are His brothers and sisters, that means you get a big family of siblings when you become a Christian. The great thing about families is that no matter what happens, good or bad, you have a group of people you are connected to who will love you. God created families to support us and help us and be there for us in happy and sad times. Just think how wonderful it is to know that's true for God's huge family of believers too!

TALK TO GOD
Thank God for giving you such a big, loving family through Jesus.

How can you be a good sibling in God's family? You can encourage and love your brothers and sisters in the kingdom of God. You can pray for them. You can be sad with them when they are sad. You can be excited when they are excited. You can share what you have with those who don't have as much. And you can keep cheering them on as they follow Jesus.

EXPLORE MORE: What did Jesus say about His family in Mark 3:31–35?

DID YOU KNOW?
One of the largest families in Canada is the Ionce family. The parents were born in Romania and moved to Canada in the 1990s. They have eighteen children.

I can be a part of God's big family.

Jesus Understands

We have a high priest who can feel it when we are weak and hurting. We have a high priest who has been tempted in every way, just as we are. But he did not sin. —Hebrews 4:15 NIrV

There's an old song that says, "Nobody knows the trouble I've seen. Nobody knows my sorrow. Nobody knows the trouble I've seen. Nobody but Jesus."

Sometimes it can seem like no one understands how we feel, especially when we're in the middle of a hard time. But like this song says, Jesus sees what happens to us, and He knows how we feel. He knows because He's watching us as He cares for us. But He also knows because He lived a human life.

In the Old Testament, God gave the Israelites a high priest to go to God on their behalf to have their sins forgiven. The high priest came from Aaron's family. He would sprinkle blood in the holiest part of the temple once a year. This day was called the Day of Atonement because it was the day the priest "paid" for the people's sins. Hebrews tells us that Jesus is our High Priest now and forever. He shed His blood to take away our sins. Even though Jesus is perfect and fully God, He still understands what it means to be human. He lived on earth as a human. Jesus knows how you feel when you're afraid, sad, angry, and happy. Hebrews 4 tells us Jesus can feel it when we are weak and hurting and that He hurts with us.

> **TALK TO GOD**
> What is something you want to talk to God about? Go to Him boldly as you pray.

Because Jesus understands how we feel, Hebrews 4:16 says we can boldly go to God's throne. That means we can talk to God without fear. And just like the Israelites received forgiveness on the day of Atonement, we will receive mercy from God because Jesus has gone to God as our High Priest.

EXPLORE MORE: What does Hebrews 7:23–25 say about Jesus being our High Priest?

Jesus is my High Priest.

> **DID YOU KNOW?**
> "Nobody Knows the Trouble I've Seen" is an African American song that started during the period of slavery in the United States. It was first published in 1867 and was later recorded by several great musicians including Louis Armstrong, Marian Anderson, Paul Robeson, and Mahalia Jackson.

Once and For All

With one sacrifice Christ made his people perfect forever. They are the ones who are being made holy. —Hebrews 10:14 ERV

Wouldn't it be nice if you only had to take out the trash once and it never had to be taken out again? Or what if you took one shower, and it kept you clean for the rest of your life? What if you did your math homework on the first day of school, and every assignment was completed for the rest of the year?

Homework, chores, and other responsibilities have to be done over and over again. That's how it was in the Old Testament when the Israelites had to make sacrifices for their sins over and over. They could never be perfect by obeying the law of Moses, so God told them to make sacrifices to cleanse them from their sins.

Hebrews 10 tells us that when Jesus came into the world He said, "You don't want sacrifices and offerings, but you have prepared a body for me. You are not pleased with the sacrifices of animals killed and burned or with offerings to take away sins." Then Jesus said, "Here I am, God. . . I have come to do what you want."

The sacrifices the priests offered covered the people's sins, but they could never take them away forever or change the people's hearts. When Jesus died on the cross, He offered His life as one sacrifice for all of our sins. And that sacrifice is good forever. Unlike the sacrifices in the Old Testament, Jesus's sacrifice takes away our sins and makes us perfect before God. And because of the Holy Spirit in us, Jesus's sacrifice changes our hearts. Jesus has taken care of everything once and for all.

TALK TO GOD
Tell Jesus how thankful you are that His life, death, and resurrection took away your sins once and forever.

EXPLORE MORE: The words Jesus said in Hebrews 10 are also found in Psalm 40:6–8. Look them up in Psalms to read them.

DID YOU KNOW?
The National Center for Education Statistics found that elementary students in the United States get an average of 4.7 hours of homework each week. That means elementary students complete about 165 hours of homework in a school year.

Jesus is the perfect sacrifice.

Hold on to Courage

So do not lose the courage that you had in the past.
It has a great reward. —Hebrews 10:35 ICB

Can you think of a time when you had to be brave? How about when you first learned how to swim or when you had to talk in front of your class at church or school? When we've been brave in the past, it can help us be brave again in the future.

The book of Hebrews was written to Jews who believed in Jesus and were being treated badly because of their faith. We don't know for sure who wrote Hebrews, but the writer gave some good advice to the Jewish Christians that is also for us today. Hebrews 10:35–36 says, "So do not lose the courage that you had in the past. It has a great reward. You must hold on, so you can do what God wants and receive what he has promised."

TALK TO GOD
Ask God to help you hold on to courage in Jesus.

The Jewish Christians faced many struggles when they first believed in Jesus. But Hebrews tells us they stayed strong. Even though they were treated badly because of their faith, they helped others and stayed joyful. They knew their love for Jesus would last forever, so it didn't matter what others did or said to them.

We might face problems or hard times because we follow Jesus too. When that happens we can think back to times when we had courage and use that to help us be strong. Jesus saves us, and Hebrews promises us, "The One who is coming will come. He will not be late. The person who is right with me will have life because of his faith." While we wait for Jesus to come back, we can stay strong with courage. We will be glad we did!

EXPLORE MORE: What does 2 Timothy 1:7 tell us about the spirit God gave us?

I can have courage to stand strong for Jesus.

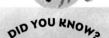

DID YOU KNOW?
King George VI of England struggled with a stutter from a young age. When he became king, he worked with a speech therapist from Australia to help him face his fear of speaking in front of people.

The Famous Faithful

People who lived in the past became famous because of faith.
—Hebrews 11:2 ICB

Some people want to be famous. They might try to become famous by getting followers on social media or posting a video that gets a lot of views. They might try to get on TV or become a famous athlete or musician.

Do you know what made people famous in the Bible? It wasn't how many followers they had or how good they were at sports. Hebrews 11:2 tells us men and women became famous because of their faith in God. Hebrews 11 is often called the "faith chapter" of the Bible. It talks about different people who had faith to obey God. They did amazing things because they bravely followed Him. These stories are wonderful because they show us great things that have happened, and also because they encourage us to have faith too.

Some of the people listed in Hebrews 11 are Abel, Noah, Abraham, Sarah, Joseph, Moses, Rahab, Samson, and David. Hebrews 11:39 says, "All these people are known for their faith." These heroes had gigantic faith, but did you know we have something they didn't have? Hebrews 11:40 says, "God planned to give us something better." The famous faithful didn't get a chance to totally understand and enjoy the work of Jesus, but we do! They hoped for a Messiah who would come and do His great work. We get to look back through the Bible and see the Messiah for ourselves. Jesus is the one who brought the heroes of faith to God even though He hadn't come to earth yet. And Jesus is the one who brings us to God too. He deserves all the fame.

EXPLORE MORE: What does Hebrews 11:6 say about faith?

Faith comes from Jesus.

TALK TO GOD
Thank God for the faithfulness of the heroes in the Bible, and ask Him to help you walk in faith too.

DID YOU KNOW?
Cristiano Ronaldo is considered one of the most famous people in the world. He is a Portuguese footballer who plays for Manchester United. In 2022 he was the most popular person on Instagram with over 450 million followers.

Good Gifts

Every good and perfect gift is from God. This kind of gift comes down from the Father who created the heavenly lights. —James 1:17 NIrV

Everyone likes to get gifts. Whether they're for your birthday, Christmas, or for no reason at all, gifts are fun to receive! Gifts don't always come wrapped in pretty paper with a fancy bow. A gift can be a plate of warm cookies from your mom, a cozy blanket your brother or sister shares with you, or a compliment from your teacher.

When someone gives you a gift, the polite thing to do is say, "thank you." This lets the giver know you appreciate their act of kindness. Saying thank you also reminds you that someone did something nice for you.

Many of your gifts might come from your family or friends, but nobody gives you more gifts than God. He gives you gifts like food, water, and the air you breathe every day. Your home, your family, and your toys and games are also gifts from God. He gave you a mind so you can think and learn, a nose to smell a warm loaf of bread, and a voice so you can sing your favorite songs. Those are gifts too!

TALK TO GOD
Think of a good gift God has given you and thank Him for it.

We can also enjoy God's gifts in His creation. A refreshing rain, a sunny day, a field full of flowers, and a glowing rainbow are gifts God gives for everyone to enjoy. It would be impossible to make a list of all the gifts God gives us, but it's fun to try. And the greatest gift God has given us is the gift of Jesus! When you think about all of God's good gifts, your heart can't help but say, "thank you."

EXPLORE MORE: What does the apostle Paul say about the gift of Jesus in 2 Corinthians 9:15?

God gives me good gifts every day.

DID YOU KNOW?
Flowers and jewelry are two of the most common gifts grown-ups give to each other. Some popular gifts for kids are Hot Wheels, Legos, and the game Monopoly.

God Is Near

Come near to God, and God will come near to you.
—James 4:8 ICB

Have you ever heard the word *omnipresent*? It's a big word that we use to describe God, and it means that God is everywhere all the time. It's hard for us to understand because we can only be in one place at a time. But God can be everywhere all at once because He is a spirit and doesn't have the kind of body that we have.

Since God is everywhere, He is close to you no matter where you are. Sometimes if you are having a hard day, you might feel like God is far away. If you ever feel that way, just talk to God and remember that He's with you. When you talk to God, or when you read your favorite Bible verses, or listen to a song that praises Him, you will feel close to God again.

When David wrote Psalm 139, he said, "You are all around me, in front and in back. You have put your hand on me. . . . If I go up to the skies, you are there. . . . If I rise with the sun in the east, and settle in the west beyond the sea, even there you would guide me."

When God sent Jesus to earth, one of the names Jesus was given is "Immanuel," which means "God is with us." When you remember that God is with you no matter where you are, it can help you on days when you feel sad or alone. On the best days, the worst days, or in-between sort of days, you can always come near to God because He is always near to you.

TALK TO GOD
Ask God to help you feel close to Him and to remember that He is always near to you.

DID YOU KNOW?
The states of Colorado, Utah, Arizona, and New Mexico meet in one place called the Four Corners Monument. People who visit the monument can be in four states at one time.

EXPLORE MORE: What is the sign Isaiah foretold in Isaiah 7:14?

God is always near me.

God's Word Lasts Forever

For you have been born again, but not to a life that will quickly end. Your new life will last forever because it comes from the eternal, living word of God. —1 Peter 1:23 NLT

Do you like getting a new pair of shoes? New shoes look good for a while. But soon they get scuffed and worn out. And as your feet grow, your shoes become too small. New games are fun to get too. But whether it's a board game, or a game for your tablet or computer, games don't last forever either. You might get tired of playing the game, you might lose some of the pieces, or your electronic device might stop working. Can you think of other things that don't last long? What about your birthday cake? That might disappear in a day or two!

When the apostle Peter was teaching Christians about God to help them grow in their faith, he used some verses from the Old Testament book of Isaiah. The prophet Isaiah said that people are like grass in the spring, and their beauty is like a flower. But grass dries up, and flowers fall to the ground. They do not last forever. Then he said, "But the word of God lasts forever."

God's word is the Bible, and the stories, prophecies, and truth in the Bible will last forever. The Word of God is also Jesus. Jesus was with God in the beginning, and He is our Lord and Savior who lives forever.

Peter explained that when we believe in Jesus, we are born again, and our spirit will never die. Our earthly bodies will not last forever. If we believe in Jesus, one day we will get a new body, and we will live forever with Him. Things on earth will not last, but things in heaven will last forever.

EXPLORE MORE: Read the words Peter quoted from Isaiah in Isaiah 40:7–8.

TALK TO GOD
Thank God that His word lasts forever and that you can live forever with Him by believing in Jesus.

Jesus's followers will live with Him forever.

DID YOU KNOW?
A perennial is a plant that blooms year after year from a bulb or seed that's planted in the ground. The flowers last for two to three weeks, but they will continue to bloom for a few years.

Cast It Away

Cast all your anxiety on him because he cares for you. —1 Peter 5:7 NIV

Have you ever seen someone cast a fishing line into a lake or the ocean? Maybe you've even done it yourself! When someone casts a line, they don't just throw it out a foot or two in front of them. They try to cast it out as far as they can.

The apostle Peter taught the people in the church many important things. He told the older people to be like shepherds for the younger people. He told all believers to be humble instead of proud. And then he told them to cast all their anxiety on God because God cared about them. Another way to say that is, "Give all your worries to God because He cares about you."

When we are upset or worried about too many things, it's hard to remember to trust God. It's also hard to think about others when our minds are full of our worries and problems. Worrying can keep us from enjoying all of God's good gifts and blessings. If you are worried about something, you might not pay attention to the birds chirping or notice the pretty flowers showing off their colors. You might miss the chance to have fun with a sibling or a friend. Worrying can also keep you from getting a good night's sleep.

TALK TO GOD
Think of something you are worried about and then give it to God.

God cares about you and doesn't want you to worry. The next time you're worried about something, give it to God. Cast that worry as far away as you can, and tell God you don't want to think about it anymore. God wants you to give Him all of your worries, so He can give you all of His peace.

EXPLORE MORE: What does Jesus say He will give us in John 14:27?

DID YOU KNOW?
A longer fishing rod can cast the line farther than a shorter rod, and a thinner line will cast farther than a thicker line.

I will give my worries to God.

Love One Another

Dear friends, we should love each other, because love comes from God. The person who loves has become God's child and knows God.
—1 John 4:7 ICB

The Bible is the great big story of God's great big love. God shows us His love in many ways, but His greatest act of love was sending Jesus to die on the cross for our sins. When we believe in Jesus, we belong to God, and we are His children.

God wants us to show love to others because it shows them what God is like. It also shows that God is working in our hearts to make us more like Jesus.

Showing love to others is something you can do every day, and there are many different ways you can do it. First of all, you can show love to others with your words. Saying, "I love you," to your parents, grandparents, or siblings can put a smile on their faces. You can also say words like "good job," "thank you," or "you're awesome."

TALK TO GOD
Ask God to help you think of someone you can show love to today.

We can show love to others with our actions. Holding the door for someone, making a card for a friend who is sick, or inviting a new kid in your neighborhood to play with you are simple and fun ways to show God's love.

Another way to show love is to pray with people who are sad or going through hard times. God loves to hear your prayers, and He loves when you help others by praying for them. There are so many ways to show love to other people that it's impossible to list them all. No matter how you choose to show love to others, it shows that God's love is in your heart.

EXPLORE MORE: Read 1 John 4:15–16. How can we know that God lives in us?

I will love others because God loves me.

DID YOU KNOW?
World Kindness Day is a holiday in the United States that was formed in 1998 to promote kindness throughout the world. It is celebrated on November 13 as part of the World Kindness Movement.

Write Down What You See

"So write what you see. Write the things that happen now and the things that will happen later." —Revelation 1:19 ERV

Revelation is the last book of the Bible. It was written by John, who was a disciple and close friend of Jesus. At the time John wrote Revelation, many Christians were being punished. The Roman Emperor sent John to the Island of Patmos as a punishment for preaching about Jesus.

While John was on the island, he heard a loud voice like a trumpet that said, "Write down in a book what you see, and send it to the seven churches: to Ephesus, Smyrna, Pergamum, Thyatira, Sardis, Philadelphia, and Laodicea."

Jesus gave John incredible visions about heaven. In the first three chapters of Revelation, John writes about the visions he had for each of the seven churches. Then in Revelation 4, John describes Jesus's throne in heaven. He said that the person on the throne looked like precious stones, and an emerald rainbow was around the throne. Surrounding Jesus's throne were twenty-four other thrones with twenty-four elders sitting on them. The elders were dressed in white and wore golden crowns on their heads. Flashes of lightning and sounds of thunder came from the throne. Four heavenly creatures circled the throne saying, "Holy, holy, holy is the Lord God All-Powerful. He always was, He is, and He is coming."

TALK TO GOD
Tell Jesus that He deserves all of our praise and worship.

Anyone who reads the book of Revelation will learn how beautiful heaven is. Someday when we get to heaven, we will see that Jesus is filled with God's power and glory. God's beauty is all around Him because Jesus is God. Heaven is a beautiful place where everyone will be filled with joy as they worship Jesus.

EXPLORE MORE: Read Revelation 4:9–11 to find out how the twenty-four elders worship Jesus.

DID YOU KNOW?
Patmos is a Greek Island in the Aegean Sea. It's 13.15 square miles (34.1 square kilometers) and has a population of nearly 3,000 people.

Heaven is a beautiful place.

The Bright Morning Star

"I, Jesus, have sent my angel to give you this witness for the churches. I am the Root and the Son of David. I am the bright Morning Star." —Revelation 22:16 NIrV

The planet Venus is the brightest light in the nighttime sky after the moon. Astronomers are scientists who study the planets and stars. They tell us that Venus doesn't twinkle like stars do, but it has a steady glow. Venus is called the morning star because it appears just before the sun rises and daylight begins. It's the first light to shine in the darkness, announcing the beginning of a new day.

TALK TO GOD

Praise Jesus for being the bright Morning Star who shines the brightest light.

Don't you love waking up in the morning when it's getting light outside? It's fun to get dressed, eat breakfast, brush your teeth, and start your day. You might be getting ready to go to school. You might be looking forward to playing outside. Maybe you will practice the piano, read a book, or play a game. Mornings are a time of joy and excitement as you look forward to a new day.

In one of the visions John saw while he was on the Island of Patmos, Jesus said He is the bright Morning Star. Like the planet Venus, Jesus is the first light. Jesus created light on the first day of creation, and He is the light that shines in the darkness. Nothing shines brighter than Jesus.

Every morning before you begin your day, ask Jesus to shine His light through you by the way you live. Ask Him to help you do your best in whatever you do. You can also thank Jesus for loving you and being your Savior. Thank Him that He is always with you. Just like the morning light gives us hope for a new day, Jesus gives us hope every day of our lives.

EXPLORE MORE: Read Psalm 148:1–6. Why should everything in the heavens praise God?

Jesus is the bright Morning Star.

DID YOU KNOW?
Venus is the hottest planet in the solar system. It is sometimes called "Earth's sister" since the two planets are similar in mass and size, but there's no way people could ever live there.

The Alpha and the Omega

I am the Alpha and the Omega. I am the First and the Last. I am the Beginning and the End. —Revelation 22:13 NIrV

In Revelation, Jesus calls himself the Alpha and the Omega three times. The New Testament was first written in Greek. Alpha is the first letter of the Greek alphabet, and Omega is the last letter. So when Jesus says He is the Alpha and the Omega, He's saying that He is the beginning and the end—He has always been and will always be!

Jesus has existed from the beginning. Colossian 1:15 NIrV says, "The Son is first, and he is over all creation." As we read stories from Genesis to Revelation, we see how Jesus is everywhere. The story of Abraham and Isaac at the altar is a picture of Jesus becoming our sacrifice. Jesus is like the ladder in Jacob's dream that reaches from heaven to earth. Jesus is like manna in the wilderness because He is the Bread of Life. Jesus is like water from a rock that saves thirsty people.

The scarlet cord in Rahab's window represents the blood of Jesus. The story of Boaz caring for Ruth shows us Jesus's love. Many verses tell us Jesus would come from David's family. Psalm 23 describes our Good Shepherd. Isaiah talks about Jesus's birth and life and the meaningful names He would be called.

Jesus fulfills the prophecies of the Old Testament prophets. The Gospels tell about Jesus's miracles, parables, His death, and His resurrection. The rest of the New Testament tells how Christians spread the good news throughout the world. And in Revelation we learn that Jesus is coming back to be our King. He will reign forever as the Lamb who gave His life for the world. Jesus is the Alpha and the Omega—the first, the last, and everything in between.

TALK TO GOD
Thank Jesus that He is coming back someday.

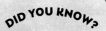

EXPLORE MORE: What does Jesus promise in Revelation 22:20?

Jesus is eternal.

Glossary

The first time the word appears in this book is listed after the definition.

Altar: A holy place where people may give gifts (sacrifices) to God. (July 10)

Apostle: A follower of Jesus who was sent out to spread the good news about Him. Paul, Peter, and John were some of Jesus's apostles. (January 27)

Birthright: During biblical times, rights were normally given to the first-born son in a family. It can include the family's land or home. Esau gave up his birthright to his younger twin brother, Jacob. (January 15)

Blessing: Kind words or a special gift from an important person. Jacob tricked his father into giving him his brother's blessing. (January 15)

Christian: A person who believes in Jesus and follows Him. (January 22)

Crucify: To kill by nailing a body to a cross. Jesus was crucified. (November 2)

Descendant: The sons and daughters of a person; family members who are born after someone. Abraham lived after Noah and was related to him; Abraham was a descendant of Noah. (January 9)

Disciple: A person who follows a leader. In the Bible, Jesus called twelve disciples who followed Him, learned from Him, and told others about Him. (April 23)

Eternal: Lasting forever, or not ending. We have eternal life when we believe in Jesus. (January 4)

Forgiveness: Giving up anger toward someone who has hurt you. (January 24)

Gentile: Anyone who is not an Israelite. (September 8)

Gospel (books): The books of the Bible that tell about Jesus's life—Matthew, Mark, Luke, John. (March 20)

Gospel (message): The message about Jesus forgiving our sins. The word *gospel* means "good news." (July 27)

Grace: The help and love God gives even though we don't deserve it. (March 16)

Holy: Set apart as very special. God is holy, and so is His name. That means God deserves a lot of respect. (January 14)

GLOSSARY

Holy Spirit: One of the three "persons"—along with God the Father and Jesus—who are God. There is only one God, but He lives as one "Trinity." The Holy Spirit is the person of God who lives inside us when we believe in Jesus as our Savior. (January 2)

Israel: The name of a person and two nations in the Bible. God changed Jacob's name to Israel after Jacob wrestled with God at the Jabbok River. The great nation that came from Jacob's twelve sons was called Israel. When the nation of Israel split into two kingdoms after Solomon died, the northern kingdom kept the name Israel to show it was different from the southern kingdom, called Judah. (January 21)

Manna: The thin flakes of bread God sent to feed the Israelites when they escaped from Egypt. The word means "what is it?" The Israelites asked "what is it?" when they saw the flakes on the ground. (February 2)

Messiah: A word meaning "anointed one," or the one specially chosen by God. Jesus is the Messiah, the one chosen by God to die on the cross to save people from their sins. (January 15)

Monument: A building or statue created to remember someone or something. Jacob set up a stone monument to remember the agreement he made with Laban, his father-in-law. (January 20)

Passover: A holiday remembering how God "passed over" and protected the Israelite babies while punishing the Egyptians. (January 27)

Pharaoh: The king of the Egyptians. In Exodus, we learn about a new Egyptian king who did not treat the Israelites well. Pharaoh made the Israelites slaves and he was very mean to them. (January 24)

Pharisee: A member of one group of Jews. Jesus often scolded the Pharisees for just following religious rules instead of actually loving God and others. They didn't realize that God is pleased when people believe in Jesus. (September 14)

Plagues: The awful punishment God brought upon the Egyptians for disobeying Him. There were ten different plagues, including frogs, gnats, flies, and grasshoppers taking over the land. (January 27)

Promised land: A place that God promised to Abraham and the family that would come from him—his son, grandsons, great-grandsons, and all of those following. In Abraham's time, the promised land was called Canaan. Later it was called Israel. (January 28)

Prophet: A person chosen by God to carry His messages to other people. Bible prophets included people like Elijah, Daniel, Isaiah, and Jeremiah. (February 21)

GLOSSARY

Resurrection: To rise from the dead. Jesus was resurrected after He was crucified. (October 18)

Sabbath: A holy day to rest. (February 2)

Sacrifice: To give up something as a gift, or offering, to God. Abraham was prepared to sacrifice his son, Isaac. He didn't have to because God provided a ram as the offering. (January 11)

Salvation: The act of being saved, or rescued, from our sins. (January 11)

Savior: Someone who rescues another person from trouble or danger. Jesus is the Savior of the world, because He made a way for everyone who believes in Him to become part of God's family. (January 4)

Sin: The wrong things people do; disobedience to God's laws. The Bible says the payment for sin is death, but God offers eternal life through Jesus. (January 4)

Species: A group of living things. Scientists use the word *species* to group living things that are alike. (May 19)

Synagogue: A place where Israelites (also called Jews) worship God. (September 11)

Tabernacle: In the Old Testament, the tent where the Israelites worshiped God while they traveled through the wilderness. (February 9)

Temple: In the Bible, the place in Jerusalem where the Jews worshiped God. (February 22)

Worship: Telling God that He is good, powerful, and worth our love. We can worship God in our prayers, singing, giving, and the way we serve other people. (February 11)

Scripture Permissions

About the Authors

Crystal Bowman is a bestselling, award-winning author of more than one hundred books for children and families, which have sold more than three million copies internationally and been translated into more than a dozen languages. She is the creator and coauthor of *Our Daily Bread for Kids, M Is for Manger*, and *I Love You to the Stars: When Grandma Forgets, Love Remembers*. A conference speaker, freelance editor, and contributor to several blogs, she is also a regular contributor to *Clubhouse Jr. Magazine*, and writes lyrics for children's piano music. She and her husband enjoy spending time with their grown children and huggable grandkids. www.crystalbowman.com.

As a mother of two boys, **Teri McKinley** is passionate about helping kids understand God's love for them. An award-winning, bestselling author of more than a dozen books for children, Teri's books have been published in eight languages and have reached a wide variety of audiences. She is the coauthor and cocreator of *Our Daily Bread for Kids* and Our Daily Bread for Little Hearts series. Some of her most celebrated titles include *Our Daily Bread for Kids, M Is for Manger*, and *My Arms Will Hold You Tight*.

Teri's love for writing began in early childhood, as she often wrote short stories for fun. She was exposed to the publishing industry at a young age as the daughter of renowned children's author Crystal Bowman. Her love for writing grew as she attended book signings and writing conferences with her mom. Today Teri also enjoys writing for moms and encouraging them along with their children. Above all, Teri's heart is that her readers would be encouraged and brought closer to Christ through her writing.

Illustrator **Anita Schmidt** lives by the Baltic Sea surrounded by seven seas in northern Germany. Her passion for drawing started from the very beginning when she first held a pencil. Anita went on to study graphic design, but after having two children she rekindled her passion for illustrating and now can't stop drawing!

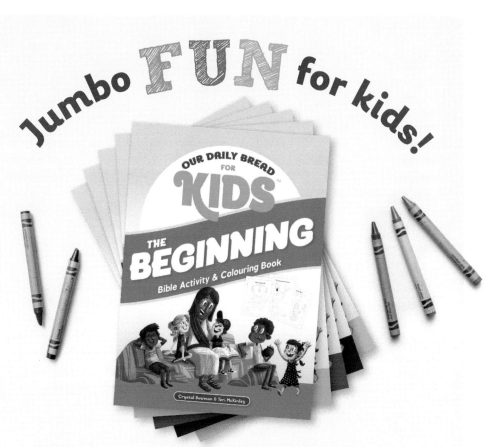

Jumbo FUN for kids!

Children ages 6 to 9 will love challenging themselves with activities and coloring pages compiled from the popular Our Daily Bread for Kids series.

Inside they'll find:

- ✱ Bible-based word searches, crossword puzzles, quizzes, and other games;
- ✱ 200 pages of interesting and challenging activities;
- ✱ fun ways to remember Bible facts; and
- ✱ hours and hours of entertainment!

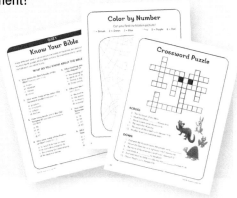

Buy it today

More **Our Daily Bread for Kids**, please!

Introduce your children to spending quality time with God each day through the *Our Daily Bread for Kids* series! The Bible reading notes, engaging activities and energetic songs will help them see how fun and exciting it is to get to know God through His Word.

ourdailybreadpublishing.org.uk

"Start children off on the way they should go...."

Proverbs 22:6 (NIV)

Teach your children about what really matters in life—loving others and loving God—with the help of *Our Daily Bread for Kids: 365 Meaningful Moments with God*. This hardcover features adorable characters and colorful illustrations to keep kids engaged and entertained every day. Each page shares a short devotion written in kid-friendly language, a Bible verse, and a fun fact that nurtures kids in their relationship with God.

Ideal for ages 6 & up.

Buy it today

Spread the Word
by Doing One Thing.

- Give a copy of this book as a gift.
- Share the QR code link via your social media.
- Write a review of this book on your blog, favourite bookseller's website, or at **ourdailybreadpublishing.org.uk**.
- Recommend this book to your church, small group, or book club.

Connect with us. 🄵 ⓘ 🕊

Our Daily Bread Publishing, PO Box 1, Carnforth,
Lancashire, LA5 9ES, United Kingdom
Email: books@odb.org